Visual Basic .NET

for complete beginners

by Ken Carney

Copyright: Home and Learn
Publisher: Home and Learn
ISBN: 978-0-9563653-6-1

Visual Basic .NET – Contents

INTRODUCTION 9

    WHAT YOU NEED TO DO THE COURSE 9
    THE FREE VISUAL BASIC EXPRESS EDITION 9
    ADDITIONAL FILES 10

GETTING STARTED 11

    THE TOOLBOX 15
    ADDING A TOOL (CONTROL) TO YOUR FORM 17

PROPERTIES 22

    SAVING YOUR WORK 28
    ADDING A SPLASH OF COLOUR 29

REVIEW NUMBER 1 34

GETTING OUR HANDS DIRTY: VARIABLES 35

    WHAT ARE VARIABLES? 36
    ADDING A BUTTON TO THE FORM 37
    STRING VARIABLES 44
    ASSIGNING VALUES FROM TEXTBOXES TO YOUR VARIABLES 48
    MORE ABOUT VARIABLES 52
    USING VARIABLES 55

A CALCULATOR PROJECT 60

    DESIGNING THE FORM 60
    THE CODE 61
    THE 0 TO 9 BUTTONS 62
    THE PLUS BUTTON 64

REVIEW NUMBER 2 67

CONDITIONAL LOGIC 68

    IF STATEMENTS 68
    SELECT CASE 71

COMBO BOXES 74

REVIEW NUMBER 3 77

    PART 1 - IF STATEMENTS 77
    HELP WITH THIS REVIEW 77
    MESSAGE BOX CONCATENATION 78
    PART 2 - SELECT CASE STATEMENTS 79

LOOPING THE LOOP 80

WHAT IS A LOOP? 80
FOR LOOPS 80
DO LOOPS 83

THE TIMES TABLE PROGRAMME 86

MORE CONTROLS - MENUS 93

CREATING SUB MENUS 99
UNDERLINE SHORTCUT 100
KEY COMBINATION SHORTCUTS 102

REVIEW FOUR 104

MORE ABOUT THE MESSAGE BOX 105

WRITING THE CODE FOR THE MENU SYSTEM 107

THE OPEN FILE DIALOGUE BOX 107
THE INITIAL DIRECTORY 110
THE TITLE PROPERTY 110
THE FILTER PROPERTY 110
SELECTING A FILE 112
THE SAVE MENU 114
THE EDIT MENU 115
THE COPY MENU 116
THE PASTE MENU 117
THE CUT MENU 118
THE UNDO MENU 118
THE VIEW MENU 118
THE VIEW TEXTBOXES MENU ITEM 118
THE VIEW IMAGES MENU ITEM 120
INSERT AN IMAGE 121

CHECK BOXES AND OPTION BUTTONS 124

CHECK BOXES 124

RADIO BUTTONS 130

REVIEW NUMBER 5 132

ERROR HANDLING AND DEBUGGING 137

TYPES OF ERROR 137
DESIGN TIME ERRORS 137
RUNTIME ERRORS 139
TRY ... CATCH 141
LOGIC ERRORS 144
BREAKPOINTS 145

HURRAY FOR ARRAYS! 149

WHAT IS AN ARRAY? 149
ARRAYS WHERE BOUNDARIES ARE NOT KNOWN 155

STRING MANIPULATION 158

THE STRING VARIABLE TYPE 158
MANIPULATING DATA FROM A TEXT BOX 161
TRIM 162
ISNUMERIC( ) 163
CHAR 164
INSTR( ) 166
SUBSTRING 167
EQUALS 168
REPLACE 168
INSERT 169
SPLIT AND JOIN 169
JOIN 171

REVIEW NUMBER 6 172

HELP WITH THIS REVIEW 172

TEXT FILES 173

OPENING A TEXT FILE FOR READING 173
READING LINE BY LINE 176
WRITING TO A TEXT FILE 176
APPENDING TEXT TO A FILE 179
CREATING A FILE IF IT DOESN'T EXIST 180
COPYING FILES 180
MOVING FILES 181
DELETING FILES 181

REVIEW NUMBER SEVEN 183

FUNCTIONS AND SUBS 186

PARAMETERS 188
BYVAL AND BYREF 192
FUNCTIONS 193
STANDARD MODULES 196

EVENTS 203

THE CLICK EVENT 203
MOUSEDOWN 204
THE KEYDOWN EVENT 208
THE FORM LOAD EVENT 211

VB.NET AND CLASSES 213

OBJECT ORIENTED PROGRAMMING 213

CLASSES AND OBJECTS...213
THE .NET FRAMEWORK 214
NAMESPACES..214
CREATING YOUR OWN CLASSES 215
CREATING METHODS IN YOUR CLASSES 218
CREATING AN OBJECT FROM A CLASS 218
CREATING AND USING METHODS THAT DON'T RETURN A VALUE........221
CREATING YOUR OWN PROPERTIES..223
ADDING A PROPERTY TO A CLASS 224
USING YOUR NEW PROPERTY 227

REVIEW NUMBER EIGHT **230**

VB.NET AND DATABASES **232**

VISUAL BASIC EXPRESS AND DATABASES – THE EASY WAY 232

THE DATABASE OBJECTS...**244**

THE CONNECTION OBJECT 244
DATA SETS AND DATA ADAPTERS 248
STRUCTURED QUERY LANGUAGE..249
NAVIGATING THROUGH THE DATASET..253
MOVE FORWARD ONE RECORD AT A TIME 257
MOVE BACK ONE RECORD AT A TIME 258
MOVING TO THE LAST RECORD IN THE DATASET............................258
MOVING TO THE FIRST RECORD IN THE DATASET 259
UPDATING A RECORD 260
ADD A NEW RECORD 262
DELETING RECORDS 265

REVIEW NINE **268**

WORKING WITH FORMS...**270**

ANCHORING AND DOCKING 270
DOCKING 272
TOOLBARS..273
CODING FOR YOUR TOOLBAR BUTTONS..278
CREATING OTHER FORMS 278
MODAL AND NONE MODAL FORMS 280
GETTING AT VALUES ON OTHER FORMS..281

GRAPHICS AND VISUAL BASIC .NET **285**

DRAWING LINES ON A FORM 285
THE PAINT EVENT 289
RECTANGLES AND ELLIPSES 295
FILLED RECTANGLE 297
HOW TO DRAW AN ELLIPSE..298

POLYGONS 302

OTHER FILL STYLES 304

DRAWING TEXT 307

PUTTING IT ALL TOGETHER – A BAR CHART PROJECT 310

HOW TO CREATE A SQL SERVER EXPRESS DATABASE **312**

HAVE YOU GOT SQL SERVER EXPRESS INSTALLED? 312

HOW TO CREATE A SQL SERVER DATABASE 314

HOW TO CREATE TABLES IN YOUR SQL SERVER DATABASE 316

ADDING DATA TO A SQL SERVER DATABASE TABLE 322

DATABASES AND DATAGRIDS 323

THE DATAGRIDVIEW CONTROL 324

CONNECTING TO A SQL SERVER DATABASE 326

GET CELL DATA FROM A DATAGRIDVIEW 332

PICTURE VIEWER – A PROJECT **335**

ADDING THE CONTROLS TO THE FORM 336

SELECTING IMAGES 338

ADDING IMAGES TO AN IMAGES LIST 341

ADDING IMAGES AND FILE PATHS TO THE LISTVIEW 342

THE BIGGER PICTURE 344

ZOOMING IN AND OUT 347

A TABBED BROWSER **350**

THE WEBBROWSER CONTROL 351

NAVIGATION BUTTONS 353

GRAPHIC BUTTONS 356

ADDING TOOLTIPS 359

CREATING NEW TABS 361

SENDING EMAIL WITH VISUAL BASIC .NET **364**

CREATE A NEW MAIL MESSAGE 368

ADDING ATTACHMENTS 372

RECEIVE EMAILS WITH VB NET **377**

POP3 SERVERS 377

POP3 COMMANDS 377

OPENING A CONNECTION TO A POP3 SERVER 378

POP3 SERVER AUTHENTICATION 383

QUITTING THE POP3 SERVER 387

DO YOU HAVE MAIL? 389

GETTING A LIST OF MESSAGES 391

GETTING THE MESSAGE 393

PARSING THE EMAIL 396

DELETING EMAILS 397

RESET THE POP3 SERVER 400

PRINTING IN VB NET 405

SIMPLE PRINTING 405
THE PRINTPAGE EVENT 407
PRINTING MULTIPLE PAGES 409
LOADING A FILE TO BE PRINTED 414
PRINTING THE FILE 416

CODE LIBRARIES 420

CREATING YOUR OWN CODE LIBRARIES 420
HOW TO USE YOUR DLL FILE 424

DEPLOYING YOUR APPS 428

VISTA'S/WIN 7 AUTHENTICATION ISSUES 428
SETTING AN ICON FOR YOUR PROGRAMME 430
PUBLISH YOUR PROGRAMME 432

Introduction

Hello, and a very warm welcome to the Home and Learn computer book for VB .NET Programming. The software you need is set out below. We assume that you have absolutely no knowledge of programming. Throughout the course of this book you will learn the fundamentals of NET programming with VB.NET or Visual Studio NET. And, of course, you will start writing your own programmes. By the end of the book, you will have acquired a good understanding of what programming is all about, and have the ability to take it further, if you so wish. At the very least, you will have given your brain a good work out!

We hope you enjoy your computer book, and our time together.

Before you make a start, though, please read the following brief sections.

What you need to do the course

To do this course you need the following:

- A PC running the Windows XP, Vista or Windows 7 operating system
- Either VB.NET, Visual Studio.NET or the free Visual Basic Express Edition (versions up to and including 2010)
- An internet connection to download the files needed for the exercises in this book

The Free Visual Basic Express Edition

If you don't have either VB.NET or Visual Studio.NET, then you can use the free Visual Basic Express Edition from Microsoft. At the time of writing, this can be downloaded from the following location:

http://www.microsoft.com/express/Windows/

Microsoft also allows you to order the software on CD, if the download is too big for you. (If the above link doesn't work, it means Microsoft have changed the location yet again! In which case, send us an email.)

We cannot, however, accept questions about the installation of the Microsoft software.

Additional Files

Throughout this book, you will see references to additional files. These can now be downloaded from our web site. Connect to the internet and go to the following web page:

www.homeandlearn.co.uk/downloads/downloads.html

Once on the page, click the link for your course book, and save the Zip file to your own hard drive. If you have any problems downloading the files, please contact us at the following email address:

enquiry@homeandlearn.co.uk

You can now make a start. Good luck with your programming!

Getting Started

Launch your Visual Basic .NET or Visual Studio software. When the software first loads, you'll see a screen something like this one:

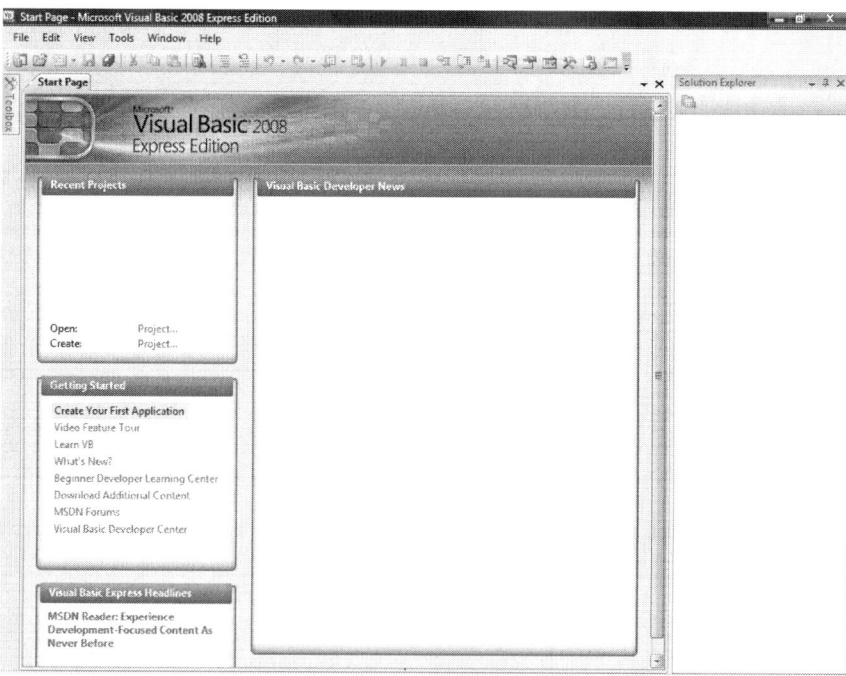

Or this, if you have downloaded the 2010 Express edition:

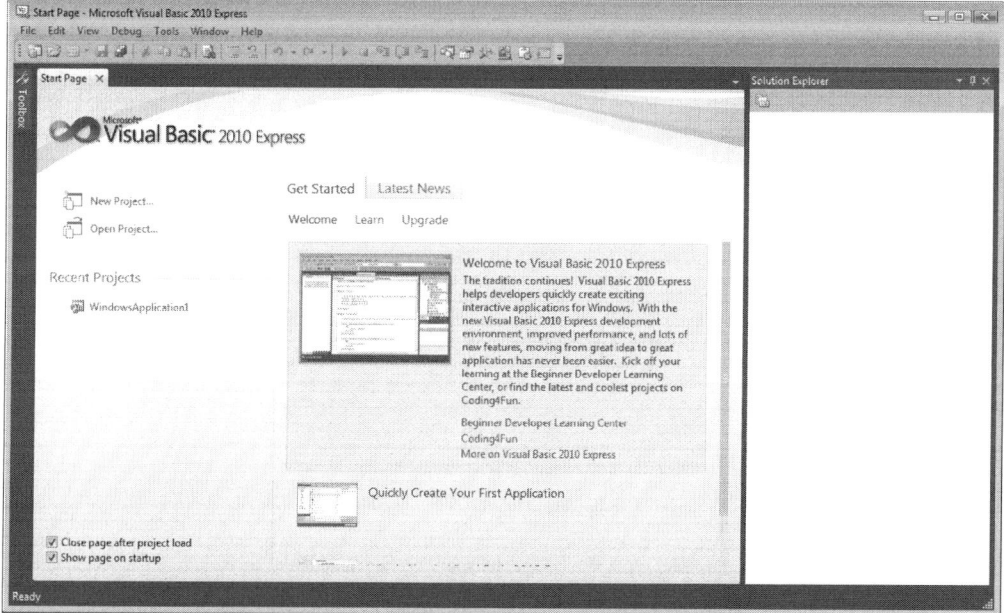

There's a lot happening on the start page. But basically, this is where you can start a new project, or open an existing one. At the moment, the area labelled "Recent Projects" is blank. This is what you'll see when you run the software for the first time (because you haven't created a project yet). When you create a project, the Name you gave it will be displayed on this page, as a hyperlink. Clicking the link will open the project.

At the bottom of the Recent Projects area, there are two links: "Open" and "Create". To get started, click the "**Create**" link. (If you can't see a **Create** link, click **File** from the menu bar. From the File menu, select **New Project**). When you do, you'll see this dialogue box appear in the version 2008:

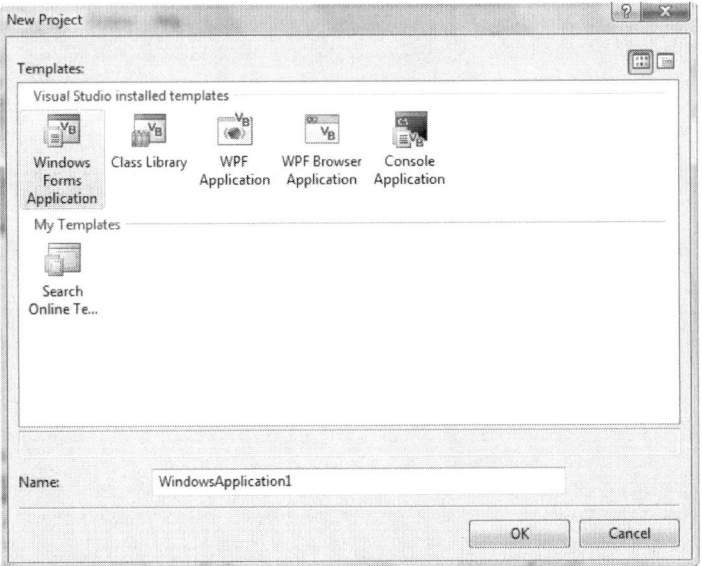

Or this one for version 2010:

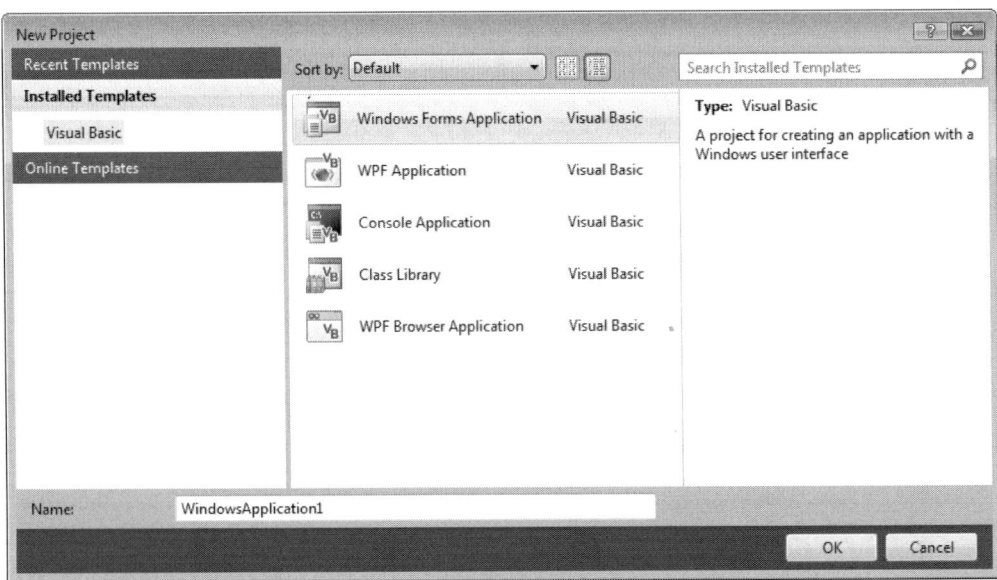

As a beginner, you'll normally want the option selected: "Windows Forms Application". This means that you're going to be designing a programme to run on a computer running the Microsoft Windows operating system.

If you look in the Name textbox at the bottom, you'll see it says **WindowsApplication1**. This is the default name for your projects. It's not a good idea to keep this name. After all, you don't want all of your projects to be called "WindowsApplication1", "WindowsApplication2", etc. So click inside this textbox and change this Name to the following:

My First Project

Keep the Location the same as the default. This is a folder inside of your "My Documents" folder called "Visual Studio Projects". A new folder will then be created for you, and its name will be the one you typed in the "Name" textbox. All of your files for your first project are then saved in this folder.

Click the OK button, and the Visual Basic NET design time environment will open. It will look like the following (version 2008):

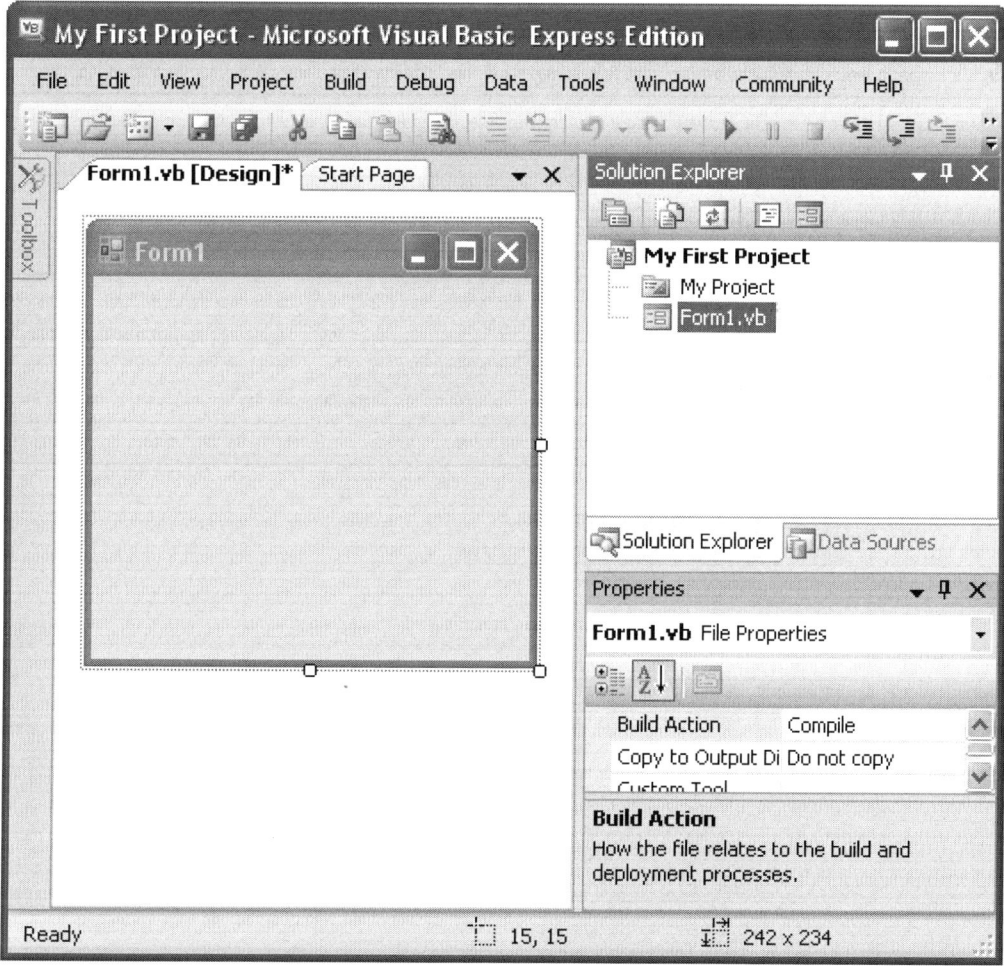

Or this, in version 2010:

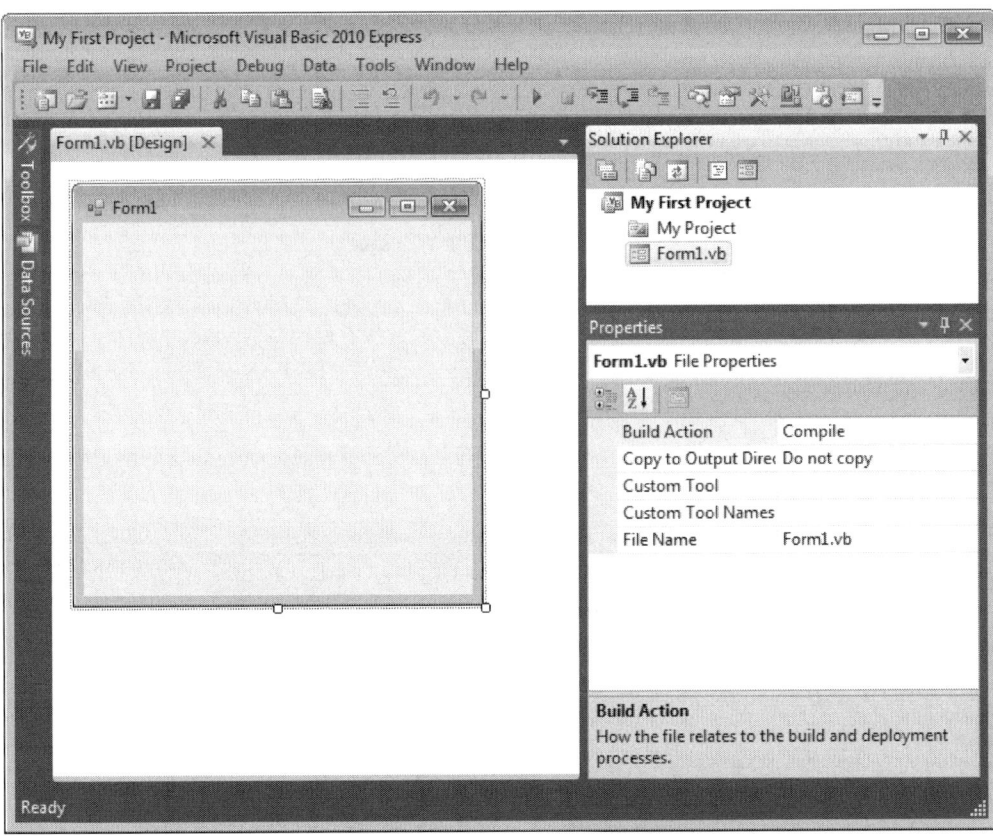

That's a very daunting piece of software, hey? Well, don't worry. We'll break it down bit by bit, and pretty soon you'll be zipping your way around it like a pro!

The first thing to concentrate on is that funny grey square in the middle. That's called a form. It's actually the pretty bit of your programme, the part that others will see when they launch your masterpiece. Granted, it doesn't look too attractive at the moment, but you'll soon discover ways to lick it into shape.

To run the form, try this:

To run the form, try this:

- From the menu bar, click **Debug**
- From the drop down menu, click **Start Debugging**
- Alternatively, press the F5 key on your keyboard
- Your programme is launched

Congratulations! You have now created your very first programme. It should look like this:

The Form Running as a Programme

Click the Red X on the form to stop it from running. You will then be returned to the software environment.

If you compare the first form with the one above, you'll see that they look very similar. But the one above is actually a real programme, something you could package and sell to unsuspecting village idiots.

So what's going on? Why the two different views? Well, Visual Basic has two distinct environments, a design environment and a Debug environment. Design Time is where you get to play about with the form, spruce it up, add textboxes, and buttons, and labels (and code, of course); Debug is where you can test your programme and see how well it performs. Or doesn't perform, as is usually the case.

But don't worry about the terminology, for the time being. Just be aware that there's a two step process to VB programming: designing and debugging.

So, let's get on and do some designing! Before we can start designing a form, though, we need some tools. And where are tools kept? In a toolbox!

The Toolbox

Things like buttons, textboxes, and labels are all things that you can add to your Forms. They are known as Controls, and are kept in the Toolbox for ease of use.

The Toolbox can be found on the left of the screen. In the picture below, you can see the toolbox icon next to Form1:

Express Edition 2008

Express Edition 2010

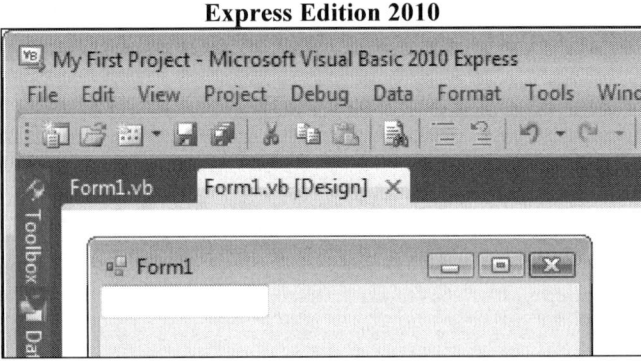

To display all the tools, move your mouse over the toolbox icon. You'll see the following automatically appear:

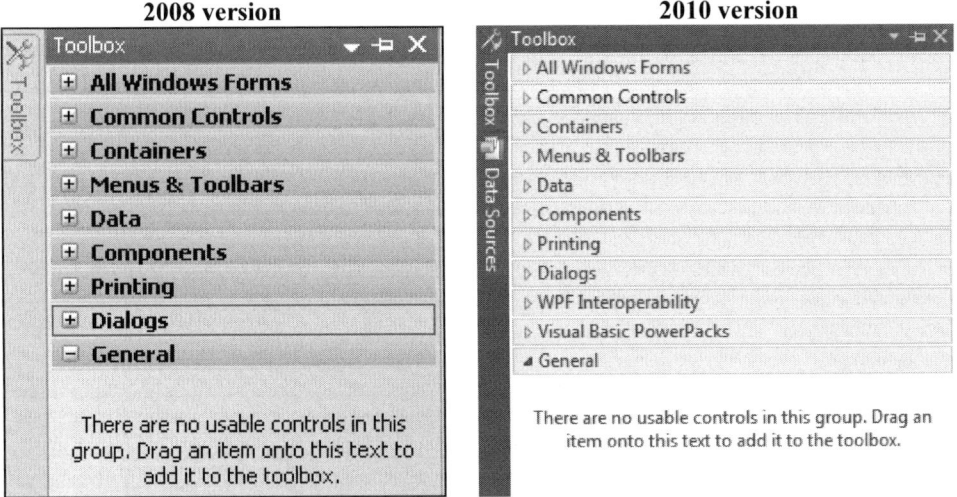

There are seven categories of tools available. The toolbox you'll be working with first is the Common Controls toolbox. To see the tools, click on the plus symbol next to Common Controls. You'll see a long list of tools:

As you can see, there's an awful lot of tools to choose from! For this first section, we'll only be using the Button, the Textbox and the Label.

If you want to keep the toolbox displayed, click the Pin icon next to the X. To close the toolbox, simply move your mouse away.

Adding a Tool (Control) to your form

Let's start by adding a textbox to our form. With the tools displayed, do the following:

- Locate the TextBox tool
- Double click the icon
- A textbox is added to your form

The textbox gets added to the top left position of your form. To move it down, hold your mouse over the textbox and drag to a new position:

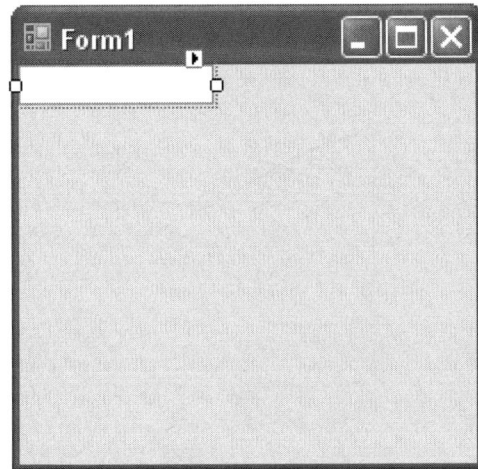

Notice the small squares around the textbox. These are sizing handles. Move your mouse over one of them. The mouse pointer turns into an extended line with arrowheads. Hold your left mouse button down and drag outwards. The textbox is resized. Play around with the sizing handles until you're happy with the size of your textbox.

One thing you will notice is that you can't make the size any higher, but you can make it wider. The reason why you can't make it any higher is because the default action of a textbox is to have it contain only a single line of text. If it's only going to contain one line of text, Microsoft reasoned, there's no reason why you should be able to change its height. A textbox can only be made higher if it's set to contain multiple lines of text. You'll see how to do this soon.

- Create two more textboxes by double clicking on the textbox icon in the toolbar (Or Right-Click on the selected textbox and choose Copy. Then Right-Click on the Form and choose Paste.)
- Resize them to the same size as your first one
- Line them up one below the other with space in between
- Try to create something that looks like the one below

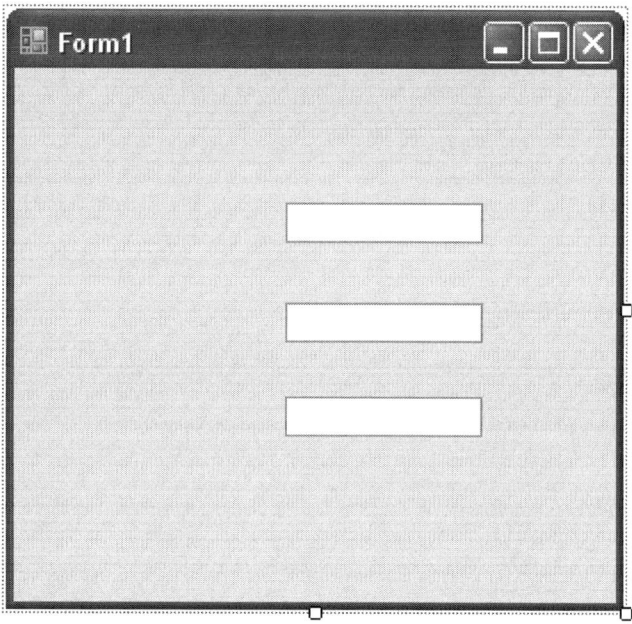

Let's add some labels near the textboxes, so that your users will know what they are for.

- Locate the label control in the toolbox
- Double click the label icon
- A new label is added to your form
- It should look like the one below

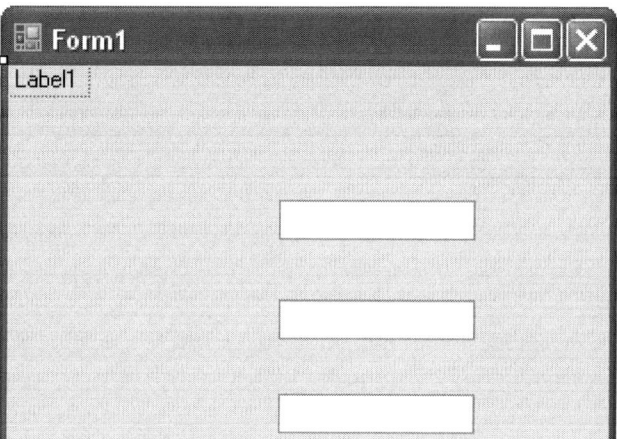

Click on the label to select it. Now hold your left mouse button down on the label. Keep it held down and drag it to the left of the textbox.

Create two more labels, and position them to the left of the textboxes. You should now have a form like this one:

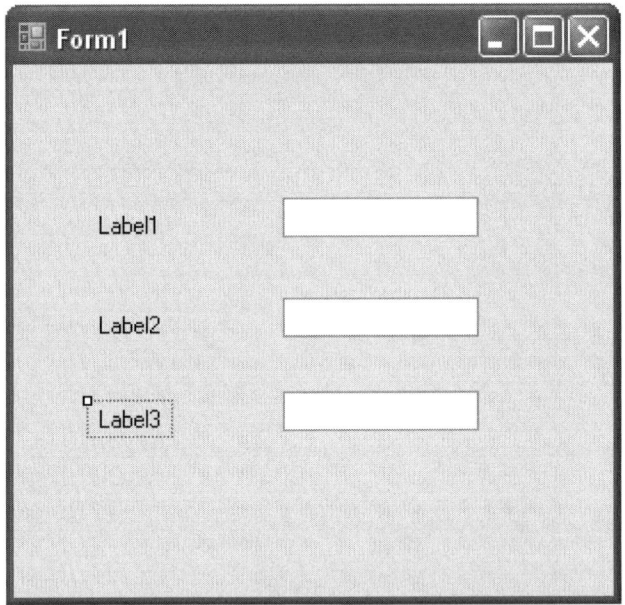

To see what your Form looks like as a programme, click **Debug > Start Debugging** from the menu bar. Or press F5 on your keyboard:

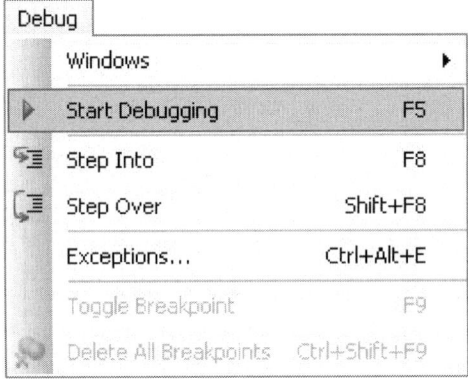

To stop the programme from running, you can do one of the following:

- Click the Red X at the top right of your Form
- Click **Debug > Stop Debugging** from the menu bar

You can also click the **Stop** button on the VB toolbars at the top, as in the image below:

All right, we're getting somewhere. We now have a form with textboxes and labels, something that looks like a form people can fill in. But those labels are not exactly descriptive, and our textboxes have the default text in them. So how can we enter our own text for the labels, and get rid of that default text for the textboxes?

To do those things, we need to discuss something called a Property.

Properties

I'm sure you've noticed the area to the bottom right of the design environment, the area with the textboxes in a grid that has those daunting names like AccessibleDescription, AccessibleName, AccessibleRole. That's the Properties box.

Click anywhere on the form that is not a label or a textbox, somewhere on the form's grey areas. The form should have the little sizing handles now, indicating that the form is selected.

On the right of the design environment there should be the following Properties box:

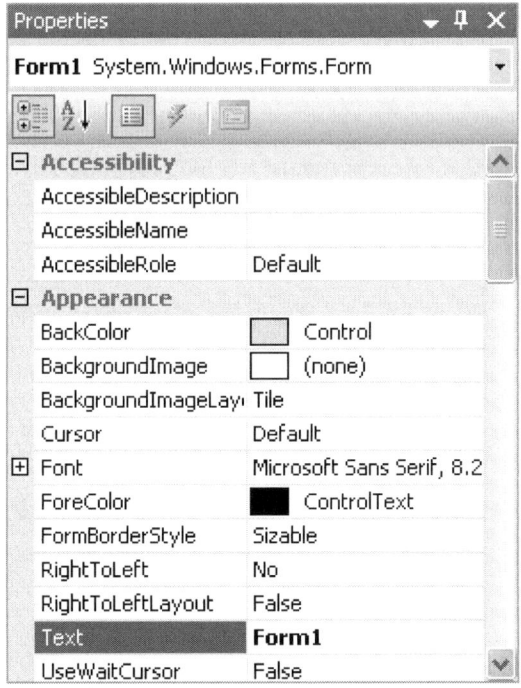

If your Properties box says "**Textbox1** Textbox" or "**Label1** Label" then you haven't yet selected the Form. Click away from the textbox or label until the Properties box reads "**Form1**"

What you are looking at is a list of the properties that a form has: Name , BackColor, Font, Image, Text, etc. Just to the right of these properties are the values for them. These values are the default values, and can be changed. We're going to change the value of the Text property.

First, you might want to display the list of Properties in a more accessible form. You can display the list properties alphabetically. To do that, click the **Alphabetic** icon at the top of the Properties box, as in the image below:

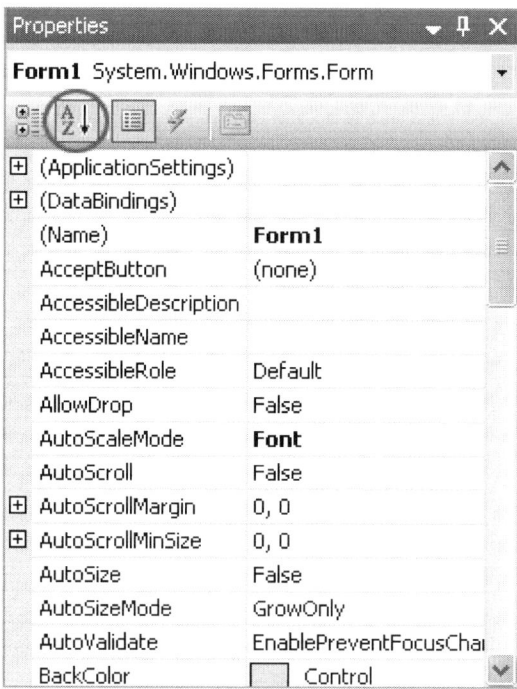

This will make the properties easier to find.

Before we change anything in the Properties box, let's clear up what we mean by "Property".

Those controls you added to the form (textboxes and labels), and the form itself, are called control objects. You can think of controls as things, something solid that you can pick up and move about. Controls (things) have properties. If your television were a control, it too would have properties: an On/Off button property, a colour property, a volume property, and a ... well, what other properties would your television have? Think about it.

The properties of your television will have values. The On/Off button would have just two values - On or Off. The volume property could have a range of values, from zero to ten, for example. If the value of the volume property was set to ten, the loudest value, then you'd probably have some very angry neighbours!

In VB.NET, you can change a property of a control from the Properties Box. (You can also change a property using code, which you'll do quite a lot.) If we go back to our Form object, and the properties and values it has, we can see how to change them using the Properties Box. We'll change only one of these values for now - the value of the Text property. So, do this:

- Locate the word **Text** in the Property box, as in the image below

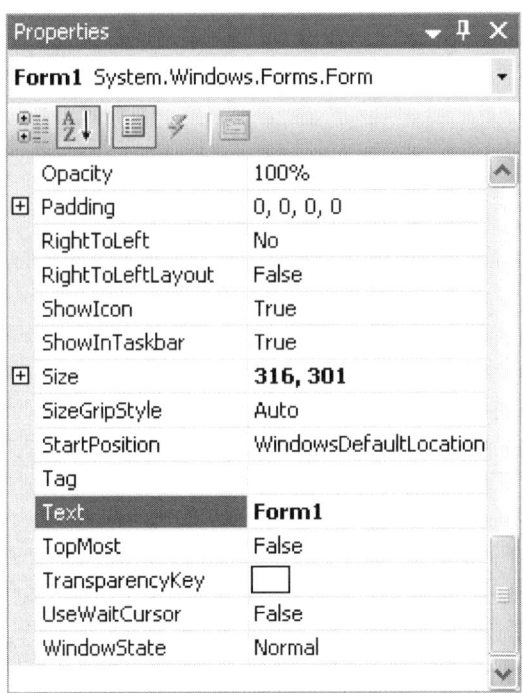

Text is a Property of Form1. Don't be confused by the word "Form1" next to the word "Text". All this means is that the current value of the Text property is set to the word "Form1". This is the default.

To change this to something of your own, do this:

- Click inside the area next to "Text", and delete the word "Form1" by hitting the backspace key on your keyboard
- When "Form1" has been deleted, type the words **My First Form**

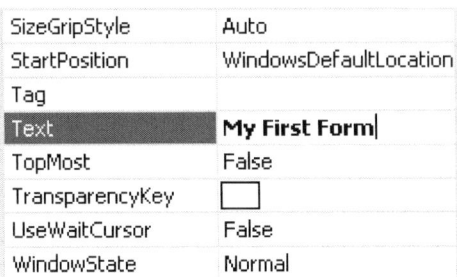

- Click back on the form itself (the one with the labels and textboxes), or hit the return key on your keyboard
- The words "My First Form" will appear as white text on a blue background at the top of the form

When you've correctly changed the Text property, your Form will then look like this one:

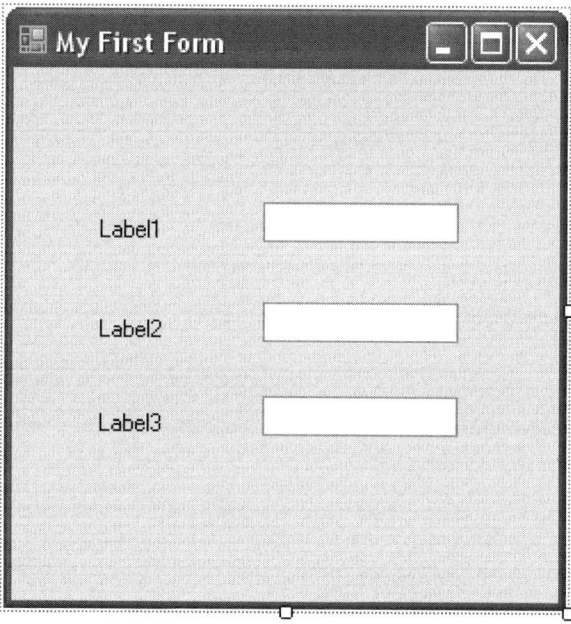

As you can see, your new text has gone at the top of the form, in white on the blue background.

So the Text Property of a form is for setting the caption you want to display in the title bar at the top. Changing the values of some properties is fairly easy. We'll now change the Text properties of our labels, and the Text properties of our Textboxes.

Click on Label1 so that it has the sizing handles, and is therefore selected. Examine the Property box for the Label:

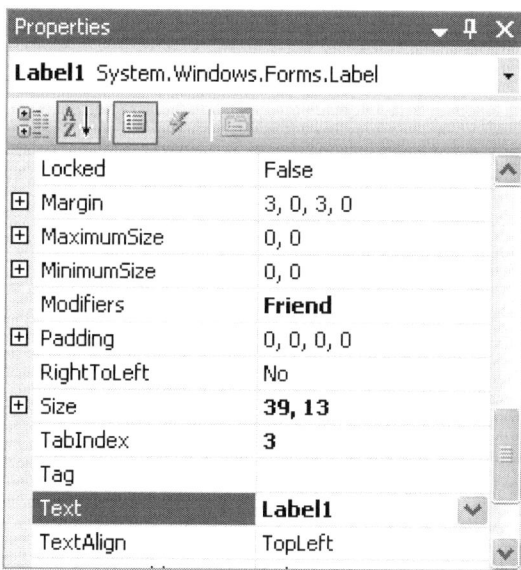

You can see that the Label control has quite a few different properties to the Form control. Think back to your television as a control. It will have different buttons and knobs to your DVD Player control. A label has different "buttons and knobs" to the Form's "buttons and knobs".

But the Label has a lot of properties that are the same. The Text property of a Label does what you'd expect it to do: adds text to your label. We'll do that now:

- With label1 selected, click inside the area next to "Text", and delete the word "Label1" by hitting the backspace key on your keyboard
- Type in the words "First Name"
- Click back onto the grey form, or hit the return key on your keyboard
- Label1 has now changed its text caption to read "First Name"
- If you've made a typing error, go back to the first step above and try again
- Your form should now look like this:

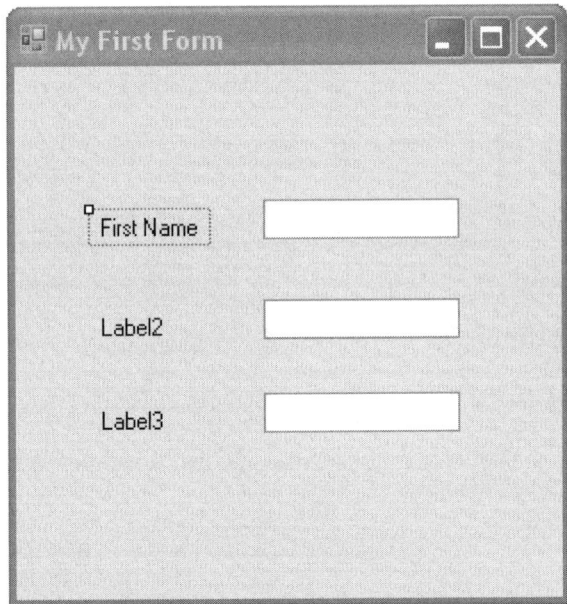

Now, change the Text property of the other two labels. Change them to these values:

Label2:   Last Name
Label3:   Telephone Number

What you should notice is that the labels resize themselves, after you press the enter key to commit the changes. You may need to drag your labels to the left a bit. But when you're finished, your form should look like ours below:

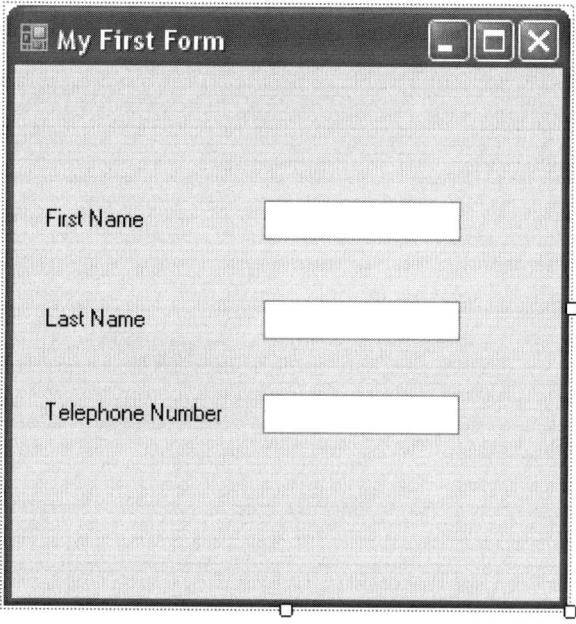

In fact, that Form looks a little squashed at the moment. Is there anything we can do to make it bigger? Well, it just so happens there is.

The Form can be resized just like the Label and the textboxes. Click anywhere on the form that is not a textbox or a label. If you look closely around the Form's edges, you'll notice our old friends the sizing handles. To make the form bigger, just stretch it like you did the labels and the textboxes. Play around with the size of the form until you're happy with it. You can now reposition and resize the textboxes and labels so that things don't look too squashed. Your form might look like this one:

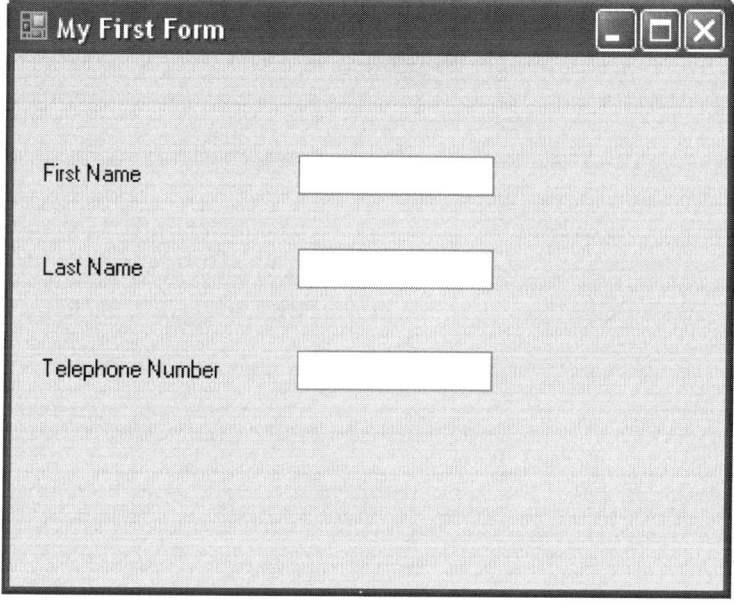

Click on **Debug > Start Debugging** to have a look at your programme. Or Press F5 on your keyboard. Click **Debug > Stop Debugging** to get back to the design environment. (Or just click the red X at the top right of the form.)

Saving your work

If you have a look in the top right of the Design Environment, you'll see the Solution Explorer. (If you can't see it, click **View > Solution Explorer** in version 2008 and **View > Other Windows > Solution Explorer** in version 2010.)

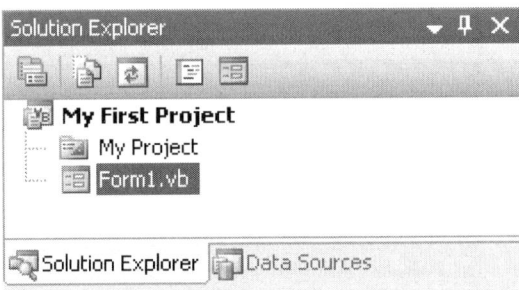

The Solution Explorer shows you all the files you have in your project (Notice that the name of your project is at the top of the tree – "My First Project").

At first glance, it looks as though there are not many files in the project. But click the Show All Files icon, circled below:

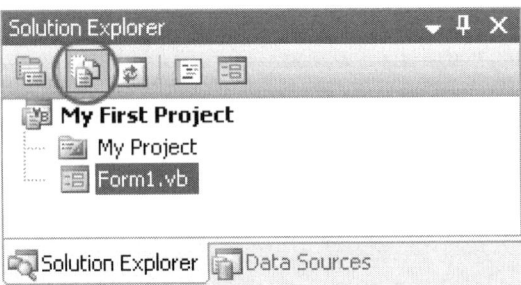

When you click **Show All Files**, the Solution Explorer will look something like this:

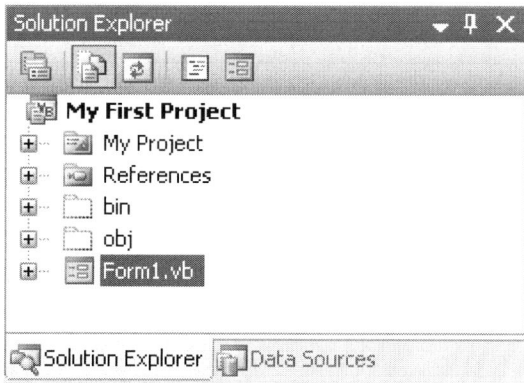

When you save your project, you are saving all these files.

To save your work, click **File** > **Save All** and you'll see the following dialogue box (we've chopped ours down a bit):

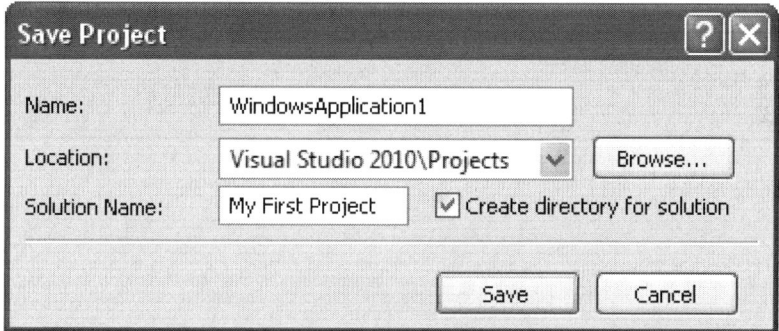

The files are usually saved in the My Document folder in XP (Document folder in Vista and Windows 7), under Visual Studio. If you want to save your projects elsewhere, click the **Browse** button.

To actually save your work as you go along, just click **File** > **Save All** from the menu bar. Or press Ctrl + Shift + S on your keyboard. Or click the icon in the Toolbar (the stack of floppy disks). If you save often then you won't lose any of your work if anything goes wrong with your computer.

Before you get to your first Review, though, let's see how to add a splash of colour to your form.

Adding a splash of colour

At the moment, our form looks a little bland. Time to liven it up with a splash of colour.

Changing the colour of the Form means we have to change one of its properties - the **BackColor** property.

So click anywhere on the form that is not a textbox or a label. If you do it right, you should see the sizing handles around the edges of the grey form. The Property Box on the right will read "Form1", and that indicates that you have indeed selected the form. When the Form is selected you can change its properties.

To change the colour of the Form, click the word "**BackColor**" in the Property Box. Next, click the black down-pointing arrow to the right. A drop-down box will appear:

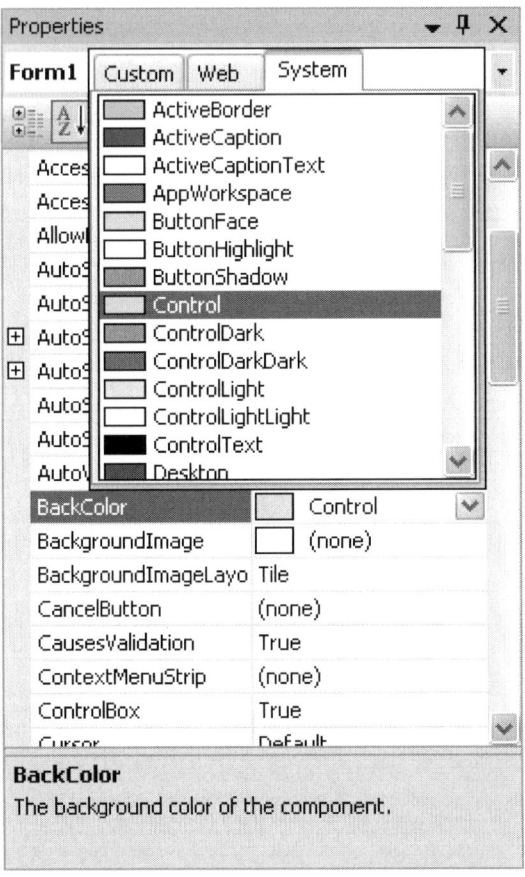

The default colour is the one selected – Control. This is on the System Tab. The System colours are set to whatever colour scheme the user has opted for when setting up their computers. For example, you can use the Display Properties dialogue box in Windows to change how things like menus and buttons look. Someone who is colour-blind might have changed his or her settings in order to see things better on the computer screen. If you stick with the System colours then a colour-blind user of your programme would not have any problems seeing your master work.

If you want to choose a colour that is not a System colour, click the Custom Tab. You'll then see this:

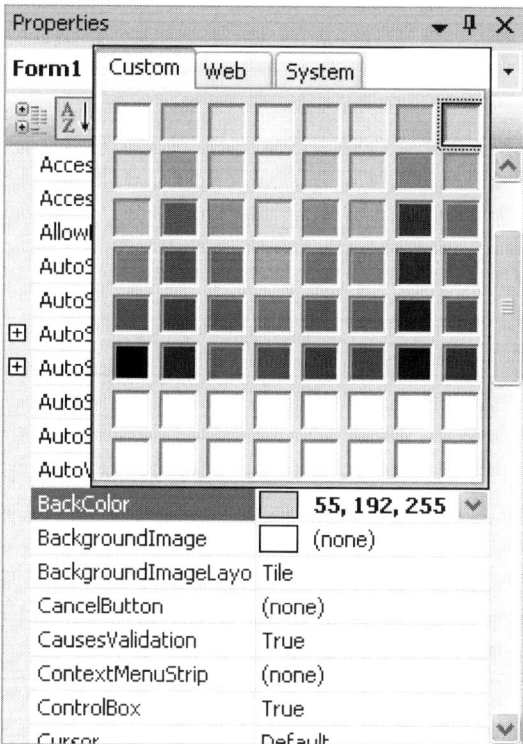

Click on any of the Colours in the colour palette and the background colour of your form will change.

You can also select the Web tab. When you do, you'll see a list of Web-Safe colours to choose from. A Web-Safe colour is one that displays correctly in a web browser, regardless of which computer is being used (that's the theory, anyway). You might want to use a Web-Safe colour if you're designing a project for the internet. But you can choose one even if you're not.

To change the colour of the labels, click on a label to select it. Look in the Property box to see if it reads Label. If so, you can now go ahead and change the BackColor property of the Label in exactly the same way that we changed the BackColor property for our Form.

Change the colour of the other two labels to anything you like. To change the colour of more than one Label at a time, click on one Label to select it. Now, hold down the "Ctrl" key on your keyboard and click another Label. You'll see that two Labels now have sizing handles around them. Click the third Label with the "Ctrl" key held down, and all three Labels will be selected. You can change the BackColor property of all three at once.

If you want to change the Font size of the Labels and Textboxes, select a control. Let's start with Label1.

- So click on Label 1
- Scroll down the Property Box until you see Font
- Click on the word "Font" to highlight it
- Microsoft Sans Serif is the default Font

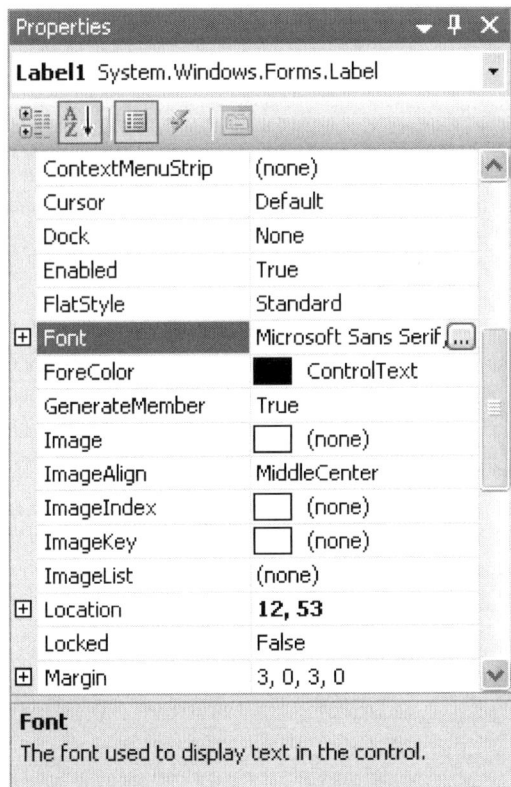

Notice that the Font property has a cross next to it. This indicates that the property is expandable. Click the cross to see the following:

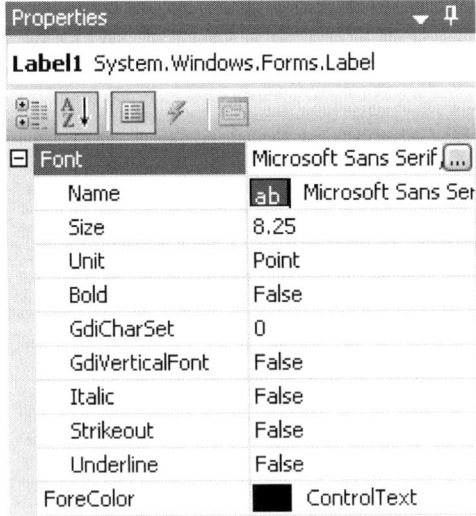

As you can see, you can change a lot of Font properties from here: the Name of the font, its Size, whether it should be Bold or not, etc. You can also click the square box with the three dots in it. This brings up a dialogue box where you can change the font properties in the same place.

Make the following changes to the three labels:

Font:	Arial
Font Style:	Bold
Font Size:	10

Change the Font of the three Textboxes so that they are the same as the Labels

And now it's time for your first review.

Review Number 1

The textboxes are blank, at the moment. For Review Number 1, locate the Text Property of the all three textboxes. Enter the following

Textbox1:	Please Enter Your First Name
Textbox2:	Please Enter Your Last Name
Textbox3:	Please Enter Your Telephone Number

Your form should have a splash of colour by now; the labels should have colour and a change of font; and the textboxes should have had their default font changed.

Here's one we played around with. It's a bit on the garish side!

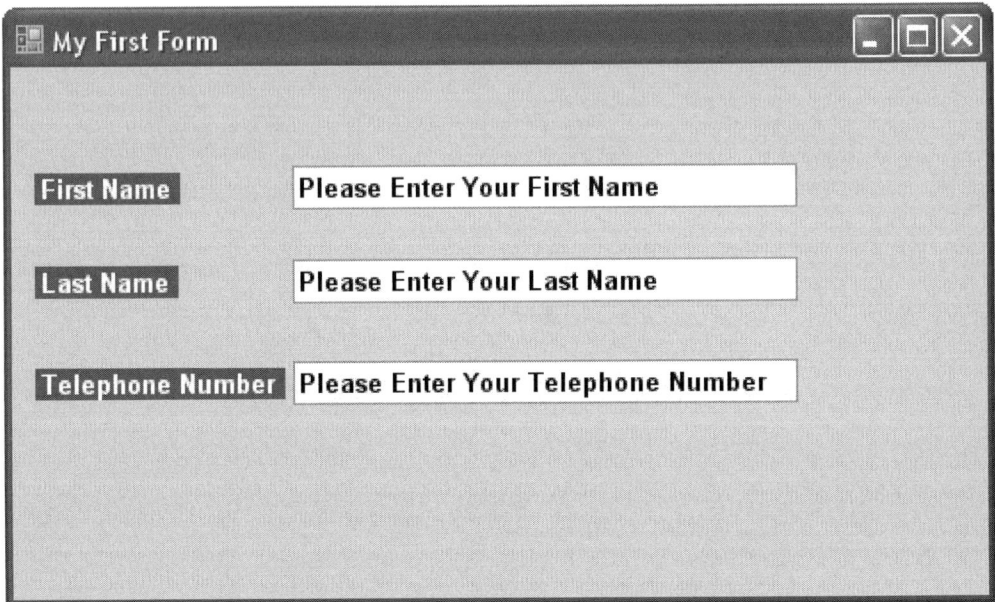

To get the white text on a coloured background, explore the ForeColor property.

When you're satisfied with your form, you can move on to the next section.

Getting our Hands Dirty: Variables

Time to get our hands dirty with a bit of programming. There's no putting it off any longer, I'm afraid! We'll create a new project for this section.

So, if you already have your VB NET software open, you can get rid of the current project by clicking **File** from the menu bar. From the drop down menu, choose **Close Project**. You will be returned to the Start Page. Click **File > New Project** from the menu bars. When you get the dialogue box popping up, choose **Windows Application** at the top. Then change the **Name** from **WindowsApplication** to **Variables**:

When you click the OK button, a new form will appear.

If you look at the Solution Explorer at the top, you'll see the name of the project has changed to the Name you gave it.

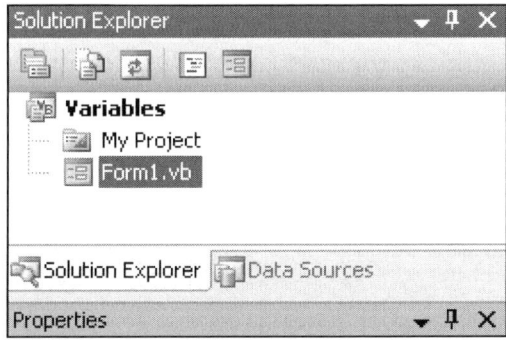

The name of the Project is now Variables – the same name as the folder that is created for you to hold all your project files.

What are Variables?

Why are we discussing variables? And what is a variable?

With Visual Basic, and most programming languages, what you are doing is storing things in the computer's memory, and manipulating this store. If you want to add two numbers together, you put the numbers into storage areas and "tell" Visual Basic to add them up. But you can't do this without variables.

So a variable is a storage area of the computer's memory. Think of it like this: a variable is an empty cardboard box. Now, imagine you have a very large room, and in this room you have a whole lot of empty cardboard boxes. Each empty cardboard box is a single variable. To add two numbers together, write the first number on a piece of paper and put the piece of paper into an empty box. Write the second number on a piece of paper and put this second piece of paper in a different cardboard box.

Now, out of all your thousands of empty cardboard boxes two of them contain pieces of paper with numbers on them. To help you remember which of the thousands of boxes hold your numbers, put a sticky label on each of the two boxes. Write "number1" on the first sticky label, and "number2" on the second label.

What have we just done? Well, we've created a large memory area (the room and the cardboard boxes), and we've set up two of the boxes to hold our numbers (two variables). We've also given each of these variables a name (the sticky labels) so that we can remember where they are.

Now examine this code:

```
Dim number1 As Integer
Dim number 2 As Integer

number1 = 3
number2 = 5
```

That's code from Visual Basic Net. It's VB's way of setting up (or declaring) variables.

Here's a breakdown of the first line of code (**Dim number1 As Integer**):

Dim
Short for Dimension. It's a type of variable. You declare (or "tell" Visual Basic) that you are setting up a variable with this word. We'll meet other types of variables later, but for now just remember to start your variable declarations with **Dim**.

number1
This is the cardboard box and the sticky label all in one. This is a variable. In other words, our storage area. After the Dim word, Visual Basic is looking for the name of your variable. You can call your variable almost anything you like, but there are a few reserved words that VB won't allow. It's good practice to give your variables a name appropriate to what is going in the variable.

As Integer
We're telling Visual Basic that the variable is going to be a number (integer). Well meet alternatives to Integer later.

And here's an explanation of the third line of code:

Number1 = 3
The equals sign is not actually an equals sign. The = sign means assign a value of. In other words, here is where you put something in your variable. We're telling Visual Basic to assign a value of 3 to the variable called number1. Think back to the piece of paper going into the cardboard box. Well, this is the programming equivalent of writing a value on a piece of paper

Now that you have a basic idea of what variables are, let's write a little piece of code to test them out. First, though, let's have our first look at the coding window.

To make life easier, we're going to put a button on our form. When our button is clicked, a little message box will pop up. Fortunately, there's no coding to write for a button, and very little at all for a message box.

Adding a Button to the Form

Instead of double clicking the Button tool in the toolbox to add the control to the form, we'll explore another way to do it.

With your Form displayed in the Visual Basic Design environment, do the following:

- Click on the Button tool in the toolbox with the left hand mouse button, but click only once
- Move your mouse to a blank area of your form - the mouse pointer will turn into a cross
- Press and hold down the left mouse button
- Drag across the form with the button held down
- Let go of the mouse button when you're happy with the size
- A Button is drawn

You can use the above method to draw most of the controls onto the form - labels, buttons, textboxes, etc.

The Button control, just like all the other controls we've seen so far, has a list of properties. One of these properties is the Text property. At the moment, your button will say "Button 1". You can change that to anything you like.

- Click on the Button to highlight it
- Click on Text in the Property Box
- Click in the box next to the word "Text"
- Delete the word "Button 1"
- Type "Add two numbers"
- Click back on the Form

Now add a Textbox to your form using one of the methods outlined (either double-click, or draw).

Your Form should now look something like this:

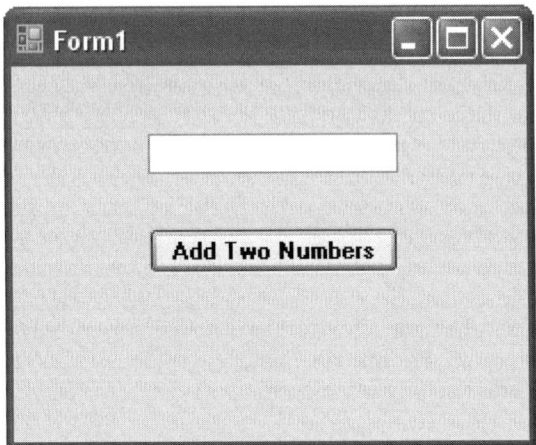

The Font property of the Button has also been changed, here, in exactly the same way as we changed the Font property of the Label and Textbox previously.

To get our first look at the code window, double click your Button control. The code window will appear, and will look like this:

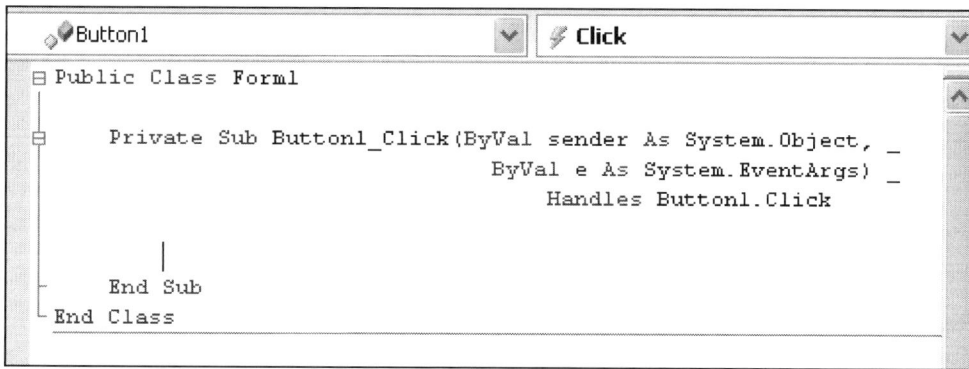

Notice that we've used the underscore character (_) to spread the code over more than one line. You can do this in your own code, if it becomes too long. But you don't have to.

The part to concentrate on for the moment is where your cursor is flashing on and off. Because you double-clicked the Button control, the cursor will be flashing between the lines Private Sub … and End Sub.

Here's the parts we're concentrating on, the parts in bold:

> **Private Sub Button1_Click**(ByVal sender As System.Object, _
> ByVal e As System.EventArgs) _
> Handles Button1.Click
>
> **End Sub**

And here's what each part means:

Private
Private means that no other part of the programme can see this code except for our button

Sub
Short for Subroutine. The "Sub" word tells VB that some code follows, and that it needs to be executed

Button1
This is the name of our button. You might think that we've just erased the word "Button1" when we changed the Text property, so why does VB insist that it's still called Button1? We'll, the Name property of the control is the important one. If you change the Name property, VB will change this button name for you.

_Click ( )
This is something called an Event. In other words, when the button is clicked, the Click Event will fire, and the code we're going to write will be executed

End Sub
The subroutine ends right here. This signifies the end of our code.

Don't worry if you don't understand all of that. It will become clearer later. Let's add our code.

Click your mouse on the blank line after **Private Sub Button1_Click**, etc, but before **End Sub**. Type the following code:

> **Dim number1 As Integer**
> **Dim number 2 As Integer**
> **Dim answer As Integer**
>
> **number1 = 3**
> **number2 = 5**
>
> **answer = number1 + number2**
>
> **MsgBox answer**

After typing all that, your code window should now look like this:

```
Private Sub Button1_Click(ByVal sender As System.Object, _
                          ByVal e As System.EventArgs) _
                          Handles Button1.Click

    Dim number1 As Integer
    Dim number2 As Integer
    Dim answer As Integer

    number1 = 3
    number2 = 5

    answer = number1 + number2

    MsgBox(answer)

End Sub
```

Before we explore what's happening here, save your work and then click **Debug** > **Start Debugging** from the Visual Basic Menu, or press F5 on your keyboard. This will launch your programme. Click the Button once, and you should get the following:

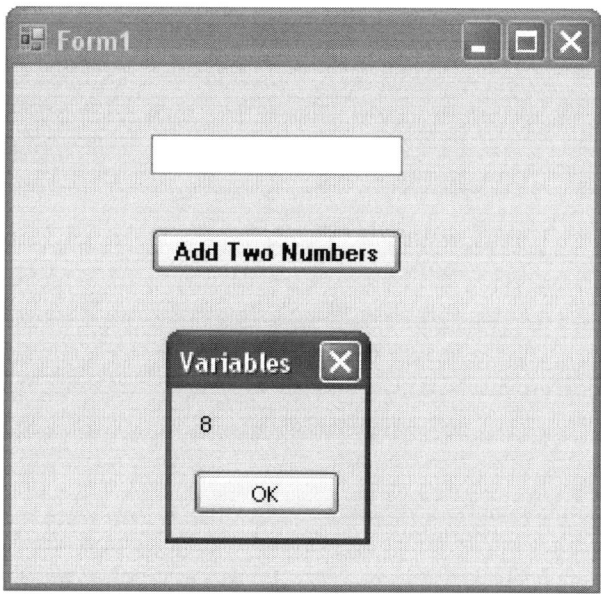

Stop your programme, and return to the Design Environment. If you can't see your code, you can click the Tabs at the top of the Window, as in the image below:

Click the "Form1.vb [Design]" tab to see your Form.

OK, what happened there? Well, what happened is we've just written a programme to add two numbers together, and we displayed the result by using a Message Box - your very first real programme! But let's break that code down a little more.

> **Dim number1 As Integer**
> **Dim number 2 As Integer**
> **Dim answer As Integer**
>
> **number1 = 3**
> **number2 = 5**
>
> **answer = number1 + number2**
>
> **MsgBox answer**

- First, we started with the Dim word, indicating to Visual Basic that we wanted to set up a variable
- Then we gave the variable a name (**number1**)
- Next, we "told" VB that what is going inside the variable is a number (**As Integer**)
- Two more variables were set up in the same way, **number2** and **answer**

After setting up the three variables, here's what we did:

- Told Visual Basic that what is going into the first variable was the number 3, and what is going into the second variable was the number 5. To put something into a variable, you use the equals (=) sign. But it's not really an equals sign – it's an assignment operator. You are assigning the value of 3 to the variable called number1.

number1 = 3
number2 = 5

The next part is a little bit more complicated, but not too complicated. What we wanted to do was to add two numbers together. So we said

number1 + number2

Visual Basic already knows how to add up: all we need to do is "tell" it to add up. We do the "telling" in the traditional, mathematical way - with the plus sign (+). What Visual Basic will do is to look at what we've stored inside **number1**, and look at what's inside **number2**. It sees the 3, sees the five, and also sees the plus sign. Then Visual Basic adds them up for you.

Except we also did something else. We said to Visual Basic "When you've finished adding up the two variables **number1** and **number2**, store the result in that other variable we set up, which is called answer."

So, the whole line

answer = number1 + number2

means:

"Add the variable called number1 to the variable called number2. Then store the result in the variable called answer."

Think of it as working from the right-hand side of the equals sign first. Then when you have the answer, assign it the variable on the left of the equals sign.

The final part of the programme used Visual Basic's in-built Message Box. We'll learn a more about the Message Box later. For now, think of it as a handy way to display results.

Message boxes are quite handy when you want to display the result of some code. But we have a textbox on the form, and we might as well use that.

So delete the line: **MsgBox answer**. Type the word **Textbox1**, then type a full stop. You should see a drop-down box appear. This is a list of the Properties and Methods that the Textbox can use.

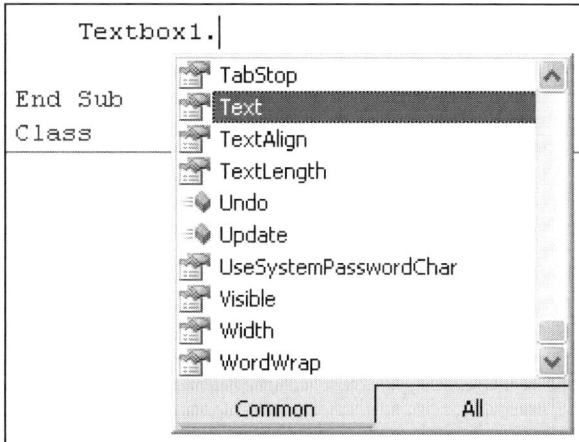

Scroll down until you see the word "Text". Double click the Text property and the drop-down box will disappear. (This drop-down box is known as IntelliSense, and is very handy. It means you can just select a property or method from the list without having to type anything.)

The Text property you have chosen is the same Text property that you set from the Properties Window earlier. Here, we're setting the property with our code; before, we set it at design time. But the result is the same – the Text property of the textbox will be set to a value of our choosing.

To set a value, type an equals sign, then type a value for the Text property. We want the contents of the variable called answer to appear in the textbox. So the rest of the code is just this:

Textbox1.Text = answer

Your code window should then look like this:

```
Private Sub Button1_Click(ByVal sender As System.Object, _
                          ByVal e As System.EventArgs) _
                          Handles Button1.Click

    Dim number1 As Integer
    Dim number2 As Integer
    Dim answer As Integer

    number1 = 3
    number2 = 5

    answer = number1 + number2

    TextBox1.Text = answer

End Sub
```

Run your code again, and press the Button on the form. You should see the number 8 appear in the textbox.

OK, time for your first exercises. They're not too painful, and hopefully they'll give you a better idea of what variables are. And besides, programming is about doing, not talking. So off we go!

Exercise
Delete the values "3" and "5" and replace them with numbers of your own

Exercise
Delete the plus sign in between number1 and number2, and replace them with each of the following in turn

        -          (the minus sign)
        *   (the multiplication sign in VB is the asterisk sign)
        /   (the divide sign in VB is the forward slash)

Exercise
Set up another Integer variable. Give it the name number3. Assign a value of 10 to this new variable. Multiply the value of your new variable by the variable called answer. Display the result in your textbox.

(Another way to assign values to variables is when you first set them up. You can do this:

Dim number3 As Integer = 10

This is exactly the same as saying:

Dim number3 As Integer

number3 = 10

It's up you which method you use. But the objective is the same – to assign a value to a variable.)

String Variables

So we've just learnt something about variables, what they are and how to set one up. We learnt about the word "integer", and that integer variables held numbers. But what if we don't want numbers? After all, our first Form asked users to type in their First Name and Last Name. Names are not numbers, so what do we do then? Well that's where Strings come in.

What is a String? Actually a string is nothing more than text. And if we want Visual Basic to store text we need to use the word "String". To set up a variable to hold text we need to use **As String** and not **As Integer**. If the information we want to store in our variables is a First Name and a Last Name, we can set up two variables like this.

Dim FirstName As String
Dim LastName As String

Again we've started with the **Dim** word. Then we've called the first variable **FirstName**. Finally, we've ended the line by telling Visual Basic that we want to store text in the variable - **As String**.

So we've set up the variables. But there is nothing stored in them yet. We store something in a variable with the equals sign (=). Let's store a first name and a last name in them

FirstName = "Bill"
LastName = "Gates"

Here, we said to Visual Basic "Store the word 'Bill' into the variable **FirstName** and store the word 'Gates' into the variable called **LastName**. But pay attention to the quotation marks surrounding the two words. We didn't say Bill, we said "Bill". Visual Basic needs the two double quotation marks before it can identify your text, your String.

So remember: if you're storing text in a variable, don't forget the quotation marks!

To test all this out, add a new Button to your Form. Set the Text property of the Button to "String Test". Your Form would then look like this:

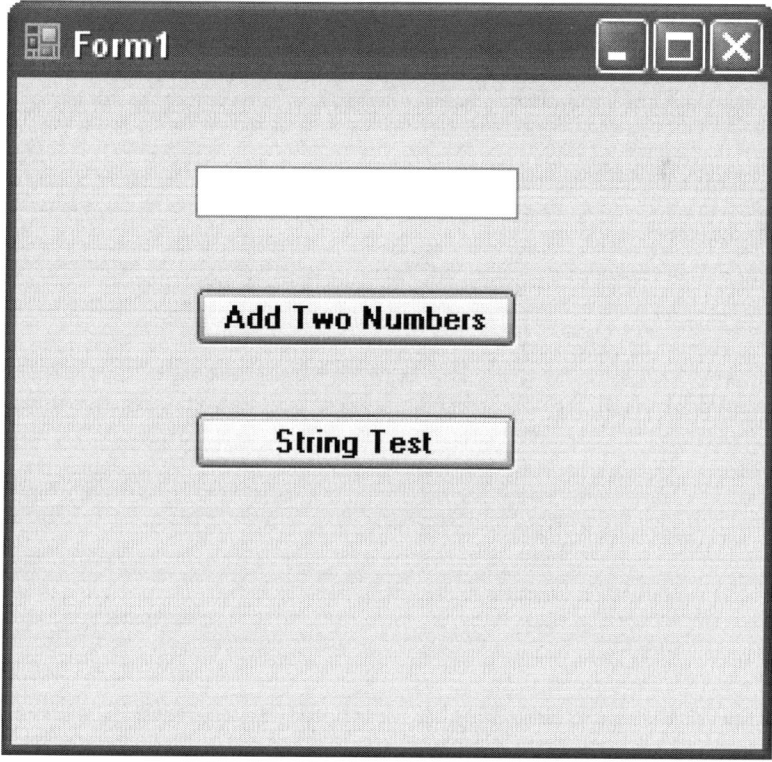

Double click your new button, and add the following code:

Dim FirstName As String
Dim LastName As String
Dim FullName As String

FirstName = "Bill"
LastName = "Gates"

FullName = FirstName & LastName

TextBox1.Text = FullName

Your code window should now look like this:

```
Private Sub Button2_Click(ByVal sender As System.Object, _
                          ByVal e As System.EventArgs) _
                          Handles Button2.Click

    Dim FirstName As String
    Dim LastName As String
    Dim FullName As String

    FirstName = "Bill"
    LastName = "Gates"

    FullName = FirstName & LastName

    TextBox1.Text = FullName

End Sub
```

There's a line there that needs explaining

FullName = FirstName & LastName

In the two lines of code above that one, we stored the string "Bill" and the string "Gates" into two variables. What we're doing now is joining those two variables together. We do this with the ampersand symbol (**&**). The ampersand is used to join strings together. It's called **Concatenation**.

Once Visual Basic has joined the two strings together (or concatenated them), we're saying "store the result in the variable called **FullName**".

After that, we tell VB to display the result in our Textbox.

So, once you've typed the code, start your programme and test it out.

Once the programme is running, click the Button and see what happens. You should have a Form that looks something like this one:

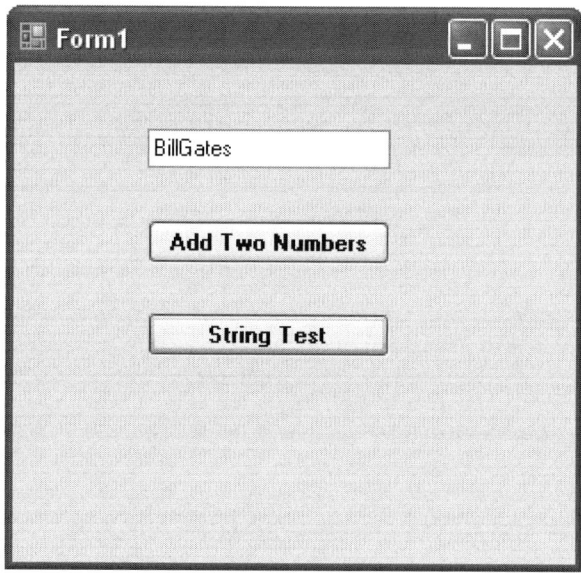

The textbox has displayed the text stored in our variables, "Bill" and "Gates". We joined them together with the ampersand (&). But as you can see, the two words are actually joined as one. We can add a bit of space between the two words by using another ampersand. Change this line **FullName = FirstName & LastName** to this:

FullName = FirstName & " " & LastName

What we're saying here is join this lot together: the variable called FirstName **and** a single blank space **and** the variable called LastName. When you've finished concatenating it all, store the result in the variable **FullName**.

Notice that we don't surround **FirstName** and **LastName** with quotation marks. This is because these two are already string variables; we stored "Bill" into FirstName and "Gates" LastName. So VB already knows that they are text.

Exercise
Remove one of the ampersand symbols (&) from this line in your code:

FullName = FirstName & " " & LastName

Move your cursor down a line or two. You should see that part of your code has a wiggly blue line under it.

VB is telling you that it has problems with this line of code. If you hold your mouse over the wiggly blue line, VB tries to provide an explanation:

```
FullName = FirstName & " " LastName
                             End of statement expected.
```

The explanations VB provides are sometimes enigmatic. But you will know that there is a problem. If you run the code, you'll get this popping up at you:

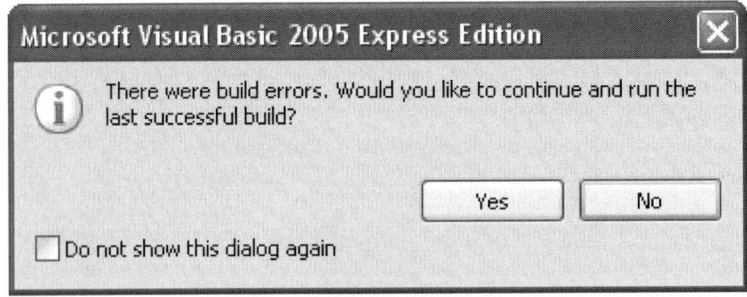

Click the NO button. Put the ampersand back in, and all will be well.

Exercise
Amend your code so that the textbox reads Gates Bill when the button is clicked.

Exercise
Add another string variable to your code. The variable should hold a middle name. Display the first name, the middle name and the last name in the textbox.

Points to remember:

- Your variable names cannot include spaces. So **MiddleName** would be all right, but **Middle Name** will get you an error message
- When you're putting text into your new variable, don't forget the two double quotes
- Remember to put in enough ampersands in your **FullName** = line of code

Assigning values from Textboxes to your Variables

Instead of putting direct text into your variables, such as "Bill" or "Gates", you can get text from a textbox and put that straight into your variables. We'll see how that's done now. First, do this:

- Add a new textbox to your form
- With the textbox selected, locate the Name property in the Properties area:

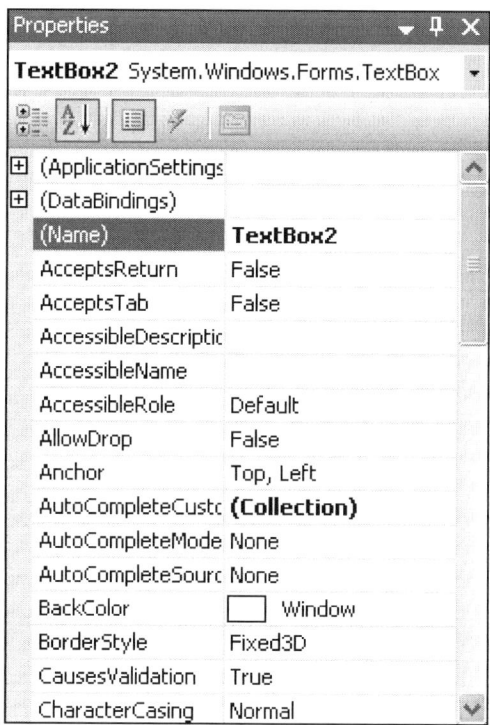

The current value of the Name property is Textbox2. This is not terribly descriptive. Delete this name and enter **txtLastName**. Scroll down and locate the Text property. Delete the default text, and just leave it blank.

Click on your first textbox to select it. Change the Name property from Textbox1 to **txtFirstName**.

What we've done is to give the two textboxes more descriptive names. This will help us to remember what is meant to go in them.

Unfortunately, if you view your code (click the Form1.vb tab at the top, or press F7 on your keyboard), you'll see that the blue wiggly lines have returned (though the 2010 edition of the software may actually change the name in the code as well, so you won't see the errors below):

```
TextBox1.Text = FullName
```

If you hold your cursor over the Textbox1, you'll see this:

```
TextBox1.Text = FullName
```
Name 'TextBox1' is not declared.

It's displaying this message because you changed the name of your Textbox1. You now no longer have a textbox with this name. Change Textbox1 into txtFirstName and the wiggly lines will go away. (Change it in your Button1 code as well.) Your code should now read:

txtFirstName.Text = FullName

Run your programme again. If you see any error messages, stop the programme and look for the wiggly lines in your code.

We'll now change our code slightly, and make use of the second textbox. You'll see how to get at the text that a user enters.

Locate these two lines of code

FirstName = "Bill"
LastName = "Gates"

Change them to this

FirstName = txtFirstName.Text
LastName = txtLastName.Text

Remember: the equals (=) sign assigns things: Whatever is on the right of the equals sign gets assigned to whatever is on the left. What we're doing now is assigning the text from the textboxes directly into the two variables.

Amend your code slightly so that the WholeName is now displayed in a message box. Your code should now be this:

Dim FirstName As String
Dim LastName As String
Dim WholeName As String

FirstName = txtFirstName.Text
LastName = txtLastName.Text

WholeName = FirstName & " " & LastName

MsgBox(WholeName)

Run your programme. Enter "Bill" in the first textbox, and "Gates" in the second textbox. Then click your "String Test" button. You should get this:

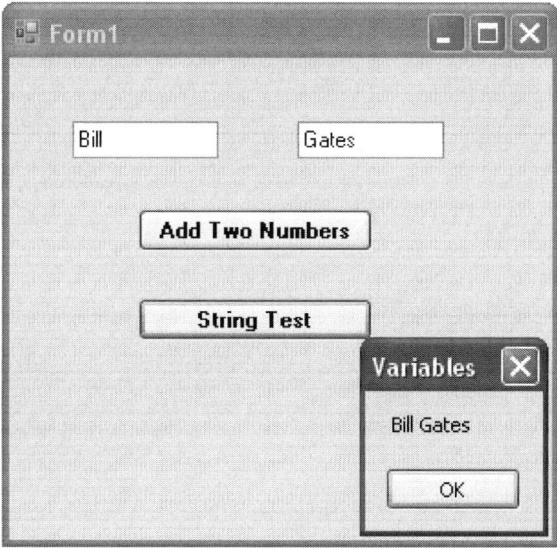

Before we changed the code, we were putting a person's name straight in to the variable **FirstName**

FirstName = "Bill"

But what we really want to do is get a person's name directly from the textbox. This will make life a whole lot easier for us. After all, not everybody is called Bill Gates! In the line **FirstName = txtFirstName.Text** that is what we're doing - getting the name directly from the textbox. What we're saying to Visual Basic is this

- Look for a Textbox that has the Name **txtFirstName**
- Locate the Text property of the Textbox that has the Name **txtFirstName**
- Read whatever this Text property is
- Put this Text property into the variable **FirstName**

And that's all there is too reading values from a textbox - just access its Text property, and then pop it into a variable.

Exercise

- Add a third textbox to your form
- Change its Name property to **txtWholeName**
- Add labels to your form identifying each textbox (A quick way to add more labels is to use the toolbox to add one label. Then right click on that label. Choose Copy from the menu. Right click on the form, and select Paste.)
- Write code so that when the "String Test" button is clicked, the whole of the person's name is displayed in your new textbox

When you complete this exercise, your form should look like this one (we've deleted the first button and its code, but you don't have to):

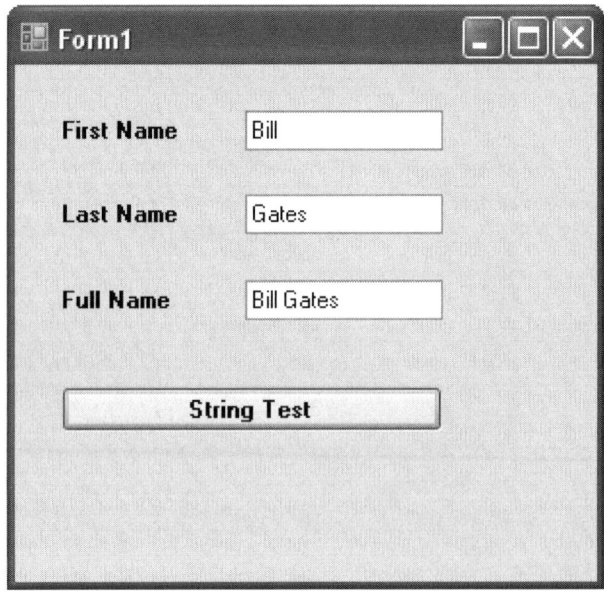

More about Variables

We've met two variable types so far - As String and As Integer. But there are quite a few more you can use. Let's start by examining number variables.

Start a new project for this. If you have the old one displayed, you can click **File > Close Project** from the menu bar. You will then be returned to the Start Page. Click **File > New Project** from the menu bar. In the dialogue box, give your project a name.

Put a textbox and a Button on your new form. Change the Properties of the Textbox to the following

> **Name**:   txtNumbers
> **Font**:   MS Sans Serif, Bold, 10
> **Text**:   Leave the textbox blank

Change the Properties of the Button to the following

> **Text**:   Answers
> **Font**:   MS Sans Serif, Bold, 10

Your Form should look something like this:

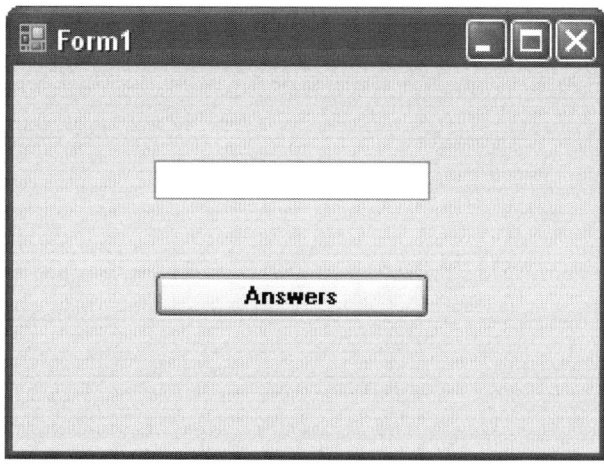

Double click on the Button to bring up the code window. Type the following code for your Button (The Button1_Click part is spread over three lines only for ease-of-reading in this book. You can keep yours on one line in your code):

Private Sub Button1_Click(ByVal sender As System.Object, _
                          ByVal e As System.EventArgs) _
                          Handles Button1.Click

Dim testNumber As Short
testNumber = Val(txtNumbers.Text)
MsgBox testNumber
End Sub

Notice that there is a new Type of variable declared – **As Short**. This means "Short Integer". We'll see what it does. The **Val** part converts the **Text** into a number.

Run your programme. While it's running, do the following:

- Enter the number 1 into the textbox, and click the Answers button
- The number 1 should display in the Message Box
- Add the number 2 to the textbox and click the Button
- The number 12 should display in the Message Box
- Add the number 3 to the textbox and click the Button
- The number 123 should display in the Message Box
- Keeping adding numbers one at a time, then clicking the button
- How many numbers did you get in the textbox before the following error message was displayed?

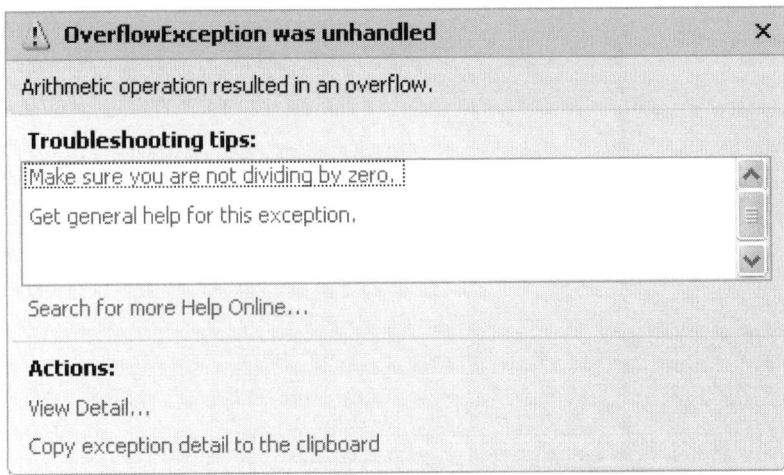

You should have been able to enter 12345 quite safely. When you entered 123456 and clicked the button, that's when the error message displayed. You are then returned to the coding environment. You'll see the problem line highlighted in yellow:

```
testNumber = Val(txtNumbers.Text)
```

But your programme will still be running. So click **Debug > Stop Debugging** to return to the normal code window.

An Overflow happens when you try to put too much information into a variable that can't handle it.

The reason we got an error message after just 6 numbers was because of the variable type. We had this:

Dim testNumber As Short

And it's **As Short** that is causing us the problems. If you use **As Short** you're only allowed numbers up to a certain value. The range for a Short variable is -32 768 to 32 767. When we entered 6 numbers, Visual Basic decided it didn't want to know. If you run your programme again, and then enter 32768, you'll get the same Overflow error message. If you change it once more to –32769, you'll get the error message as well. So it's not just 6 numbers a Short Type can't handle – it's 5 numbers above or below the values specified.

So what's the solution? Change the variable Type, of course!

Change the variable to this:

Dim testNumber As Integer

Now start the programme and try again, adding numbers one at a time to the textbox, and then clicking the button. How far did you get this time?

If you started at 1 and added the numbers in sequence, you should have been allowed to enter 1234567890. One more number and Visual Basic gave you the Overflow error message, right?

That's because variable types with **As Integer** also have a limitation. The range you can use with the **As Integer** variable type is –2,147,483,648 to 2,147,483,647. If you want a really, really big number you can use As Long.

Dim testNumber As Long

But these will get you whole numbers. Leave your number on **As Integer**. Run your programme again and enter a value of 123.45 into your textbox. Press the button and see what happens.

VB will chop off the point 45 bit at the end. If you want to work with floating point numbers (the .45 bit), there are three Types you can use:

Dim testNumber As Single
Dim testNumber As Double
Dim testNumber As Decimal

Single and Double mean Single-Precision and Double-Precision numbers. If you want to do scientific calculations, and you need to be really precise, then use Double rather than Single: it's more accurate.

The **As Decimal** Type is useful when you want a precise number of decimal places. It's not as accurate as the Double Type, though.

In terms of the space used in the computer's memory, Short Types use 2 Bytes, Integer Types use 4 Bytes, Long Types use 8 Bytes, Single Types use 4 Bytes, Double Types use 8 Bytes, and Decimal Types use 16 Bytes.

Exercise
Write a programme to calculate the following sum.

0.123345678 * 1234

Use the Single Type first, then change it to As Double. Use a Message box to display the answer. Was the number rounded up or rounded down for the Single Type?

Using Variables

In this next section, we're going to learn how to transfer the contents of one textbox to another textbox. We'll also learn to transfer the text from a label to a textbox, and whatever was in the textbox we'll transfer it to a label. This will get us a little more practice with variables, and how to use them.

Start a new Visual basic project. You should know how to do this by now, and what the design environment looks like. But you should have a plain grey Form on your screen. By default it will be called Form1.

Make sure the Form is selected (has it got the white squares around it?), and then click the Name property in the Properties window. Change the Name of the form to **frmVariables**.

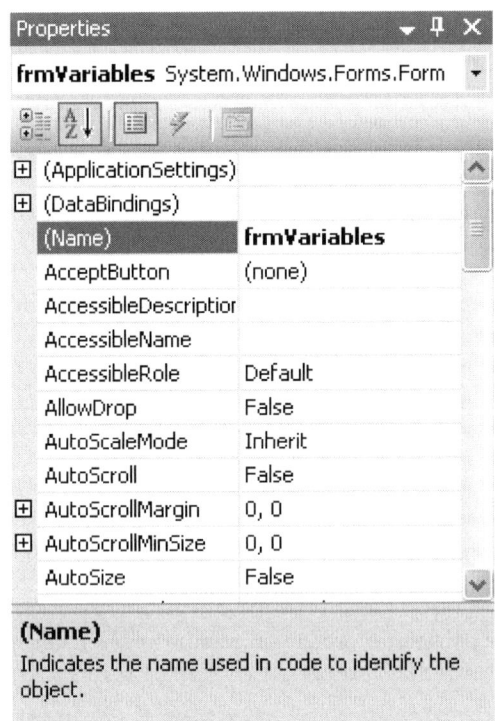

Set the Text property of the Form to "Transferring information". You can choose any background colour you like for the form, or leave it on the default.

Put the following controls on the Form, and change their properties to the ones specified below (NOTE: lbl is short for label):

Textbox

Name:	txtVariables
Font:	MS Sans Serif, Bold, 10
Text:	Delete the default text "Text1" and leave it blank

Label

Name:	lblTransfer
BackColor:	A colour of your choice
Text:	Label Caption
Font:	MS Sans Serif, Bold, 10

Button

Name:	btnTransfer
Text:	Transfer to TextBox

The height of your controls is entirely up to you.

If you double click your Button to bring up the code window, you will see that the first line of the code no longer says Button1_Click (etc). The first line should say this

Private Sub btnTransfer_Click(ByVal sender As System.Object, _
ByVal e As System.EventArgs) _
Handles btnTransfer.Click

End Sub

The reason it has changed is because you changed the Name property of the Button. The button now has the Name btnTransfer. If you wanted to, you could change the Name property back to Button1. Then when you double clicked the button, the code window would pop up and the first line would be **Button1_Click** (etc).

What we're going to do now is to transfer the Text on the label ("Label Caption") to our empty textbox. And all with the click of a button.

As you'll see, there isn't much code.

Type the following into your code window:

Dim LabelContents As String

LabelContents = lblTransfer.Text

txtVariables.Text = LabelContents

Your code window should now look something like this:

```
Private Sub btnTransfer_Click(ByVal sender As System.Object, _
                             ByVal e As System.EventArgs) _
                                Handles btnTransfer.Click


    Dim LabelContents As String

    LabelContents = lblTransfer.Text

    txtVariables.Text = LabelContents

End Sub
```

Now Run your programme and test it out. When you click on the "Transfer" button, you should see that the contents of the label will be inserted into the textbox.

But let's break the code down and see what's going on.

Dim LabelContents As String
Here is where we set up a variable called LabelContents. Because it will be holding text, we've used the variable type **As String**.

LabelContents = lblTransfer.Text
Here is where we put something into our empty variable. We changed the Name property of our Label from the default Label1 to lblTransfer. A Label has lots of properties you can manipulate. One of those properties is the Text property. After you typed the word "lblTransfer" and then typed a full stop, you probably saw a drop down box appear. Inside the box is a list of all the properties and Methods that a Label has. We wanted to manipulate the Text property of our label so we selected the word Text after the full stop. So we were saying "Access the value of the Text property of the label called lblTransfer, and put this value into the variable called LabelContents." Because our Text was ""Label Caption", the variable LabelContents now holds the text "Label Caption."

txtVariables.Text = LabelContents
Finally, we want to transfer whatever is in the variable LabelContents to the Textbox. Our Textbox is called txtVariables. Again, after typing the full stop the drop down box would appear, showing you a list of all the properties that a Textbox has. The one we're interested in is the Text Property. So we're saying, "Take whatever text is in the variable LabelContents, and transfer it to the Text property of the Textbox called txtVariables.

And with three lines of code we can transfer text from a label to a Textbox. But can we do it the other way round? Can we transfer whatever is in a Textbox to a Label? Well, sure we can.

Add another button to your form. Change its Name property from Button1 to **btnTransferToLabel**, and change the Text property to "Transfer To Label". Again, there are just three lines of code.

So double click your new button to bring up the code window. Then type in the following code:

Dim TextBoxContents As String

TextBoxContents = txtVariables.Text

lblTransfer.Text = TextBoxContents

Now, see if you can work out how it works. It's the same thing as the first three lines of code: set up a variable, transfer the Text property of the Textbox to the variable, transfer the variable to the Text property of the Label.

Run your programme and test it out. Type something into the Textbox, and then click the "Transfer To Label" button.

Exercise
A button also has a Text Property. Write code to transfer the Text of a button to the Textbox. It's probably better for this exercise to create a new Button. Set its Name property to whatever you like. And give its Text Property a new value (The Text property will be Button1 by default)

But the process is exactly the same as the two bits of code above - you should only need 3 lines of code for this exercise.

- Set up a Variable
- Transfer the Text property of the button to the variable
- Transfer the variable to the Textbox

A Calculator Project

For your second Review, you're going to create a Calculator. It won't be a very sophisticated calculator, and the only thing it can do is add up. That's because the coding for subtraction, division and multiplication is a little too difficult at this stage. What the project will give you is more confidence in variables, and shifting values from one control to another. So create a new project, call it Calculator, and let's get started.

Designing the Form

Let's design the form first. What does a calculator need? Well numbers, for one. A display area for the result. A plus sign button, an equals sign button, and a button to clear the display.

Here's how our calculator is going to work. We'll have 10 button for the numbers 0 to 9. When a button is clicked its value will be transferred to a display area, which will be a Textbox. Once a number is transferred to the Textbox we can click on the Plus button. Then we need to click back on another number. To get the answer, we'll click on the equals sign. To clear the display, we'll have a Clear button.

If you haven't already, create a new project. Save it as Calculator. To your new form, first add ten Buttons (You can add one, then copy and paste the rest). The Buttons should have the following Properties:

Name: btn Plus a Number (btnOne, btnTwo, btnThree, etc)
Text: A number from 0 to 9. A different one for each button, obviously
Font: MS Sans Serif, Bold, 14

Next, add a Textbox. Set the following properties for the Textbox:

Name: txtDisplay
Font: MS Sans Serif, Bold, 14
Text : Leave it blank

Three more buttons need to be added:

Plus Button
    Name: btnPlus
    Font: MS Sans Serif, Bold, 14
    Text: +

Equals Button
    Name: btnEquals
    Font: MS Sans Serif, Bold, 14
    Text: =

Clear Button
    Name: btnClear
    Font: MS Sans Serif, Bold, 14
    Text: Clear

When your form design is finished, it might look something like this:

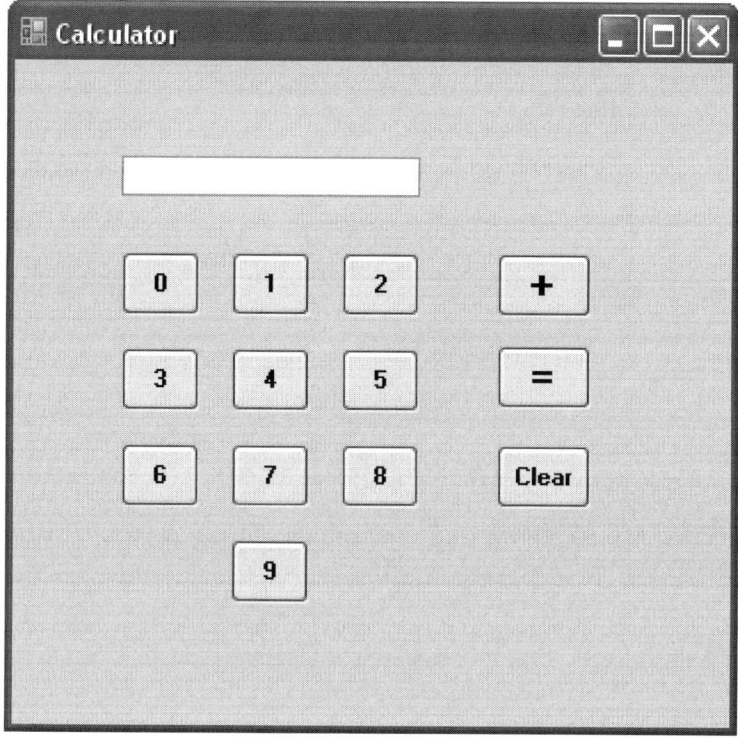

So if you wanted to add 5 + 9, you would click first on the 5. A 5 would appear in the textbox. Then you would click the + symbol. The 5 would disappear from the textbox. Next, click on the 9. The number 9 would appear in the textbox. Finally, click on the = symbol. The 9 would disappear from the textbox, and the answer to our sum would replace it. We would then click the Clear button to clear the display.

The Code

You might be thinking that all this is terribly complicated at such an early stage. But it isn't really. All we are doing is transferring the Text Properties from the Buttons to the textbox. And you already know how to do that. The number buttons don't do anything else. All the work is done with the Plus button and the Equals button. And there are only two lines of code needed for the Plus button, and three for the Equals button.

For this to work, though, a little word about Scope.

So far, when you've set up a variable, you've set them up behind a Private Subroutine. Like this:

Private Sub Button1_Click(ByVal sender As System.Object, _
ByVal e As System.EventArgs) _
Handles btnZero.Click

Dim MyVariable As String

End Sub

Suppose you had another button on the form, Button2, and the code was this

Private Sub Button2_Click(ByVal sender As System.Object, _
ByVal e As System.EventArgs) _
Handles btnZero.Click

Dim MyOtherVariable As String

End Sub

How can you access what's in **MyVariable** from Button2? The answer is, you can't. It's like two people sitting at desks in cubicles. Each person has written something on a piece of paper. They can't see into the other person's cubicle, only whatever is their own cubicle. So how do they share their information?

Well suppose there is a screen in front of them. A big screen. They can both see the screen in front of them; it's each other they can't see. What they could do is project their information onto the screen. Then one person could see what the other has written.

Similarly, in VB you can set up your variable declarations outside of the code for a Button. That way, more than one Button can see the code.

You can place your variable declarations right at the top of the code window, just beneath the line that begins "Public Class Form1". We'll set up two Integer variables there, **total1** and **total2**.

```
1 Public Class Form1
2       Dim total1 As Single
3       Dim total2 As Single
4
```

Now all the controls on your form can see these two variables. Those Buttons you set up can put something in them, and every button has the ability to see what's inside them.

The 0 to 9 Buttons

The Buttons with the Text 0 to 9 only need to do one thing when the button is clicked - have their Text Properties transferred to the Textbox. You've already wrote code to do that.

So double click the 0 Button and enter the following code:

Private Sub btnZero_Click(ByVal sender As System.Object, _
ByVal e As System.EventArgs) _
Handles btnZero.Click

txtDisplay.Text = btnZero.Text

End Sub

This code will transfer the Text Property of a Button called btnZero to the Text Property of a Textbox called txtDisplay.

Run your programme and try it out. When the programme is running, click the 0 button to see that it does indeed transfer the Text on the Button to the textbox

Except, there's a problem with that code. If you wrote similar code for all ten of your number buttons, the calculator wouldn't be right. Why is that? Have you spotted what's wrong? It's a good idea to set this book aside for a while and think about why this code on its own wouldn't work. In fact you could write code for a few more of the number buttons and test it out.

What happens when you transfer the number 2 to the Textbox, and then click the number 3? The number 2 will disappear, to be replaced by the number 3. Which is all right if all you wanted to do was add up single numbers, but not much good if you actually wanted the number 23 in the Textbox. With this code, you could have **either** the number 2 in the Textbox or the number 3, but not both!

So how do we solve this problem? How do we fix it so that we can have two or more numbers appearing in our Textbox?

What we need is a way to get whatever is in the Textbox to stay where it is, and not disappear on us when we click a different number. It's quite easy. It's this:

txtDisplay.Text = txtDisplay.Text & btnZero.Text

So now we're saying the textbox doesn't just contain the Text on the Button. It must also keep whatever is inside the textbox as well.

txtDisplay.Text =
Assign a value to the Text Property of the Textbox called txtDisplay

= txtDisplay.Text
One of these values will be the Text property of the textbox itself (In other words, keep whatever is inside the textbox).

&
We don't want to add the two numbers together. We use the ampersand symbol to concatenate the numbers

btnZero.Text
Combine whatever was in the textbox with the Text Property of the Button called btnZero

So what you need to do now is to add that code to all of your ten number Buttons. Obviously it won't be exactly the same. For the button called btnOne the code would be this:

txtDisplay.Text = txtDisplay.Text & btnOne.Text

When you've finished coding all ten buttons, run the programme and click all ten number buttons to see if they do indeed transfer the numbers on the caption to the textbox. Not only that, but test to see if you can have more than one number in the textbox.

Now that we can get numbers into our Textbox display area, we'll write code to do something with those numbers - add them together, in other words.

The Plus Button

Let's remind ourselves how our calculator works. To add up 5 + 9, we'd do this:

1. Click first on the 5
2. A 5 appear in the textbox
3. Click the + symbol
4. The 5 disappears from the textbox
5. Click on the number 9
6. A 9 appears in the textbox
7. Click on the = symbol
8. The 9 disappears from the textbox
9. The answer to 5 + 9 appears in the textbox
10. Click the "Clear" button to clear the textbox

We've done numbers 1 and 2 on that list. We're now going to do numbers 3 and 4 on the list. What we're trying to do is this: Click on the Plus symbol and make the number in the Textbox disappear. Before the number vanishes, we can store it in a variable. The variable we're going to be storing the number in is one of those variables we set up at the top of the code. It's this one:

Dim total1 As Integer

We've already seen how to retain a value from a textbox and add it to something else:

txtDisplay.Text = txtDisplay.Text & btnZero.Text

Here, we kept the value that was already in the textbox and joined it to the Text property of the button.

We can do something similar if we want to retain a value that is already in a variable. Examine this:

variable1 = variable1 + 1

The "= variable1 + 1" part just says "Remember what is in the variable **variable1**, and then add 1 to it". So if **variable1** contain the number 3, what would **variable1** now hold after that bit of code is executed? The whole code might be this

> **variable1 = 3**
> **variable1 = variable1 + 1**

(If you don't know the answer to that, please send an email and ask for some further clarification on the subject.)

The above is known in programming terms as "Incrementing a variable". There is even a shorthand you can use:

> **variable1 += 1**

This says "variable1 equals variable1 plus 1". Or "Add 1 to variable1". You can also use the other mathematical operators with the same shorthand notation:

> **variable1 = 10**
> **variable1 *= 3**

This new code says "Multiply whatever is inside of variable1 by 3".

The shorthand notation can be tricky to read (and to get used to), so we won't use it much. But it's there if you want it.

Back to our code.

If we're going to be adding two numbers together, we need Visual Basic to remember the first number. Because when we click the equals sign, that first number will be added to the second number. So if we haven't asked VB to remember the first number, it won't be able to add up.

The variable we're going to be storing the first number in is **total1**. We could just say this:

> **total1 = txtDisplay.Text**

Then whatever is in the textbox will get stored in the variable total1.

Except we want VB to remember our numbers. Because we might want to add three or more numbers together: 1 + 2 + 3 + 4. If we don't keep a running total, there's no way for our programme to remember what has gone before, it will just erase whatever is in total1 and then start again.

So just like the code above (varaible1 = variable1 + 1), we need to "tell" our programme to remember what was in the variable. We do it like this:

> **total1 = total1 + Val(txtDisplay.Text)**

That **Val( )** part just makes sure that a number in a textbox is kept as a number, and not as text. It's short for Value. The important part is the **total1 + txtDisplay.Text**. We're saying "The variable total1 contains whatever is in total1 added to the number in the textbox." An example might clear things up. Suppose we were adding 5 + 9. Now, suppose **total1** already contained the number 5, and that number 9 was in the textbox. It would work like this:

$$=5 \qquad =5 \qquad\qquad =9$$
total1 = total1 + txtDisplay.Text

total1 =   5 +   9

total1 =   14

Finally, we need to erase the number in the textbox. To erase something from a textbox, just set its Text property to a blank string. We do this with two double quotation marks. Like this:

txtDisplay.Text = ""

That tiny bit of code will erase the Text a textbox. Another way to erase text from a textbox is to use the Clear method. After you typed a full stop, you probably saw the drop down list of Properties and Methods.

But scroll up to the top, and locate the word Clear. Double click "Clear" and the drop down list will close. Hit the return key and VB adds two round brackets to your code:

txtDisplay.Clear( )

Notice that we're not setting the textbox to equal anything. We're using something called a Method. You can tell it's a Method because there's a purple block icon next to the word. A Method is a built-in bit of code that VB knows how to execute. In other words, it knows how to clear text from a textbox. You'll learn more about Methods later.

So the whole code for our Button called btnPlus is this:

```
Private Sub btnPlus_Click(ByVal sender As System.Object, _
                         ByVal e As System.EventArgs) _
                         Handles btnPlus.Click

    total1 = total1 + Val(txtDisplay.Text)

    txtDisplay.Clear()

End Sub
```

Add that code to your Plus button. All we've done with that code is to store numbers into our variable **total1** and then erase whatever was in the textbox.

We now need to add the numbers up.

Review Number 2

Write the code for the equals button. There are only three lines in total, and here's a little help.

You need to use the other variable that was set up at the top of the coding window, **total2**. The variable **total1** will be added to whatever is in **total2**

The first line of code will be this:

total2 = total1 + (something missing here)

Your job is to supply the missing code. In other words, replace "(something missing here)"

Remember that **total1** contains the first number to be added. And you know where that came from. The only thing left to do is to add the second number.

For the second line of code, you need to transfer the **total2** variable to the textbox.

For the third line of code, all you are doing is resetting the variable **total1** to zero. That's because after the equals button has been pressed, we have finished adding up. If you wanted to do some more adding up, that **total1** will still hold the value from the last time. If you reset it to zero, you can start adding some new numbers.

The only thing left to do is to write a single line of code for the Clear button. All you are doing there is erasing text from a textbox. Which you already know how to do.

To recap what needs to be done for Review Number 2

- Write code for the Equals button (This code will be three lines long (not counting Private Sub, End Sub)
- Write a single line of code for the Clear Command button

Conditional Logic

In this section we'll learn about the power of conditional logic. It might get a bit tricky, so hold on to your hats! If at any stage you get totally stumped, send an email and we'll do our utmost to help you out. We'll start with conditional logic, though.

If Statements

What is conditional logic? Well, it's something you use in your daily life all the time, without realising you're doing it. Suppose that there is a really delicious cream cake in front of you, just begging to be eaten. But you are on a diet. The cake is clearly asking for it. So what do you do, eat the cake and ruin your diet? Or stick to your diet and let somebody else have that delicious treat? You might even be saying this to yourself:

> **If** I eat the cake **Then** my diet will be ruined

> **If** I don't eat the cake **Then** I will be on course for a slimmer figure

Note the words **If** and **Then** in the above sentences. You're using conditional logic with those two words: "I will eat the cake on condition that my diet is ruined". Conditional logic is all about that little **If** word. You can even add **Else** to it.

> **If** I eat the cake **Then** my diet will be ruined

> **Else**

> **If** I don't eat the cake **Then** I will be on course for a slimmer figure

And that is what conditional Logic is all about - saying what happens if one condition is met, and what happens if the condition is not met. Visual Basic uses those same words - If, Then, Else for conditional Logic. Let's try it out.

Start a new project. Give it any name you like. In the design environment, add a Button to the new form. Double click the button and add the following code to it:

```
Private Sub Button1_Click(ByVal sender As System.Object, _
                          ByVal e As System.EventArgs) _
                          Handles Button1.Click

    Dim firstname As String
    firstname = "Bill"
    If firstname = "Bill" Then MsgBox("firstname is Bill")

End Sub
```

Run the programme and see what happens. You should get a Message Box with the words "firstname is Bill" in it.

What we did was to set up a string variable and put the name "Bill" into it. When then used conditional logic to test what was in the variable. In fact, we used an If statement. We said:

If the variable called firstname holds the value "Bill" **Then** display a Message Box

We can tidy that up a bit, because a single line of code can get very long with If statements. We can use this format instead.

> **If firstname = "Bill" Then**
>   **MsgBox "firstname is Bill"**
> **End If**

That's a lot tidier. Note that we start a new line after the word **Then**.

- The first line contains our condition: "**If** the following condition is met".
- The second line is what we want to do if the condition is indeed met.
- The third line tells Visual Basic that the If statement ends right here.

Try this. Delete the two quotation marks around the word Bill. Your code should now be this:

> **Dim firstname as String**
>
> **firstname = "Bill"**
>
> **If firstname = Bill Then**
>   **MsgBox "firstname is Bill"**
> **End If**

VB.NET puts a blue wiggly line under **Bill**. If you try to start your programme, you'll get a message box telling you that there were Build Errors, and asking if you want to continue.

Say No to return to the design environment. The reason for the blue wiggly line is that VB insists on you using double quotes to surround you text. No double quotes and VB insists it's not a string of text.

Change you code to this.

> **firstname = "Phil"**
>
> **If firstname = "Bill" Then**
>   **MsgBox "firstname is Bill"**
> **Else**
>   **MsgBox "firstname is not Bill"**
> **End If**

Now run the programme and see what happens when you click the button.

You should have gotten a Message Box popping up saying "firstname is not Bill". The reason is that we included the **Else** word. We're now saying, "If the condition is met **Then** display one Message Box. If the condition is not met, display a different Message Box." Notice that the **Else** word is on a line of its own.

Let's try another one. We'll use that delicious cream cake this time. Amend you code to this

```
Dim creamcake As String

creamcake = "Eaten"

If creamcake = "Eaten" Then
        MsgBox "Diet is ruined"
Else
        MsgBox "Diet is not Ruined"
End If
```

Run the programme to test it out. Stop the programme. Change the line **creamcake = "Eaten"** to **creamcake = "Not Eaten"**. Run your programme again, and test it out.

Now, after you have tested your programme, try this. Add a textbox to your form. Then change this line in your code:

creamcake = "Not Eaten"

To this:

creamcake = Textbox1.Text

What the code does is to transfer the text in the Textbox directly to the **creamcake** variable. We can then test what is in the variable with an **If** statement.

When you've finished the code, test it out by typing the word "Eaten" (with a capital E) into the textbox, and then clicking the button. Then try it with a lower case "e".
Was the diet ruined or not ruined with a lowercase "e"?

Exercise
Set up another String variable called DietState and add it to your code. Use an If statement to test the DietState variable. If the diet is ruined then assign the text "Diet is ruined" to the DietState variable. Else, assign the text "Diet is not ruined" to the DietState variable.

For this exercise, you can keep the textbox and assign the text entered to the creamcake variable. You are then testing this creamcake variable to see what is in it.

In the IF statement, delete the code for the two MsgBox lines. In place of these two lines, you can assign your text to the DietState variable. After End If but before End Sub, you can add a new Message Box

MsgBox DietState

Select Case

So far, we've explored only simple If statements, and we're going to leave it that way for now. But they can get quite complex, because you can have one If statement inside another, and multiple Else statements. However, the code you have just written does demonstrate how you can find out what is in a variable, and take action if the condition is either met or not met. We're now going to explore another way to do that - the Select Case statement

The Select Case statement is another way to test what is inside of a variable. You can use it when you know there is only a limited number of things that could be in the variable. For example, suppose we add another choice for that cream cake. We've only said that the consequences of eating the cream cake is that the DietState will be either "Ruined" or "Not Ruined". But what if we add another option - "Diet State Not Tested". In other words, we ate the cake but refused to climb onto the scales to weigh ourselves!

With three choices, we can still use an **If ... Else** statement. But let's change it to a Select Case statement. Remember: all we are doing is testing what is inside a variable, in this case the creamcake variable. Once we decide what is inside the variable we can set our DietState. So let's look at how the Select Case works.

```
creamcake = TextBox1.Text

Select Case creamcake

        Case "Eaten"
                DietState = "Diet Ruined"
        Case "Not Eaten"
                DietState = "Diet Not Ruined"
        Case Else
                DietState = "Didn't check"
End Select

MsgBox DietState
```

Select Case
We tell Visual Basic that we want to start a Select Case statement by simply using the words "Select Case". This is enough to set up the statement

creamcake
The variable **creamcake** follows the words Select Case. We're saying, "Set up a Select Case statement to test what is inside the variable **creamcake**"

Case "Eaten"
We ask Visual Basic to check if the variable **creamcake** contains the word "Eaten". If it does, VB will drop down to the line or lines of code below and read that. If the variable **creamcake** doesn't contain the word "Eaten", the programme will skip the line or lines of code below and jump to the next **Case**. The programme will continue to check all the words after **Case** to see if one of them contains what is in the variable **creamcake**. If it finds one, it will read the code

below the **Case** word; if it doesn't find any matches, it will not do anything at all. Note also that it will only look for an exact match

Case Else
We can use the **Else** word after **Case**. If the programme doesn't find any matches, it will then execute the code below the **Case Else** line

End Select
Tell Visual basic to end the Select Case statement

So the Select Case checks a variable for any number of different choices. If a match is found, it will then execute code below the Case option it has found. In our code, we've just told the programme to store some text in the **DietState** variable. After the Select Case statement has ended we displayed the variable in a Message Box.

As you have probably noticed, the words in double quotes have to be typed exactly before a match is found. According to the programme, "Eaten" is different from "eaten". But you can tell VB to look for both forms by using the **To** word. Try amending your code to this:

> **Case "Eaten" To "eaten"**

Now if you enter either the lower case version or the upper case version, Visual Basic will consider it a match.

You can use Select Case statement with numbers, as well, and the **To** word comes in very handy here. If you were checking a variable to see if the number that was in the variable fell within a certain age-range, you could use something like this:

```
Select Case agerange
        Case 16 To 21
                MsgBox "Still Young"
        Case 50 To 64
                MsgBox "Start Lying"
End Select
```

In fact, before we go any further let's use that age-range Select Case statement in a little programme.

Add a label to your form. Set the Text property of the label to "Enter you Age in the Textbox".

We can now amend our code so that it doesn't check for cream cakes, but age ranges. Delete or amend your code to the following:

```
Dim agerange As Integer
Dim message As String

agerange = Val(Textbox1.Text)

Select Case agerange
```

```
                Case 16 To 21
                        message = "Whole life ahead of you!"
                Case 21 To 40
                        message = "You're not a kid anymore!"
                Case 41 To 50
                        message = "You're definitely not a kid anymore!"
                Case 51 To 60
                        message = "Time to start Lying"
                Case Is > 60
                        message = "Hope you've got a good pension!"
                Case Else
                        Message = "Too young to measure"
        End Select

        MsgBox message
```

When you've finished typing all that code, run the programme. Test it works by entering different ages in the textbox, and then clicking the button.

The code first sets up an integer variable and a string variable. The integer will hold the number from the textbox, and the string will hold our message. Then we put the value in the textbox directly into the agerange variable:

agerange = Val(Textbox1.Text)

Again, we've used **Val( )** to make sure that VB recognises the value as an integer.

Next, we use a Select Case statement. We use the **To** word to specify a range of different values. When the programme finds the right value, it will execute the code below the Case it has matched. Note the case **Case Is > 60**. The > symbol stands for "Greater Than". So the whole line reads "Case is greater than 60". Finally, we display the result in a message box.

OK, we're coming to a Review real soon. Before you can do the Review, you need to know how to set up and use Combo Boxes.

Combo Boxes

Locate the Combo Box on the Visual Basic toolbar. It looks like this:

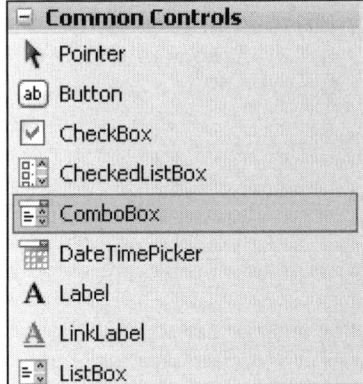

Double click the icon to add a Combo Box to your form. Or click once with the left hand mouse button, and then draw one on the form.

A combo box is a way to limit the choices your user will have. When a down-pointing arrow is clicked, a drop down list of items appears. The user can then select one of these options. So let's set it up to do that.

Click on your Combo Box to select it. Then locate the Item property from the Properties Box:

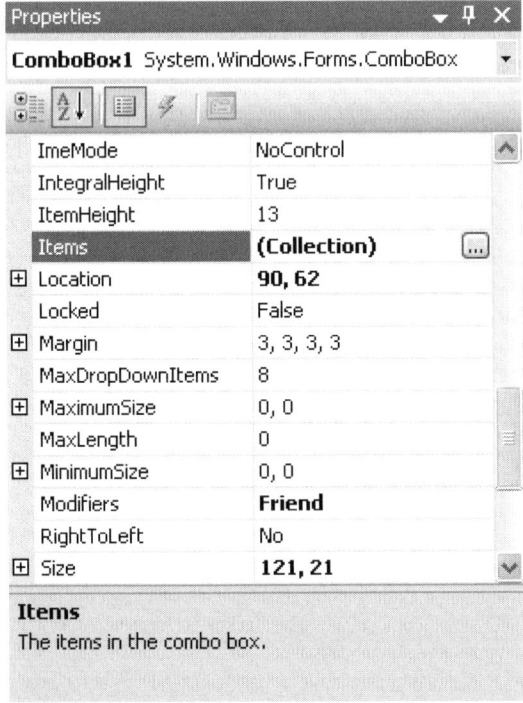

Click the grey button to the right of **(Collection)**, in the image above. The one with the three dots in it. When you do, you'll get the following box popping up:

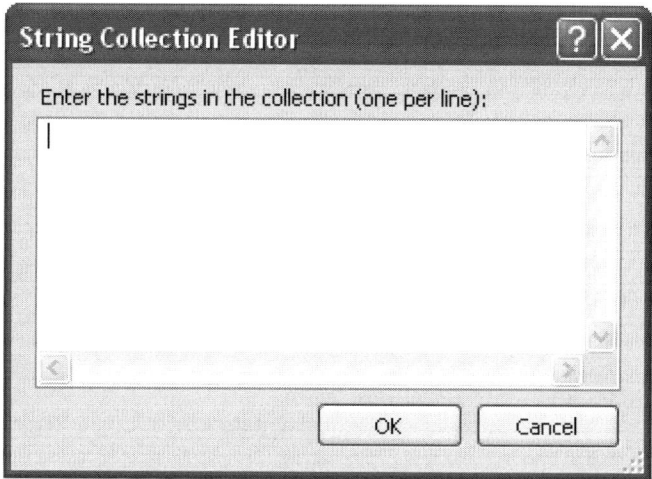

To use the String Collection Editor, type an item and press Return (it's just like a normal textbox. Each item will be one item in your drop-down box.)

Enter five items, as in the image below:

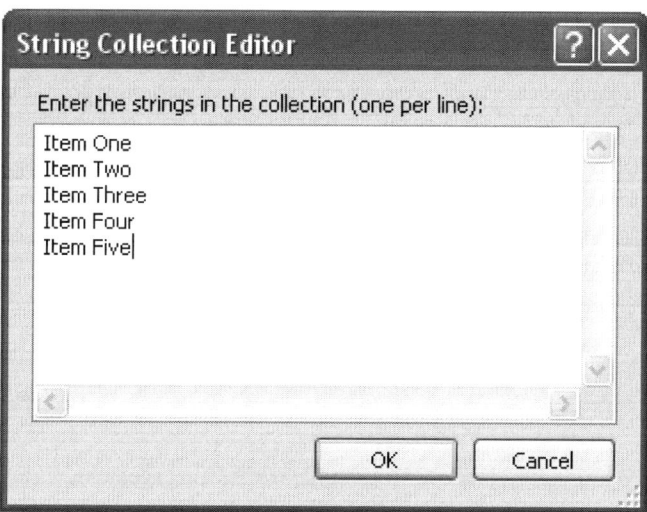

Then click the OK button at the bottom. The Editor will close, and it will look like nothing has happened. However, run your programme and test out your new Combo Box. You should have something like this:

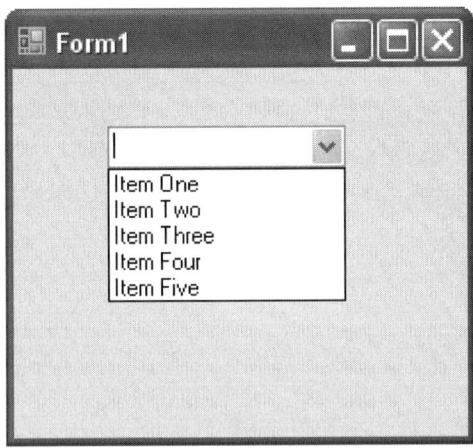

You now need to know how to get values from the list. Once you know how to get a value from the list, you can put the value into a variable and test it with some Conditional logic.

Getting a value from a Combo Box is fairly straightforward, because it acts just like a Textbox. A Textbox has a Text property, and so does a Combo Box. To get a value from a Textbox, you would code like this:

MyVariable = Textbox1.Text

Whatever is in the Textbox will be transferred to the variable called **MyVariable**. The process is exactly the same for a Combo Box. The code is like this:

MyVariable = Combobox1.Text

Now we are transferring whatever is selected from the Combo Box to the variable called MyVariable.

Let's try it. Put a Button on your Form, and double click the button to open the code window. Then enter the following code:

Dim MyVariable as String
MyVariable = Combobox1.Text
MsgBox MyVariable

Run your programme. When the programme is running, select an item from your Combo Box. Then click your button. Whatever was in the Combo Box window should have ended up in the Message Box.

And that's all there is to getting a value from a Combo Box - just access its Text Property and pass it to a variable.

Finally, the Combo Box has a DropDownStyle property. Locate this property and you'll notice its value has a drop down box. The box contains three different Combo Box styles to choose from. Experiment with all three and see how they differ.

And now on to Review Number 3

Review number 3

Review Number 3 will test your knowledge of If Statements and Select Case Statements. It's split into two parts.

Part 1 - If statements

Start a new project. Add a textbox, a Label and a button to your new Form. What the programme will do is ask users to enter a number between 10 and 20. The number will be entered into the Textbox. When the Button is clicked, your Visual Basic code will check the number entered in the Textbox. If it is between 10 and 20, then a message will be displayed. The message box will display the number from the Textbox. If the number entered is not between 10 and 20 then the user will be invited to try again, and whatever was entered in the Textbox will be erased.

Help with this Review

The first thing to do is set up an integer variable to hold the number. Whatever was in the textbox can then be passed directly to this variable.

Then you construct your If Statement to test what is in the variable. To help you test this variable, you are going to need to use some of the following operators:

>	This symbol means Is Greater Than and is used like this:
	
	If number > 10 Then
	    MsgBox("The Number was Greater Than 10")
	End If

<	This symbol means Is Less Than and is used like this:
	
	If number < 10 Then
	    MsgBox("The Number was Less Than 10")
	End If

>=	This symbol means Is Greater Than or Equal to, and is used like this:
	
	If number >= 10 Then
	    MsgBox("The Number was 10 or Greater")
	End If

<=	This symbol means Is Less Than or Equal to, and is used like this:
	
	If number <= 10 Then
	    MsgBox("The Number was 10 or Less")
	End If

And	You can combine the logical operators with the word And. Like this:
	
	If number > 5 And number < 15 Then
	    MsgBox("Greater than 5 And Less than 15")
	End If

Or	You can combine the logical operators with the word Or. Like this:
	
	If number > 5 Or number < 15 Then
	    MsgBox("Greater than 5 Or < Less than 15")
	End If

< >	A less than symbol followed by a greater than symbol means "Is Not Equal to". It is used like this:
	
	If number1 <> number2 Then
	    MsgBox("Is Not Equal to")
	End If

A word about **And** and **Or**. Notice the format with **And** and **Or**. The variable is repeated twice:

If VariableName = 7 Or VariableName = 10 Then MsgBox VariableName

If you just put something like this:

If VariableName > 7 Or < 10 Then MsgBox VariableName

then Visual Basic will give you an error message. What you have to say is

If [test the variable for this value] **And** [test the variable for that value] **Then**

Your **If** statement should contain an **Else** part, too. It will be in this format:

    If [conditional logic here] **Then**
        Message Box code here
    Else
        Message Box code here
        Erase Textbox code here
    End If

Remember, you are testing your variable to see if it between 10 and 20 (including the numbers 10 and 20 themselves).

Message Box Concatenation

So far with a Message Box you have been displaying either text in double quotes

MsgBox "This is my message"

Or you have been displaying what is inside the variable

MsgBox MyVariable

The difference is that direct text is surrounded by double quotation marks, and the variable itself is displayed without using quotation marks. But you can combine the two. Like this: (Note the round brackets, which you should also use. VB puts them in most of the time, if you miss them out, but not always.)

MsgBox("This is my message " & MyVariable)

To combine direct text and a variable, you use the & symbol (the concatenate symbol). If you miss out the & symbol when trying to join direct text and a variable, VB gives you an error message. To demonstrate joining direct text with a variable, try this code with a button:

Dim YourNumber as Integer

YourNumber = 7

MsgBox("The number entered was " & YourNumber)

So, to recap on what is need for Part 1

- A form with a Textbox, a Label and a button
- The Label will say something like "Please Enter a number between 10 and 20"
- When a number is entered into the Textbox, and the button is clicked, your code will test what the number is
- If the number is greater than or equal to 10 And less than or equal to 20 then display a suitable message
- If the number is not in the required range, ask the user to try again
- If the number is not in the required range, erase whatever is in the Textbox

Part 2 - Select Case Statements

Add a Combo box and another button to your form. The list of items in your Combo box can be anything you like - pop groups, football teams, favourite foods, anything of your choice. Use a select case statement to test the selected Combo Box choice, and give the user a suitable message when the button was clicked.

This part of the assignment shouldn't cause you too many problems, because it's practically the same as the Select Case section we did previously.

Looping the Loop

There are three types of loop for us to cover with VB.NET: a **For** loop, a **Do** loop, and a **While** loop. This last one is almost the same as a Do loop, and we won't be covering it here. But the other two types of loop come in very handy, and a lot of the time you can't programme effectively without using loops.

What is a Loop?

A loop is something that goes round and round and round. If you were asked to move your finger around in a loop, you'd know what to do immediately. In programming, loops go round and round and round, too. In fact, they go round and round until you tell them to stop. You can programme without using loops. But it's an awful lot easier with them. Consider this.

You want to add up the numbers 1 to 4: $1 + 2 + 3 + 4$. You could do it like this

> **Dim answer As Integer**
>
> **answer = 1 + 2 + 3 + 4**
>
> **MsgBox answer**

Fairly simple, you think. And not much code, either. But what if you wanted to add up a thousand numbers? Are you really going to type them all out like that? It's an awful lot of typing. A loop would make life a lot simpler. We'll discuss the For Loop first.

For Loops

Don't get hung up too much on the name of the Loop. Just remember what they do: go round and round until you tell them to stop. This first type of loop just happens to be called a For Loop. We'll use one to add up our 4 numbers, and then discuss the code. Study the following. In fact, create a new Project. Add a button to your new Form. Double click your new button and type the following code for it.

> **Dim answer As Integer**
> **Dim startNumber As Integer**
>
> **answer = 0**
>
> **For startNumber = 1 To 4**
>   **answer = answer + startNumber**
> **Next startNumber**
>
> **MsgBox answer**

Run the programme, and see what happens when you click the button. The number 10 should be displayed in your message box.

The For loop code

We start by setting up two integer variables. We set one of these to zero. Then we start our loop code. Let's examine that in more detail.

For startNumber = 1 To 4

answer = answer + startNumber

Next startNumber

Here's a table of the relevant parts.

For

We start our loop by telling Visual Basic what type of loop we want to use. In this case it is a **For** loop.

startNumber = 1

The next thing you have to do is tell Visual Basic what number you want the loop to start at. Here we are saying "Start the loop at the number 1". The variable **startNumber** can be called anything you like. A popular name to call a start loop variable is the letter **i** (i = 1). So what we're doing is setting up a variable - the start of the loop variable – and putting 1 into it

To 4

The **To** word, followed by a number or variable, tells Visual Basic how many times you want the loop to go round and round. We're telling Visual Basic to loop until the **startNumber** variable equals 4

Next startNumber

When Visual Basic reaches this line, it checks to see what is in the variable **startNumber**. It then adds one to it. In other words, "Get me the next number after the one I've just used."

The next thing that happens is that Visual Basic will return to the word **For.** It returns because it's in a loop. It needs to know if it can stop looping. To check to see if it can stop looping, it skips the **startNumber = 1** part, and then jumps to your end number. In our case, the end number was 4. Because **Next startNumber** adds one to whatever is in **startNumber**, then **startNumber** is now 2 (It was 1 at the start. The next number after one is ... ?). So if startNumber is now 2, can Visual Basic stop looping? No it can't. Because we've told it to loop until it reaches number 4. It's only reached number 2, so off it goes on another trip around the loop. When the startNumber is greater than the end number, Visual Basic drops out of the loop and continues on its way.

But remember why we're looping: so that we can execute some code over and over again.

To clarify things, change the above code to this:

```
Dim startNumber As Integer

For startNumber = 1 To 4
    MsgBox("Start Number = " & startNumber)
Next startNumber
```

Run the programme, and click your button. What happens? You should have seen this in the message box, one after the other:

```
Start Number = 1
Start Number = 2
Start Number = 3
Start Number = 4
```

Each time round the loop, the code for the message box was executed. You had to click OK four times - **startNumber = 1 To 4**.

So to sum up, a For loop needs a start position and an end position, and all on the same line. A For loop also needs a way to get the next number in the loop. A loop without any code to execute looks like this:

```
For i = startNumber To endNumber

Next i
```

The above code uses two variables for the start and end numbers. The start number for the loop goes directly into the variable **i**. When Visual Basic wants the next number, it just adds one to whatever is in the variable **i**. You could use it like this:

```
Dim startNumber As Integer
Dim endNumber As Integer
Dim i As Integer

startNumber = 1
endNumber = 4

For i = startNumber To endNumber
    Msgbox i
Next i
```

Change the code for your button to that new code, and test it out. Study the code so that you understand what is going on.

For Loops might not be easier to understand than just typing **answer = 1 + 2 + 3 + 4**, but they are a lot more powerful if you want to add up a thousand numbers!

Exercise
Put two textboxes on your form. The first box asks users to enter a start position for a For Loop; the second textbox asks user to enter an end position for the For loop. When a button is clicked,

the programme will add up the numbers between the start position and the end position. Display the answer in a message box. You can use this For Loop code

For i = startNumber To endNumber

answer = answer + i

Next i

Get the startNumber and endNumber from the textboxes.

Exercise

Amend your code to check that the user has entered numbers in the textboxes. You will need an If statement to do this. If there's nothing in the textboxes, you can halt the programme with this code:

Exit Sub

For this exercise, you will be passing whatever is in the textboxes to integer variables. It is these variables you are checking with your If Statement. Because numbers will be entered into the textboxes, remember to convert the text to a value with Val( ).

But the Text property will return a zero if the box is empty. So your If statement will need to check the variables for a value of zero. If it finds a zero, **Then** you can use the **Exit Sub** code. The If statement should come first, before the For Loop code.

Do Loops

We saw with the For Loop that a specific number of times to loop was coded into it. We said

For startNumber = 1 To 4

We knew that we only wanted to loop four times. But what if we don't know how many times around the loop we want to go? Later, we'll be opening text files and reading the data from them. If we used a For loop to get every line of text, we'd have to know beforehand how many lines the text file held. A For Loop would not be very efficient in this case.

But a Do Loop would be. With a Do Loop we can use word s like "While" and "Until". And then we can say, "Go round and round the loop While there's still text to be read from the file." An example might make things clearer.

Load the form you created for the last exercise, the one that has two textboxes and a Button and tested your understanding of For loops.

Add another button to the Form. Your form might look something like this:

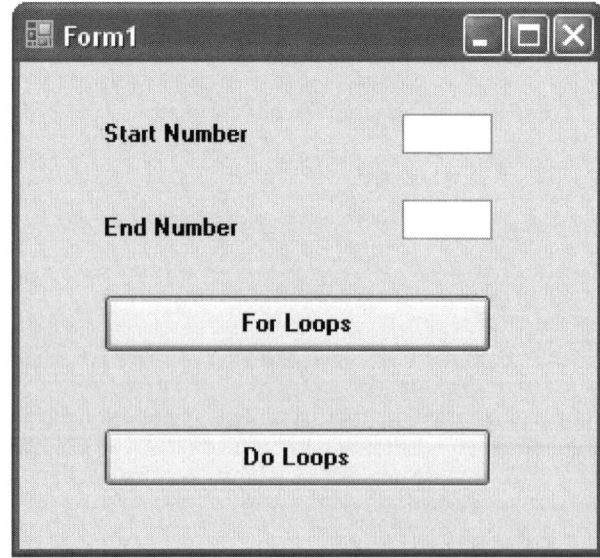

Double click the new button to open the code window, and then type the following code:

```
Dim number as Integer

number = 1

Do While number < 5
        MsgBox number
        number = number + 1
Loop
```

When you've finished, run the programme and see what happens. The numbers 1 to 4 should have displayed in your message box.

So the Do loop keeps going round and around. And when it gets to the top, it tests the "While" part - Do While number is Less Than 5. It's really answering a Yes or No question: is the number inside the variable called **number** Less Than 5? If it is Less Than 5, go round the loop again. If it's not Less than 5, Visual Basic jumps out of the Loop entirely.

You can add the "While ... " part to the bottom, just after the word "Loop". Like this:

```
Do
        number = number + 1

Loop While number < 5
```

Try it and see what difference it makes.

None, right? But there is a difference between the two. With the "While ... " part at the bottom, the code above it gets executed at least once. With the code on the first line after the word "Do", the code might not get executed at all. After all, the number inside the variable might already be Greater Than 5. If it is, Visual Basic won't execute the code.

You have another choice for Do Loops - **Do ... Until**.

There's not much difference between the two, but a **Do ... Until** works like this. Change your Loop code to the following:

> **Do Until number < 5**
>
> > **MsgBox number**
> > **number = number + 1**
>
> **Loop**

Run the code and see what happens.

Nothing happened, right? That's because we "Keep looping UNTIL the number in the variable called **number** is Less Than 5" The problem is, the number inside the variable is already Less Than 5. And if the number is Less than 5, then the code won't execute - because it has already met the end condition.

Change that Less Than sign to a Greater Than sign, and then test your code again. Now what happens?

The numbers 1 to 5 should have displayed. Again, the loop keeps going round and around testing to see if our end condition is met, in this case Is Greater Than 5. If the condition is met, VB breaks out of the Loop; if not, keep going round.

Change the Greater Than sign to Greater Than or Equal to (>=), and test it again. It should now print 1 to 4.

The "Until" part can go at the bottom, just after the word Loop. Like this

> **Do**
>
> > **MsgBox number**
> > **number = number + 1**
>
> **Loop Until number >= 5**

To sum up, use a Do Loop if you don't know what the end number is going to be, otherwise a For Loop might be better. You're now going to write a programme that uses a For Loop inside a Do Loop. The programme works out the times table.

The Times Table Programme

Start a new project for this. Onto your new Form, place two textboxes and a Button. Set the Text property of Textbox1 to 1, and the Text property of Textbox2 to 10. Set the Text property of the button to "Go".

When the Go button is clicked, the programme will put the numbers from the Textbox into two variables. We'll then put a value into a variable called **multiplier**. If you're doing the times tables, the format is

X multiplied by Y = Z
(2 multiplied by 3 = 6)

The Do Loop will work out the multiplier (that's the Y part); The For Loop will work out the rest. We'll then display the results in something called a List box.

So add a List Box to your form. It looks like this in the toolbox:

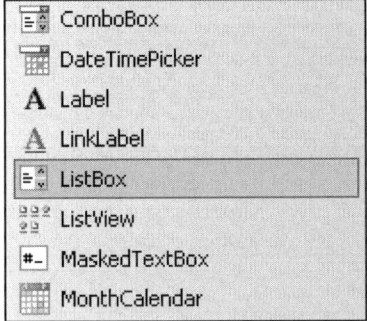

Your form should look something like this:

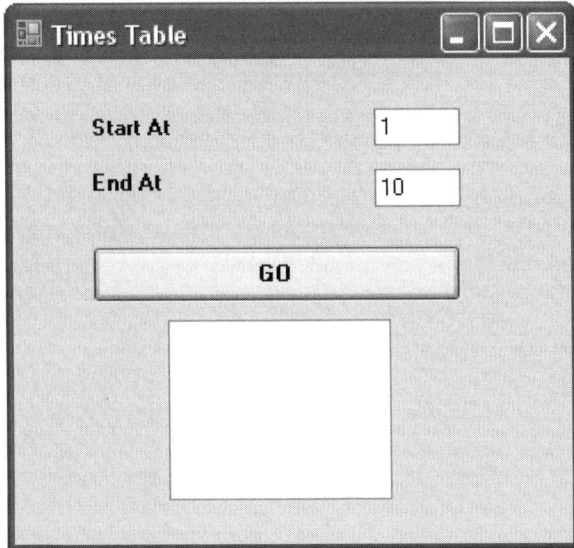

A List box is similar to a Combo Box, in that you have a list of items that the user can select. Here, we're just using it display the results of our programme. We'll add items to the List box with our code, rather than in design time like we did for the Combo box.

So, here's the code for the entire programme. Double click your Go button, and add the following:

```
Dim number1 As Integer
Dim number2 As Integer
Dim multiplier As Integer
Dim answer As Integer
Dim i As Integer

number1 = Val(TextBox1.Text)
number2 = Val(TextBox2.Text)
multiplier = 2

Do While multiplier < 3

  For i = number1 To number2

    answer = i * multiplier
    ListBox1.Items.Add(i & " Times " & multiplier & " = " & answer)
  Next i

  multiplier = multiplier + 1

Loop
```

When you've finished, run the programme and see how it works. You should see this appear in your List box:

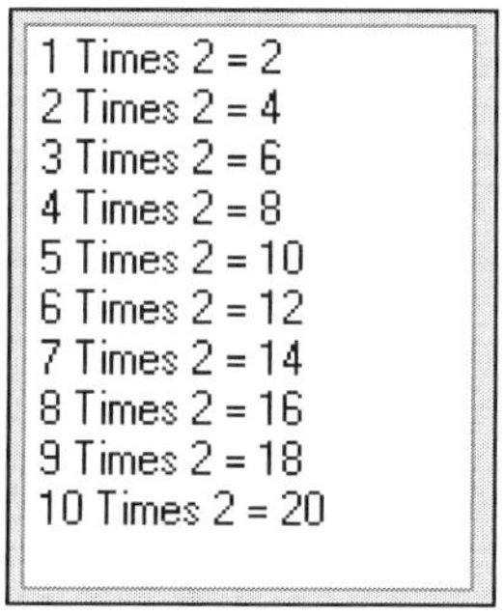

```
1 Times 2 = 2
2 Times 2 = 4
3 Times 2 = 6
4 Times 2 = 8
5 Times 2 = 10
6 Times 2 = 12
7 Times 2 = 14
8 Times 2 = 16
9 Times 2 = 18
10 Times 2 = 20
```

Let's run through the code to see how it works.

The code

As you can see, we've set up five Integer variables - **number1**, **number2**, **multiplier**, **answer** and **i**.

The next thing we did was to pass whatever is in our two Textboxes straight into the two variables, **number1** and **number2**. The start number goes into textbox one, and the end number goes into textbox2.

Then we set a starting value for the multiplier: **multiplier = 2**.

Then we have our two Loops, one inside the other. The first is the Do Loop:

> **Do While multiplier < 3**
>
> **multiplier = multiplier + 1**
> **Loop**

This Do loop is exactly the same as the one you met before. All it does is go round and round While the variable called **multiplier** is Less Than 3. The bit of code between Do and Loop just keeps adding one to whatever is in **multiplier** (incrementing the variable).

The other thing the Do Loop does is to execute our second loop - the For Loop. The For Loop gets executed each time around. The For Loop was this:

> **For i = number1 To number2**
>
> answer = i * multiplier
> ListBox1.Items.Add(i & " Times " & multiplier & " = " & answer)
>
> **Next i**

Remember: the **number1** and **number2** variables hold our numbers from the Textboxes. We set these to 1 and 10. So our first line of the For Loop is really this:

> **For i = 1 To 10**

We're saying, Start a For Loop. Whatever is in the variable called number1, make that the starting number for the Loop. Put this value into the variable called i. The end of the Loop will come when the variable called i has the value 10. Stop looping when you reach this value.

The next part of the code reads this

> **answer = i * multiplier**

This means, Put into the variable called **answer** the following sum: whatever is in the variable called i multiplied by whatever is in the variable called **multiplier**.

A digression

Yes, the * symbol means multiply in Visual Basic. The basic Math symbols are these

+   The Plus sign adds numbers together

-           The minus sign takes one number away from another

*   The symbol above the number 8 on your keyboard tells Visual Basic to
            multiply two numbers

/   The forward slash on your keyboard is the divide by symbol

=   The equals sign

A word or two about how to use the mathematical symbols in Visual Basic. You can use the operators by themselves:

> **answer = 8 + 4**
> **answer = 8 - 4**
> **answer = 8 * 4**
> **answer = 8 / 4**

Or you can combine them by using parentheses.

> **answer = (8 - 4) + (4 - 2)**
> **answer = 6**

Here, Visual Basic will work out the sums in parentheses first, and then add the two sums together

> **answer = (8 - 4) + (4 -2)**
> **answer = 4 + 2**
> **answer = 6**

But you've got to be careful with parentheses, because there is a strict order that VB uses when it's doing maths. Consider this sum

> **answer = 8 - 4 + 4 + 2 * 2**

Try that code behind a new button. Display the result in a MsgBox. What answer did you get? 12! It's wrong! But why?

You would think it would work out the sum like we do - left to right

> **8 - 4 = 4**
> **+ 4 = 8**
> **+ 2 = 10**
> *** 2 = 20**

But VB doesn't work it out like that. Visual basic will do the multiplying first. So it will calculate like this

> **2 * 2   = 4**
> **8 - 4 + 4   = 8**
> **8 + 4   = 12**

To make sure Visual Basic does your sums correctly you have to be careful of the parentheses. Try changing the code to this:

$$answer = (8 - 4) + (4 + 2) * 2$$

Now what happens? That's right - you get 16! It's still wrong! At least it is if you are working from left to right. But Visual Basic isn't. It will do the (4 + 2) * 2 part first, and then add that to 8 - 4. Which gives you 16.

In order to force Visual Basic to get the sum right, you need even more parentheses. Try this code and see what happens:

$$answer = ((8 - 4) + (4 + 2)) * 2$$

Finally we get the answer we've been expecting - 20! The parentheses above have grouped our sums into separate sections, thereby forcing VB to do the sums in the right order.
So take care when using parentheses to do your sums! But the order that Visual Basic does its sums is this:

Multiplication	*
Division	/
Addition	+
Subtraction	-

End of Digression

But back to our For Loop. You'll remember we had this sum

$$answer = i * multiplier$$

So that says, put into the variable **answer** the sum of **i** times **multiplier**. We're getting whatever is in **i** from the For loop. But we're getting whatever is in the variable called **multiplier** from the Do Loop.

So Visual Basic will read the **Do While** line after noting that the number 2 has been put into the variable called **multiplier**. It will then check to see if the end of the loop condition has been met - multiplier is Less Than 3. As 2 is not Less Than 2, VB drops down to the next line.

The next line is a For Loop - For i = 1 To 10. This entire loop will be executed, and the code inside the For loop worked out.

So the For loop gets executed 10 times. Which means that our sum will get executed 10 times. When the end condition of the For loop is met, Visual Basic will exit the For Loop and drop down to the line of code below **Next i**. The code below **Next i** is this

$$multiplier = multiplier + 1$$

What was inside the variable called **multiplier** was the number 2, so 2 + 1 = 3. And three is the new number inside the variable **multiplier**.

Then, Visual Basic drops down to the next line, which is Loop. So it goes back up to the **Do While** line of code

Do While multiplier < 3

The same question is asked again: Have we met the end condition for the Do Loop? The end condition was "Keep looping while the variable called **multiplier** is Less Than 3".

Because the value in **multiplier** is now equal to 3 and not less than 3, the end condition has been met. When the end condition is met, VB exits the Do loop.

Exercise
Change the Do While line to this:

Do While multiplier < 5

Can you guess what will appear in your list box? Run your programme and find out.

Finally, a word about the line that displays your text in the list box. It was this:

ListBox1.Items.Add(i & " Times " & multiplier & " = " & answer)

To add items to a list box with code, first you type the name of your list box:

ListBox1

Type a full stop and a drop down list will appear. Select **Items** from the list.

ListBox1.Items

Type another full stop and again a drop down list will appear. Select the **Add** Method

ListBox1.Items.Add

This method, not surprisingly, lets you add items to your list box. Whatever you want to add goes between a pair of round brackets:

ListBox1.Items.Add( )

In between the round brackets, we have this for our code:

i & " Times " & multiplier & " = " & answer

It might be a bit long, but there are 5 parts to it, all joined together by the concatenate symbol (&):

i
" Times "

multiplier
" = "
answer

The variable **i** holds the current value of the For Loop; " Times " is just direct text; **multiplier** holds the value we're multiplying by (our times table); " = " is again direct text; and **answer** is the answer to our times table sum.

If you want to clear the items from a List box you can do this. At the top of the code, enter this line:

ListBox1.Items.Clear()

So instead of selecting Add from the final drop down list, select Clear.

Exercise
Add another textbox to your form. This will represent the "times table". So far you have been getting this value directly from the code. For this exercise, get the multiplier value directly from the textbox. Add appropriate labels to all your textboxes.

The multiplier variable is the starting point for your "times tables". What else do you need to amend in the code? Think about what happens if you entered a 5 into your new Textbox.

If you enter a number 5 or greater, the code doesn't get executed! Can you understand why that is? If not, I suggest you go over this looping section again.

Exercise
Amend the above code to solve the problem of the programme not being executed.

If you successfully solved the problem, what else did you notice? Assuming that you added two labels to your new textboxes - "Start At" and "End At" - what happens if you enter a 3 in the Start At textbox and a 5 in the End At textbox? Will you actually get the 5 times table? What can you do so that the 5 times table is displayed? (Consider using a different Do Loop. What about a Do ... Until loop?)

More Controls - Menus

All right, let's have a breather from all that Looping. We'll now explore some more of the controls from the Visual Basic toolbox, and see how they can enhance the look of your Form. First, let's have a look at what you can do to the Form itself.

You can add dropdown menus to your Form. These types of menus are very common to Windows programme. Visual Basic itself has many of these dropdown menus - File, Edit, View, Project, Format, etc. And they're very easy to add.

Start a new project. To your new form, use the toolbox to add a MenuStrip:

Double click the control to add one to your form. When you do, you'll notice two things. At the top of your form, you'll see this:

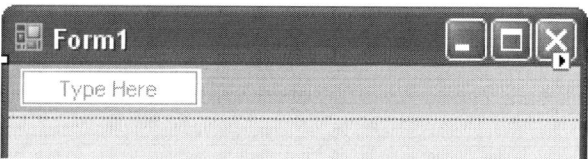

We'll see how to construct our menu soon. But notice the other thing that gets added to your project. Examine the bottom of your screen, on the left. You'll see this:

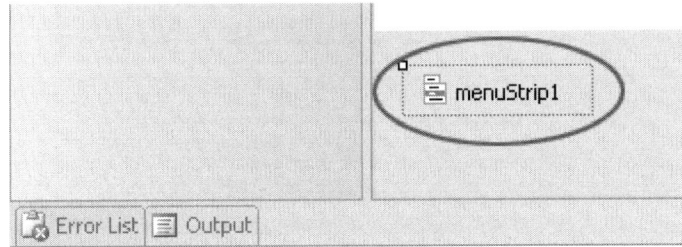

This is the control itself. If you click on this, you'll see that the Properties box on the right changes. There are many properties for the control. But there are lots of properties for the MenuItem object, as well. The MenuItem object is the one at the top of the form – the one that says Type Here.

Click inside the area that says "Type Here". Type the word **File**:

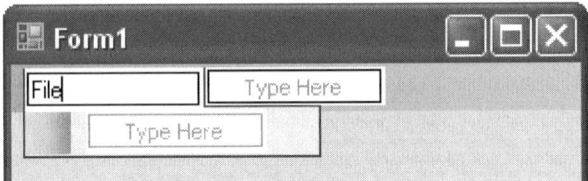

Now press the enter key on your keyboard. Your menu will look like this:

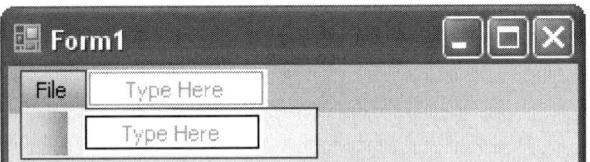

To create items on your File menu, click inside the Type Here box. Enter the word **New**, and press the enter key on your keyboard again. Your menu will then look like this:

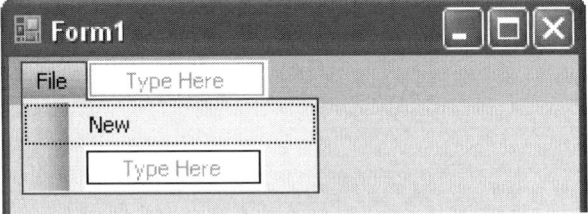

Add an "Open" and a "Save" item to your menu in the same way. It should look like this:

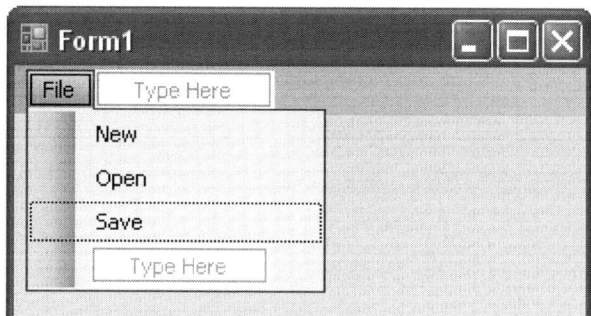

The final item we'll add to our menu is an "Exit" item. But you can add a separator between the "Save" and "Exit".

To add a separator, click inside the blue "Type Here" box. Instead of typing a letter, type the minus character "-" (in between the "0" key and the "+/=" key on your keyboard). When you hit your return key, you'll see the separator appear:

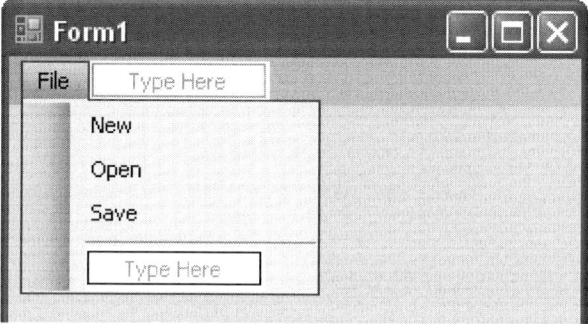

Click inside the "Type Here" area, and add an Exit (or Quit) item. Click back on your form, away from the menu, to finish off. You should now have a File menu like this one:

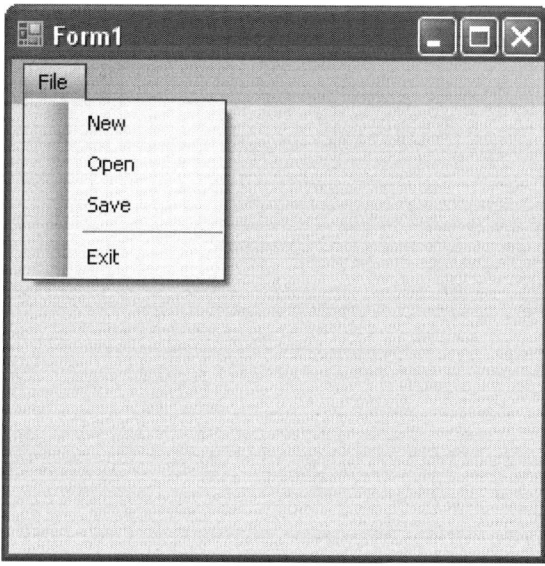

To see what your menu look like, Run your programme. Click the File menu. We haven't added any code to the menu yet, so nothing will happen if you click an item on the menu.

Stop your programme and return to the design environment. Click **File** in Design Time to see your drop down menu. You can double click an item to open up the code window. But don't do that yet.

Another way to get to the code for an object is this:

- Press F7 on your keyboard to go to the code window
- Click the arrow at the top, where it says General:
- From the drop down box, have a look at the list of items:

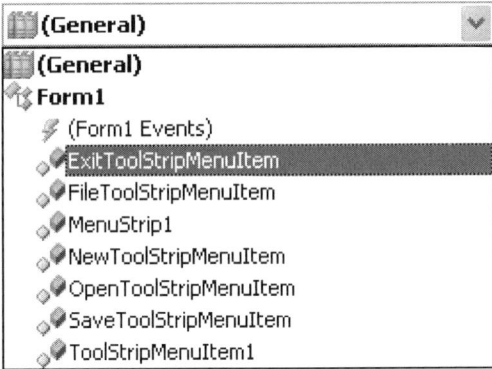

The Exit menu here is "ExitToolStripMenuItem". If you were to click that item, a code stub would open, ready for you to type your code.

However, "ExitToolStripMenuItem" is very difficult to remember. We can rename our menu items so that they are more descriptive. So do this:

- Get back to your form by pressing Shift + F7 on your keyboard
- Click the File menu to select it
- Select the Exit item (Careful not to click in the middle as this may open the code window. Click near the left edge somewhere.)
- When you have the Exit item selected, look at the properties box on the right:

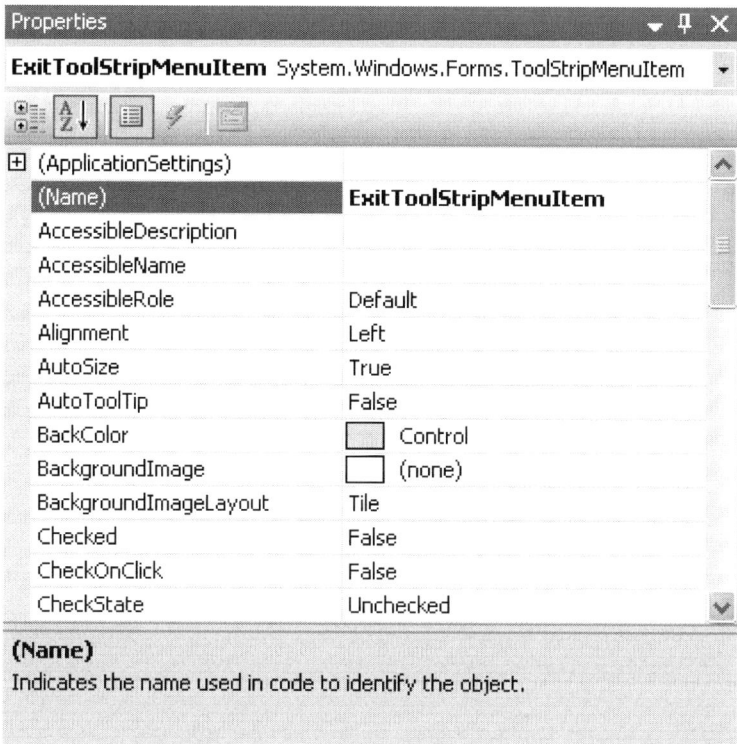

- Click inside the Name property
- Change it to mnuExit
- Press your return key to confirm the change

Now press F7 again to bring the code window up. Click the drop down arrow of the General box, and you should see the new name appear (Notice that the item called ExitToolStripMenuItem has vanished):

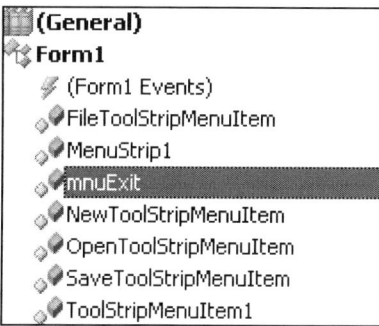

Click on your new mnuExit item.

Nothing will happen!

To jump straight to the code, you need to look at the drop down box opposite. It will probably say "Declarations". Click the arrow and you'll see a new list:

The items in the new box are called Events. The Event you want is the Click event. So select that one from the list (we'll cover Events in more depth later). When you select Click from the list, you are taken straight into the code for that event. It should be like this one:

```
Private Sub mnuExit_Click(ByVal sender As Object, _
                          ByVal e As System.EventArgs) _
                          Handles mnuExit.Click


End Sub
```

The code above has been tidied up to fit on this page; yours will all be on one line. But notice that it says **mnuExit_Click**.

Don't worry too much about what it all means; we'll get to that in a later section. What we want to do is add some of our own code, so that out Exit menu item actually does something.

There's only one line of code to add. It's this:

```
Private Sub mnuExit_Click(ByVal sender As Object, _
                          ByVal e As System.EventArgs) _
                          Handles mnuExit.Click


      Me.Close()


End Sub
```

(Again this has been tidied up to fit on this page.)

To test out your new code, run your programme. Click your File menu, and then click the Exit item. Your form should close down, and you'll be returned to the design environment.

Creating Sub Menus

A sub menu is one that branches of a menu item. They usually have an arrow to indicate that there's an extra menu available. You will have seen these plenty of times in Windows programmes.

You can create your own sub menus quite easily. Try this:

- Return to the Form view (Shift + F7 is a shortcut)
- Click on your File menu so that you can see it all
- Select the New item (Careful where you click. Click once on the left edge)
- You should see this:

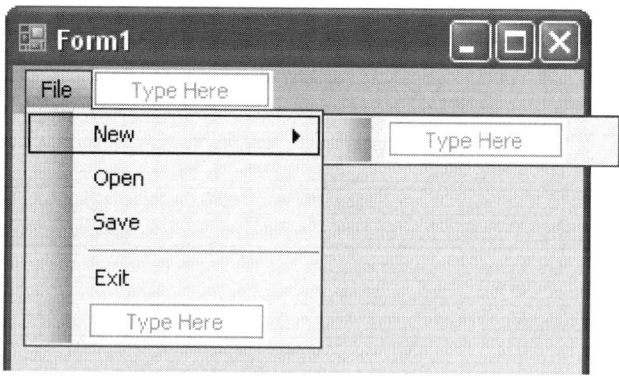

- Click on the "Type Here" just to the right of New
- You'll see yet more "Type Here" areas:

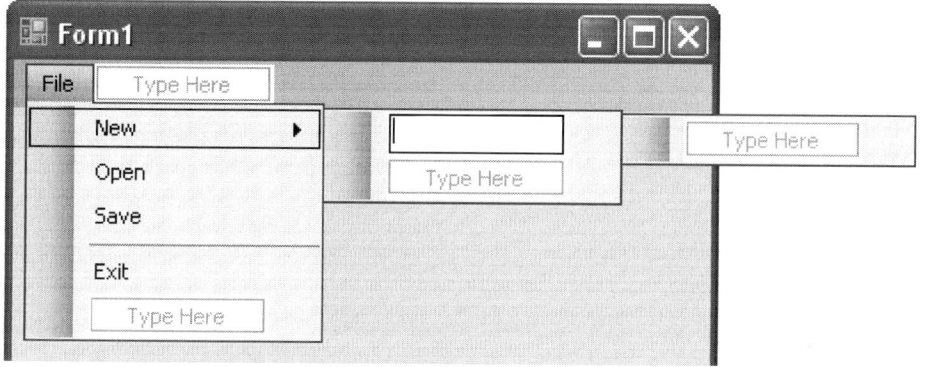

- Type "New Project" (without the quotes), and then hit the return key on your keyboard
- Type in "New File" and then click away from the menu, somewhere on the form
- You will then have a menu like this one:

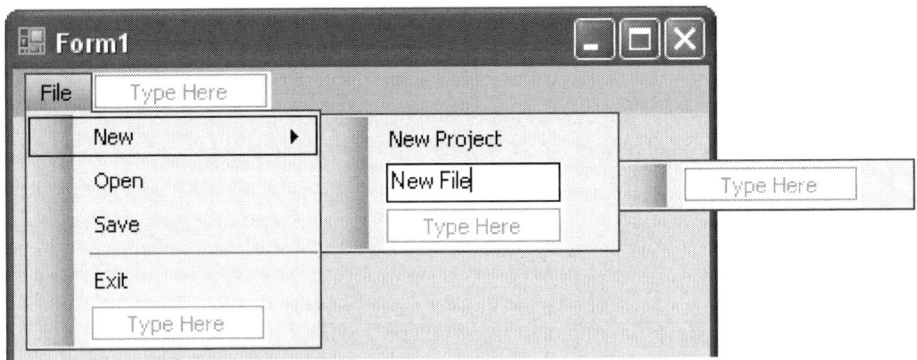

Save your work, and then run your programme. Click your new menu to see the following:

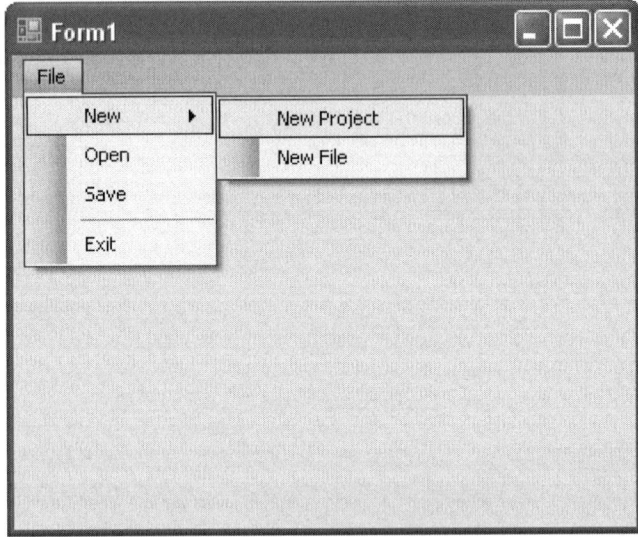

Of course, none of the menu items work except the Exit menu. But you should have found that adding menus to your programmes is an easy matter with VB.NET.

One more thing we can do. If you look closely at a lot of menu items, you see that they have shortcuts attached. There are two types of shortcuts: An underline shortcut, and a key combination shortcut.

Underline Shortcut

To add an underline, do this:

- Click on your New menu item once. This will select it
- Now locate the Text property:
- Type an ampersand symbol (&) before the "N" of New:

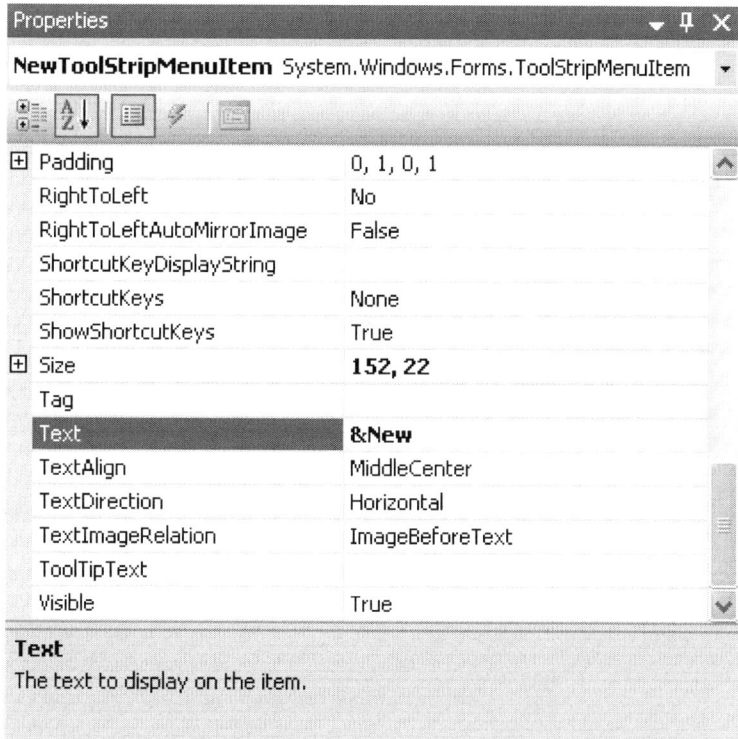

- Hit the return key on your keyboard
- You should see this on your menu:

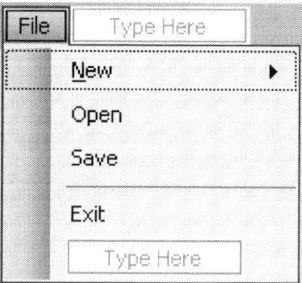

Notice that "N" of New is now underlined. If you want an underline shortcut, the ampersand character should be typed before the letter you want underlined.

Add underlines for the "F" of File, the "O" of Open, the "S" of Save, and the "E" of Exit. When you're done, your menu should look like this one:

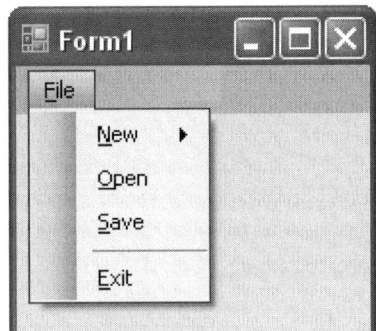

Key combination shortcuts

A key combination shortcut is one that appears at the end of a menu item (Ctrl + N, for example). You can easily add this option to your own programmes. So try this:

- In Design time, select the New item on your menu
- Look at the properties box on the right
- Locate the ShortcutKeys item:

- Click the down arrow to reveal the following:

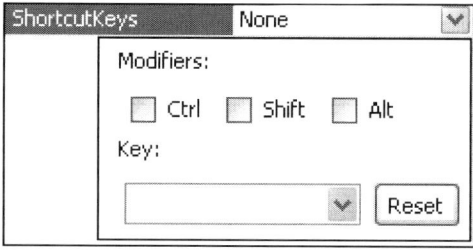

The Modifier is the key you press with your shortcut. For example, the CTRL key then the "N" key on your keyboard. Place a check inside the Ctrl box. Then select the letter "N" from the Key dropdown list, as in the next image:

Click back on your menu to see what it looks like:

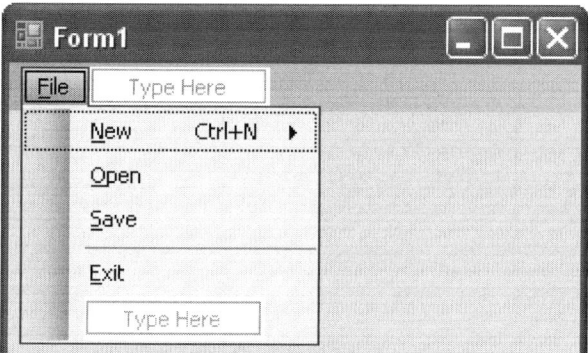

Using the same technique, add a shortcut key combination to your exit menu. Run your programme and test it out. Your programme should quit when you press your exit shortcut.

You can add these types of shortcuts to any menu item. Just remember to choose a different key stroke combination for each one. And don't have too many of them – they'll spoil the look of your menu!

OK, time for another review.

Review Four

For review Four, there are two parts to complete.

Part One

Add the following menus to the menu bar you have already designed in this section: Edit, View

On the Edit Menu, place the following menu items: Undo, Cut, Copy, Paste

On the View Menu, place the following menu items: View Textboxes, View Labels, View Image

Just like you did with the Exit menu item, Change the Name property of ALL menu items. Do not leave them on the defaults of "MenuItem1", "MenuItem2", etc. (You should change the Name property to something relevant, and use the prefix mnu. For example, the Undo item could have the Name mnuUndo.)

- Add an underline shortcut for ALL menu items
- Add at least one key combination shortcuts per drop down menu (you already have one on the File menu, so this doesn't count)

When you have finished part one, your menus should look like these (though you can use different key combinations, if you like):

Edit Menu

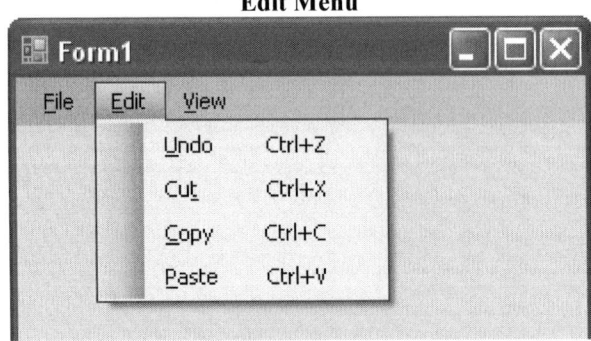

View Menu

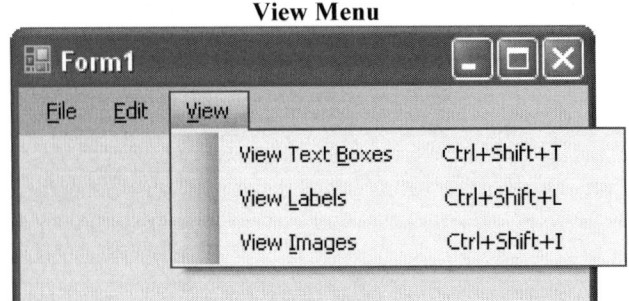

Review Four Part Two

Write code to display a message box whenever a menu item is clicked, or its shortcut used. The message box should explain what the menu item will do when it's fully implemented.

There's only one line of code to write for each menu item. You can get at the code for the click event of each menu item in exactly the same way that you did for the Exit menu item.

To help you display your messages in a better light, you can format the message boxes quite easily. Here's how.

More about the Message Box

The message box function you have used so far is the old message box function. It is the one left over from VB6:

MsgBox("Your Message Here")

The newer VB.NET message box function is very similar, but the syntax is slightly different. It's this:

MessageBox.Show("Your Message Here")

So you type the word "MessageBox" then a full stop. Double click the "Show" method on the menu that appears. Then type a round bracket. You should get a rather long and complex tool tip appearing.

What it all means is there are options you can use with your message box. The first one is "Text As String". The text in question is the text that will appear for your message – the message itself, in other words. The next one is "Caption As String". This sets the white caption at the top of the message box.

So if your message box function was this:

MessageBox.Show("This menu will Undo an Operation", "Undo")

You would get this message box popping up:

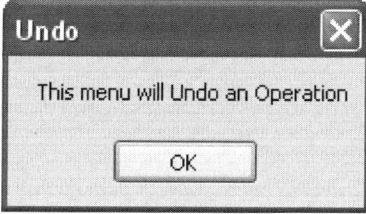

Each option for your message box is separated by a comma. If you type a comma after the **"Undo",** you'll get another pop-up menu. On this menu, you can specify which buttons you want on your message box:

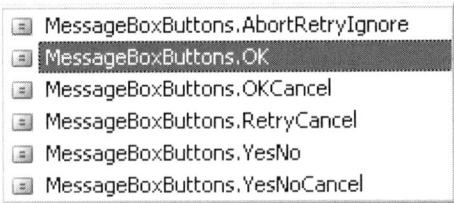

You only need the OK button on your message boxes. Double click this item, then type another comma. Yet another pop-up menu will appear. On this menu, you can specify the symbol that appears in the message box:

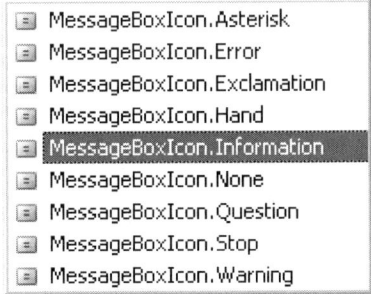

It's up to you which symbol you choose. Experiment with all of them and see what they look like. In the image below, we've gone for the Information symbol:

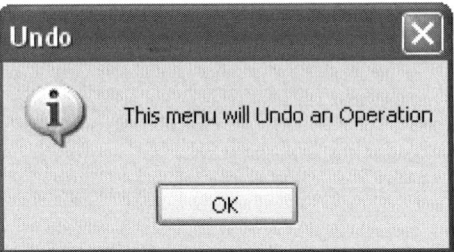

The message box above is a lot better than the first one we tried.

Writing the Code for the Menu System

For the last review, you designed a form interface that had a File, Edit and a View menu. In this section, we'll write code so that your menu items actually do something other than displaying message boxes. In other words, the Edit > Cut menu will really cut text, and the Edit > Paste menu will really paste text.

So open up your work for review four. Comment out or delete your message box code. (You comment out code by typing a single quote character at the start of the line. The line will then turn green, and will be ignored when the programme is run.)

We'll start with the File > Open menu.

The Open File Dialogue Box

In most programmes, if you click the File menu, and select the Open item, a dialogue box is displayed. From the dialogue box, you can click on a file to select it, then click the Open button. We'll see how to do that from our menu.

First, place two textboxes on your form. In the properties box, locate the MultiLine property. It is set to False by default (which is why you can't change the height of textboxes). Change this value to True.

Type some default text for the Text Property of textbox1.

Your form should now look something like this one:

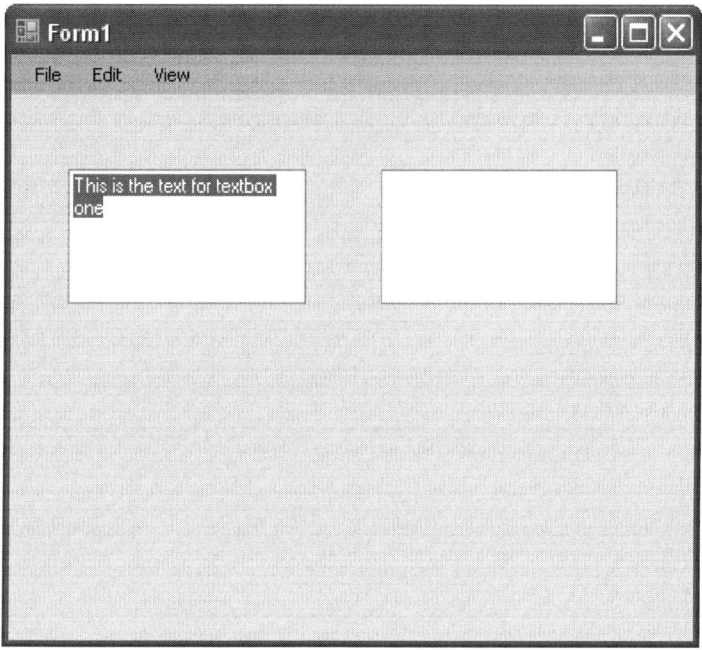

We'll work with these textboxes when we do the Edit menu. So let's leave them for now.

When we click on File > Open from our menu, we want the Open dialogue box to appear. This is fairly straightforward in VB.NET. In fact there is even a control for it!

Open up your toolbox, and locate the control called "OpenFileDialog":

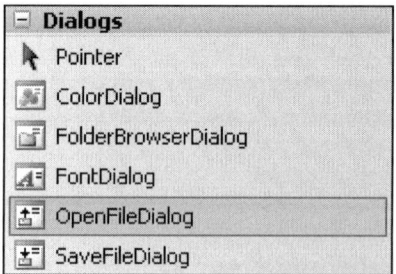

Double click the control to add one to your project.

But notice that the control doesn't get added to your form. It gets added to the area at the bottom, next to your menu control:

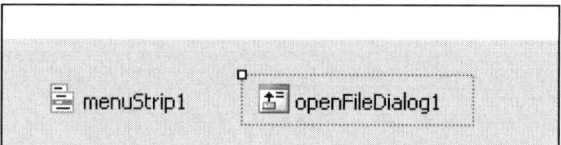

The shaded area surrounding the control means that it is selected. If you look to your right, you'll see the properties that you can use with the control.

Click on the Name property and change the name to **openFD**. When you change the name in the properties box, the name of the control at the bottom will change:

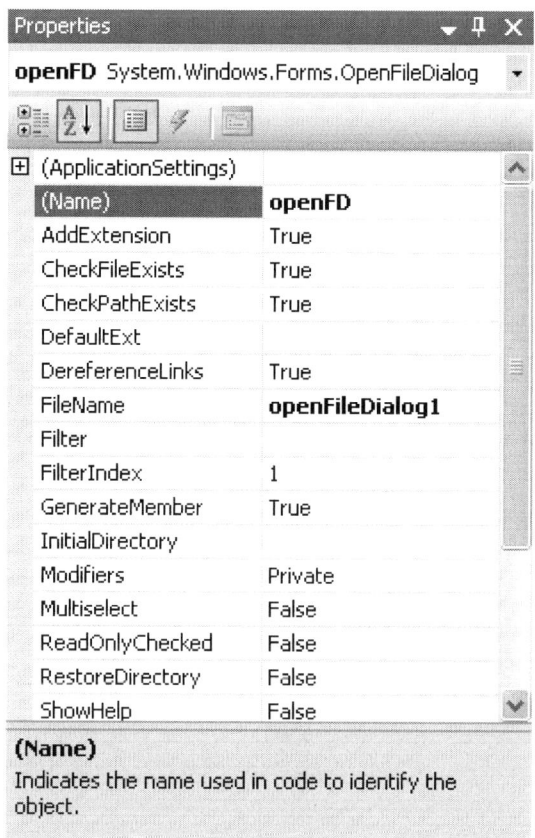

We'll now write some code to manipulate the properties of our new control.

Access the code for your **File > Open** menu item. To do this quickly, you can simply double click the Open item on your menu bar. Or, press F7 to access the Code View. Click the name of your menu item from the left dropdown box at the top of the code. Then select the Click event from the dropdown box to the right. Your empty code should be this (the code below has underscore characters added, so that it can fit on this page):

```
Private Sub mnuOpen_Click(ByVal sender As Object, _
                          ByVal e As System.EventArgs) _
                          Handles mnuOpen.Click

End Sub
```

With your cursor flashing between the two lines of your code, add the following:

openFD.ShowDialog( )

When you typed a full stop after the **openFD**, you probably saw a list box appear. You can just double click the **ShowDialog** item to add it to your code.

But this method of the **OpenFileDialog** control does what you'd expect it to do: Shows the dialogue box. You can even test it out right now. Press F5 to run your programme. Then click the Open item on your File menu. You should see an Open dialogue box display.

Return to the design environment, and we'll explore some more things you can do with this Dialogue box control.

The Initial Directory

You can set which directory the dialogue box should display when it appears. Instead of it displaying the contents of the "My Documents" folder, for example, you can have it display the contents of any folder. This is done with the Initial Directory property. Amend your code to this:

> **openFD.InitialDirectory = "C:\"**
> **openFD.ShowDialog( )**

Run your programme again, and see the results in action. You should see the contents of the "C" folder on your hard drive.

The Title Property

By default, the dialogue box will display the word "Open" as a caption at the top of your dialogue box. You can change this with the Title property. Add the line in Bold to your code:

> **openFD.InitialDirectory = "C:\"**
> **openFD.Title = "Open a Text File"**
> **openFD.ShowDialog( )**

Run your code again, and Click File > Open from your menu. You should see this at the top of the Open dialogue box:

The Filter Property

In most dialogue boxes, you can display a list of specific files that can be opened. These are displayed in the "Files of Type" drop down list. To do this in VB.NET, you access the Filter property. We'll restrict our users to only opening Text files, those that end in the extension ".txt".

The following is used for the filter property:

> **openFD.InitialDirectory = "C:\"**
> **openFD.Title = "Open a Text File"**
> **openFD.Filter = "Text Files|*.txt"**
> **openFD.ShowDialog( )**

Run your code. Click File > Open on your menu, and then click the arrow on the drop down box for "Files of Type". You should see this:

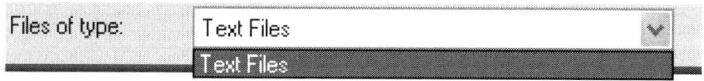

Or this, in Windows 7:

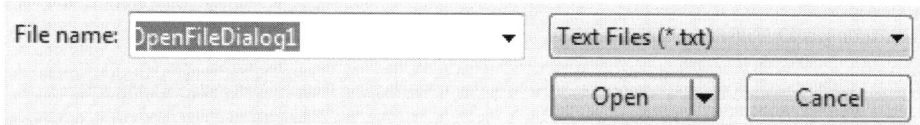

You can add a little bit extra to the description part of the filter, if you like (for Windows XP users). This will serve as a reminder of just what the extension is. Try amending the line to this:

> **openFD.Filter = "Text Files(*.txt)|*.txt"**

When you run your code, you'll see this in the Files of Type area:

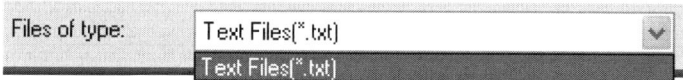

If you scroll across your Open dialogue box, you should see only text files displayed (you'll still see folders). If you can't see any files at all, double click a folder and explore. You'll soon see something like this:

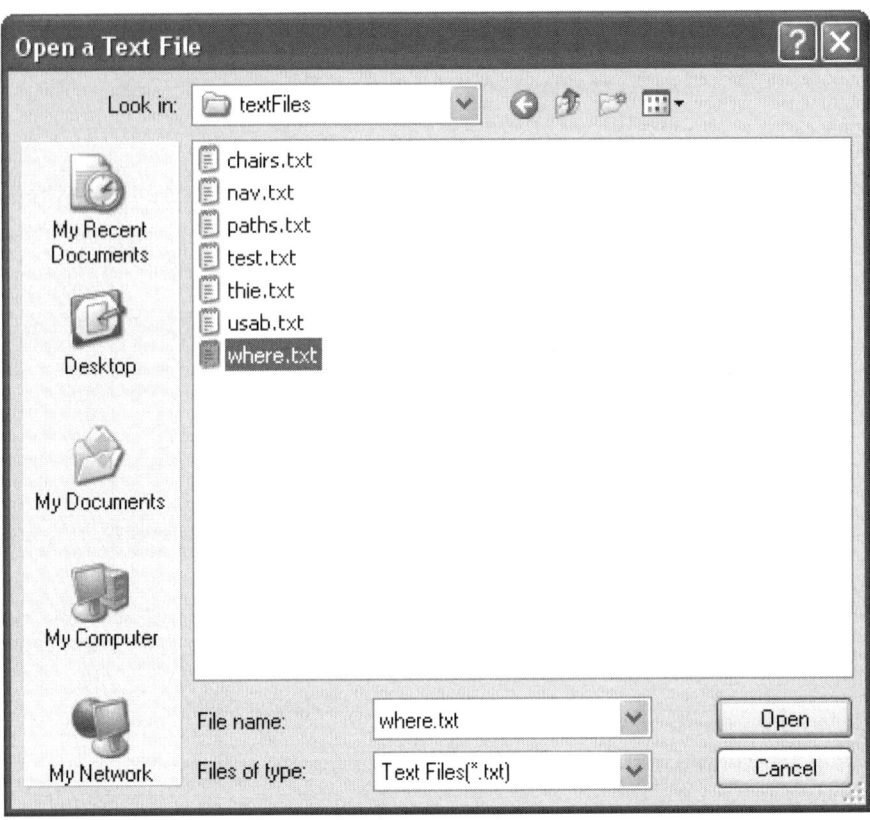

To display files of more than one type, add a Pipe character between each filter. In the code below, two file types are specified, text files and Microsoft Word documents:

openFD.Filter = "Text Files|*.txt|Word Files|*.doc"

When the programme is run, you should be able to see two file types in the list:

Windows XP   **Windows 7**

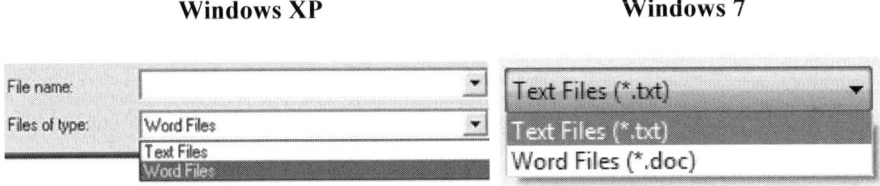

Selecting a File

You'll notice that if you select a file and click the Open button, nothing happens. That's because the Open dialogue box doesn't actually open files! It only displays a list of files that CAN be opened, if you were clever enough to write the code. We'll be writing the code that does the opening (and the saving) in a later section. But you need to be able to get the name of the file. The Open Dialogue box has a property that returns the file name that was selected. Not surprisingly, it's called FileName:

OpenFD.FileName

However, this is a property that returns a value (a string value). The value is the name of a file. So you have to assign this value to something. We can assign it to a new variable:

Dim strFileName As String

strFileName = OpenFD.FileName

The value in the variable **strFileName** will then hold the name of the file selected. So change you code to this (new lines in bold):

Dim strFileName As String

openFD.InitialDirectory = "C:\"
openFD.Title = "Open a Text File"
openFD.Filter = "Text Files|*.txt"
openFD.ShowDialog()
strFileName = OpenFD.FileName

MsgBox strFileName

Run your programme, and click your File > Open menu. Navigate to where you have some text files. Click one to select it. Then click the Open button. You should see the name of the file displayed in your message box:

Notice that the location (the path) of the file is also displayed.

One thing you may have noticed is that if you select a file, then click the Cancel button, the message box still displays. But it will be blank. In your code, you will only want to do something with a file if the Cancel button is NOT clicked.

You can test to see if it was clicked by assigning the openFD.ShowDialog() to an integer:

Dim DidWork As Integer = openFD.ShowDialog()

You can then test what is inside of the **DidWork** variable. The result of the action is also stored by VB.NET in this property:

DialogResult.Cancel

You can compare the two in an IF statement:

If DidWork = Windows.Forms.DialogResult.Cancel Then
        MsgBox("Cancel Button Clicked")
Else
        strFileName = openFD.FileName
        MsgBox(strFileName)
End If

In the code above, you're only opening the file if the Open button was clicked. The code is a bit more complicated, but study it for a while and it will make sense!

The Save Menu

The save dialogue box works in the same way as the Open dialogue box. However, you can't use the same control. If you examine the Toolbox, you'll see a control called SaveFileDialog:

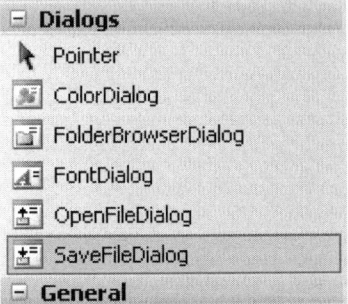

Double click this control to add one to your project. If you look at the bottom of the screen, you'll see the control added there, rather than onto your form:

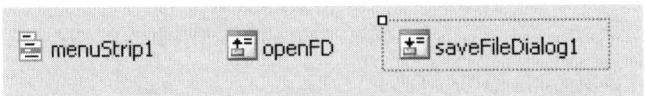

In the image above, the control is selected. Change the Name property of your control to something more manageable. Change it to **saveFD**.

Access the code for your File > Save menu item. Then add the following code:

saveFD.ShowDialog()

Your code window should look like this one (Again, underscores have been added to the first line to fit on this page):

```
Private Sub mnuSave_Click(ByVal sender As Object, _
                              ByVal e As System.EventArgs) _
                              Handles mnuSave.Click


    saveFD.ShowDialog()


End Sub
```

Run your programme, then click your File > Save menu item. You should see the Save As dialogue box appear.

Just like the Open control, you can use the properties of the Save control on your dialogue boxes. Try changing these properties, just like you did with the Open properties:

Initial Directory
Title
Filter
FileName

There's another useful property you can use with the Save control – the Overwrite prompt. When you set this property, a message box pops up warning you that the file will be overwritten, and do you want to continue. To use this property, the code is this:

saveFD.OverwritePrompt = True

However, just like the Open box, when you click the Save button no file is actually being saved. You have to write your own code for this. You'll learn how to do this in a later section. For now, let's move on to the Edit menu.

The Edit Menu

If you haven't already, add two textboxes to your form and set their **MultiLine** property to **True**. As a reminder, your form should look like this:

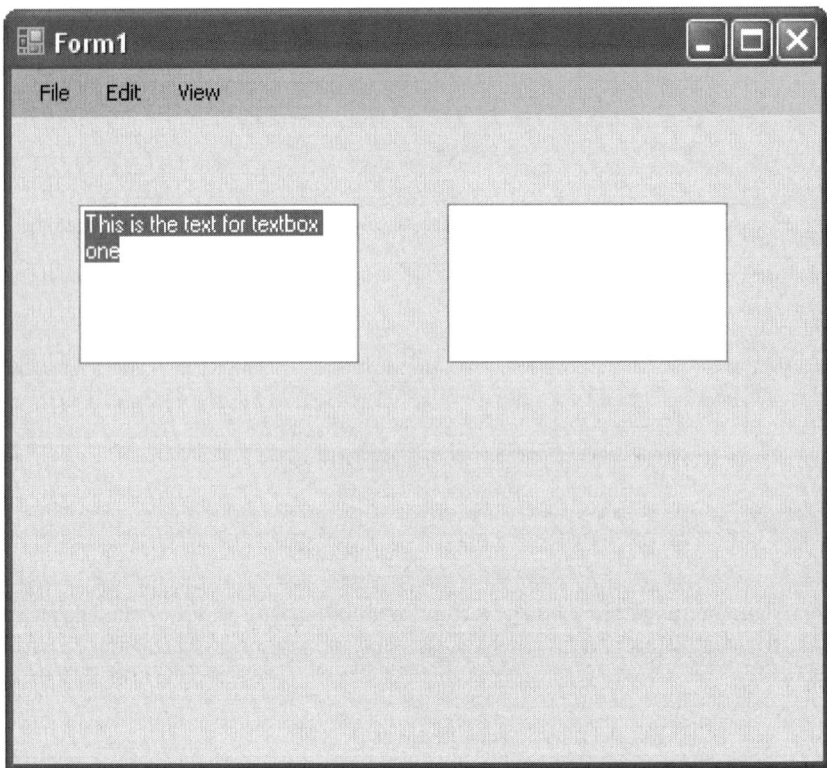

What we'll do now is to get the following menu items to work: Undo, Cut, Copy and Paste. We'll start with Copying:

The Copy Menu

If you type Textbox1 then a full stop, you get a list of properties and methods available to the textbox. Scroll up to the top and locate the Copy method:

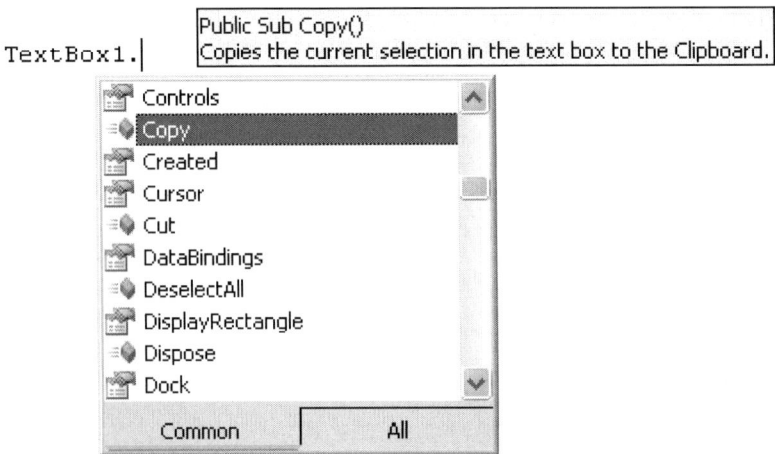

Notice the tool tip in yellow. It's telling you what this method does – copies the current selection to the clipboard. The clipboard is a temporary storage area available to most Windows applications. When you invoke the Copy method of the textbox, any selected text is place in this temporary storage area for you. You don't have to write any other code.

So access the code for your Copy menu item, and add this line to it:

Textbox1.Copy( )

Your code window will then look like this:

```
Private Sub mnuCopy_Click(ByVal sender As Object, _
                          ByVal e As System.EventArgs) _
                          Handles mnuCopy.Click

    TextBox1.Copy()

End Sub
```

That's all there is for the copy menu! But nothing visible will happen when you run your code. Let's paste it into the second textbox.

The Paste Menu

Again, there's only one line of code to write. It's this:

TextBox2.Paste( )

Notice that we're saying paste to textbox2. Because the copy menu places the text from textbox one onto the clipboard, you only need this one line of code.

So add that line to your Paste menu item:

```
Private Sub mnuPaste_Click(ByVal sender As Object, _
                           ByVal e As System.EventArgs) _
                           Handles mnuPaste.Click

    TextBox2.Paste()

End Sub
```

Time to test it out. Run your programme. Select all the text in textbox one (it might already be selected), then click **Edit > Copy** from your menu.

Click inside the second textbox. Then click **Edit > Paste** from your menu. The text should appear in textbox two.

The Cut Menu

Access the code for you Cut menu item. Add the following code to it:

TextBox1.Cut( )

Run your programme, and select the text in textbox one. From your menu, click Edit > Cut. The text should disappear (it's on the clipboard, though). Click inside textbox two, and click Edit > Paste. The text should be pasted over.

The Undo Menu

For the Undo menu, add this line of code:

TextBox1.Undo( )

Run your programme. Then select the text in textbox one. Click **Edit > Cut** and the text disappears. Now click **Edit > Undo**. The text reappears.

The Edit menu we implemented is only a simple one. But it does demonstrate what you can do with VB.NET and menus.

We'll complete our look at menus by coding for the View menu you added to your form. In the process, we'll take a look at pictures boxes, as well as seeing how easy it is to hide and disable controls on a form.

The View Menu

The items on our view menu are:

View Textboxes
View Labels
View Images

Although these are not terribly practical examples of what to place on a View menu, they will help us to demonstrate a few useful techniques. The first of these is how to show and hide controls.

The View Textboxes menu item

Controls on a form can be hidden or shown as the need arises. The process is quite easy.

Access the code for your View Textboxes menu item. Type the following for the menu item:

Textbox1.Visible = False
Textbox2.Visible = False

Run your code and test it out. Click **View > View Textboxes**. The two textboxes you added should disappear.

To hide a control, simply set its **Visible** property to **False**. If you want to get it back, show a control by setting the **Visible** property to **True**.

A good idea is to have the ability to toggle a control on and off: One click of a menu item could hide the control, and a second click could show it again. You can do that with your menus.

Each item on your menu has a **Checked** property. If set to **True**, you'll see a tick appear next to the menu item. As in the image below:

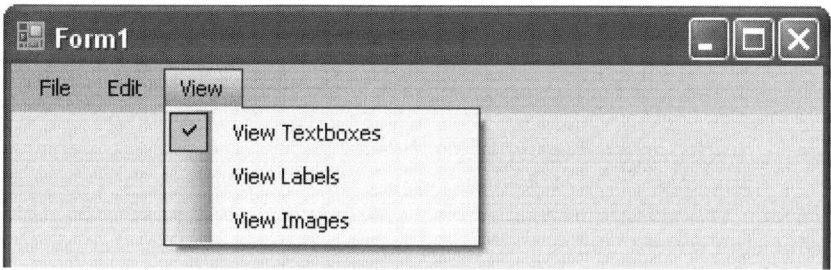

You can use this **Checked** property as a toggle: If the menu item is ticked, display the textbox; if it's not ticked, hide the textbox.

Delete or comment out the line of code for your **View Textboxes** menu item. Add the following line in its place (this assumes that you've named your View Textboxes menu item as **mnuViewTextboxes**. If you've named it something else, change the part before the full stop):

mnuViewTextboxes.Checked = Not mnuViewTextboxes.Checked

This line toggles the Tick on and off. The part before the equals sign sets the **Checked** property of our menu item. The part after the equals sign sets it to whatever it's NOT at the moment. So if Checked is **True**, it's NOT False. In which case, set it to **False**.

Run your code and test it out. Click **View > View Textboxes**. Have a look at the menu again, and you'll see a tick appear. Click **View > View Textboxes** again and the tick will disappear.

We can show the textboxes if there's a tick next to **View Textboxes**. Just test the value of the Checked property in an If Statement. Add this If Statement just below your first line:

If mnuViewTextboxes.Checked = True Then
        TextBox1.Visible = True
        TextBox2.Visible = True
Else
        TextBox1.Visible = False
        TextBox2.Visible = False
End If

So the If Statement examines the **Checked** property of the menu item. If it's **True**, make the textboxes **Visible**; Else, we set the **Visible** property of the textboxes to **False**.

Before you run your code, return to Form view by holding Shift + F7 on your keyboard. When you have your form displayed, and not the code, click on textbox1 to select it. In the property box, locate the **Visible** property and set it to **False**. Do the same for texbox2. When your form runs, the two textboxes will then be hidden.

Now run your programme and test out your new menu. Click **View > View Textboxes** and see if they toggle on and off.

Exercise
Add two labels to your form. Write code to toggle the labels on and off. The two labels should disappear with the textboxes. And they should reappear when the menu item is toggled to the on position.

The View Images menu Item

It's easy to add an image to your form with VB.Net. To insert an image, locate the **PictureBox** control in the toolbox. Either double click the control, or hold down your mouse on the form and draw one out. You should see something like this:

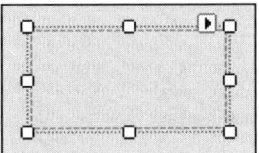

Change the Height and Width properties of the Picture Box to 100, 100. You'll have a small square. To make it stand out more, locate the BorderStyle property. Change the value to Fixed3D. Your Picture Box will then look like this:

To add a picture at design time, locate the Image property in the properties box:

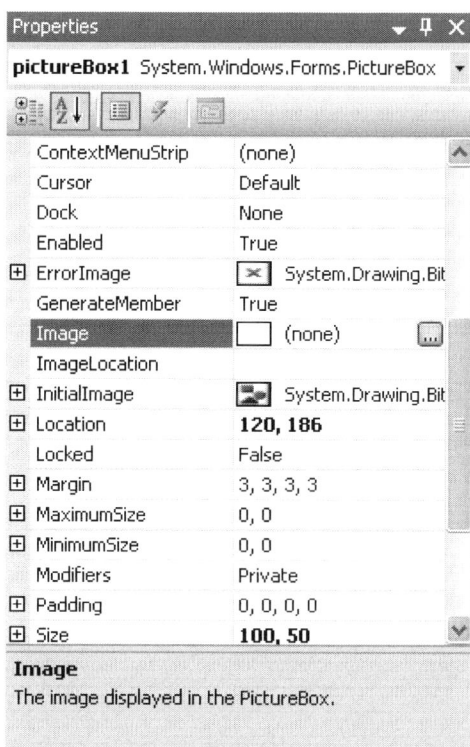

Click the button with the three dots on it, and a dialogue box appears (called Select Resource). Click the Import button and search for an image file. There are some images amongst the files you downloaded at the start of this book (in the Additional Files section). Locate an image. Select it, and then click Open in the dialogue box. The image will appear in your Picture Box:

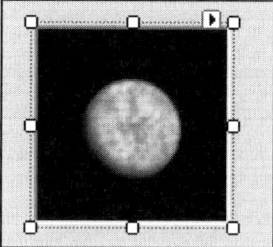

If you select an image that is too big for the picture box, only part of it will be visible. The Picture Box control does not resize your image.

You can, however, set another property of the picture box – the SizeMode property. Set this to AutoSize and your picture box will resize to the size of your image.

Insert an Image

You can use your open file dialogue box again to specify an image for the user to select. We'll do this from the View Images menu item.

Highlight your code for the **mnuOpen** item. Copy the first five lines, these lines:

Dim strFileName As String

openFD.InitialDirectory = "C:\"

openFD.Title = "Open an Text File"
openFD.Filter = "Text Files|*.txt"
Dim DidWork As Integer = openFD.ShowDialog()

Paste them to your mnuViewImages menu item code. Change the Title property to this:

openFD.Title = "Open an Image"

And change the Filter property to this:

openFD.Filter="jpegs(JPEG)|*.jpg|gifs(GIF)|*.gif|Bitmaps(BMP)|*.bmp"

Run your code and click your **View Images** menu item. You should see the Open dialogue box appear. If you look at the "Files of type" box, you should see this:

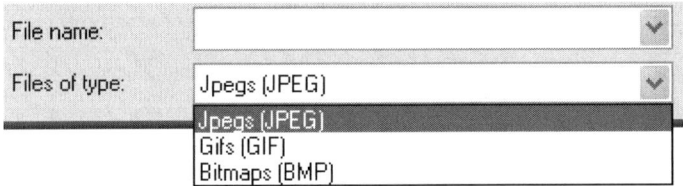

Or this in Windows 7:

You should now be able to see only the three image formats we've specified.

To insert an image into your Picture Box, some new code is needed. Again though, we'll wrap it up in an If Statement.

Add the following code below the lines you've just added:

If DidWork <> Windows.Forms.DialogResult.Cancel Then
strFileName = openFD.FileName
PictureBox1.Image = Image.FromFile(strFileName)
openFD.Reset()
End If

There are only two lines you haven't met yet. The first is this line:

PictureBox1.Image = Image.FromFile(strFileName **)**

Previously, you were loading the image into the Image property of PictureBox1 directly from the Properties Box (by clicking the grey button with the three dots in it). Here, we're loading an image into the Image property using code. The way you do it is with the **FromFile** method of the Image Class. Although that might be a bit baffling at this stage of your programming career, all it means is that there is some in-built code that allows you to load images from a file. In between round brackets, you type the name and path of the file you're trying to load. Since our file name has been placed inside of the **strFileName** variable, we can just use this. You can then assign this to the Image property of a Picture Box.

The last line, **openFD.Reset( )**, will reset the initial directory of the open file dialogue box. To see what this does, comment out the line (put a single quote at the start of the line). Run your programme and Click **View > View Images**. Insert an image and then click **File > Open**. You'll notice that the files displayed in your dialogue are from the last directory you opened, rather than the one you set with "InitialDirectory = "C:\". By resetting the open dialogue box control, you're fixing this problem.

OK, that concludes our brief look at menus. We'll create a new programme now, and explore checkboxes, radio buttons and GroupBoxes.

Check Boxes and Option Buttons

Two more useful controls in the Visual Basic toolbox are the Check box and the Option Button. You use these when you want to give your users a choice of options. We'll add both of these to a new Form, and then combine them with a Select Case statement to read what the user has chosen.

Check Boxes

So start a new project. Locate the Checkbox control in the toolbox. Double click the control and a Checkbox appears on your new Form

You'll see that the Checkbox has the Text property of CheckBox1 by default, and a Name of CheckBox1. If you were to double click again on the Checkbox icon in the toolbox, the new control would be called CheckBox2.

The problem with this approach is that by double clicking each Checkbox, you have several individual Checkboxes. And if you wanted to move them around you'd have to move each Checkbox separately. There is a way to group all your CheckBoxes together, and move them around as one - by using a GroupBox. (You can use a Panel control as well, but we'll stick with the GroupBox.)

So, click on your Checkbox with the right mouse button. From the menu that pops up, select delete to get rid of it.

Now locate the GroupBox control in the toolbox, under Containers:

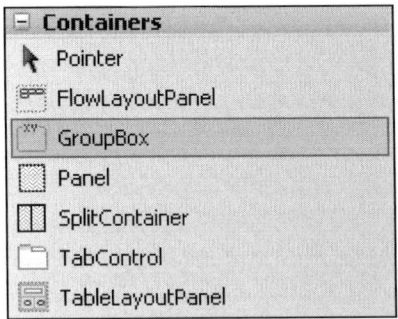

It's better to draw this one on the form, rather than dragging and dropping. When you've added one, the only thing you should have on your Form is a GroupBox.

We're not going to be using many of the Properties in the GroupBox Property box. But click on your GroupBox to select it, and change to the Text Property to "Soaps". Change the Font Property to anything you like. You should now have a Form like this one:

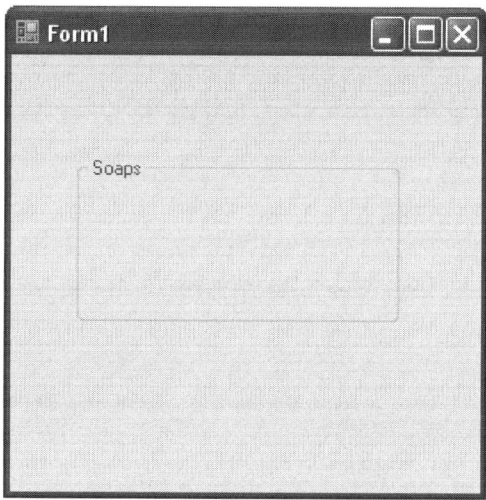

The GroupBox we just added will hold our Checkboxes. It acts as a container for the controls. To move the Checkboxes about, we can just click on the GroupBox to select it, and drag and drop the GroupBox somewhere else. The Checkboxes will all move with the GroupBox. Let's add some Checkboxes to it.

You **CAN'T** double click a checkbox and add it to a GroupBox. The only way to add a control to a GroupBox is to draw one on the GroupBox.

- Click once with your left mouse button on the Checkbox icon in the VB toolbox
- Move your mouse pointer over to the inside of the GroupBox. The mouse pointer will change to a cross
- Hold down you left mouse button inside the GroupBox. Keep the button held down, and drag outwards. Release the left button when you're happy with the size. You can always resize it later.
- Add 5 Checkboxes to your GroupBox
- Change the Text property of each of your Checkboxes to any five Soap Operas. Your Form should now look something like the one below:

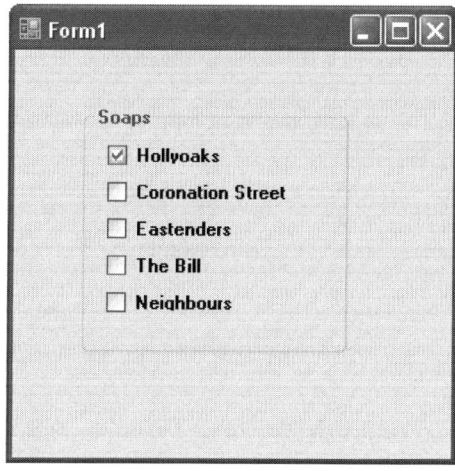

Run your programme to test it out. Click inside a Checkbox to select an item. Click again to deselect it. When you've finished, return to the Design Environment and click on the GroupBox itself to select it. Make sure the GroupBox IS selected, and not one of your Checkboxes. You can now drag the GroupBox around your Form and all the Checkboxes will move with it.

The point about having Checkboxes is to offer your users multiple choices. We'll now write some code to get the choices made by the user. All the Checkboxes with ticks inside them will have their Text displayed in a Message Box.

If you click on any one of your Checkboxes and examine its Properties in the Property box, you'll notice that it has a CheckState Property. Click the down arrow to see the options this CheckState has:

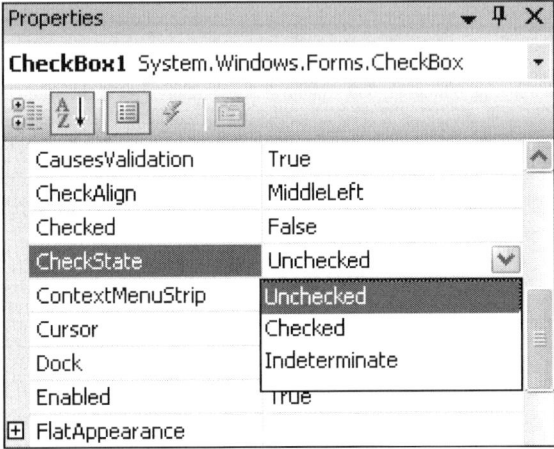

As you can see, you are given three options: Unchecked, Checked, Indeterminate.

If a checkbox has been selected, the value for the CheckState property will be 1; if it hasn't been selected, the value is zero. (The value for the Indeterminate option is also zero, but we won't be using this.)

We're only going to test for 0 or 1, Checked or Unchecked. You can do the testing with a simple If Statement. Like this:

If CheckBox1.CheckState = 1 Then
    MsgBox("Checked")
End If

After you type the equal sign, though, VB will give you a drop down box of the values you can choose from. So the above code is the same as this:

If CheckBox1.CheckState = CheckState.Checked Then
    MsgBox("Checked")
End If

Whichever you choose, the Statement will be True if the checkbox is ticked and False if it isn't.

Add a Button to your Form and put that code behind it (either of the two, or test both). When you've finished typing the code, run your programme. Put a tick inside Checkbox1, and click your button. You should get a Message Box popping up.

Amend your code to this:

> **If CheckBox1.CheckState = CheckState.Checked Then**
> > **MsgBox("Checked")**
> **Else**
> > **MsgBox("Not Checked")**
> **End If**

An alternative to Else is ElseIf. It works like this:

> **If CheckBox1. CheckState = 1 Then**
> > **MsgBox "Checked"**
> **ElseIf Checkbox1. CheckState = 0 Then**
> > **MsgBox "Unchecked"**
> **End If**

When using the **ElseIf** clause, you need to put what you are testing for on the same line, just after **ElseIf**. You put the word **Then** right at the end of the line. You can have as many **ElseIf** clauses as you want. In other words, it's exactly same as the first "If" line only with the word "Else" in front "If".

Add 4 more If Statements to check for the values in your other Checkboxes - Checkbox2.CheckState, Checkbox3.CheckState, etc.

We're now going to get rid of the Message Boxes inside the If Statements. So either comment out all your MsgBox lines, or delete them altogether.

Instead, we'll build up a String Variable. So add a String Variable to the code for your button, and call it **message**.

The **message** variable needs to go inside the If Statement. If the user has checked a Box (If its CheckState property is 1), then we build the message. We need to remember what is inside the **message** variable, so we can just use this:

> **message = message & Checkbox1.Text & vbNewLine**

That way, every time an option is Checked, Visual Basic will keep what is in the variable called message and add to it whatever the text is for the Checkbox.

So add that line to your If Statements. Something like this:

> **If Checkbox1.CheckState = 1 Then**
>
> > **message = message & Checkbox1.Text & vbNewLine**
>
> **End If**

If Checkbox2.CheckState = 1 Then

message = message & Checkbox2.Text & vbNewLine

End If

And at the end of your If Statements, on a new line, add this:

MsgBox "You have chosen " & vbNewLine & message

Here, we're building a text message for our Message Box. We're saying our Message Box is to contain the text "You have chosen " **And** a New Line **And** whatever is inside the variable called **message**.

When you've finished, run your Programme to test it out. Put a tick inside all of your Checkboxes. When you click your button all your Soap Operas should appear in the Message Box. Check and Uncheck some options, and click the button again. Only those items that are selected should appear in your Checkbox.

So, we can test to see which Check Boxes a user has ticked, and we can keep a record of those choices for ourselves.

What we can also do is count how many Check Boxes were ticked. We can then use a Select Case Statement to display a suitable message.

Keeping a count is straightforward. First we set up an integer variable called counter, and set its value to zero.

Dim counter As Integer = 0

Then we can just keep adding one to whatever is in this counter variable. In other words, every time a Checkbox has a value of 1 (is ticked), we can add one to our counter (increment our variable).

We can add this straight into our If Statement, on a new line after the **message** code.

counter = counter + 1

So your code would be this:

If Checkbox1.CheckState = 1 Then
        message = message & Checkbox1.Text & vbNewLine
        counter = counter + 1
End If

To test that your counter is working, you can add a second message box to the end of the code, just below your first message box:

MsgBox("Counter = " & counter)

Or adapt your first message box:

MsgBox("You have chosen " & counter & " soaps")

Now that we have a way to count how many Checkboxes are ticked, we can add a Select Case Statement.

Exercise

Add a Select Case Statement to the end of your code to test whatever is inside the variable called **counter**.

Remember what the format is for a Select Case? It's this:

> **Select Case VariableName**
>   **Case 0**
>   **MsgBox "You obviously don't watch soaps!"**
> **End Select**

If you have 5 Check Boxes on your Form, then the maximum value that counter will hold is 5. So you only need to go up to Case 5.

Add suitable messages for each Case that you're testing for.

Radio Buttons

Radio Buttons, sometimes called Option Buttons, are used when you want to restrict a user's choice to one: Male/Female, for example. A Checkbox would be no good here, because a user could tick both boxes. You want to force your users to pick only one from your list of options.

Adding Radio Buttons to a Form is exactly the same process as adding a Checkbox. Again, we'll add some Radio Buttons to a GroupBox, and write code to extract what the user has chosen.

- Add a GroupBox to your Form.
- Set the Text Property of the GroupBox to "Best Sit Com of all time"
- Set the Font options to anything you like
- Place five Radio Buttons into your GroupBox (By default, they'll be called "RadioButton1", "RadioButton 2", "RadioButton 3", etc
- Set the Text Property of the Five Radio Buttons to Only Fools and Horses, Dad's Army, Blackadder, Fawlty Towers, Vicar of Dibley
- Your Form should now look something like this:

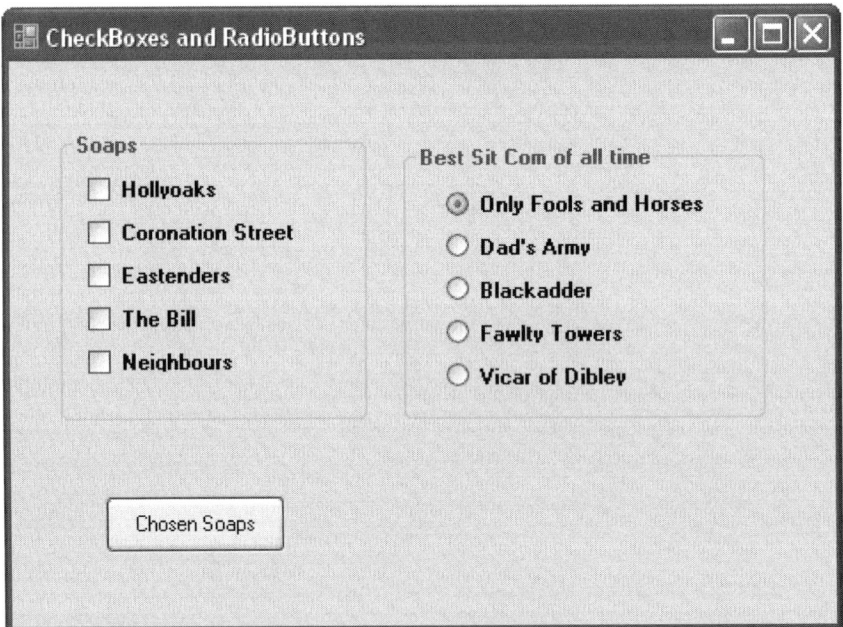

Run your programme and test to see if you can indeed only select one item from the list.

The reason you can only select one is that all the radio buttons are placed in the same GroupBox. You can place another set of radio buttons in a second GroupBox, and these would work independently of the set of radio buttons in the first GroupBox.

To test which Sit Com was chosen, you can use an If … Elseif Statement. You can do this because only one of the radio buttons will be True if selected: all the others will then have a value of False.

So place a Button on your form. Set the Text property to something appropriate. Then double click your new button to open up the code window. Type the following code (Notice that the Property is now Checked, and not CheckState):

Dim ChosenSitCom As String

If RadioButton1.Checked = True Then
  ChosenSitCom = RadioButton1.Text
ElseIf RadioButton2.Checked = True Then
  ChosenSitCom = RadioButton2.Text
ElseIf RadioButton3.Checked = True Then
  ChosenSitCom = RadioButton3.Text
ElseIf RadioButton4.Checked = True Then
  ChosenSitCom = RadioButton4.Text
ElseIf RadioButton5.Checked = True Then
  ChosenSitCom = RadioButton5.Text
End If

MsgBox("You voted for " & ChosenSitCom)

By using If ... ElseIf we can check which radio button a user selected. The Text property from the chosen radio button is then placed in a String variable called ChosenSitCom. At the end, we then display the selected radio button in a message box.

Run your programme and test it out. Select a Sit Com, and then click your Button. You should see the item you selected displayed:

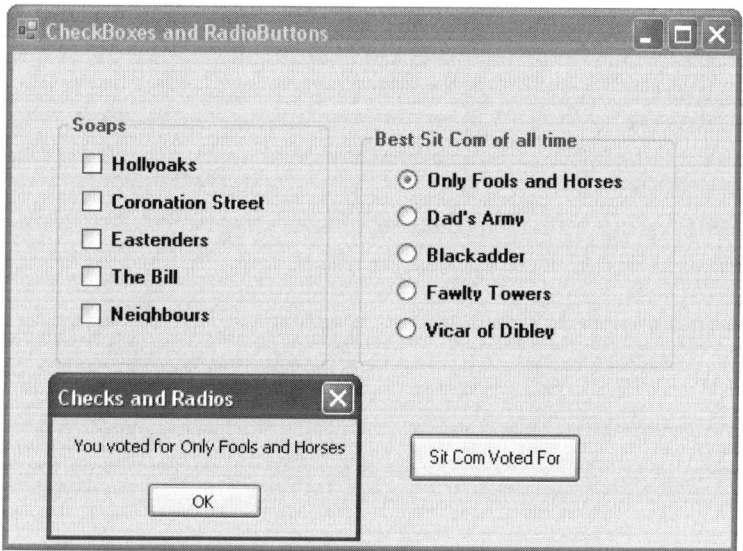

Exercise
Add a Textbox to your Form. Write code to transfer a chosen Sit Com to the Textbox when the button is clicked. Add a label next to the Textbox with the Caption "You Voted For. . ."

Review Number 5

Your boss at work has discovered that you know something about Visual Basic NET programming. She asks you to write an Order Form programme. The Order Form must have textboxes for First Name, Last Name, Address, Email Address. There must be Checkboxes on the Form for at least 5 items. The items will be computer components that customers can buy (CD ROM drive, Monitor, Keyboard, Mouse, etc). Your boss also needs to know how they are paying for the items they are buying: Direct Debit, Credit Card, Cheque, or Cash. They can only pay by one of these methods, so you decide on Option Buttons for this.

For the person using the form, there will be a menu bar. The menu bar will consist of three main menus: File, Save and Tools. On the File menu there will be options for "New Record", and "Exit". On the Save menu there will be an option for "Save Details" On the Tools menu there will be an option for "Erase Checkboxes and Options".

First, design the order Form your boss wants. The Form should have the properties set out below. When you've finished, it might look something like the one above. (But by all means create your own design.)

You'll notice something else on the form. A textbox and a label on the right hand side. The label is self explanatory. The Textbox has a special function. When your user clicks Save > Save Details from your Menu Bar, all the details will appear in this textbox: First Name, Last Name, Address, Email Address, all of their Ordered Items, and their method of payment. In real life, these details would be transferred straight to a database. In a later section of your course, you'll be doing just this – saving the order details to a database (an Access database).

The controls on your Form, then, should have the following Properties.

The Form

Name	frmOrderForm
Text	Order Form
BackColor	If you decide to go with a colour, a colour of your choice
Picture	If you decide to go with a picture, any picture of your choice

Textboxes (5)

Name	txtFirst
Text	Enter any default First Name of your choice
Font	MS Sans Serif Bold 10 point

Name	txtLast
Text	Enter any default Last Name of your choice
Font	MS Sans Serif Bold 10 point

Name	txtAddress
Text	Enter any default Address of your choice
Font	MS Sans Serif Bold 10 point

Name	txtEmail
Text	Enter any default Email Address of your choice
Font	MS Sans Serif Bold 10 point

Name	txtDetails
Text	Leave Blank
MultiLine	True
Font	MS Sans Serif Bold 10 point

Labels (5)

Name	lblFirst
Backcolor	Any colour of your choice
Text	First Name

Font	MS Sans Serif Bold 10 point
Name	lblLast
Backcolor	Any colour of your choice
Text	Last Name
Font	MS Sans Serif Bold 10 point
Name	lblAddress
Backcolor	Any colour of your choice
Text	Address
Font	MS Sans Serif Bold 10 point
Name	lblEmail
Backcolor	Any colour of your choice
Text	Email
Font	MS Sans Serif Bold 10 point
Name	lblDetails
Backcolor	Any colour of your choice
Text	Customer's Details
Font	MS Sans Serif Bold 10 point

GroupBoxes (2)

Name	fraOrdered
Text	Ordered Items
Font	MS Sans Serif Bold 12 point
Name	fraPayment
Text	Method of Payment
Font	MS Sans Serif Bold 12 point

For the Check Boxes and Radio Buttons, you can just leave them with the default Names - Checkbox1, Checkbox2, Checkbox3, etc. Set the Text properties for the Check Boxes and Option Buttons to any computer items you like, and any payment methods you like.

The Menu Bar

1. **Main Menu Item:**

Text	File
Name	mnuFile

   ▪ **Options on the File Menu**

Text	New Record
Name	mnuNew
Text	Exit
Name	mnuExit

2.   **Main Menu Item**
                Text   Save
                Name   mnuSave

- **Option on the Save Menu**

                Text   Save Details
                Name   mnuSaveDetails

3.   **Main Menu Item**
                Text   Tools
                Name   mnuTools

- **Option on the Tools Menu**

                Text   Erase Checkboxes and Radio Buttons
                Name   mnuEraseChecks

Once you've designed your Form, and set all the Properties, you can start to write the code.

The Code

The File Menu

The first bit of coding is for the New Record item on the File Menu. This is quite easy. All you are doing here is erasing whatever is in a Textbox, and setting the CheckState Properties of the Checkboxes and Radio Buttons to False. You'll also want to clear whatever is any variables. If it's a String variable you can use **MyString = ""**; if it's an integer, you can use **MyInteger = 0**.

The code for the Exit menu is the same as for a previous part of this book. You're just using the Close Method of **Me**.

The Save Menu

The Save Details item of the Save menu has to do one thing - write the details from the Textboxes, Checkboxes and Radio Buttons to the Textbox called txtDetails.

You need to consider how you are going to get the data from those controls. You already know how to get data from a Textbox. You also know how to get data from a Checkbox. And you know how to get data from a Radio button.

Once you have all the data in variables, you can build up a string and then transfer it all to the txtDetails textbox

The Tools Menu

The Tools menu is there if the user makes a mistake. Suppose the person entering the details gets it wrong, and ticked the first three Checkbox items when it should have been the last three. By clicking on **Tools > Erase Checkboxes and Radio Buttons**, they can remove all the ticks from the Check Boxes, and erase whatever item was selected from the Radio choices. But the data in the Name, Address, and Email boxes gets left alone. They can try again and select new items from the Checkboxes and select a new Radio Button. Of course, you could have two items on the Tools menu, if you wanted - Tools > Erase Check Boxes and Tools > Erase Option Button. But the code should be easy enough for you.

But remember what the objective of this Review is: to get the details from the Textboxes, the Checkboxes and the Radio Buttons into the Textbox called txtDetails.

When you're done, you should have some valuable experience with form design.

Error Handling and Debugging

Debugging your code is something you will need to do. Unless you write perfect code every time, there's no getting away from it. In this section, we'll take a look at ways you can track down errors using VB.NET.

Types of Error

Programming errors are generally broken down into three types: Design-time, Runtime, and Logic errors.

A Design-time error is also known as a syntax error. These occur when the environment you're programming in doesn't understand your code. These are easy to track down in VB.NET, because you get a blue wiggly line pointing them out. If you try to run the programme, you'll get a dialogue box popping up telling you that there were Build errors.

Runtime errors are a lot harder to track down. As their name suggests, these errors occur when the programme is running. They happen when your programme tries to do something it shouldn't be doing. An example is trying to access a file that doesn't exist. Runtime errors usually cause your programme to crash. If and when that happens, you get the blame. After all, you're the programmer, and you should write code to trap runtime errors. If you're trying to open a database in a specific location, and the database has been moved, a Runtime error will occur. It's your job to predict a thing like this, and code accordingly.

Logic errors also occur when the programme is running. They happen when your code doesn't quite behave the way you thought it would. A classic example is creating an infinite loop of the type "Do While x is greater than 10". If x is always going to be greater than 10, then the loop has no way to exit, and just keeps going round and round. Logic errors tend not to crash your programme. But they will ensure that it doesn't work properly.

We'll take a closer look at all three types of error.

Design Time Errors

Create a new Windows project. Add a button and textbox to your form. Leave the Name properties on the defaults of Button1 and Textbox1. Double click your button to access its code, and type the following:

Textbox2.Text = "Debug"

When you finish typing the line, VB.NET puts a blue wiggly line under Textbox2:

```
Private Sub Button1_Click(ByVal sender As System.Object, _
                          ByVal e As System.EventArgs) _
                          Handles Button1.Click


    TextBox2.Text = "Debug"


End Sub
```

If you hold your mouse over **Textbox2**, you'll see a yellow tool tip appear, like the following:

```
Private Sub Button1_Click(ByVal sender As System.Object, _
                          ByVal e As System.EventArgs) _
                          Handles Button1.Click


    TextBox2.Text = "Debug"
       Name 'TextBox2' is not declared.
End Sub
```

The error is occurring because you don't have a textbox called Textbox2. You'll also see this same "Not declared" error if you try to set up a variable on the fly (which you were allowed to do in previous version of VB.) As an example, change your code to this:

strText = "Debug"
TextBox1.Text = strText

Here, we're trying to put the word "Debug" into a variable called **strText**. We then want to assign this variable to the Text property of Textbox1. However, VB.NET protests about this, and puts a wiggly line under all occurrences of strText:

```
strText = "Debug"
TextBox1.Text = strText
```

Hold your mouse over the variable strText and you'll see the "not declared" tip again:

```
strText = "Debug"
TextBox1.Text = strText
              Name 'strText' is not declared.
```

The problem this time is that we haven't declared the variable strText. Change the code to this:

Dim strText As String

strText = "Debug"
TextBox1.Text = strText

Now that we have declared a variable, the wiggly lines will go away. If we added the variable declaration in the wrong place, however, the wiggly lines would come back. Change your code to this:

```
strText = "Debug"
TextBox1.Text = strText

Dim strText As String
```

The wiggly lines will be back. That's because the declaration comes on the third line. When VB.NET meets the first two lines, it knows nothing about the strText variable.

If you have the **Error List** window open, you'll see a report of your error (If you can't see the Error List window, from the menu bars click **View > Other Windows > Error List**):

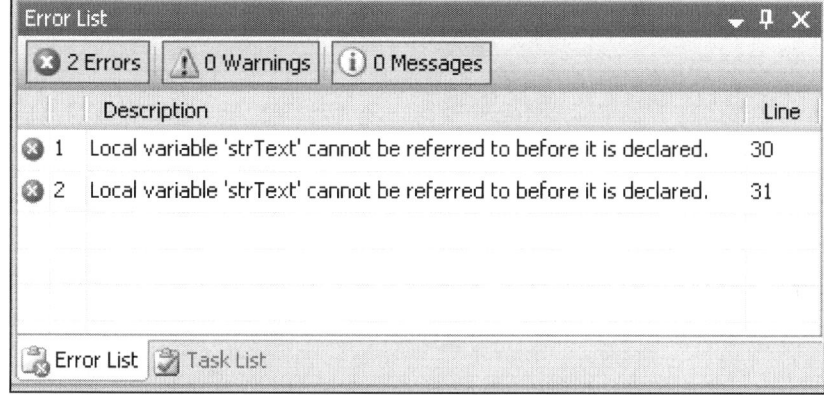

The description of the error is "Local variable 'strText' cannot be referred to before it is declared". If you double click the icons on the left, VB.NET will highlight the error in your code.

Move the "Dim ... " Line back to the top, and not only do the blue wiggly lines go away, but the Task List will be erased.

Design-time errors like the one above can be quite straightforward to correct. Others can be quite difficult, and you'll see the blue wiggly line but not understand how to correct the error. The Task List should be your first port of call when faced with such an error.

Runtime errors

As was mentioned, Runtime errors are the ones that crash your programme. A simple way to crash a programme is to divide by zero. Change the code for your button to this, and try it out:

```
Dim Num1 As Integer
Dim Num2 As Integer

Num1 = 10
Num2 = 0

TextBox1.Text = CInt(Num1 / Num2)
```

The CInt( ) part means Convert to an Integer. We're just making sure to convert the answer to the sum into a number. But run your programme and test it out. Click your button and see what happens.

What happens is that you'll get the following error message popping up:

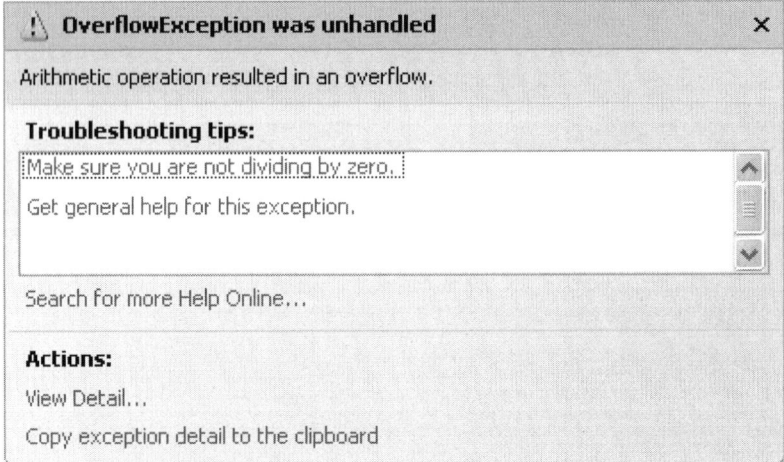

Stop your programme from running to get rid of the error message.

When you try to divide by zero, VB.NET throws up the Overflow error message – there would be just too many zeros to go into the Integer variable type. Even if you changed the Type into a Single or a Double, you'd still get the same error message. Programming environments just don't like you dividing a number by zero. If this were in a real programme, chances are it would crash, or "bug out". And you'll get the blame!

If you think the answer to a calculation could result in zero, you should check for this. We'll see how to write code to trap Runtime errors in a moment. But here's another example of one.

From the controls toolbox, add a RichTextBox control to your form. Change the Name property of your RichTextBox to **rt1**. A RichTextBox is just like a normal textbox but with more functionality. One of these extra functions is the ability to load a file directly. Delete or comment out any code you have for your button, and add the following line:

rt1.LoadFile("C:\test10.txt", RichTextBoxStreamType.PlainText)

All the line does is to load (or try to) the text file called "test10.txt" into the RichTextBox. The second argument just specifies that the type of file we want to load is a Plain Text file.

Run your programme, and then click the button. If you don't have a text file called "test10.txt" in the root folder of your C drive, you'll get the following Runtime error message:

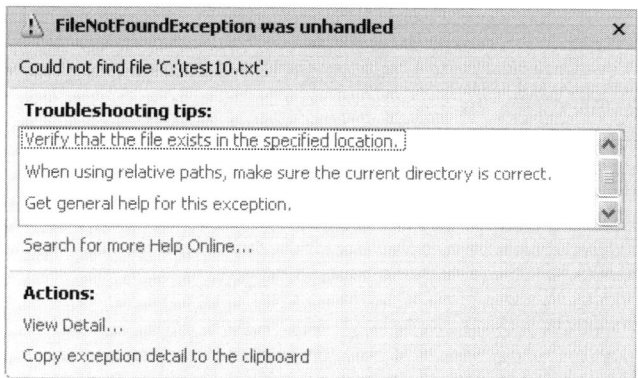

The additional information is quite useful this time. It's saying that the file "C:\test10.txt" could not be found. If the error occurred in a normal programme, it would shut down. Not something you want a programme to do in mid stream! But let's see how to deal with it.

Try ... Catch

VB.NET has an inbuilt class that deals with errors. The Class is called Exception. When an exception error is found, an Exception object is created. The coding structure VB.NET uses to deal with such Exceptions is called the Try ... Catch structure.

In the coding area for your button, type the word Try. Then hit the return key on your keyboard. VB.NET completes the rest of the structure for you:

> **Try**
>
> **Catch ex As Exception**
>
> **End Try**

The Try word means "Try to execute this code". The Catch word means "Catch any errors here". The ex is a variable, and the type of variable it is is an Exception object.

Move your line of code to the Try part:

> **Try**
>
>> **rt1.LoadFile("C:\test10.txt",**
>> **RichTextBoxStreamType.PlainText)**
>
> **Catch ex As Exception**
>
> **End Try**

When you run your programme, VB will Try to execute any code in the Try part. If everything goes well, then it skips the Catch part. However, if an error occurs, VB.NET jumps straight to Catch. Add the following to your Catch part:

MessageBox.Show(ex.Message)

Your coding window should look like this:

```
Private Sub Button1_Click(ByVal sender As System.Object, _
                        ByVal e As System.EventArgs) _
                            Handles Button1.Click

    Try
        rt1.LoadFile("C:\test10.txt", RichTextBoxStreamType.PlainText)
    Catch ex As Exception
        MessageBox.Show(ex.Message)
    End Try

End Sub
```

Because **ex** is an object variable, it now has its own Properties and methods. One of these is the Message property. Run your programme and test it out. Click your button. You should see the following error message:

The message is coming from the "additional Information" section of the error message we saw earlier, the one we didn't handle. But the point about this new message box is that it will not crash your programme. You have handled the Exception, and displayed an appropriate message for the user.

If you know the kind of error that a programme might throw, you can get what Type it is from the Error message box you saw earlier. This one:

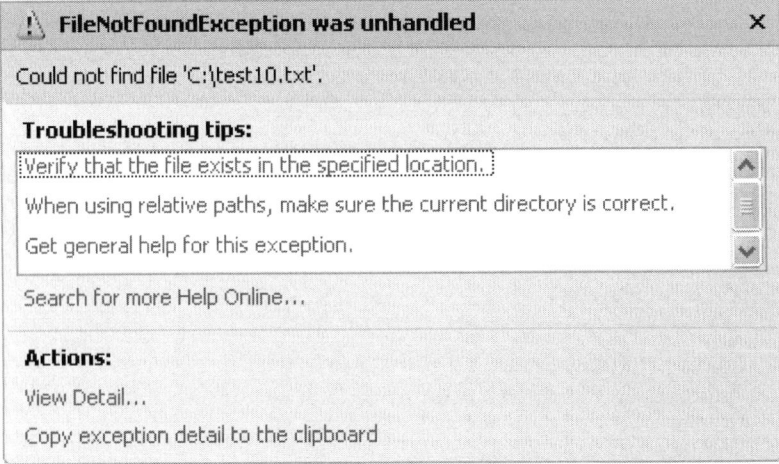

Click the **View Details** links under **Actions** to see the following:

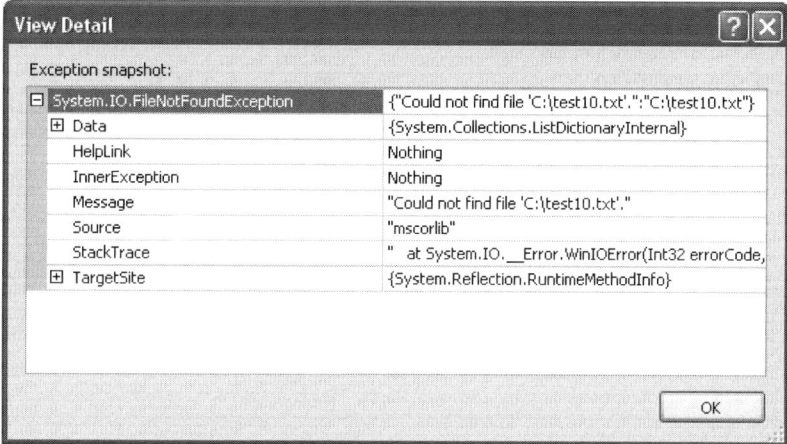

The first line tells us the Type of Exception it is:

System.IO.FileNotFoundException

You can add this directly to the catch part. Previously, you were just catching any error that might be thrown:

Catch ex As Exception

But if you know a "file not found" error might be thrown, you can add that to the Catch line, instead of Exception:

Catch ex As System.IO.FileNotFoundException

You can keep the Exception line as well. (You can have as many Catch parts as you want.) This will Catch any other errors that may occur:

```
Try
    rt1.LoadFile("C:\test10.txt", RichTextBoxStreamType.PlainText)
Catch ex As System.IO.FileNotFoundException
    MsgBox("Can't find this file")
Catch ex As Exception
    MsgBox(ex.Message)
End Try
```

There is one last part of the Try … Catch Statement that VB.NET doesn't add for you – Finally:

```
Try

Catch ex As Exception
```

Finally

End Try

The **Finally** part is always executed, whether an error occurs or not. You typically add a **Finally** part to perform any cleanup operations that are needed. For example, you may have opened a file before going into a **Try ... Catch** Statement. If an error occurs, the file will still be open. Whether an error occurs or not, you still need to close the file. You can do that in the **Finally** part.

But Microsoft advise that you always use **Try ... Catch** Statements in your code. However, throughout the rest of this book, for convenience sake, we won't be using them. Even when we should be!

Logic Errors

The third category of errors are the Logic errors. These can be thought of as coding errors. Your coding errors. They can be quite tricky to track down, and have you tearing your hair out with frustration. You will often hear yourself saying "But that should work! Why won't it!"

Add another button to your form, and try this code as an example:

```
Dim x As Integer
Dim y As Integer
Dim answer As Integer

x = 10.5
y = 3
answer = x * y
TextBox1.Text = answer
```

When you've added the code to your button, run your programme and test it out. Before you click the button, what answer did you expect to get?

You'd think that 10.5 multiplied by 3 would give you the answer 31.5. Click your button. The answer that appears in your textbox is 30!

This is a logic error: when you don't get the answer you thought you'd get. The problem, if you were paying attention during the variable types sections, is that we are trying to put floating point numbers into an Integer variable type. The Integer variable only works with whole numbers. When you assign 10.5 to the variable x, the point 5 on the end gets chopped off. So only the 10 gets stored in x. 10 times 3 is thirty, and this is the answer that appears in the textbox.

But the point is that VB.NET did not raise a Design-time error. Nor did it raise a Runtime error. The programme executed, and did not "bug out" on you. It just didn't give you the answer you expected – it was a logic error.

Logic errors can be fairly simple to track down and solve. (The problem above can be solved by changing the variable types from Integer to Single or Double.) But they can also be quite difficult to track down. Especially as your code gets longer and longer. Here's another example of a logic error.

Erase the code you have for button2, and add the following instead:

```
Dim i As Integer
Dim LetterCount As Integer
Dim strText As String
Dim letter As Char

strText = "Debugging"

For i = 1 To strText.Length - 1

        letter = strText.Substring(1)

        If letter = "g" Then
                LetterCount = LetterCount + 1
        End If
Next

TextBox1.Text = "G appears " & LetterCount & " times"
```

All the code does is to try and count how many times the letter "g" appears in the word "Debugging". We're using a For loop, and Substring to get one letter at a time. This single letter is then placed inside the variable called letter. An If Statement is used to check if the letter is a "g". If it is, we increment the LetterCount variable. The answer we're expecting in the textbox is 3. Except, we don't get 3. We get zero:

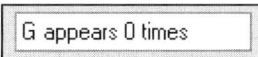

There were no wiggly lines, and therefore no Build errors. When the button was clicked, a Runtime exception did not crash the programme. So that leaves a logic error. But where is it?

Breakpoints

Another weapon in your debugging armoury is the Breakpoint. A breakpoint is like a note to VB.NET to stop your programme at a particular place. You add one to your code by clicking in the margins. A brown circled then appears, indicating where the code will break. The following two images show how to add one:

Click in the Margins

```
For i = 1 To strText.Length - 1
    letter = strText.Substring(1)

    If letter = "g" Then
        LetterCount = LetterCount + 1
    End If
Next
```

A brownish circle appears

```
For i = 1 To strText.Length - 1
    letter = strText.Substring(1)

    If letter = "g" Then
        LetterCount = LetterCount + 1
    End If
Next
```

Notice that the line where you want VB.NET to break is highlighted brown.

Run your programme, and click the button. You are immediately returned to the coding window. The place where you put the breakpoint will now have a yellow arrow on top of the brown circle. The brown highlighted line will now be yellow:

```
For i = 1 To strText.Length - 1
    letter = strText.Substring(1)

    If letter = "g" Then
        LetterCount = LetterCount + 1
    End If
Next
```

The yellow highlight indicates where in your code VB.NET is. To continue checking your code, press F10 on your keyboard (you can also press F11, but this will jump into any Subs or Functions you've set up. VB 2008 users may need to press F8 instead of F10. Or just use the toolbars at the top, or the Debug menu. This applies from now on, when we say "press F10".)

The next line in your code will be highlighted:

```
For i = 1 To strText.Length - 1
        letter = strText.Substring(1)

        If letter = "g" Then
            LetterCount = LetterCount + 1
        End If
Next
```

The yellow arrow, and the yellow highlight, jump down one line. Press the F10 key again (or F8). Then hold your mouse of the **letter** variable. The value this variable currently holds will be displayed:

```
letter = strText.Substring(1)
      letter "e"c
```

The first time round the loop, the value in **letter** is "e" (The "c" next to it means that the variable type is Character).

If the "e" of "Debugging" is getting checked first, what happened to the "D"? Straight away, this indicates a problem. And the problem is that the Substring method starts counting from zero. So halt your programme by clicking "Debug > Stop Debugging", or click the Stop icon on the toolbar. Change the line in question to this:

letter = strText.Substring(0)

Run your programme again, and click the button. When you are returned to your code, press the F10 key and check the value of the **letter** variable. It should now be this:

```
letter = strText.Substring(0)
      letter "D"c
```

This time, the code is catching the first letter of the word when the loop begins, and not the second one.

Is that it? Have we found the cause of our problems? Stop your programme. Click on the brown circle to get rid of the Breakpoint. Run it again, and see what happens.

The number of G's counted is still zero! So the logic error has not yet been tracked down. Create another Breakpoint at the same place, and try again.

You can continue pressing the F10 key until you've spotted the error. Or you can use another debugging tool – the Locals window.

While your programme is still in Debug mode (the yellow line will still be there, if it is), click **Debug > Windows > Locals** from the menu bar. You should see the following in the bottom left of your screen:

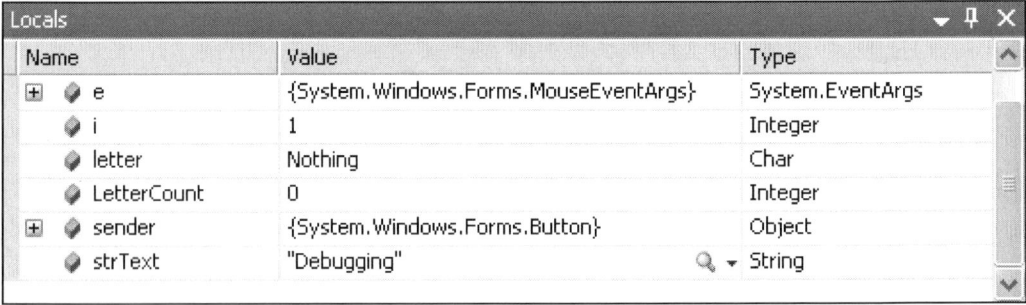

Locals means "Local variables". That is, variables declared in this section of the code. The variables **i**, **letter** and **LetterCount** are showing in the window. The value of these variables is also displayed: 1, Nothing and 0. Press F10 and these values will change. This is the Locals window after a few goes round the loop:

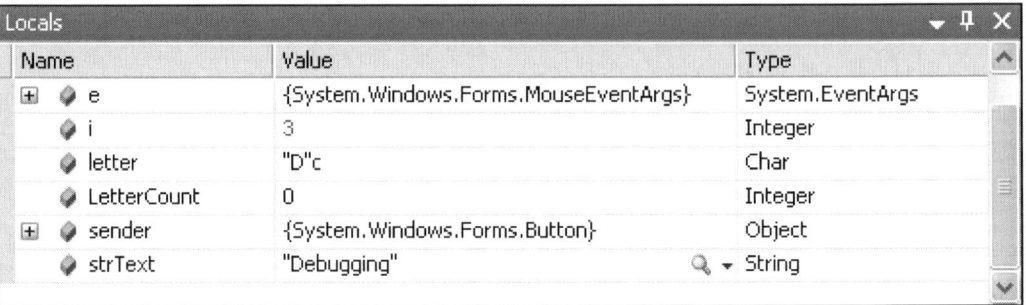

The variable i is now 3; letter is still "D", and LetterCount is still 0. Keep pressing F10 and go round the loop a few times. What do you notice?

You should notice that the value in letter never moves on. It is "D" all the time. And that's why LetterCount never gets beyond 0.

Exercise
Why does **LetterCount** never gets beyond 0? Correct the code so that your textbox displays the correct answer of 3 when the programme is run.

And that's it for Error checking and debugging. It can often be an art form in itself. But one well worth persevering with: it could save you a lot of headaches!

Hurray For Arrays!

In this section, you are going to learn all about the power of arrays, and how easy they can make your programming life. First, you need to know what an array is.

What is an array?

By now, you've been using variables quite a lot. You've put numbers into variables, and you've put text into variables. But so far, you've only done this one at a time: you've put one number into a variable, or one string of text. You've been doing this:

Dim MyNumber As Integer

MyNumber = 5

Or this

Dim MyText As String

MyText = "A String is really just text"

Or even this:

Dim MyNumber As Integer = 5

So one variable was holding one piece of information. An array is a variable that can hold more than one piece of information at a time. The MyNumber variable above held one number 5. If you had an array variable called MyNumbers - plural - you could hold more than one number at a time. You set them up like this:

Dim MyNumbers(4) As Integer

MyNumbers(0) = 1
MyNumbers(1) = 2
MyNumbers(2) = 3
MyNumbers(3) = 4
MyNumbers(4) = 5

When you set up an array with the Dim word, you put the name of your array variable, and tell Visual Basic how many items you want to store in the array. But you need to use parentheses around your figure. You then assign your data to a position in the array. In the example above we've set up an Integer array with 5 items in it. We've then said put number 1 into array position 0, put number 2 into array position 1, put number 3 into array position 2, and so on.

You might be thinking that the array was set to the number 4 - MyNumbers(4) - but always remember that an array starts counting at zero, and the first position in your array will be zero.

So that's what an array is - a variable that can hold more than one piece of data at a time - but how do they work? A programming example might help to clear things up.

- Start a new VB project.
- Add a Button to your Form.
- Set the Text property of the Button to "Integer Array"
- Put the following code behind your button

Dim MyNumbers(4) As Integer

MyNumbers(0) = 10
MyNumbers(1) = 20
MyNumbers(2) = 30
MyNumbers(3) = 40
MyNumbers(4) = 50

MsgBox("First Number is: " & MyNumbers(0))
MsgBox("Second Number is: " & MyNumbers(1))
MsgBox("Third Number is: " & MyNumbers(2))
MsgBox("Fourth Number is: " & MyNumbers(3))
MsgBox("Fifth Number is: " & MyNumbers(4))

Test out the programme when you are finished. The numbers 10 to 50 should have been displayed in your message boxes.

In the code, we first set up an Integer array with 5 items in it.

Dim MyNumbers(4) As Integer

We then assigned values to each position in the array.

MyNumbers(0) = 10

To get at the values in the array, and display them in messages boxes, we just used the array name, followed by the position in the array.

MsgBox("First Number is: " & MyNumbers(0))

So we've said, "Display whatever number is in array position 0, then display whatever number is in array position 1 ... " and so on.

Add another messages box statement on a line below the others. Put this

MsgBox("Sixth Number is: " & MyNumbers(5))

Run your programme again, and click the Button.

What happened? You probably got this error message:

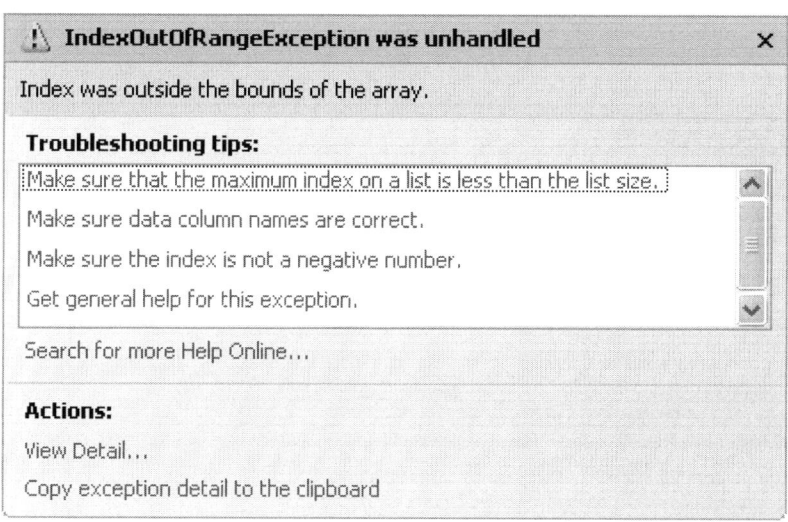

The Index the error message is talking about is the figure in parentheses in your array. We set up this array:

MyNumbers(4) As Integer

And the highest Index number is therefore 4. But we tried to display something at index number 5:

MyNumbers(5)

Visual Basic said "Wait a minute, the idiot hasn't got a position number 5!" So it stopped the programme and gave you an error message.

Delete **MsgBox("Sixth Number is: " & MyNumbers(5))** from your code.

So the way to get at information held in an array is through its Index number - "What's at array position 0? What's at array position 1?" A very handy way to get at the information in your array is by accessing its Index number in a For Loop.

So that you don't have all those message boxes popping up, we can display the results in a List Box.

Add a List Box to your form. Make it fairly wide, and just leave it on the default Name of ListBox1. Then change your code to the following (the new code is in Bold text):

```
Dim MyNumbers(4) As Integer
Dim i As Integer

MyNumbers(0) = 10
MyNumbers(1) = 20
MyNumbers(2) = 30
MyNumbers(3) = 40
MyNumbers(4) = 50
```

```
For i = 0 To 4
        ListBox1.Items.Add( MyNumbers(i) )
Next i
```

Run your programme, and click your button. Your form might look something like this one:

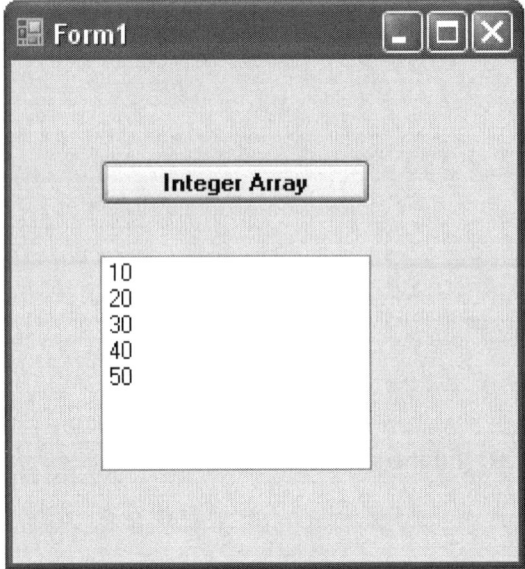

The first time round the loop, the variable called **i** will hold the number 0. Visual Basic will test to see if our end condition is met. The end condition was "Loop until the variable **i** holds the number 4". The variable **i** only holds the number 0, so Visual Basic drops down to the next line - **ListBox1.Items.Add(MyNumbers(i))**. And what is inside the variable **i**? The number 0. So what's really getting adding to the List Box is this:

MyNumbers(0)

In other words, "Add to the List Box whatever is inside the array at position number 0"

The next time round the loop, the variable i will hold the number 1. So this gets executed

ListBox1.Items.Add(MyNumbers(1))

And the loop continues round and around, adding whatever is inside our array until the end condition for the loop is met.

Change the first line of the For loop to this:

For i = 0 To 5

Can you guess what will happen? Try it and see. Make sure you know why you get the error message before moving on.

Arrays can hold other types of data, too. They can hold Strings of text.

- Put another Button on your Form
- Set the Text property to "String Array"
- Put the following code behind your Button

```
Dim MyText(4) As String
Dim i As Integer

MyText(0) = "This"
MyText(1) = "is"
MyText(2) = "a"
MyText(3) = "String"
MyText(4) = "Array"


For i = 0 To 4
        ListBox1.Items.Add( MyText (i) )
Next i
```

When you have finished, run the programme and click your new button. The text you put into the 5 array positions should display in the List Box.

Again, the same process is at work: Set up an array, and specify how many items you want to hold in the array; assign your data to each position; go round a loop and access whatever is in each position of the array.

Assigning values to an array

There are a number of ways you can put data into each position of an array. The code we just wrote for the two buttons had known values stored into each position. We knew that we wanted the numbers 1 to 5 to be stored into our Integer array, and we knew that we wanted the text "This is a String Array" stored into our String array.

But you don't have to know what the values are. You can assign values straight from a Textbox into the positions of your array. Like this:

```
MyNumbers(0) = Val(Textbox1.Text)
MyNumbers(1) = Val(Textbox2.Text)
MyNumbers(2) = Val(Textbox3.Text)
MyNumbers(3) = Val(Textbox4.Text)
MyNumbers(4) = Val(Textbox5.Text)
```

With that code, whatever you typed into the 5 Textboxes on your Form would be stored into the 5 positions of your array. The same would be true of a String Array:

```
MyText(0) = Textbox.1Text
MyText(1) = Textbox.2Text
MyText(2) = Textbox3.Text
MyText(3) = Textbox4.Text
MyText(4) = Textbox5.Text
```

But do we have to keep typing out a value for each and every position of our array. What if we had an array with a hundred items in it, **MyText(99)**? Would we have to type out text for all one hundred positions of the array?

Well, obviously not. You can use code to assign values to your array. Here is an example where we don't type out values for all positions of an array. It's a times table programme. We'll use an array. And we'll write a line of code to assign values to each position of the array.

- First, though, add another Button to your form.
- Set the Text Property to "Times Table Array"
- Add a Textbox to your Form
- Set the Text Property to a blank string (in other words, delete Textbox1 from the Text property)
- Add a Label near the Textbox
- Set the Text property of the Label to "Which Times Table do you want?"
- Now double click your new button to get at the code window
- Add the following code:

```
Dim numbers(10) As Integer
Dim times As Integer
Dim StoreAnswer As Integer
Dim i As Integer

ListBox1.Items.Clear()

times = Val(TextBox1.Text)
For i = 1 To 10

        StoreAnswer = i * times
        numbers(i) = StoreAnswer
        ListBox1.Items.Add(times & " times " & i & " = " & numbers(i))

Next i
```

Run the programme. Enter a number in your new text box, and then click the Times Table Array button. The times table for the number should have been printed.

At the top of the code we set up three normal Integer variables, **i**, **times** and **StoreAnswer**. (We didn't really need the StoreAnswer variable, but it is here to make the code more readable.) We also set up an array. (Notice that we set it to 10. This actually gives us 11 positions in the array. But we're only putting something in positions 1 to 10. This is because it is more convenient for us, and for our Loop.)

Dim numbers(10) As Integer

We need to know what number we are going to be multiplying by, which times table we're working out. We get this number from the Textbox, and can assign it directly to the variable **times**

times = Val(Textbox1.Text)

We can then set up a For Loop. Inside the For Loop is where we'll assign values to each position of our array:

numbers(i) = StoreAnswer

First time around the loop, the variable **i** will hold a value of 1. So the second position of our array, **numbers(1)** will be assigned whatever is in the variable **StoreAnswer**

The second time around the loop, the variable **i** will hold a value of 2. So the second position of our array, **numbers(2)**, will again be assigned whatever is in the variable **StoreAnswer**

We go round and round the loop assigning values to all ten positions of our array.

The other two lines of code inside the array just work out the times tables, and adds the answer to the List Box. Study them, and make sure you understand how they work.

But the point of this is to demonstrate that you can use code to assign a value to a position in an array.

Arrays where Boundaries are not known

Study the following Form:

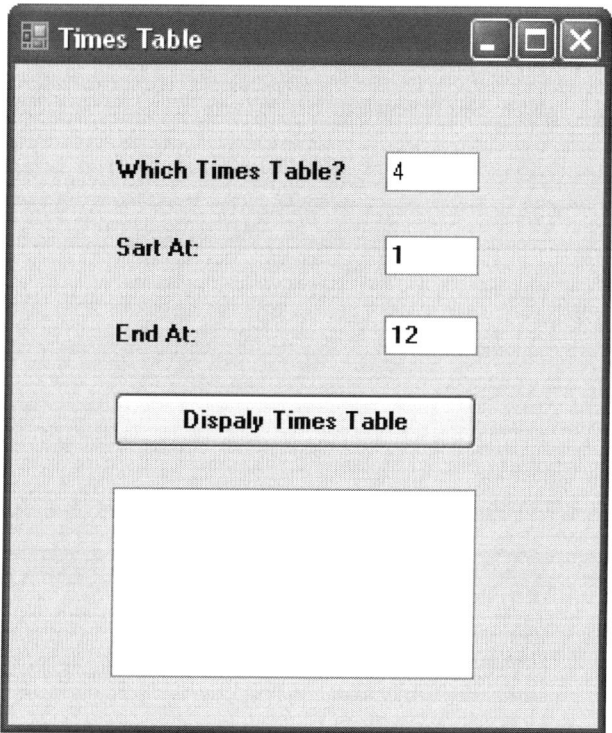

In the above Form, the user is invited to enter values into three Textboxes. The first Textbox is for whatever times table he or she wants. The second Textbox asks for the starting value of the times table. The third Textbox is for the end number of the times table. In other words, 1 times 4, 2 times 4, 3 times 4, right up to 12 times 4.

The point is that the user can enter any values he or she wants. We won't know until they are entered, and the button is clicked. Up until now, we've used an array with a fixed size. Our previous times table programme only went up to 10, and it started at 1. We used this to set up our array

Dim numbers(10) As Integer

But that array would be no good for the above Form. Our array only held 11 positions. The user definitely wants the 4 times table right up to 12. Is there any way we can set up an array where the number of positions is not known? How can we set up a Non-Fixed size array?

You do it like this. First set up an array with empty brackets

Dim numbers( ) As Integer

Next, pass the values from the Text Boxes to some variables

times = Val(Textbox1.Text)
startAt = Val(Textbox2.Text)
endAt = Val(Textbox3.Text)

We can then use these values to reset the array. You reset an array by using the **ReDim** word. You then specify the new values. Like this:

ReDim numbers(endAt)

Our original array did not have its size set - **Dim numbers( ) As Integer**. So we've got the end number from the Textbox. When we reset an array, we can use this new value. Since our user entered the value 12 for the end number, our array is now really this:

Dim numbers(12) As Integer

We can use the same variables for our For Loop. Then we can go round and round the loop assigning values to our array.

To test this concept out, either start a new project, or amend the one you have displayed. Create three textboxes and labels. And add a new Button. Double click your button to open the code window. Then add the following code:

```
Dim numbers( ) As Integer
Dim startAt As Integer
Dim endAt As Integer
Dim times As Integer
Dim StoreAnswer As Integer
Dim i As Integer
```

```
times = Val(TextBox1.Text)
startAt = Val(TextBox2.Text)
endAt = Val(TextBox3.Text)

ReDim numbers(endAt)

For i = startAt To endAt
        StoreAnswer = i * times
        numbers(i) = StoreAnswer
        ListBox1.Items.Add( times & " times " & i & " = " & numbers(i) )
Next i
```

When you're finished, run your programme and test it out. Click the button and the times table should appear in the List Box.

And that is how to set up an array when you don't know what size the array is going to be - set up an array with empty brackets. Reset the array with the **ReDim** word, and then give it some new values.

But we'll leave arrays for now and move on to another subject – working with Strings of text.

String Manipulation

Humans are far from perfect. Especially when they are entering data into textboxes! Sometimes they won't enter any details at all in the boxes you want them to. And then when they do enter something, they often get it wrong. Sometimes on purpose, just to trip you up. By manipulating Strings of data, we can check things like text in a textbox to see if it is correct, and thereby gain some control of the user's actions.

The String Variable Type

There's more to the string variable type than meets the eye. You've used them a lot to store text. But the string variable types come with a lot of inbuilt power. Strings have their own properties and methods, just like a textbox or label or form does. That's because strings are objects. (In fact, all variables are objects in VB.NET, including the number variables.) In a later section, we'll be going into a bit more detail on objects. For now, think of them as things that can be manipulated – like the textbox, label and form just mentioned.

And strings variables can be directly manipulated, too. An example should clear things up.

Start a new project. Add two textboxes and a button to your new form. For Textbox1, set the Text property to "string variables". Double click the button to open the coding window. Then type the following:

```
Dim strUpper As String

strUpper = TextBox1.Text
TextBox2.Text = strUpper.ToUpper( )
```

Run your code and see what happens when you click the button.

You should have found that the text from textbox1 gets converted to uppercase letters.

The reason it gets converted is because we used the **ToUpper** method of the string variable. When you typed the full stop after the variable name, you probably saw this pop up box:

Simply double click the method you want, and it's added to your code.

strUpper.ToUpper( )

Notice that the name of the variable you want to do something with comes first. Then, after the full stop, you add the name of the method.

It's easy to guess what some of the methods do (like **ToLower**), but others are a bit more enigmatic (Like **Substring**).

We'll now go through some of the string methods to see what they do, and how useful they can be in your code.

Before we start, here's a full list of the methods that a string variable can access (next page):

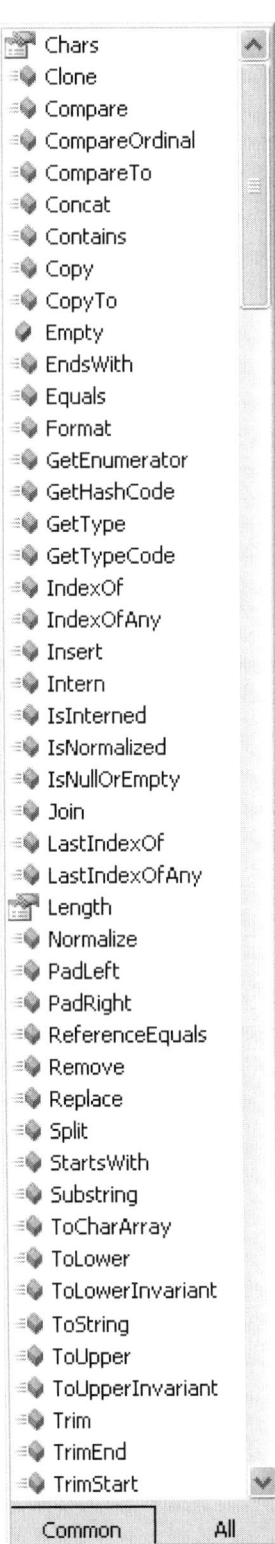

Length and **Chars** on that list are properties and not methods. We'll be using these two, and they come in quite useful.

Manipulating data from a Text Box

You already know how to pass data from a Textbox into a variable. Just do this:

> **Dim FirstName As String**
>
> **FirstName = txtFirst.Text**

Then whatever was in the Textbox you called **txtFirst** will get transferred directly to the String variable you set up. Once the data is in the variable, you can test it to see if it's the type of data you want. After all, the user could have entered numbers to try and trip you up. Or they could have left it blank.

Add a new textbox to your form. Change the Name property to txtFirst. Add a second button to your form, and set the Text property to whatever you want.

> **Dim FirstName As String**
>
> **FirstName = txtFirst.Text**
>
> **If FirstName = "" Then**
>
> > **MsgBox "Please enter your First Name in the text box"**
> > **Exit Sub**
>
> **End If**

In this code, we are passing whatever is in the text box directly to the variable called **FirstName**. We are then testing what is inside the variable with an If statement. We want to test if the user has actually entered something into the text box. If they've left it blank, we want to tell them to try again. We also want to exit the Subroutine. After all, if they got it wrong, we don't want to proceed with any code we might have written.

The way we are testing to see if the user has left the text box blank is this:

> **If FirstName = "" Then**

We've put two sets of double quotes together. This signifies a string of text that is blank. If the user didn't enter anything at all, then our variable **FirstName** will contain a blank string. This is what we're testing for.

Run the programme and try it out. Don't type anything at all in the textbox, but just click the button. The message box should display.

Now, click inside the textbox. Hit the space bar three times. And then click the button. Did the Message box display?

So why didn't it? After all, there was nothing in the textbox. Isn't that an blank string? What was passed to the variable?

Well, when you press the space bar Visual Basic counts that as a text character. So when you press the space bar three times what is in the variable is this:

FirstName = "   "

and not this:

FirstName = ""

The two are entirely different, according to Visual Basic. After all, you might have wanted three spaces!

So how can we check to see if there is anything at all in our textbox? How do we defeat the user who has tried to fool us by hitting the space bar a number of times?

Trim

One of the methods on our list is Trim. What this does is to trim any leading or trailing blank spaces from a string. So if the string was "   Text", then Trim would delete those spaces for you, leaving just "Text".

You use it in your code like this:

```
FirstName = txtFirst.Text
FirstName = FirstName.Trim
```

First, we put the text from the textbox into the variable **FirstName**. Then we said "assign to the variable FirstName (FirstName =) the value of FirstName trimmed (FirstName.**Trim**)".

Again, though, we're just adding the method we want after the variable name. VB will take care of the trimming for us.

Another way to Trim is to use the **Trim( )** function directly. Like this:

FirstName = Trim(txtFirst.Text)

What you are trimming here is any blank spaces from around text entered directly in the text box called **txtFirst**

But we now have a way to thwart that user who is trying to trip us up by entering blank spaces into our text box. If you were programming a Form where the First Name was going into a database, then it's essential you trap anything like this.

OK, we've tested to see if the First Name text box was empty. Is there anything else we can do? What if our clever-clogs user tries to fool us again. This time he (they're always "he's"!) decides to enter some numbers. He claims his name is "123456". Is there anything we can do to stop his little games? Is there a way to test that the data entered into a text box was text and not numbers?

IsNumeric( )

Comment out your If statement. A quick way to comment out a whole block of code is to highlight it first. Then click the comment icon on the toolbar:

The icon next to it removes the comments from highlighted code.

But type this code just below your commented block:

If IsNumeric(FirstName) Then

MsgBox "Those were numbers, my friend"

End If

To check if a variable is a number, you can use the **IsNumeric( )** function. This function will return either True or False. In other words, if the variable being checked is a number, then **IsNumeric( )** is True; if **IsNumeric( )** is not a number then False gets returned.

But notice that we're not using one of the string methods here. There is no IsNumeric on the list. You have to use the in-built function, if you want to test if the entire string is a string of numbers.

There's a good reason why you'd want to do this. If you tried to put a string of numbers into an Integer variable, VB would give you an error message. You have to convert the string of numbers first. (You saw one way to do this - with the Val( ) function).

By using the IsNumeric() function, you can test to see whether a string of text is actually a string of numbers.

But what if our mischievous little imp claimed his first name was "George12345". Is there anything we can do to check that numbers have been used with text?

Indeed there is. We can use a variable Type that you haven't met before - Char. But we're going to have to use it in a For loop. We can then loop round each keyboard character in the variable and check what's inside it.

Char

The variable type Char can hold one character at a time (the Char is short for Character). You set it up like this:

Dim OneCharacter As Char

You can then store a character in the variable like this:

OneCharacter = "A"

Or like this:

Dim OneCharacter As Char = "a"

You can even do this:

Dim OneCharacter As Char = "apple"

But if you try to put a whole word into a Char variable, only the first letter will be retained.

So what good is the Char variable type?

Well, a common use for it is to transfer one letter at a time from a string, and then test to see what this character is. You can test to see if it's a number, for example. Or perhaps to test if the string contains an "@" symbol for a valid email address. We'll test for a number. In the process, we can study the Length property of string variables.

Add another textbox and a button to your form. Change the Name property of the textbox to txtChars. For the Text property of the Textbox, enter "George123". Double click the new button and enter the following variable declarations:

Dim OneCharacter As Char
Dim FirstName As String
Dim i As Integer
Dim TextLength As Integer

Remember what we're going to be doing here. We're going to put the text from the textbox into a string variable. Then we'll loop round every character in the string to see if it's a number.

So the next line to add to your code is the one that transfers the text from the textbox to the string variable. Add this:

FirstName = Trim(txtChars.Text)

The next thing we need is how long the string is. We need this for the end value of our loop. The length property will give us this answer. So add this line:

TextLength = FirstName.Length

The length property of a string variable tells you how many characters are in the string. You can add a message box to test out your code so far:

MsgBox("Number of characters is: " & TextLength)

Run your programme. Click the button and test out your code. You should see a message box like this one:

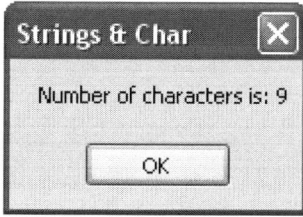

So "George123" has 9 characters.

We can now loop round each character in the string and test which ones are the numbers. Add the following For loop to your code (you can delete or comment out your message box line now):

For i = 0 To TextLength - 1

Next i

So the For loop starts at zero and ends at the length of the text, minus 1. (It will loop from 0 to 8 in our code: 9 characters. We'll see why you have to deduct 1 soon.
Inside of our loop, we need to grab one character at a time, and then put it into our Char variable. You can do that with the **Chars** Property of the string variable type. Here's the line:

OneCharacter = FirstName.Chars(i)

You type the name of your variable, then after the full stop you add **Chars( )**. Inside of the round brackets, you need a number. This number is the position in the string you want to grab. So if you wanted the third letter of a string variable, you'd put this:

Dim SomeString As String
Dim OneCharacter As Char

SomeString = "George123"
OneCharacter = SomeString.Chars(2)

The variable **OneCharacter** would then hold the third letter – "o".

The reason we've put 2 inside of the round brackets and not 3 is because VB starts counting the characters from zero, and NOT 1. And that's why the For Loop is this:

For i = 0 To TextLength – 1

You have to deduct 1 because the **Chars()** count starts at zero. So amend your For Loop to this:

> **For i = 0 To TextLength - 1**
> **OneCharacter = FirstName.Chars(i)**
> **MsgBox(OneCharacter)**
> **Next i**

Run your code, and then click your button. You should get a message box displaying. In fact, you'll get 9 message boxes, one for each character in the string.

Ok, try these exercises to test your new knowledge.

Exercise
Add an If statement to your For Loop. Check each character of the string "George123". If you find a number, display a suitable message, something like "A number was found". Exit the for loop when the first number is found

Exercise
Amend your code to keep a count of how many characters in the string are numbers. Display the count in a message box.

InStr( )

The **InStr( )** method of string variables tells you what the position of one string is inside another. For example, if your string was "me@me.com" and you wanted to know if the string contained the @ symbol, you could use InStr( ) Method. You would use it like this:

> **FirstString = "me@me.com"**
> **SecondString = "@"**
>
> **position = InStr(FirstString, SecondString)**

The variable **FirstString** is the string we want to search; **SecondString** is what we want to search for. You can specify a starting position for the search to begin. If you do, this number goes at the start (the default is zero):

> **position = InStr(1, FirstString, SecondString)**

The variable **position** is an integer variable. That's because the InStr() Method returns a number, and not text. In the code above, **position** would have a value of 3. That's because the @ symbols starts at the third letter of "me@me.com".

(**Note:** the InStr( ) Method starts counting at 1, and not zero like Chars(), which is very confusing!)

If the string you're searching for is not found, then the value placed inside of your integer variable (**position** in our case) is zero. That enables you to code something like this:

```
If position = 0 Then
          MsgBox "Not a Valid email address: There was No @ Sign"
End If
```

Substring

Another useful string method is Substring. This allows you to grab one string within another. (For example, if you wanted to grab the ".com" from the email address "me@me.com.")

In between the round brackets of Substring( ), you specify a starting position and then how many characters you want to grab (the count starts at zero again). Like this:

```
Dim Email as String
Dim DotCom as String

Email = "me@me.com"
DotCom = Email.Substring(5, 4)

MsgBox(DotCom)
```

The message box would then display the characters grabbed from the string, in this case the ".com" at the end (start at position 5 in the string and grab 4 characters).

You could also do a check to see if the email address ended in ".com" like this. Here's some code to do the job:

```
Dim Email As String
Dim DotCom As String

Email = "me@me.con"
DotCom = Email.Substring(Email.Length - 4, 4)

If DotCom = ".com" Then
          MsgBox("Ends in Dot Com")
Else
          MsgBox("Doesn't End in Dot Com")
End If
```

The starting position for Substring( ) this time is "**Email.Length - 4**". This is the length of the string variable called **Email**, minus 4 characters. The other 4 means "grab four characters"

You have to be careful, though. If there wasn't four characters to grab, VB would give you an error message.

We could replace the **Chars( )** For loop code we wrote earlier with a Substring method. The result would be the same. Here's the code:

```
For i = 0 To TextLength - 1
        OneCharacter = FirstName.Substring(i, 1)
        MsgBox OneCharacter
Next i
```

So we're saying, "Start grabbing characters from the position i. Just grab one character".

Substring and Chars are very useful methods to use when you want to check the letters in a string of text.

Equals

In code previously, we had this:

```
If DotCom = ".com" Then
        MsgBox("Ends in Dot Com")
Else
        MsgBox("Doesn't End in Dot Com")
End If
```

You can use the **Equals** method of string variables in the first line, instead of an equals sign:

```
If DotCom.Equals(".com") Then
```

So after the name of your string variable comes the full stop. Then select "Equals" from the popup list. In between the round brackets, you type the string (or variable name) that you want VB to compare.

The Equals method is used to compare one string of text against another. If they're the same a value of True is returned, else it's False.

Replace

You can replace text in one string with some other text. The process is fairly straightforward. Here's some code that uses Replace. Add a button to your form and test it out:

```
Dim OldText As String
Dim NewText As String

OldText = "This is some test"
NewText = OldText.Replace("test", "text")

MsgBox(OldText)
MsgBox(NewText)
```

When you run the programme, the first message box will say **"This is some test"** and the second box will say **"This is some text"**.

The text you want to get rid of comes first. Then after a comma, type the new text. You can use string variables rather than direct text surrounded by double quotes, for example:

```
Dim NewWord As String = "Text"
NewText = OldText.Replace("test", NewWord)
```

Insert

You can also insert some new text into a string. Here's some code to try out:

```
Dim SomeText As String
Dim NewText As String

SomeText = "This some text"
NewText = SomeText.Insert(5, "is ")

MsgBox(SomeText)
MsgBox(NewText)
```

The 5 in round brackets means start at position 5 in the string variable **SomeText** (the count starts at zero). You then type the text that you want inserted. You can use a variable name instead of direct text surrounded by quotes.

Split and Join

Two very useful string variable methods are Split and Join. Split allows you to split a line of text and put each element (word or phrase) into an array; Join allows you to join elements of an array into one line of text. An example or two might clear this up.

In a later project, you'll have to open up a text file and read its contents. You can read the text file line by line, and each line might be something like this:

"UserName1, Password1, UserName2, Password2, UserName3, Password3"

The programming problem is to separate each word. You can use Split for this. Each word would then be separated, ready for you to place into an array.

Here's an example for you to try out. (It's better to put this code behind a new button):

```
Dim LineOfText As String
Dim i As Integer
Dim aryTextFile() As String

LineOfText = "UserName1, Password1, UserName2, Password2"

aryTextFile = LineOfText.Split(",")
```

For i = 0 To UBound(aryTextFile)
        MsgBox(aryTextFile(i))
Next i

Notice the line that sets up an array:

Dim aryTextFile() As String

We don't know how many elements will be in the array (how many words on each line), so we leave the round brackets blank.

The next line just put some text into a variable called **LineOfText**. But this can come from a text file that you open with code.

The line that does the splitting comes next:

aryTextFile = LineOfText.Split(",")

Notice that **aryTextFile** has now lost its round brackets. If you put them in, you get an error. The use of the **Split** method, though, is this:

LineOfText.Split(",")

After the name of your variable and the full stop, select (or type) the word Split. In between round brackets you put what is known as the separator. This is the symbol or punctuation mark that you are using to separate each element of your line. In our case, we're using a comma to separate the words in the line. But you can use anything you like (a hyphen, for example).

When VB finishes the splitting, it fills up your array. Each element will occupy one slot in your array. So in our example, **aryTextFile(0)** will hold a value of **UserName1**, **aryTextFile(1)** will hold a value of **Password1,** etc.

The For loop is there to show you how to loop round each element in your array, and displays the results in a message box:

For i = 0 To UBound(aryTextFile)
        MsgBox(aryTextFile(i))
Next i

The first line includes this:

UBound(aryTextFile)

UBound means Upper Boundary of an array. In between the round brackets of **UBound()** you type the name of your array. Notice, though that the round brackets of the array have gone missing again.

So if your array was this:

MyArray(9)

The Upper Boundary of the array would be 9. So the end of the For Loop would then be 9. You code like this when you don't know how many elements are in your array.

The message box just displays what is in each position of your array:

MsgBox(aryTextFile(i))

Join

The Join method is used when you want to join the elements of an array back together again. Here's some code which does exactly that:

Dim LineOfText As String
Dim i As Integer
Dim aryTextFile(3) As String

aryTextFile(0) = "UserName1"
aryTextFile(1) = "Password1"
aryTextFile(2) = "UserName2"
aryTextFile(3) = "Password2"

LineOfText = String.Join("-", aryTextFile)

MsgBox(LineOfText)

The line that joins each element in the array is this:

LineOfText = String.Join("-", aryTextFile)

After typing the word "**String**", which is a generic string object, you type a dot then the word "Join". In between the round brackets of Join(), you first type what you want to use as a separator. Here, we're using an hyphen as a separator. Next, you put the name of your array. Again the round brackets from the array have gone missing.

When the line executes, the variable **LineOfText** will hold the following:

"UserName1-Password1-UserName2-Password2"

Once you have the array elements joined together, you could then write the line back to your text file.

Split and Join can be very useful indeed.

Now that we've had a look at the methods of string variable, it's time for a review.

Review Number 6

Design a Form with a two textboxes and a Button

Write a programme that swaps around the first two letters of a person's first and last name. For example, if the person's name was "Bill Gates" the "Ga" of the last name will be swapped with the "Bi" of the first name. The result would then be "Gall Bites"

Use only ONE text box for the full name. So "Bill Gates" should be in the first textbox, and when the button is clicked, "Gall Bites" will appear in the second textbox.

Help with this Review

The only string methods you really need for this programme are Split and Substring.

The first job is to get the name from the textbox and put into a variable. You can then split the name in two with the Split() method.

Because there's only a First Name and a Second Name, your array only needs to hold two elements (Unless you want to handle names with more than two words!) You can then use Substring to grab the first two characters of each name.

Once you've chopped both names into four separate parts, you can then join the bits together again using concatenation (&).

Finally, display your results in the second textbox.

Text Files

There is a very useful object in VB.NET called System.IO (the IO stands for Input and Output). You can use this object to read and write to text files.

We're going to be having a closer look at objects (and what System is) in the next section. For now, let's just see how to open up a text file using the System.IO object.

First, here's an explanation of just what we mean by "text file".

The files on your computer all end in a three letter extensions. Microsoft Word files will have a different three letter extension from Microsoft Excel files. The extension is used to identify one file type from another. That way, Excel won't try to open Word files, or vice versa. You can just write some code to strip the last three letters from the file name, and then check that these three letters are the ones you want. Rather like the code you wrote to strip the last three letters from an email address.

Text files have an extension that ends in **.txt**. The Windows operating system gives you a good, basic Text Editor in Notepad. The Notepad programme allows you to save files with the **.txt** extension. In other words, as Text Files. And that is what is meant by Text Files in this section of the book.

A simple text file like this is called a Sequential File, and that is what we will be opening here. So let's begin.

Opening a Text File for Reading

The ability to open up a text file and read its contents can be very useful to you in your programming life. You might have a text file containing quiz questions and answers, for example. You could read the questions and answers from a text file and create your own "Who wants to be a Millionaire" game.

To open up a text file, you need to create something called a "StreamReader". This, as its name suggests, reads streams of text. The StreamReader is an object available to System.IO. You create a StreamReader like this:

Dim FILE_NAME As String = "C:\Users\Owner\Documents\test.txt"

Dim objReader As New System.IO.StreamReader(FILE_NAME)

The first line just sets up a string variable called FILE_NAME. We store the path and name of our text file inside of the string variable:

= "C:\Users\Owner\Documents\test.txt"

We're saying that there is a text file called **test** which is at the location (path) specified.

You set up the StreamReader to be a variable, just like a String or Integer variable. But we're setting up this variable differently:

Dim objReader As New System.IO.StreamReader(FILE_NAME)

We've called the variable **objReader**. Then, after the "As" word, comes "New". This means "Create a New Object". The type of object we want to create is a StreamReader object:

System.IO.StreamReader

Sysytem is the main object. **IO** is an object within System. And **StreamReader** is an object within IO.

StreamReader needs the name of a file to Read. This goes between a pair of round brackets:

System.IO.StreamReader(**FILE_NAME**)

VB will then assign all of this to the variable called **objReader**. So instead of assigning say 10 to an Integer variable, you are assigning a StreamReader to a variable.

But this won't do you any good. We haven't actually opened the text file yet. We've just told VB where the text file is and what object to open it with. You do the opening like this:

TextBox1.Text = objReader.ReadToEnd

Now that **objReader** is an object variable, it has its own properties and methods available for use (in the same way that the textbox has a Text property).

One of the Methods available to our new StreamReader variable is the **ReadToEnd** method. This will read the whole of your text, right to the end. We're then popping this in a textbox.

Let's test all this theory out. Start a new project. Add a textbox to your new form, and just leave it on the default Name of Textbox1. Set its MultiLine property to True. Add a Button to your form. Double click the button and add the following code for it:

Dim FILE_NAME As String = "C:\Users\Owner\Documents\test.txt"

Dim objReader As New System.IO.StreamReader(FILE_NAME)

TextBox1.Text = objReader.ReadToEnd

 objReader.Close( )

The last line closes the StreamReader we set up. You have to close your stream objects after you've used them, Otherwise you'll get errors messages.

When you're done, run your programme and click your Button.

Unless you already have a file called test.txt at the location specified you'll get this error message popping up:

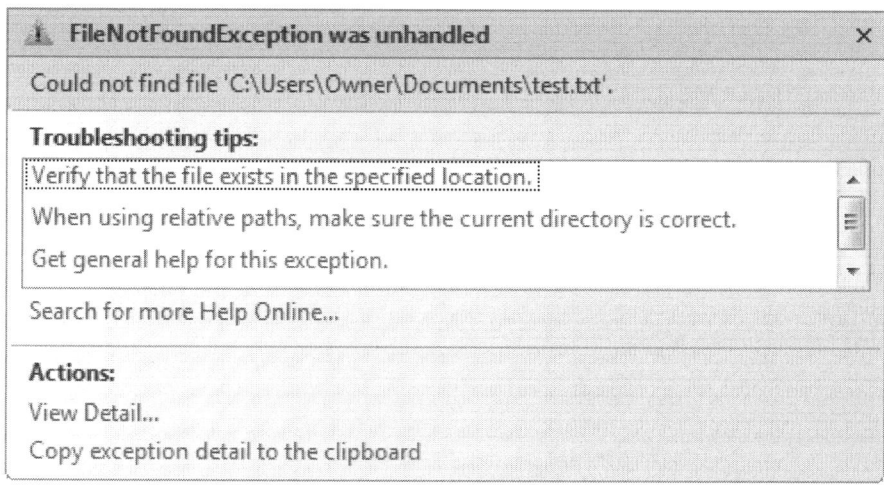

The second line spells it out clearly: Could not find file "C:\Users\Owner\Documents\test.txt". So we were trying to read a text file that doesn't exist.

You can, though, test to see if the file exists. If it does, you can open it; if not, you can display an error message. Amend your code to this:

Dim FILE_NAME As String = "C:\Users\Owner\Documents\test.txt"

If System.IO.File.Exists(FILE_NAME) = True Then
       Dim objReader As New System.IO.StreamReader(FILE_NAME)
       TextBox1.Text = objReader.ReadToEnd
       objReader.Close()
Else
       MsgBox("File Does Not Exist")
End If

We've now wrapped up our code in an If Statement. The first line of the If Statement is this:

If System.IO.File.Exists(FILE_NAME) = True Then

This tests to see whether or not a file exists. Again, you start with **System.IO.** Then you access another object of **System.IO** – the **File** object. This has a method called **Exists**. In between the round brackets, you type the name (or variable) of the file you want to check. The value returned will either be True (if it does exist) or False (if it doesn't).

If the file exists, then we can go ahead and create our StreamReader; If it doesn't, we can display a error message for the user.

So that your programme will work, there is a file called "test.txt" to download. (The download location can be found at the start of this book). Copy the file to your hard drive, in the main C:\ folder. When you have done that, run your programme again. Click the button again and you should see the text from your file appear in the textbox. (If you get the error message, it means you haven't copied the file to the right place.)

Reading Line by Line

Quite often, however, you don't want to read the whole file at once. You want to read it line by line. In which case, instead of using the **ReadToEnd** method, you can use the **ReadLine** method.

The **ReadLine** method, as its name suggests, reads text one line at a time. In order to do this, though, you need to use a loop. You can then loop round each line and read it into a variable. Here's a coding example:

Dim TextLine As String

Do While objReader.Peek() <> -1
 TextLine = TextLine & objReader.ReadLine() & vbNewLine
Loop

The first line of the **Do While** Loop is rather curious:

Do While objReader.Peek() <> -1

The Peek method takes a peek at the incoming text characters. It's looking ahead one character at a time. If it doesn't see any more characters, it will return a value of minus 1. This will signify the end of the text file. Our loop checks for this minus 1, and bails out when Peek has this value.
Inside the loop, we're reading each line from the text file and putting it into a new variable. (We're also adding a new line character on the end. Delete the **&vbNewLine** and see what happens).

objReader.ReadLine()

So the ReadLine method reads each line for you, instead of the ReadToEnd method which gets the whole of the text file.

Once you have a line of text, though, it's up to you to parse it. For example, suppose the line of text was this:

"UserName1, Password1, UserName2, Password2"

You would then have to chop the line down and do something which each segment. VB won't do this for you! (But you saw how to do this in the last section, when you used things like Split and Substring.)

Writing to a Text File

Writing to a text file is similar to reading a text file. Again we use System.IO. This time, instead of using the StreamReader we use the StreamWriter. The StreamWriter is used to write a stream of text to a file.

Add another Button to your form. Set the Text property of the button to "Write to File". Double click your new button to open up the coding window. Add the following:

```
Dim FILE_NAME As String = "C:\Users\Owner\Documents\test2.txt"

If System.IO.File.Exists(FILE_NAME) = True Then
        Dim objWriter As New System.IO.StreamWriter( FILE_NAME
)
        objWriter.Write(TextBox1.Text)
        objWriter.Close()
        MsgBox("Text written to file")
Else
        MsgBox("File Does Not Exist")
End If
```

Run your programme, and then click your new button.

Unless you have a file called "test2.txt", you should see the message box display: "File Does Not Exist."

Once again, VB insists that the file must exist before it can actually do something with it. Which is not unreasonable!

Stop your programme and change this line:

```
Dim FILE_NAME As String = "C:\Users\Owner\Documents\test2.txt"
```

To this:

```
Dim FILE_NAME As String = "C:\Users\Owner\Documents\test.txt"
```

In other words, just change the file name back to test.txt. (Hopefully, you haven't deleted the test.txt file from your hard drive.)

Run your programme again. Type something into the textbox, and then click your button. You should see the message box **"Text written to file"** appear.

But notice that if you open up the text file itself, any text you had previously will be gone – it has been overwritten, rather than appended to. (We'll see how to append text to a file shortly.)

Let's have a look at the code we wrote, though.

Once again, we check to see if the File Exists. If it's True that the file exists, then the first line that gets executed is setting up our variable:

```
Dim objWriter As New System.IO.StreamWriter(FILE_NAME)
```

It's almost the same as last time. Only two things have changed: we created a new variable name, **objWriter**, and we're now using StreamWriter instead of StreamReader. Everything else is the same.

To write the text to our file, we've used this:

objWriter.Write(TextBox1.Text)

After the name of our variable (objWriter), we typed a full stop. The drop down box appeared showing available properties and methods. The "Write" method was chosen from the list. In between round brackets, you put what it is you want VB to write to your text file. In our case, this was the text in textbox1. You can also do this:

objWriter.Write("Your Text Here")

The above uses direct text surrounded by double quotes. This is also acceptable:

Dim TheText As String = "Your Text Here"
objWriter.Write(TheText)

This time, we've put the text inside of a variable. The name of the variable is then typed inside of the round brackets of "Write".

But you don't have to write the whole text at once. You can write line by line. In which case, select WriteLine from the available properties and methods. Here's an example of how to use WriteLine:

```
Dim FILE_NAME As String = "C:\Users\Owner\Documents\test.txt"
Dim i As Integer
Dim aryText(4) As String

aryText(0) = "Mary WriteLine"
aryText(1) = "Had"
aryText(2) = "A"
aryText(3) = "Little"
aryText(4) = "One"

Dim objWriter As New System.IO.StreamWriter(FILE_NAME)

For i = 0 To 4
        objWriter.WriteLine( aryText(i) )
Next

objWriter.Close( )
```

The error checking code has been left out here. But notice the new way to write text to the file:

objWriter.WriteLine(aryText(i))

We're looping round and writing the contents of an array. Each line of text from the array gets written to our text file. But each line is appended. That is, the text file doesn't get erased after each line has been written. All the lines from the array will be written to the text file. However, if you were to run the code a second time then the contents of the file are erased before the new WriteLine( ) springs into action. In other words, you'd only get one version of "Mary WriteLine had a little one" instead of two.

Appending Text to a File

There will be times when you won't want to erase all the text from your file. You'll only want to add text to what you currently have. In which case you need to Append.

Appending text to your file is quite easy.

When you set up the object variable for the StreamWriter, you just typed the name and path of the file:

> Dim objWriter As New System.IO.StreamWriter(**FILE_NAME**)

To append text to a file, you type a comma after your file name then type the word True:

> Dim objWriter As New System.IO.StreamWriter(FILE_NAME, **True**)

If you want to add some text to the file, you need that True value. If you leave out the True or False, a new file is not created.

Here some code that appends text to the file we wrote to:

```
Dim FILE_NAME As String = "C:\Users\Owner\Documents\test.txt"
Dim i As Integer
Dim aryText(4) As String

aryText(0) = "Mary WriteLine"
aryText(1) = "Had"
 aryText(2) = "Another"
aryText(3) = "Little"
aryText(4) = "One"

Dim objWriter As New System.IO.StreamWriter(FILE_NAME, True)

For i = 0 To 4
        objWriter.WriteLine( aryText(i) )
Next

objWriter.Close( )
MsgBox("Text Appended to the File")
```

The lines that have changed are in bold. Try both version and see how it works.

Creating a file if it doesn't exist

If you want to create a file if one doesn't exist, the process is again quite simple:

Dim objWriter As New System.IO.StreamWriter(FILE_NAME, **False**)

This time, we've just added the word "False" to the end of FILE_NAME. This will ensure that a new text file is created if one doesn't exist.

Copying files

You can also copy a file that you've created. This time, we don't need the StreamWriter or StreamReader of System.IO. We need the File object:

System.IO.File

This just means "System.IO has an object called File. Use this File object".

File has its own properties and methods you can use. One of these is **Copy**. Here's some code that makes a copy of our test file.

```
Dim FileToCopy As String
Dim NewCopy As String

FileToCopy = "C:\Users\Owner\Documents\test.txt"
NewCopy = "C:\Users\Owner\Documents\NewTest.txt"

If System.IO.File.Exists( FileToCopy ) = True Then
        System.IO.File.Copy( FileToCopy, NewCopy )
        MsgBox("File Copied")
End If
```

The file we want to copy is called **"test.txt"**. We've put this inside of a string variable called **FileToCopy**. The name of the new file, and its location, are assigned to a variable called **NewCopy**.

Next, we have to check to see if the file we're trying to copy exists. Only if it does should we go ahead and copy it. You've met this code before.

Inside of the If Statement, we have this:

System.IO.File.Copy(FileToCopy, NewCopy **)**

We use the Copy method of **System.IO.File.** In between the round brackets, you first type the name of the file you want to copy. After a comma, you then type the name of the new file and its new location.

Moving files

You move a file in a similar manner – specify a source file and a new destination for it. This time, we use the Move method of **System.IO.File.** Here's some code:

```
Dim FileToMove As String
Dim MoveLocation As String

FileToMove = "C:\Users\Owner\Documents\test.txt"
MoveLocation = "C:\Users\Owner\Documents\TestFolder\test.txt"

If System.IO.File.Exists(FileToMove) = True Then
        System.IO.File.Move(FileToMove, MoveLocation)
        MsgBox("File Moved")
End If
```

The above code assumes that you have created a folder on your hard drive called "TestFolder":

MoveLocation = "C:\Users\Owner\Documents\TestFolder\test.txt"

The file called test.txt will then be moved inside of this new location. You can give it a new name, if you want. In which case, just change the name of the file when you're moving it:

MoveLocation ="C:\Users\Owner\Documents\TestFolder\NewName.txt"

Again though, the thing to type in the round brackets of the method is first the Source file, then the Destination.

System.IO.File.Move(FileToMove, MoveLocation)

Deleting files

Deleting a file is quite simple – but dangerous! So be very careful when you're trying out this code. Make sure the file you're going to delete is not needed – you won't be able to restore it from the recycle bin!

To delete a file from your computer, you use the Delete method of **System.IO.** Here's some new code for you to try:

```
Dim FileToDelete As String

FileToDelete = "C:\Users\Owner\Documents\testDelete.txt"

If System.IO.File.Exists(FileToDelete) = True Then
        System.IO.File.Delete(FileToDelete)
        MsgBox("File Deleted")
End If
```

First, we've set up a string variable called **FileToDelete**. We've then assigned the name of a file to this variable - **"testDelete.txt"**. (We created this file first, and made sure that it was safe to junk it.)

Next, we test to see if the File Exists. In the IF Statement, we then had this:

System.IO.File.**Delete(FileToDelete)**

After selecting the Delete method, you type the name of the file you want to get rid of. This goes between a pair of round brackets.

And that's it! That's all you need to do to delete a file from your computer, never to see it again. So be very careful when you test out the code!

You can now move on to a review.

Review Number Seven

In this modern world of ours, a new type of English seems to have evolved – Texting English. Just one example is the abbreviation LOL, the meaning of which is "Laughing out loud". Your project for review number seven is to write a programme that will serve as a Texting English/Real English dictionary. Here's how Part One of your programme will work (the review is in two parts).

Part One

There is a text file to download called "dictionary". (The download location can be found at the start of this book). This contains Texting English followed by its Real English translation. For example:

LOL = Laughing out loud

Each line uses an equals sign to separate the Texting English from its Real English translation. When a button is clicked on your form, you job is to write the code that opens this "dictionary" text file and read its contents. Once the text file is opened, write code to place the Texting English in one List Box and the Real English in a second List Box.

That's clearly not enough, though. When a user clicks on a term in a List Box, display the translation in a Textbox. So if LOL was selected from your List Box, the translation "Laughing out loud" should appear in the textbox. But if "Laughing out loud" was selected, the Texting version, LOL, should appear in the textbox.

Part Two

Add two new textboxes and a button. Write code so that the user can add a new Text/Real English pair to the dictionary.

Help for this Review

Part One Help

When you create your form, you're going to need a Button and two List boxes. When the button is clicked, you first have to open the text file called **dictionary**. We'll assume that this text file is in the root folder of C. So the file path would be:

TextFile = "C:\dictionary.txt"

Once you have opened the file, you need to read it line by line (you can use a Do While loop for this). Each line will have two parts: the Texting English and the Real English:

LOL = Laughing out loud

What you have to do is to Split each line in two. The line separator is the equals sign. You can then use the Split method of a string variable to search for this separator. Because each line has only two parts, you can set up an array with two elements in it:

Dim AryLine(1) As String

When you use Split, you can put the first part into array position zero, and the second part into array position 1.

Once you have split the line in two, you can then add each part to the list boxes. The way to add items to a list box is like this, remember:

Listbox1.Items.Add()

In between the round brackets, you put what it is you want to add. In your case, you'll want to put something from your array:

Listbox1.Items.Add(AryLine(0))

When you've finished looping round the text file, you'll then have two list boxes filled with the dictionary pairs. Once you have that working correctly, you can move on to your next objective – selecting an item from a List Box.

How to Select an item from a List Box

When you add an item to a list box, you're creating a collection. The first item in the collection is placed at position zero, the next at position 1, the next at position 2, etc. You can use the index position of the collection to get at the items. The property of the List Box that does this is the **SelectedIndex** property. Here's some code that's been added to the Click event of a List box with the Name of **lstText**:

```
Private Sub lstText_Click(ByVal sender As Object, _
                        ByVal e As System.EventArgs) _
                        Handles lstText.Click

    Dim selIndex As Integer

    selIndex = lstText.SelectedIndex
    MsgBox(selIndex)

End Sub
```

The **SelectedIndex** will be a number. This number is the position of the item in the list Box. If you were to run that code, then click on an item in the list box, a number would be displayed. If you clicked on the first item, this number would be 0; if you clicked on the third item, this number would be 2 (the count starts from zero, remember).

You can use this number to get at the Text property of the item – in other words, what the item is that was selected. The way you use the number is like this:

ItemChosen = lstText.Items.Item(selIndex)

This somewhat unintuitive line says "There is a property of the List Box called Items. This Items property has a property of its own called Item. Access this Item property."

But the Item property needs a number between its round brackets. The number corresponds to its position in the List Box. This will then return the text of the item chosen.

(HINT: The item position in each of your two list Boxes will be the same. So if LOL is at position 2 in your first list box, "Laughing out loud" will be at position 2 in your second list box. So if a user selects item 2 from list box one, you can grab item 2 from list box two. This will then be the translation you need)

Once you have the translation you need, you can place it into your textbox. Part One will then be completed.

Help with Part Two

For part two, you have to allow a user of your programme to add a new entry to the dictionary. The Text English will be entered into one textbox, and the Real English entered into the other. When a button is clicked, the item is added to the dictionary.

Part two should be a lot easier. All you're doing here is taking text from two textboxes and joining it together, along with an equals sign in the middle. Once you've joined the text, you can then append the text to your dictionary text file.

You should test for errors. What if a user leaves one textbox blank? What if your text file has been moved or deleted? Make sure you code for this.

Functions and Subs

So far, the code you have been writing has mostly been lumped together under one button. The problem with this approach is that your code can get quite long and complex, making it difficult to read, and difficult to put right if something goes wrong. Another approach is to separate some of this code into its own routine. This is where functions and subs come in.

The two terms refer to segments of code that are separate from your main code. You've already met some string functions - Equals( ) and Substring( ), for example. These functions are built into Visual Basic. But if you could see under the hood, what you'd find is some code to do these jobs for you. All you have to do is to specify, for the Substring( ) function, what the string is, where you want to start, and how many characters you want to grab. You don't have to worry about how Visual Basic gets your answer, because the code is all wrapped up in a function, ready for you to use over and over again.

And that's the point about Functions and Subs: it's code that you might want to use over and over again. You don't have to keep writing the same code every time you want a specific job doing. Just write the code once, and then when you want to use it, just let Visual Basic know.

An example might help to clear things up.

Think about an Order Form. We'd have a lot of Text Boxes, and we'd want to check that the user was entering the correct data. We don't want people entering numbers in our First Name text box, for instance. To check that the user has entered the correct data, we'd write some code. Except we'd have a lot of text boxes on the form. If we wanted to check all the text boxes, we'd have to write the same "checking" code for each text box. Instead of doing that, we can write our own Function or Sub. We only have to write it once. Then when we want to use it, we just refer to it by name, and the code will get executed. We'll now write a Sub that we can use over and over again.

First, though, in case you are wondering what the difference is between a Function and a Sub, it's this: Functions return a value, and Subs don't. Substring( ) is a Function, because you want some sort of answer back, and an answer that you can then use elsewhere. You assign the answer to the Substring( ) function to a variable.

But here's what we're going to do. We'll set up a text box on a form. The text box will be a first name text box, and we'll be checking that the user has actually entered something into it. So, start a new project, and put a Text Box on your new Form. Put a button on the Form, too. Write the following code for the button:

```
Dim TextBoxData As String

TextBoxData = Trim(TextBox1.Text)

If TextBoxData = "" Then
        MsgBox("Please Enter your First Name")
End If
```

Run the programme and test it out. Don't enter anything in your textbox, but just click your button. Your message box should display.

Now, all that code is inside the button. More likely than not, we'd be writing more code for that button. In fact, we could be writing lots of code. The code we write could get a bit long and complex. Do we have to have that error checking code in there? And wouldn't we have to type it out all over again, if we wanted to check another textbox from a different button?

The answer to our two questions are, Not at all, and Yes we would.

To solve the problem, we'll chop that code from the button, and write a Sub for it. To write your own Sub, your cursor needs to be outside of the button code, and on a new line. But before the "End Class". So, on a new line outside the button code type the following:

Private Sub ErrorCheck( )

When you've typed that, hit the enter key on your keyboard. Visual Basic will add the End Sub for you. The name "ErrorCheck" is entirely our own, and we could have called it almost anything we liked. But it's better to stick to something descriptive.

Your code window will then look like this one:

```
Private Sub Button1_Click(ByVal sender As System.Object, _
                          ByVal e As System.EventArgs) _
                          Handles Button1.Click

    Dim TextBoxData As String

    TextBoxData = Trim(TextBox1.Text)

    If TextBoxData = "" Then
        MsgBox("Please Enter your First Name")
    End If

End Sub

Private Sub ErrorCheck()
    |
End Sub
```

Now, cut and paste the code from your button between these two lines, where the cursor is in the image above.

You have just created your own Subroutine.

But the Sub is not doing much good where it is. We need a way to use that code. To use our new Sub, we have to tell Visual Basic to execute the code. We do that simply by referring to the Sub by name.

So click inside the button code, just before the **End Sub** of the button. Type the following:

Call ErrorCheck( )

You don't have to use the "Call" word. Try taking that word out altogether, and then testing the programme again. The programme should run exactly the same. But using the "Call" word makes your code easier to read, and tells you that you are executing your own Subroutine on this line.

Your coding window should now look like this:

```
Private Sub Button1_Click(ByVal sender As System.Object, _
                          ByVal e As System.EventArgs) _
                          Handles Button1.Click

    Call ErrorCheck()

End Sub

Private Sub ErrorCheck()

    Dim TextBoxData As String

    TextBoxData = Trim(TextBox1.Text)

    If TextBoxData = "" Then
        MsgBox("Please Enter your First Name")
    End If

End Sub
```

Run your programme and test it out. You should get the Message Box again, when nothing is in the Textbox.

Add another button to your form. Type **Call ErrorCheck()** as the code for it. Run your programme again, and then click your new button. You should get the Message box popping up, when nothing is entered into the Textbox.

The point about this is that you have created your own code segment. You can use this segment of code whenever you like, just by referring to it by name. Of course, you can have your code check more than one Textbox. You can check as many as you like. And for whatever you like. You can include the code you wrote to check for a correct email address, as well. But all that error checking code is no longer clogging up your button code.

Parameters

Add two more textboxes to your form. Set the Name property of the first Textbox to txtFirstNumber. Set the Name property of the second Textbox to txtSecondNumber. Add a new button to your Form and set the Text property to "Get Answer". The two text boxes are for numbers. We'll write code to add the two numbers together, but in our own Sub. When the button is clicked, a Message Box will pop up revealing the answer to the sum of the numbers in the textboxes.

Double click your button to bring up the code window. Click outside of the button code, just after End Sub, but before End Class. Type the following code:

```
Private Sub AddNumbers( )

        Dim first As Integer
        Dim second As Integer
        Dim answer As Integer

        first = Val(txtFirstNumber.Text)
        second = Val(txtSecondNumber.Text)

        answer = first + second

        MsgBox("The total is " & answer)

End Sub
```

We have created a Sub to add together the two numbers from the Textboxes. The code is very simple, and you should be able to follow it without any problems.

Now add this line to the code for your "Get Answer" button:

```
Call AddNumbers( )
```

Run your programme. Type a number in each of the two Textboxes, and click your button to make sure your programme works. Stop the programme and return to the design environment.

Chop the two lines of code for the Textboxes from the Sub and put them into the button. Your two sections of code should now look like this:

```
Private Sub btnAnswer_Click(ByVal sender As System.Object, _
                            ByVal e As System.EventArgs) _
                            Handles btnAnswer.Click

    Dim first As Integer
    Dim second As Integer

    first = Val(txtFirstNumber.Text)
    second = Val(txtSecondNumber.Text)

    Call AddNumbers()

End Sub

Private Sub AddNumbers()
    Dim answer As Integer

    answer = first + second

    MsgBox("The total is " & answer)
End Sub
```

The reason why there are two wiggly lines under **first** and **Second** is that the AddNumbers Sub knows nothing about these two variables. We've only declared one variable inside the Subroutine – **answer**. To get rid of the wiggly lines, we can set up something called a Parameter. Well, two parameters.

To put it simply, a Parameter is a value that we want to pass from one code section to another. What we want to do is to pass the values we gathered from our button code and hand them over to our **AddNumbers** Sub. So how do we do that?

Change the **Private Sub AddNumbers()** line to this:

Private Sub AddNumbers(first As Integer, second As Integer)

When you press your return key, VB changes the part in round brackets to this:

(ByVal first As Integer, ByVal second As Integer)

It's added a curious term – **ByVal**. We'll explain what that is in a moment. For now, concentrate on the Parameters. The parameters are what we want to hand to our Subroutine. We want to hand an integer variable called **first**, and an integer variable called **second**. Whatever values are currently stored in these two variables will be handed to our Sub

But we need to change our Calling line, the one from our button. This line now has a wiggly line under it, signifying that something is wrong. Remember, it was this:

Call AddNumbers( )

If you hold your mouse over the AddNumbers() you might see this tip appear:

```
Call AddNumbers()
```
Argument not specified for parameter 'second' of 'Private Sub AddNumbers(first As Integer, second As Integer)'.

What this is telling you is that your **AddNumbers** Sub takes some Parameters (They are called Arguments when you pass them, and Parameters when they are received. Because this is somewhat confusing, we'll stick to calling them Parameters.) In other words, you don't have any option: if you want to call this Sub, you have to add values for the parameters you set up.

So change your Calling line to this

Call AddNumbers(first, second)

(If the **second** inside your Sub has changed to **Second( )**. Delete the round brackets.)

Again, we use the parentheses. And in between the parentheses are our two variables. They don't have to have the same names. Whatever you call your variables in the **AddNumbers** Sub does not have to be the same names as the calling line. The variable names can be entirely different. But the values in the variables get passed in the order you set them up. In our case the value in the variable **first** will get passed to the first variable in our **AddNumbers** Sub; the value in the variable **second** will get passed to the next variable we set up in our **AddNumbers** Sub.

Run your programme and check that it is working properly, now that you have changed the calling line. When you are done, change the variable names for your **AddNumbers** Sub to this:

> **Private Sub AddNumbers(ByVal first2 As Integer, ByVal second2 As Integer)**
>
> **Dim answer As Integer**
>
> **answer = first2 + second2**
>
> **MsgBox "The total is " & answer**
>
> **End Sub**

Here, we have changed the names in our Sub. The variable names are now different from the ones in the calling line. They are now **first2** and **second2**. But will it still work? Test your programme out and check it. You should find that it does.

So to sum up, we can use a Sub to create our own code segment. We use this Sub just by referring to it by name. If we want to pass any values to our Sub, we can set up Parameters in between the parentheses.

Exercise
Create a Sub to check a Textbox for a valid email address, or adapt the one you already have. Pass whatever is entered in the Textbox to a variable called "email". Pass the value from this variable to your Sub by using a Parameter. When a button is clicked, a message box should pop up telling the user if the email address was wrong.

ByVal and ByRef

The word ByVal is short for "By Value". What it means is that you are passing a copy of a variable to your Subroutine. You can make changes to the copy and the original will not be altered.

ByRef is the alternative. This is short for By Reference. This means that you are not handing over a copy of the original variable but **pointing** to the original variable. Let's see a coding example.

Add a new button your form. Double click the button and add the following code:

Dim Number1 As Integer

Number1 = 10
Call IncrementVariable(Number1)

MsgBox(Number1)

You'll get a wiggly line under **IncrementVariable(Number1)**. To get rid of it, add the following Subroutine to your code:

Private Sub IncrementVariable(ByVal Number1 As Integer)
Number1 = Number1 + 1
End Sub

When you're done, run the programme and click your new button. What answer was displayed in the message box?

It should have been 10. But hold on. Didn't we increment the variable Number1 with this line?

Number1 = Number1 + 1

So **Number1** started out having a value of 10. After our Sub got called, we added 1 to **Number1**. So we should have 11 in the message box, right?
The reason **Number1** didn't get incremented was because we specified ByVal in the Sub:

ByVal Number1 As Integer

This means that only a copy of the original variable got passed over. When we incremented the variable, only the copy got 1 added to it. The original stayed the same – 10.

Change the parameter to this:

ByRef Number1 As Integer

Run your programme again. Click the button and see what happens.

This time, you should see 11 displayed in the message box. The variable has now been incremented!

It was incremented because we used ByRef. We're referencing the original variable. So when we add 1 to it, the original will change.

The default is ByVal – which means a copy of the original variable. If you need to refer to the original variable, use ByRef.

Functions

A function is more or less the same thing as a Sub - a segment of code you create yourself, and that can be used whenever you want it. The difference is that a Function returns a value, while a Sub doesn't. When you Called a Sub you did this

Call AddNumbers(first, second)

Visual Basic will go off and execute that code for you, and then drop down to the next line. The Sub **AddNumbers** is not a value, it's not equal to anything. It's not like a normal variable where you assign something to it. It's just the name of your Subroutine.

A Function is different. It is a value, will be equal to something, and you do have to assign a value to it. You create a Function in the same way you did a Sub, but this time your code will be like this:

Private Function ErrorCheck ( ) As Boolean

End Function

First, we've changed the word "Sub" to "Function"; second we've added "As" something, in this case "As Boolean". The name we called our Function is ErrorCheck, and ErrorCheck is now just like a variable. And just like a variable, we use one of the Types. We can use "As Integer", "As Long", "As Double", "As String", or any of the variable types.

Let's write some code, and try an example.

Add a new button and a textbox to your form. Change the name of the textbox to txtFunction. Double click your button and add the following code to it (add it after the **End Sub** of the button, but before the **End Class**):

```
Private Function CheckError ( ) As Boolean

    Dim TextBoxData As String

    TextBoxData = Trim(txtFunction.Text)

    If TextBoxData = "" Then
            MsgBox("Blank Text Box detected")
            CheckError = True
    End If
End Function
```

This is almost the same code from our Sub called ErrorCheck. The difference is the one added line - **CheckError = True**. Remember that CheckError is now like a variable. In this case it was a Boolean variable. So if there's nothing in the Textbox, we have set **CheckError** to True.

Again, this code is not doing much good by itself. We need a way to use it. This time, because we've set up a Function, we have to assign the value of the function to a variable. Like this:

> **Dim IsError As Boolean**
>
> **IsError = CheckError()**

Here, we are saying "Run the function called **CheckError**. When you have finished, assign the value of **CheckError** to the variable called **IsError**".

Once that code is executed we can then use the variable **IsError** and test its value. If it's true, then we know that the user did not enter anything into the Textbox; if it's False, then we know that they did. The benefit of using a Function to check for our errors is that we can halt the programme if **IsError = True**. Like this:

> **If IsError = True then**
> > **Exit Sub**
> **End If**

So double click your button and add the following:

> **Dim IsError As Boolean**
>
> **IsError = CheckError ()**
>
> **If IsError = True then**
> > Exit Sub
> **Else**
> > **MsgBox("IsError = False")**
> **End If**

Run your programme again. Click the button when the textbox is blank, and see what happens. Then enter some text into the textbox, and click your button again.

To sum up, then. A function will return a value. You put this value into the name of your Function. You then assign the value of the Function to a variable. You can then test the variable to see what's in it.

Let's set up another Function, as a further example. This time we'll add some Parameters to our Function. You use the Parameters in exactly the same way as you did for a Sub.

- So add another button to your Form
- Set its Text property to "Get Function Answer"
- Add two Textboxes to your Form
- Set the Name Property of the first Textbox to txtNumber1
- Set the Name Property of the second Textbox to txtNumber2

- Set up the following Function in your code window (The first line has been spread over two lines here. You can keep yours on one line.)

Private Function AddTwoNumbers(ByVal first As Integer, _
$$\text{ByVal second As Integer) As Integer}$$

Dim answer As Integer
answer = first + second
AddTwoNumbers = answer

End Function

So the name of this Function is **AddTwoNumbers**, and we've set it up to return an Integer value. The two parameters we're passing in are also Integers. The code inside the Function simply adds up whatever is inside the variables **first** and **second**. The result is passed to another variable, **answer**. We then pass whatever is inside **answer** to the name of our Function. So **AddTwoNumbers** will be equal to whatever is in the variable **answer**.

Instead of saying **AddTwoNumbers = answer** you can use the **Return** keyword. You use it like this:

Return answer

The result is the same: the value inside the variable answer is now the value of the function.

Open up the code for your "Get Answer" button, and add the following code to it:

Dim first As Integer
Dim second As Integer
Dim result As Integer

first = Val(txtNumber1.Text)
second = Val(txtNumber2.Text)

result = AddTwoNumbers(first, second)

If result = 0 Then
      MsgBox("Please try again ")
Else
      MsgBox("The answer is " & result)
End If

So we're telling Visual Basic to execute our Function on this line:

result = AddTwoNumbers(first, second)

We're saying, "Run the Function called **AddTwoNumbers.** Hand it the values from the two variables. When you've finished running the function, pass whatever the value of **AddTwoNumbers** is to the variable called **result**."

The next few lines are just testing what is inside the variable **result**. Remember: the variable **result** will hold whatever the value of **AddTwoNumbers** was.

When you've finished typing your code, run your programme and test it out. Type a number in the first text box, and one in the other. Then click the "Get Function Answer" button. Try typing two zeros into the textboxes and see what happens.

Setting up and using functions can be quite tricky at first, but it's well worth your while persevering: they can vastly improve your coding skills.

Standard Modules

The Subs and Functions worked perfectly well where they were – inside the two lines "**Public Class** Form1" and "**End Class**". If you tried to put them on a line underneath **End Class** you would get lots of blue wiggly lines under your code.

That's because the code all belongs to Form1. But it doesn't have to. In fact, it's better to separate all your Functions and Subs and put them somewhere else – in something called a Module. We'll explore the Standard Module, and see how to move our Functions and Subs outside of Form1. That way, we can use them in other projects.

So start a new project. Add a button to you new form. To add a Module to your project in version 2008, click **Project** from the menu bar. From the menu, click on "Add Module":

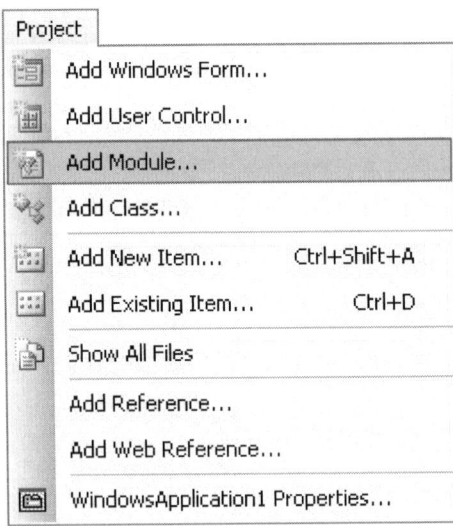

In VB .NET Express version 2010, just click Project > Add New Item.
When you click "Add Module" (or Add New Item), you'll see something like this dialogue box popping up (2008 version of the software):

Or this one, in the 2010 edition:

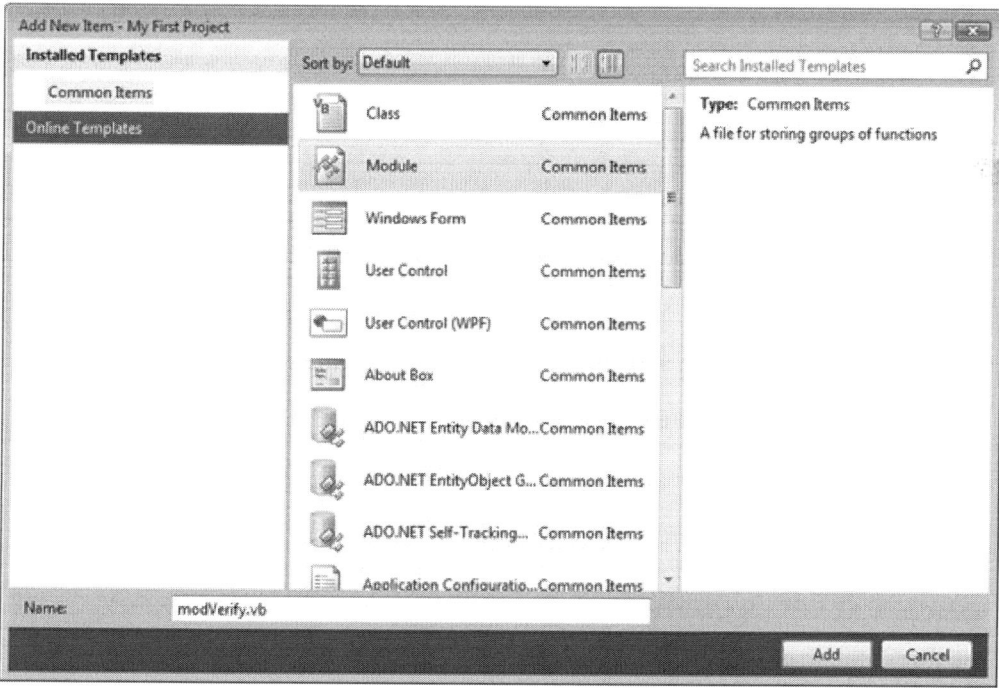

Select **Module** from the Templates window. Type a name for your new module - **modVerify.vb**. When you've typed a name, click the Open button.

You should see a blank window, with this code in it:

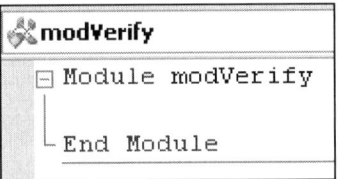

If you take a look at the Solutions Explorer on the right, you should see that your new module is listed:

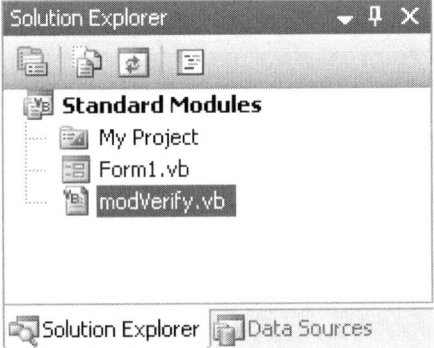

In between Module modVerify and End module, type the following Subroutine:

Private Sub AddNumbers(ByVal num1 As Integer)

Dim answer As Integer

answer = num1 + 10
MsgBox(answer)

End Sub

Your coding window should now look like this:

```
modVerify

   Module modVerify

       Private Sub AddNumbers(ByVal num1 As Integer)
           Dim answer As Integer

           answer = num1 + 10
           MsgBox(answer)

       End Sub

   End Module
```

Now click back on your form and double click the button you added. This will bring up the code window for the Form, and the cursor will be flashing inside of the button code.

Add the following code for your button:

Call AddNumbers(10)

When you press the return key, you'll see a blue wiggly line under the Sub name. If you hold your mouse over AddNumbers, you might see this:

```
Private Sub Button1_Click(ByVal sender As System.Object, _
                          ByVal e As System.EventArgs) _
                                Handles Button1.Click


      Call AddNumbers(10)
            Name 'AddNumbers' is not declared.
End Sub
```

What VB is saying is that it can't see your new Subroutine from the inside of the button code. It thinks you haven't got a Sub called AddNumbers. The reason it can't see it is we made the Sub **Private**. Only code inside of the modVerify Module can see a Private Sub. If you want the Sub or Function to be available to all the code in your project, including the button, you have to make then Public. This involves nothing more than changing the word **Private** to **Public**. Amend your Sub to this:

```
Public Sub AddNumbers(ByVal num1 As Integer)
      Dim answer As Integer

      answer = num1 + 10
      MsgBox(answer)

End Sub
```

When you make the change from **Private** to **Public**, the blue wiggly line should disappear from the Button code

Run your programme and test it out. Click your Button. You should get a message box saying "20".

We'll now add a Function to our new Module.

When you have your new Module displayed, type in the following Function:

Public Function VerifyPostcode(ByVal postcode As String) As String

postcode = StrConv(postcode, VbStrConv.UpperCase)

Return postcode
End Function

When you're finished, your coding window should look like this:

```
Module modVerify
  Public Sub AddNumbers(ByVal num1 As Integer)
      Dim answer As Integer

      answer = num1 + 10
      MsgBox(answer)

  End Sub

  Public Function VerifyPostcode(ByVal postcode As String) As String

      postcode = StrConv(postcode, VbStrConv.UpperCase)

      Return postcode

  End Function


  End Module
```

All the function does is to check a Postcode to see if the letters in it are all in capitals. That's because, quite often, people will enter a postcode as this:

ts1 4jh

What you want is a Postcode that reads:

TS1 4JH

The new function will convert a postcode handed to it, and make sure the letters are all capitals.

The inbuilt function that does the converting is worth exploring. It's this:

StrConv( )

This is short for String Conversion. In between the round brackets, VB needs you to put two things: the string you want to convert, and what sort of conversion you want. As soon as you type a comma after the string you want to convert, VB pops up a box of available conversion types:

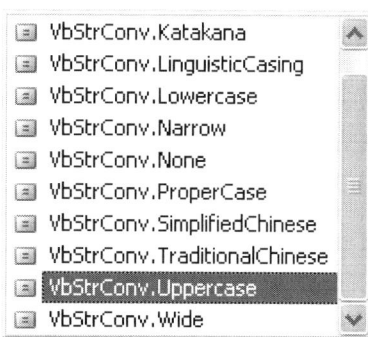

```
postcode = StrConv(postcode,
```

A lot on the list are rather baffling. But the one we used was the UpperCase one. Simply double click an item to add it to your code. This gave us the following:

StrConv(postcode, VbStrConv.UpperCase)

The function will then convert all the letters in **postcode** to capitals.

Another useful one on the list is **ProperCase**. What this will do is take a string and convert all the letters of the first word (or words) to capitals. This is useful for addresses. So if somebody entered this as an address:

49 falkland street

The **VbStrConv.ProperCase** item would convert it to this:

49 Falkland Street

But back to our code.

Select your Form again. Then add a new Button, and a Textbox to it. Change the Text property of the Textbox to **ts1 4jh**. Double click the button, and add the following code for it:

Dim CheckPostcode As String
Dim ConvertPostcode As String

CheckPostcode = Trim(TextBox1.Text)

ConvertPostcode = VerifyPostcode(CheckPostcode)

TextBox1.Text = ConvertPostcode

The first thing we do is get the Text from the textbox. This is passed to a variable called CheckPostcode. The next line calls our new function. We hand it the postcode we got from the textbox:

ConvertPostcode = VerifyPostcode(CheckPostcode)

When our function has finished the conversion, it will hand back (Return) the result and put it in the variable ConvertPostcode. This is then placed back inside the textbox.

Run your programme, and click the new button. You should find that the letters in the postcode are converted to capitals.

The point about creating a Module to house all your Subs and Functions is that they are in a separate file. You could write more Subs and Functions for your Module, ones that validate text coming from a textbox (an email checker, for example, or one that uses the ProperCase string conversion). You would then have all this code in one file that you could add to totally different projects. If the Subs and Functions were in the same code as the Form, you would have to import the whole Form before you could use the very useful Subs and Functions you created.

But that's enough about Modules. We'll move on.

Events

An event is something that happens. Your birthday is an event. So is Christmas. An event in programming terminology is when something special happens. These events are so special that they are built in to the programming language. VB.NET has numerous Events that you can write code for. And we're going to explore some of them in this section.

We'll start with all that mysterious code for the Button's Click Event.

The Click Event

Buttons have the ability to be clicked on. When you click a button, the event that is fired is the Click Event. If you were to add a new button to a form, and then double clicked it, you would see the following code stub:

Private Sub Button1_Click(ByVal sender As System.Object, _
ByVal e As System.EventArgs) _
Handles Button1.Click

End Sub

This is a Private Subroutine. The name of the Sub is Button1_Click. The Event itself is at the end: Button1.Click. The Handles word means that this Subroutine can Handle the Click Event of Button1. Without the arguments in the round brackets, the code is this:

Private Sub Button1_Click( ) Handles Button1.Click

You can have this Button1_Click Sub Handle other things, too. It can Handle the Click Event of other Buttons, for example. Try this.

Start a New project. Give it the name it Events. When your new Form appears, add two Buttons to it. Double click Button1 to bring up the code. At the end of the first line for the Button, add this:

Handles Button1.Click, Button2.Click

Add a message box as the code for the Button. Your code window might then look like this:

```
Private Sub Button1_Click(ByVal sender As System.Object, _
                      ByVal e As System.EventArgs) _
                          Handles Button1.Click, Button2.Click

    MsgBox("I can handle two buttons!")

End Sub
```

Run your programme, and then click both of the buttons in turn. The same message box appears, regardless of which one you clicked.

The reason it did so was because the Events that the **Button1.Click** Subroutine can **Handle** are at the end: the Events for Button1.Click **AND** Button2.Click.

You can add as many Events as you want on the End. As long as the Subroutine can Handle them, the Event will happen. For example, you could create two more buttons, and then add the Click Event on the end of the first button:

Handles Button1.Click, Button2.Click, Button3.Click, Button4.Click,

When you click any of the four buttons, the code inside of the **Button1_Click** Subroutine will fire.

However, if you double clicked button2 to try to bring up its coding window, you'd find that the cursor is flashing inside of the code for **Button1_Click**. Because you've attached the Click Event of button2 to the Button1 Subroutine, you can't have a separate Click Event just for Button2. This Click Event is Handled By the Subroutine called **Button1_Click**.

The arguments for a Buttons click event, the ones from the round brackets, are these two:

ByVal sender As System.Object, ByVal e As System.EventArgs

This sets up two variables: one called **sender** and one called **e**. Instead of sender being an integer or string variable, the type of variable set up for sender is System.Object. This stores a reference to a control (which button was clicked, for example).

For the **e** variable, this is holding an object, too – information about the event. For a button, this information might be which Mouse Button was clicked or where the mouse pointer was on the screen.

But because this is the Click Event, there's not much more information available: either the button was clicked or it wasn't.

But you can use other Events available to the button. One of these is the MouseDown Event. The information for the event would be which button was clicked, where the mouse pointer was when the mouse button was held down, and something called Delta (a count of how many notches have been rotated on a mouse wheel).

Let's explore the MouseDown Event.

MouseDown

The MouseDown event is available to many controls on the form. A Form can detect when the mouse was held down on it; a textbox can detect when the mouse was held down inside of it; and a Button can detect which mouse button was held down to do the clicking.

We'll see how it all works right now.

First, delete all but one of the buttons on your form. (You can right click on a control to delete it.) Go back to your coding window, and delete any code for the button on your form. Delete any Handles code except for Handles Button1.Click. Your coding window should look something like this one:

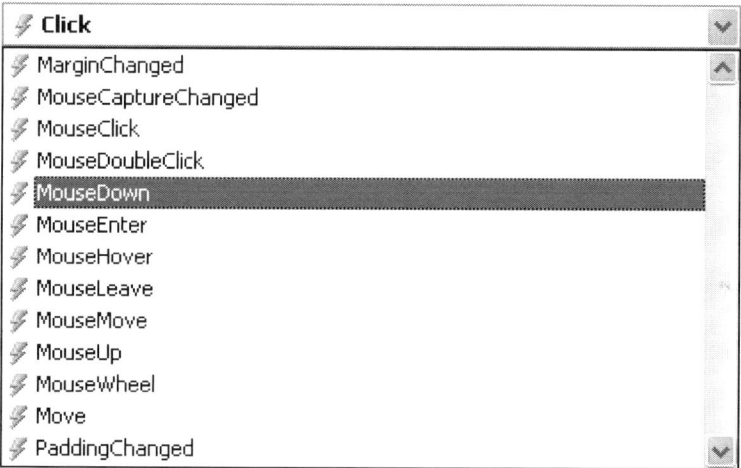

```
Button1                          Click

Public Class Form1

    Private Sub Button1_Click(ByVal sender As System.Object, _
                              ByVal e As System.EventArgs) _
                         Handles Button1.Click


    End Sub
End Class
```

Right at the top of the code window, it says Button1 and **Click**. The lightning bolt next to Click signifies that it is an Event. If you click the drop down box, you'll see a list of other available events:

```
Click

   MarginChanged
   MouseCaptureChanged
   MouseClick
   MouseDoubleClick
   MouseDown
   MouseEnter
   MouseHover
   MouseLeave
   MouseMove
   MouseUp
   MouseWheel
   Move
   PaddingChanged
```

Scroll down and find the MouseDown event, as in the image above. When you click on it, a new code stub appears. This one (it has been formatted so that the first line is spread over three lines):

```
Private Sub Button1_MouseDown(ByVal sender As Object, _
                    ByVal e As System.Windows.Forms.MouseEventArgs) _
                         Handles Button1.MouseDown

End Sub
```

This is a Private Subroutine called Button1_MouseDown. Notice that it **Handles** the Button1 MouseDown event, and not Button1.Click.

In between the round brackets of the Subroutine, we still have **ByVal sender as Object**. But we have a new argument now:

ByVal e As System.Windows.Forms.MouseEventArgs

The name of the variable is still **e**. But the type of Object being stored inside of the e variable is different:

System.Windows.Forms.MouseEventArgs

The bit on the end of all that is what we're interested in: **MouseEventArgs**. This stands for Mouse Events Arguments. What is being stored inside of the e variable is information about the Mouse Event: Did you click a button, if so which one?

The only thing you need to do to detect which button was pressed is to access a property of the **e** variable. Let's see how to do that.

Inside of the Button1_MouseDown Subroutine, type the following code:

If e.Button = Windows.Forms.MouseButtons.Right Then
             MsgBox("Right Button Clicked")
End If

As soon as you type the letter "e", you'll see this pop up box:

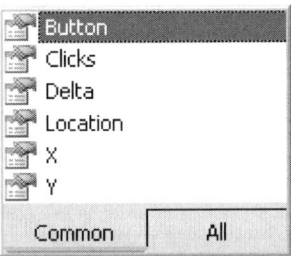

To detect which button was clicked, you need the first Property on the list: **Button**. Double click this property to add it to your code. Then after you typed the equals sign, another pop up list appears. This one:

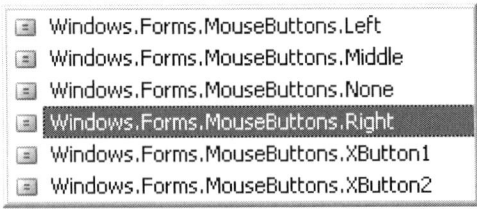

This is a list of available buttons that VB can detect. Left and Right are the ones you'll use most often.

When you've added the If Statement, your coding window should look something like this:

```
Private Sub Button1_MouseDown(ByVal sender As Object, _
                       ByVal e As System.Windows.Forms.MouseEventArgs) _
                       Handles Button1.MouseDown

   If e.Button = Windows.Forms.MouseButtons.Right Then
        MsgBox("Right button clicked")
   End If

End Sub
```

When you're finished writing your code, run your programme. Click the button with your Left mouse button and nothing will happen. Click it with the Right mouse button and you should see the message box display.

Stop your programme. When you are returned to the coding environment (Press F7 if you can't see your code), click the down arrow of Button1 at the top of the code. You'll see a drop down box like this:

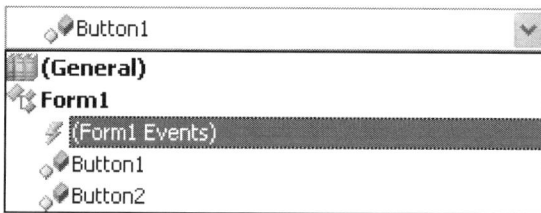

Select the one highlighted in the image, "Form1 Events". In the Events box to the right, select MouseDown from the list of available events. A new code stub will appear:

```
Private Sub Form1_MouseDown(ByVal sender As Object, _
                       ByVal e As System.Windows.Forms.MouseEventArgs) _
                       Handles Me.MouseDown
   |
End Sub
```

This time, we have a Private Subroutine called Form1_MouseDown. The two arguments are exactly the same as before. The difference is that now this code Handles the MouseDown event for something called **Me**. (This is an object that refers to the code for Public Class Form1.)

The important thing to bear in mind is that we now have a way to detect when a mouse button was clicked on the form itself.

Add the following code inside of Form1_MouseDown:

> **If e.Button = Windows.Forms.MouseButtons.Right Then**
> **MsgBox("You clicked on the Form")**
> **End If**

The only thing that has changed is the Message Box! The If Statement is exactly the same. Run your programme and test it out. Click anywhere on your Form, and you should see the new message box. However, if you right click on the button, you'll get the old message box.

Although the button is on the Form, this is considered a separate control from the Form itself. So it has its own events.

You can detect where on the Form the mouse was when the right mouse button was click. Amend your code for Form1_MouseDown. Change it to this:

```
Dim xPos As Integer
Dim yPos As Integer

If e.Button = Windows.Forms.MouseButtons.Right Then
        xPos = e.X
        yPos = e.Y
        MsgBox("The X Position is " & xPos & " The Y Position is " & yPos)
End If
```

First, we're setting up two integer variable, xPos and yPos. After that we have the same If Statement as before:

```
If e.Button = Windows.Forms.MouseButtons.Right Then

End If
```

Inside of the If Statement, we're using the X and Y properties of the **e** variable:

```
xPos = e.X
yPos = e.Y
```

The X property returns how far across, from left to right, the mouse is; the Y property returns how far down, from top to bottom, the mouse is. These values are assigned to our two variables. The result is displayed in a message box.

When you've wrote the code, run your programme and test it out. Right click anywhere on your form. The new message box should display, telling you where the mouse was when the right button was held down.

Click near the top of the form and you'll see the Y position number go down in value; Click near the bottom of the form and you'll see it go up in value. The very top of the form (or a control) has a Y value of zero.

Click from left to right and you'll see the X numbers go up in value. The very left edge of your form has an X value of zero.

The KeyDown Event

Another useful event is the KeyDown event. As its name suggests, this allows you to detect when a key on the keyboard was held down. This is useful for things like validating text in a textbox.

To test it out, add a textbox to your form. Change the Text property of the textbox to "Press F1 for help." Locate the TabIndex property in the Property Box, and change it to zero. (The Tab Index sets which control is selected when the Tab key is pressed on the keyboard. By specifying zero as the TabIndex property, you're saying that this should be the first control selected.)

Bring up your code window (you can either click the tab at the top, or press F7 on your keyboard), and click the arrow that reveals the list of controls and objects in your project:

Click on your textbox from the list to select it, as in the image above. Then click the arrow on the Event drop down box to reveal the events available to the textbox. Scroll down and select the KeyDown event:

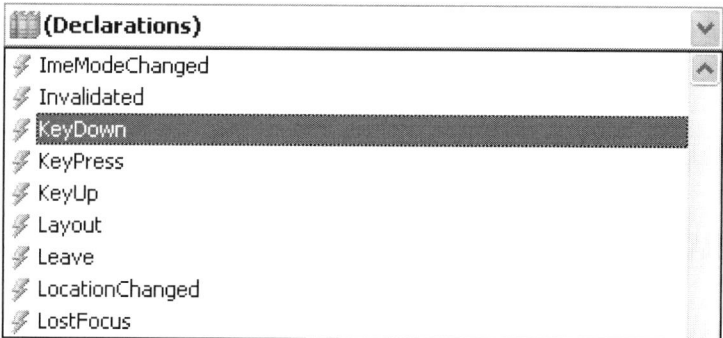

When you select the KeyDown event, a code stub appears:

```
Private Sub TextBox1_KeyDown(ByVal sender As Object, _
                    ByVal e As System.Windows.Forms.KeyEventArgs) _
                    Handles TextBox1.KeyDown

End Sub
```

The event that is being **Handled** is the KeyDown event of textbox1. Notice, though, that there is a slightly different argument in round brackets:

ByVal e As System.Windows.Forms.KeyEventArgs

Again, the variable name is still **e**. But now we have something called **KeyEventArgs** on the end. This means that the variable **e** will hold information about the Key on the keyboard that you're trying to detect.

To see what properties the **e** variable has available to it, add the following to your TextBox1_KeyDown code:

If e.KeyCode = Keys.F1 Then

TextBox1.Clear()
MsgBox("Help!!!")

End If

As soon as you type the full stop after the letter "e", you'll see this pop up box:

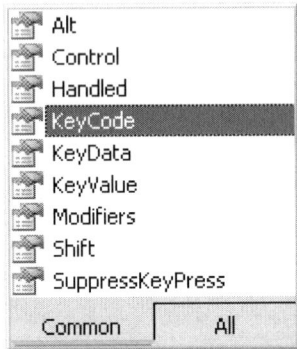

Double click a property to add it to your code. After you type an equals sign, you'll get another pop up box:

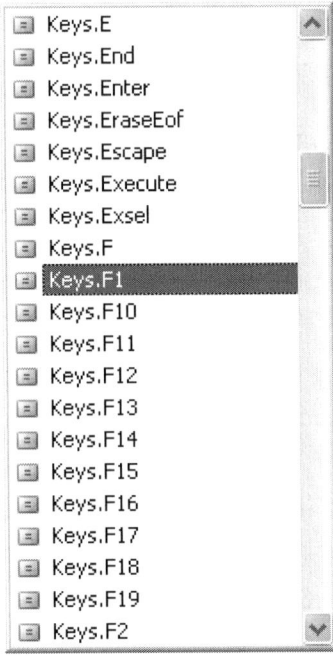

The list is a list of keys on your keyboard, some of which you'll have and others that you won't. Scroll down the list until you come to Keys.F1, and double click the item to add it to your code.

The code for the If Statement just clears the textbox and pops up a message.

Try your programme out. Press F1 (If you set TabIndex to zero then the text in the textbox should be selected, and the cursor already flashing. If it's not, click inside of the textbox and then press F1). When the F1 key is pressed, you should see the message box appear.

Another thing you can do is to record the keystrokes a user makes. For example:

Dim RecordText as String
RecordText = RecordText & Chr(e.KeyCode)
MsgBox(RecordText)

The Chr( ) function converts a KeyCode (which is an integer) to its keyboard character.

But try this exercise.

Exercise
There is an event available to the textbox called Leave. Add another textbox to your form, and write code so that the letters in a postcode are converted to uppercase when the user clicks from your first textbox and into your second textbox.

So your first textbox might read "ts1 4jh". When the user clicks inside textbox2, the text from textbox1 should change to "TS1 4JH". The code can be written in the Leave event of textbox1.

There are an awful lot of Events to explore, and we'll have a look at just one more.

The Form Load Event

An important event you'll want to write code for is the Form Load event. You might want to, for example, set the Enabled property of a control to False when a form loads. Or maybe blank out an item on your menu. You can do all this from the Form Load event.

Add another button to your form for this example, and we'll see how the Form Load event works.

Bring up your coding window, and select the Form1 Events from the drop down box:

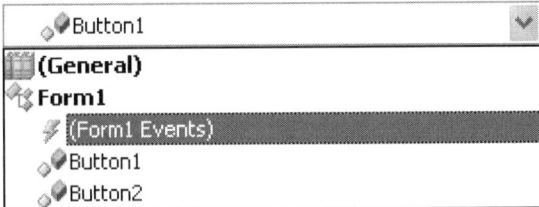

In the events drop down box, select Load:

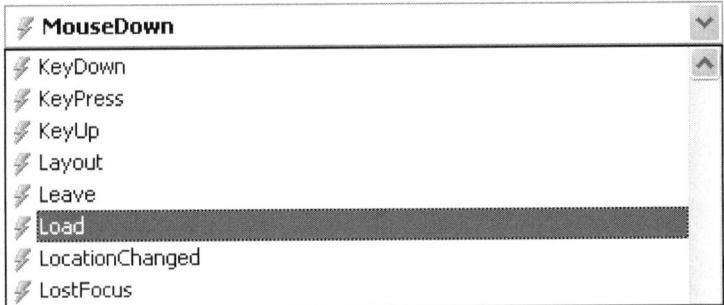

A code stub for the Form Load event is then added to your code. Type in the following as the code for the Load Event:

MsgBox("Form Load Event")

Run your programme. You should see the message box display <u>before</u> the Form loads.

To switch off your second Button before the Form loads, add this to your code:

Button2.Enabled = False

Run your programme again. You should see that button is no longer available for clicking on.

The Form Load event is a good place to set any values for your variables.

We'll now up the pace a bit. We'll have a look at just what Objects are, and how you can create your own.

VB.NET and Classes

VB.NET is an Object Oriented programming language. The Objects referred to are created from something called a Class. You've already used Classes throughout this course. But we'll now have a closer look at them.

Object Oriented Programming

The modern trend in programming languages is for code to be separated into chunks. When it's being used, each chunk of code (a chunk of code that opens text files, for example) is known as an Object. The code for the Object can then be reused whenever it is needed. Languages like C++ and Java are Object Oriented languages. Until Microsoft came out with VB.NET, the Visual Basic programming language was not OOP (object oriented programming). This time it is.

Object Oriented Programming has a steeper learning curve, and things like Encapsulation, Inheritance and Polymorphism have to be digested. We're not going quite that far in this beginner's course. But you should have a good, basic understanding of just what Objects are by the end of this section, and how to create your own Objects.

Classes and Objects

In VB.NET, a class is that chunk of code mentioned earlier. You've been using Classes all the time during this course. The Form you've started out with is a Class. If you look right at the top of the code window for a Form, you'll see:

Public Class Form1

The word "Public" means that other code can see it. **Form1** is the name of the Class
If you look at the bottom of the coding window, you'll see **End Class**, signifying the end of the code for the Class.

When you place a Button or a textbox on the Form, you're really adding it to the Form Class.

When you start the Form, VB does something called instantiation. This basically means that your Form is being turned into an Object, and all the things needed for the creation of the Form are being set up for you (Your controls are being added, variables are being set up an initialised, etc).

And that's the basic difference between a Class and an Object: A Class is the code itself; the code becomes an Object when you start using it.

The NET Framework

The NET Framework is something that Microsoft have invested a lot of time, effort and money into creating. It's big. Very big. The way that programming will be done on a Microsoft machine from now on is with NET. And not just on a Microsoft machine. There's something called ADO.NET which is used for creating web sites, and for manipulating databases. You can create applications for mobile phones and PDA's with NET. There is even a project in the making that will allow you to write a programme on a Windows machine that will then work on a computer NOT running Windows. All this is made possible with the NET Framework. But what is it?

The NET Framework is a whole lot of Classes (called Namespaces) and the technology to get those Classes to work. The main component is called the Common Language Runtime. A Runtime is the thing that gets your code to actually run on a computer. Previously, these Runtime Languages were machine or programming language specific. The Runtime that gets a Java programme to work, for example, is different to the one that gets a C programme to work. With NET, more than 15 different programming languages can use the Common Language Runtime. One of these languages is, of course Visual Basic NET. Another is C# (pronounce C Sharp). They can all use the Common Language Runtime because of something called the Intermediate Language. (This is a sort of translator for the various languages, and is too advanced to go into for us.)

Namespaces

A Namespace is a collection of Classes which are grouped together. The System.IO Namespace you met earlier groups together Classes that you use for Input and Output.

System.Windows.Forms is another Namespace you've met. In fact, you couldn't create your forms without this Namespace. But again, it is just a group of Classes huddling under the same umbrella.

System itself is a Namespace. It's a top-level Namespace. Think of it as the leader of a hierarchy. IO and Windows would be part of this hierarchy, just underneath the leader. Each subsequent group of Classes is subordinate to the one that came before it. For example Forms is a group of Classes available to Windows, just as Windows is a group of Classes available to System. A single form is a Class available to Forms:

System.Windows.Forms.Form

The dot notation is used to separate each group of Classes. A Button is also part of the Forms Class:

System.Windows.Forms.Button

As too is a Textbox:

System.Windows.Forms.TextBox

The leader of the hierarchy is still System, though. Think of it as an army. You'd have a Private who is subordinate to a Sergeant. The Sergeant would be subordinate to a Captain. And the Captain would be subordinate to a General. If the General wanted something done, he might ask the Captain to do it for him. The Captain would get the Sergeant to do it, and the Sergeant would then pick on a poor Private. So **Button** would be the Private, **Forms** would be the Sergeant, **Windows** would be the Captain, and **System** the General.

In other words, there is a chain of command in NET programming. And if you don't follow the chain of command, you're in trouble!

But you see this chain of command every time you type a full stop and a pop up box appears. When you're selecting an item from the list, you're selecting the next in the chain of command.

Take this code, for example:

Inherits System.Windows.Forms.Form

This means you don't have to keep typing the full chain of command every time you want to access a button on the form. This chain of command is inherited whenever you create a new VB.NET Form. There are plenty of times when a chain of command is not inherited though, and in that case you do have to type it all out. You did this when you referenced a StreamReader with:

System.IO.StreamReader

The IO Namespace is not inherited when you created a new Form, so you have to tell VB where it is in the hierarchy.

But that's not quite the end of the story. The reason you use all of these long Namespaces is to get at a Property or Method – the chaps that do all the actual work! When you type **Button1.Text = "Click Me"**, Text is a Property of Button1. Button belongs to Form, which belongs to Forms, which belongs to Windows … etc.

So whenever you access a Property or Method of a control, just remember that rather long chain of command.

Creating your own Classes

The big benefit of an Object Oriented Programming language is that you can create your own Objects. (It's an Object when you're using the code, remember, and a Class when you're not.)

We'll see how to do that now, as we create a very simple Class, and then turn that into an Object.

The Class we'll create is a very simple one, and is intended to show you the basic technique of setting up a class, then creating an object from it. The Class we'll create will convert the letters in a postcode to uppercase. There's already an inbuilt Class that does this. But we're writing our own so you can see how things work. We'll get the postcode from a textbox on a form. Off we go then.

- Start a new project
- Add a Textbox to your form, and leave it on the default Name, Textbox1
- Change the Text Property to ts1 4jh (make sure the letters are lowercase and not upper, because our object will convert it.)
- Add a Button to your form

Once you have a new form with a Textbox and a Button on it, you need to add a Class. This is quite easy. It's just like adding a Module. In fact, they look exactly the same!

- So from the VB menu bar, click on Project
- From the drop down menu, click **Add Class**
- You'll get this dialogue box popping up in version 2008:

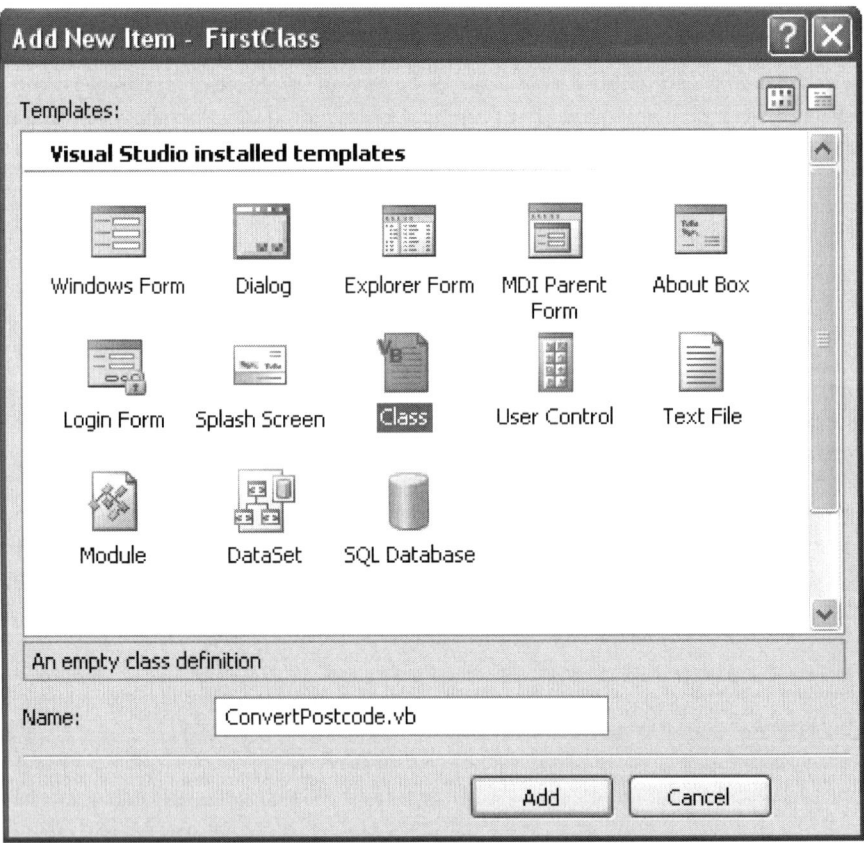

In version 2010, the dialogue box looks like this:

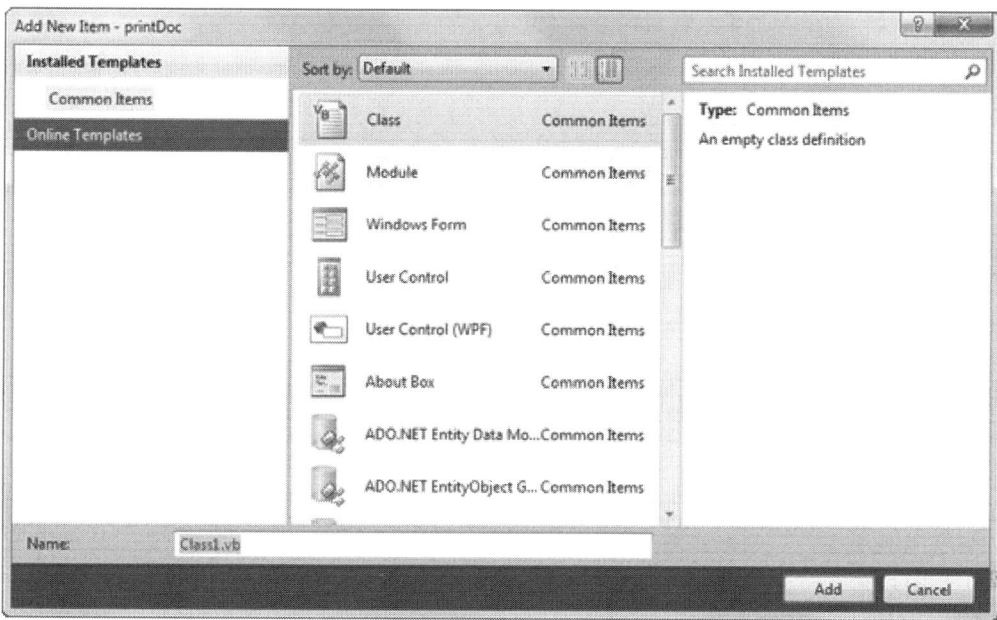

The Class Template will already be selected. The thing you need to change is the Name at the bottom. The default Name is Class1.vb. This is not terribly descriptive, and you'll have great problems working out what this class does, a few months down the line.

Change the Name from Class1.vb to **ConvertPostcode.vb**. Then click the Open button.

When the code window for the class opens up, it will look like this:

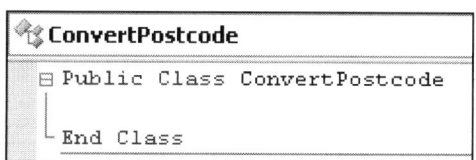

As you can see, there's not a great deal to look at! All we have is the Public Class … End Class code stub. The name of our Class is also there. But the code is in a separate window, and has a tab all to itself. It's this tab full of code that you reuse and turn into an object.

What we have to do now is add the code that does the work – converts our postcode. But we can't just write this:

Dim ConvertPostcode As String

ConvertPostcode = StrConv(TextBox1.Text, VbStrConv.UpperCase **)**
TextBox1.Text = ConvertPostcode

That would be all right for the button on our Form. But it's not all right for our Class. When you're designing a Class, your code has to go inside of things like Functions and Subs. You'll also see how to create your own properties for your objects.

When you set up a Function or Sub, you're actually creating Methods for your objects (A Method is code that actually does something, that performs an action. Converts a postcode in our case.) We'll see how to do that now.

Creating Methods in your Classes

A method created in a Class is nothing more than a Function or a Sub. You've seen how to do this in an earlier section. The process is the same. So add the following code to your Class:

Public Function DoConvert(ByVal postcode As String) As String

    Dim ConvertPostcode As String
    ConvertPostcode = StrConv(postcode, VbStrConv.UpperCase **)**
    DoConvert = ConvertPostcode

    End Function

When you've finished typing it all, your Class should look like this in the code window:

```
Public Class ConvertPostcode

    Public Function DoConvert(ByVal postcode As String) As String

        Dim ConvertPostcode As String
        ConvertPostcode = StrConv(postcode, VbStrConv.Uppercase)
        DoConvert = ConvertPostcode

    End Function

End Class
```

All we've done is to set up a Public (not private) function. We've given it the name "**DoConvert**". We've set it up to accept one parameter, a String variable called postcode. This is the value that will be handed to our function. The function itself has been set up as a String. This means that **DoConvert** will be just like a string variable that we can assign a value to.

The code itself you've met before. It uses the in-built StrConv function to do the actual job of converting the string to uppercase letters.

Now that we've set up a Method, let's see how to create an object from our Class, and put the Method to use.

Creating an Object from a Class

Our function is not much use until we can get it up and running. (Here, "Get it up and running" means create an object from our class.) To do that, double click the button on your Form, and add the following code to it:

Dim NewCode As String
Dim objConvertPostcode As ConvertPostcode

objConvertPostcode = New ConvertPostcode

NewCode = objConvertPostcode.DoConvert(TextBox1.Text)

TextBox1.Text = NewCode

The first line just sets up a new String variable called **NewCode**. Whatever is returned from our function will be stored inside of this variable.

The next line is where the action starts:

Dim objConvertPostcode As ConvertPostcode

The variable name **objConvertPostcode** is just something we made up ourselves. The "obj" prefix means Object, and this is for our benefit, to remind us that the type of data inside it holds an Object, rather than a plain old Integer or String.

After you type the word "As", then hit your spacebar, you'll see a popup box appear. If you type the letters "**conv**", you'll see the list automatically move down. The Class you created should be on that list, as in the next image:

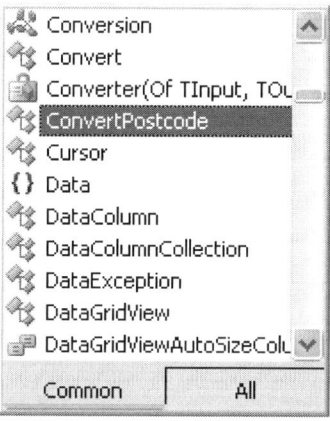

You can double click the name of your Class to add it to your code.

But what you're doing in this step is setting up a pointer to your Class. You're telling VB where the Class can be found, and then storing this inside of the variable called **objConvertPostcode**. If VB doesn't know where your Class is then it can't create an Object from it.

The next line of code is the one that creates a new object from your Class:

objConvertPostcode = New ConvertPostcode

You type the Name of your variable first, then an equals sign. To the right of the equals sign comes the word "**New**". This is what tells VB to create a New Object. And the class its creating the New Object from is the one called **ConvertPostcode**.

You can actually type all of that on the same line:

Dim objConvertPostcode As ConvertPostcode = New ConvertPostcode

This does two jobs: sets a pointer to where the Class is, and creates a new Object from the Class.

But there's reasons why you don't want to do it this way. One is that Objects take up space in memory. And you only really need to create them when they are needed. For example, what if the textbox was blank? You'd want to check for this and invite the user to try again. If you've written everything on one line, then you've already created the Object before the Textbox has been checked. Instead, you could do something like this:

If TextBox1.Text = "" Then

MsgBox "Please try again"
Exit Sub

Else
       objConvertPostcode = New ConvertPostcode
End If

Here's, the textbox is being checked first. If the user has left it blank then we bail out. If not, THEN we create an Object from our Class.

The next line in our code was this:

NewCode = objConvertPostcode.DoConvert(TextBox1.Text)

First, we type the name of the variable we want to store the result of our Method into. In our case, the one called **NewCode**. After the equals sign, we type the name of our Object variable:

objConvertPostcode

As soon as you type a full stop after your Object variable, you should see a popup box with the name of your new method on the list:

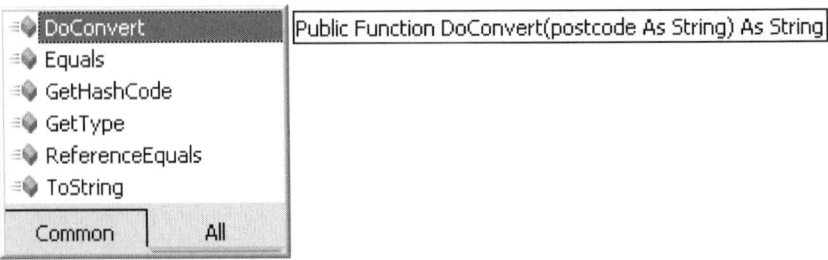

The image above shows you that the name of our Method "Do Convert" has been recognised by VB. (You can tell it's a Method because of the purple block next to it.) But notice the tool tip – it's the first line from our Function!

In between the round brackets, VB is telling us what type of data needs to be passed over to the Method – a String of text. The second "As String" tells you that the Method returns a value that needs to be stored somewhere.

So if you've set up a Method that returns a value (a Function) then you need to store it in a variable.

To get at the Method inside of your class, first type the name of your Object variable. Then type a full stop. Look for the name of your Method in the pop up list that appears.

The final line of the code just assigns the value returned from the Method back to the textbox:

TextBox1.Text = NewCode

Run your code and test it out. Click your Button and you should see the postcode change from "ts1 4jh" to "TS1 4JH".

Creating and using Methods that don't return a value

Your Methods do not have to return a value. In which case, you create a Sub and not a Function. Add the following code to your Class:

Public Sub DoMessageBox()

MsgBox("Conversion Complete")

End Sub

This is a Public Sub that doesn't do anything terribly useful. But it will illustrate how to write code to set up a Method that doesn't return a value. Here's what your coding window should look like:

```
Public Class ConvertPostcode

    Public Function DoConvert(ByVal postcode As String) As String

        Dim ConvertPostcode As String
        ConvertPostcode = StrConv(postcode, VbStrConv.Uppercase)
        DoConvert = ConvertPostcode

    End Function

    Public Sub DoMessageBox()

        MsgBox("Conversion Complete")

    End Sub

End Class
```

To run your new method, return to your Button code. You should have this, remember:

```
Private Sub Button1_Click(ByVal sender As System.Object, _
                          ByVal e As System.EventArgs) _
                          Handles Button1.Click

    Dim NewCode As String
    Dim objConvertPostcode As ConvertPostcode

    objConvertPostcode = New ConvertPostcode

    NewCode = objConvertPostcode.DoConvert(TextBox1.Text)

    TextBox1.Text = NewCode

End Sub
```

On a new line after **Textbox1.Text = NewCode**, type the following:

objConvertPostcode.DoMessageBox( )

After you type the name of your Object variable, then a full stop, you get the message box popping up. This time, your new Method is on the list:

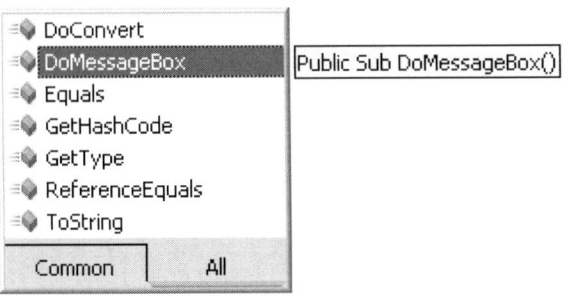

The tip next to the pop up box is telling you that the Method is a Sub, and that it therefore doesn't return a value. The Sub also has no parameters inside of the round brackets, so you don't have to hand anything to it.

You can double click the new Method to add it to your code. When you press the return key on your keyboard, VB adds a pair of round brackets to the end of the line.

So calling a Method that doesn't return a value is just like calling a Sub. The difference is that you need the name of your Object variable first. If we had set up the Sub inside of the Form1 code, we would have just done this to call it:

DoMessageBox( )

But because the Sub was inside of the Class, you first type the name of your Object variable:

objConvertPostcode.DoMessageBox( )

Run your code again. Click your button. You should see two things happen: one, the text in the textbox will change; and two, you should see the message box popping up confirming the change.

Creating your own Properties

You can add your own Properties to your Class. A Property, remember, is something that changes or sets a value. Examples are, setting the Text in a textbox, changing the background colour of a Form, and setting a Button to be **Enabled**.

You can **Get** values from a Property or **Set** them. So for a Textbox, you can **Set** the text to appear in the textbox, or you can Get what text is inside of the textbox. You use these same words, Get and Set, when you're creating your own Properties. An example might clear things up.

- Add a picture box control to your Form
- Set the **SizeMode** Property of the Picture box to **StretchImage**
- Click on the Image Property, and add the **planet.jpg** image from the files you downloaded at the start of this book
- Add two textboxes to the form. Change the Name of the first one to txtHeight, and the second one to txtWidth. Enter 300 as a the text for both textboxes
- Add two labels to the form. Set the Text of the first one to Height, and the second one to Width. Move them next to the textboxes
- Add a new button to your form. Set the Text property to "Change Height and Width"

What we'll do is to give our object the capability of setting a Height and Width property. When the object has done its work, the height and width of the picture box will change to the values from the textboxes. Off we go then.

Adding a Property to a Class

VB needs to know that you want to set up a Property for your Class. The way you do this is type "Public Property … End Property".

Access the code for your Class. Type a few lines of space between the End Sub of your DoMessageBox Method, and the line that reads "End Class". On a new line, type the following:

Public Property ChangeHeight( ) As Integer

ChangeHeight is the name of our property, and it's something we made up ourselves. After a pair of round brackets, you add the type of value that will be returned (Just like a function). Here, we want to return an Integer value.

When you press the return key after typing that line, VB finishes off the rest of the code stub for you:

Public Property ChangeHeight( ) As Integer
Get

End Get

Set(ByVal Value As Integer)

End Set
End Property

Before the code is explained, add a new variable right at the top of your code, just below "Public Class ConvertPostcode". Add this:

Private intHeight As Integer

The Private word means that only code inside of the Class can see this variable. You can't access this code directly from a button on a Form, for example.

The reason the variable is right at the top is so that other chunks of code can see and use it.

But your coding window should now look something like this next image:

```
Public Class ConvertPostcode

    Private intHeight As Integer

    Public Function DoConvert(ByVal postcode As String) As String

       Dim ConvertPostcode As String
       ConvertPostcode = StrConv(postcode, VbStrConv.Uppercase)
       DoConvert = ConvertPostcode

    End Function


    Public Sub DoMessageBox()

        MsgBox("Conversion Complete")

    End Sub

    Public Property ChangeHeight() As Integer

        Get

        End Get

        Set(ByVal Value As Integer)

        End Set

    End Property

End Class
```

Without the Get and Set parts, the Property stub is this:

Public Property PropertyName( ) As VariableType

End Property

The reason the Get and Set are there is so that you can **Set** a value for your property, and **Get** a value back out.

To Set a value, the code inside of Property is this:

Set(ByVal Value As Integer)

End Set

The **Set** word is followed by a pair of round brackets. Inside of the round brackets is **ByVal Value As Integer**. This is just like a Sub, when you hand over a value to it. The name of the variable, **Value**, is a default name. You can change this to anything you like. The type of variable, As Integer, is also a default. You don't have to pass numbers to your property. If you want your Property to handle text you might have something like this:

Set(ByVal MyText As String)

But you couldn't do this:

Set(ByVal Value As Integer, ByVal MyString As String)

In other words, you can't pass two values to your property. You can only pass one value.

But we want to pass a number to our property. For us, this value will come from the textbox on the form. Whatever number is inside of the textbox will get handed over to our Property.

Set (ByVal Value As Integer)

But we need to use this value being handed over. We can assign it to that variable we set up at the top of the Class. So add this to your code (The new line is in bold):

```
Set( ByVal Value As Integer )
        intHeight = Value
End Set
```

Whenever our Property is called into action, we're setting a Value, and then handing that value to a variable called **intHeight**. This is known as Writing to a Property.

To read from a Property, you use **Get**. This will Get a value back out of your Property. The code stub is this:

Get

End Get

You don't need any round brackets for the Get part. You're just fetching something to be read.

Add the line in bold text to your **Get** statement.

```
Get
        ChangeHeight = intHeight
End Get
```

All you're doing here is returning a value, just like you do with a function. You're handing a value to whatever name you called your property. We called ours ChangeHeight. It's an Integer. So we can pass whatever value was stored inside of intHeight over to the variable called **ChangeHeight**:

ChangeHeight = intHeight

You can also use the **Return** keyword. Like this:

```
Get
        Return intHeight
End Get
```

Let's see how to use our new Property. (It's not a terribly useful property, by the way. A Picture box already has a Height and Width property that you can use. So ours is a bit redundant. But we're keeping it simple so that you can understand how to create your own properties. And it's not a good idea to put this Property into the code for your ConvertPostcode Class. After all, what has the height and width of a picture box got to do with postcodes? But we've added it here just for convenience sake.)

Using your new Property

The property is not much good where it is. You need to be able to call it into action. The way you do that is to create a new object from the Class, and then read and write to your property.

So double click the new button you added to your form. Add the following code to it:

Dim objAlterPicBox As ConvertPostcode
Dim NewHeight As Integer

objAlterPicBox = New ConvertPostcode

Two of the lines you've already met: the one that creates a pointer to a variable (the first line), and the one that creates a new Object from your Class (the third line). The second line just sets up a variable called **NewHeight**.

(Notice that we've given the object a different name to last time. It's now called **objAlterPicBox**.)

To pass a value to your new Property (the Set part), add this line:

objAlterPicBox.ChangeHeight = Val(txtHeight.Text)

As soon as you type the name of your object variable, then a full stop, you'll see the pop up box appear:

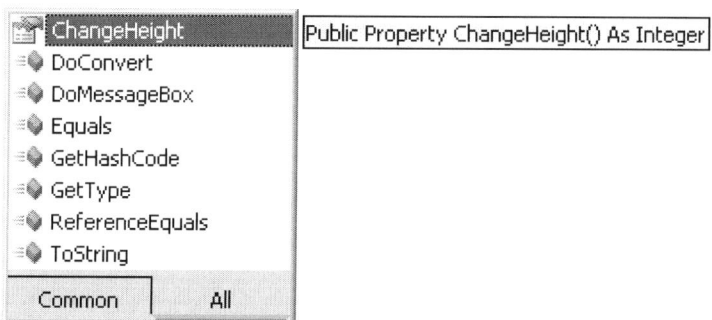

You should see your new Property on the list – **ChangeHeight**. (You can tell it's a Property because the symbol next to it is a hand holding a card.) If you double click the Property, the code is added for you.

After typing an equals sign, you then assign a value to your new property. Here, we're just passing the property whatever value is inside of the textbox called txtHeight.

But we need to Get a value back out, so that we can do something with it. The way you Get at values is to put your code that accesses the property on the right hand side of an equals sign. On the left, you need the name of a variable.

So add the following to your code:

NewHeight = objAlterPicBox.ChangeHeight

So whatever value was stored inside of ChangeHeight (or Returned), Gets handed over to the **NewHeight** variable.

You can then set the height of the picture box:

PictureBox1.Height = NewHeight

When you add that line above, your Button code should look like this:

```
Private Sub Button2_Click(ByVal sender As System.Object, _
                          ByVal e As System.EventArgs) _
                          Handles Button2.Click

    Dim objAlterPicBox As ConvertPostcode
    Dim NewHeight As Integer

    objAlterPicBox = New ConvertPostcode

    objAlterPicBox.ChangeHeight = Val(txtHeight.Text)
    NewHeight = objAlterPicBox.ChangeHeight

    PictureBox1.Height = NewHeight

    objAlterPicBox = Nothing

End Sub
```

Notice the last line:

objAlterPicBox = Nothing

Because objects take up space in memory, you can release them by setting the object to **Nothing**. VB is supposed to do the cleaning up for you, but you can't be sure that it's doing its job properly. So it's good form to release your own objects from memory.

When you've finished adding the code, run your programme and test it out. Click your new button and the Height of the picture box should change.

So just to recap:

You set up a Property by using the following code stub:

Public Property PropertyName( ) As VariableType

   Get

   End Get

   Set(ByVal Value As Integer)

   End Set

End Property

- The Set Statement is for setting values for your properties
- The Get Statement is for returning values from your properties
- Once you've created a new object variable to use your class, type the name of the variable and select your property from the pop up list
- When you're setting values for your property, the object variable and property go on the left hand side of the equals sign

ObjectVariableName.PropertyName = PropertyValue

When you're getting values from your property, the object variable and property go on the right hand side of the equals sign

VariableName = ObjectVariableName.PropertyName

Release your objects from memory by using the **Nothing** keyword

OK, that's just about it for this introduction to Classes and Objects. There's an awful lot more to learn about Objects, but this beginner's book is not the place for it. Before you leave this topic, try this exercise:

Exercise
Set up a property that changes the width of the Picture Box on your Form. Get the new width from the second textbox on your Form.

Review Number Eight

Create Methods in a Class that handle the following file operations:

- Display the Open File Dialogue box, open a selected File and display the contents of that file in a Textbox
- Copy a File to a specified location
- Moves a File to a specified location
- Deletes a File

Create a Form that uses all four Methods of your Class.

For this review, four separate Methods need to be created in your Class. You then create a form with buttons for Open, Copy, Move and Delete. When the buttons are clicked, no errors should occur.

Help with this Review

The Open Method of your Class

You need to display the Open File Dialogue Box when this Method is called. To display the Open File Dialogue Box previously, you added a control from the toolbox. But you don't have to add a control. Instead, you can set up variable:

Dim OFD As New System.Windows.Forms.OpenFileDialog

The variable OFD will then hold a reference to your Open File Dialogue Box. You can pass this object to your Method:

**Public Sub OpenFile(ByVal OpenDB As System.Windows.Forms.OpenFileDialog)
End Sub**

You then access the properties of the Open File Dialogue Box in the normal way. When you're creating the object from your Class, you'd call the OpenFile Method from the button. Like this:

**Dim objOpenFile As New Your_Class_Name
objOpenFile.OpenFile(OFD)**

A reference to your Open File Dialogue Box control is then passed to your Class. You also need to pass a textbox to your OpenFile Method. If you've added a Textbox to your form, and the Name of the textbox is Texbox1, you can assign this textbox to a variable of Type Textbox. You'd code it like this:

**Dim tb As TextBox
tb = Textbox1**

So the variable **tb** holds a reference to a Textbox. You then assign the specific textbox called Textbox1 to this variable.

To pass the textbox to your Method, you need to add a second parameter to your Sub:

> **Public Sub OpenFile(** ByVal OpenDB As System.Windows.Forms.OpenFileDialog, _ **ByVal tb1 as Textbox)**
> **End Sub**

The new call to the method is then this:

> **objOpenFile.OpenFile(OFD, tb)**

Inside of your OpenFile Method, you can then access the textbox in the same way:

> **tb1.Text = "Some Text"**

When the user chooses a file from the Open File Dialogue Box, you can then write code in your method to place the text file chosen into the textbox (you've already done this in a previous section).

The Copy, Move Delete Methods

For the other three Methods of your Class, you only need to set up Subs to handle the Copying of files, Moving files and Deleting files. Again, you've already coded for this in a previous section.

The point of this review is to create a Class that can do four things: open a file, copy a file, move a file, and delete a file. In the code for your form, you're creating objects from your new Class whenever a button is clicked. But the Form itself does not have to be too fancy. Something simple like this one will do:

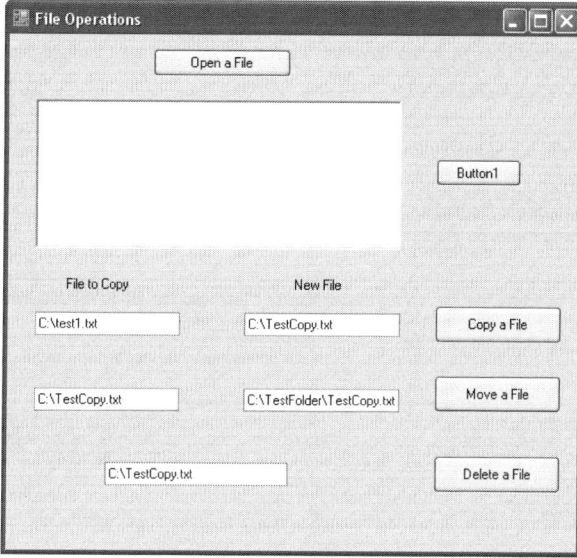

VB.NET and Databases

VB.Net allows you many ways to connect to a database or a data source. The technology used to interact with a database or data source is called ADO.NET. The ADO parts stands for Active Data Objects which, admittedly, doesn't explain much. But just like System was a Base Class (leader of a hierarchy, if you like), so is ADO. Forming the foundation of the ADO Base Class are five other major objects:

Connection
Command
DataReader
DataSet
DataAdapter

We'll see just what these objects are, and how to use them, in a later section. But we can make a start on the ADO.NET trail by creating a simple Address Book project. All we'll do is see how to use ADO to open up the database, and scroll through each entry.

Visual Basic Express and Databases – the easy way

For this tutorial, we're going to create a simple Address Book project. The names and addresses will come from a Microsoft Access database. Download the database before starting these lessons (The location of the download page can be found at the start of this book.) Once you have saved the database to your own computer, you can begin.

What we're going to be doing is to use a Wizard to create a programme that reads the database and allows us to scroll through it. The wizard will do most of the work for us, and create the controls that allow users to move through the database. The Form we create will look like this when it's finished:

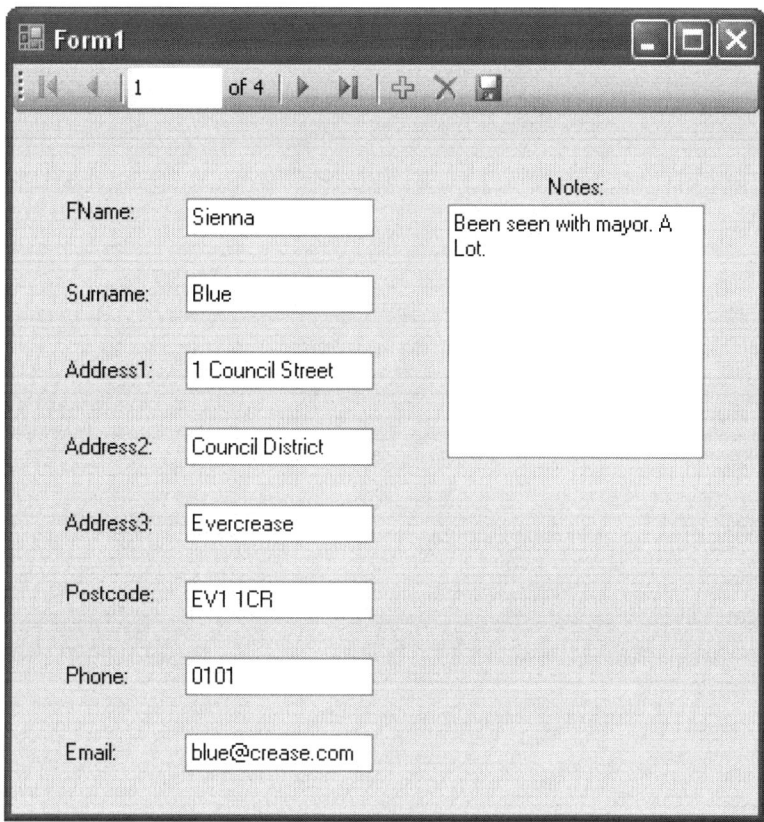

By clicking the buttons at the top, you can scroll through the database in the image above.

Let's make a start on our Database project. So, once you have your VB software open, do the following:

- Click **File > New Project** from the menu bar
- Select **Windows Application**, and then give it the Name **AddressBook**. Click OK
- Locate the **Solution Explorer** on the right hand side (If you can't see it, click **View > Solution Explorer** from the menu bar, or **View > Other Windows > Solution Explorer** in version 2010.)

We need to select a Data Source. So click on Data Sources at the bottom of the Solution Explorer in version 2008:

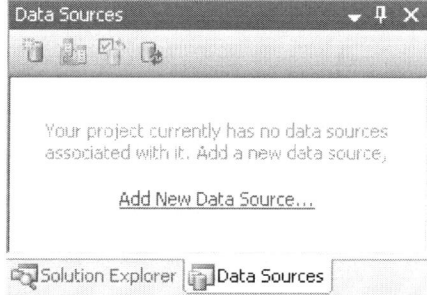

If you have VB NET 2010 then the Data Source tab is on the left, just below the Toolbox:

To Add a New Data Source in both versions, click on the link "Add New Data Source". When you do, you'll see a screen welcoming you to the Data Source Configuration Wizard. Just click **Next**, to get to the screen below:

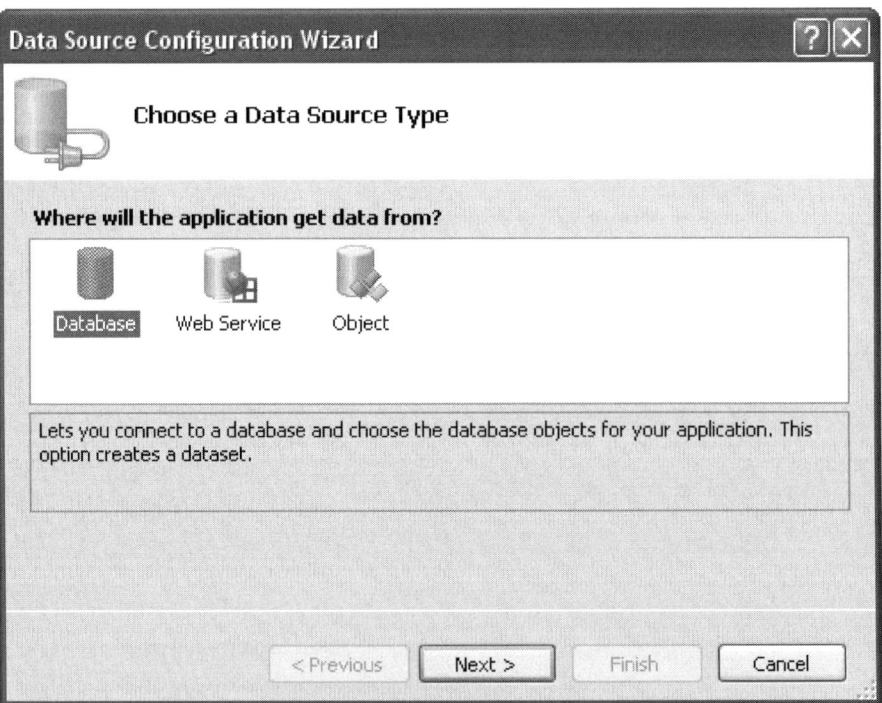

You want to connect to a Database. So select this option, and click **Next**. In version 2010 of VBN NET, you'll see this screen appear (you won't see it if you have version 2008):

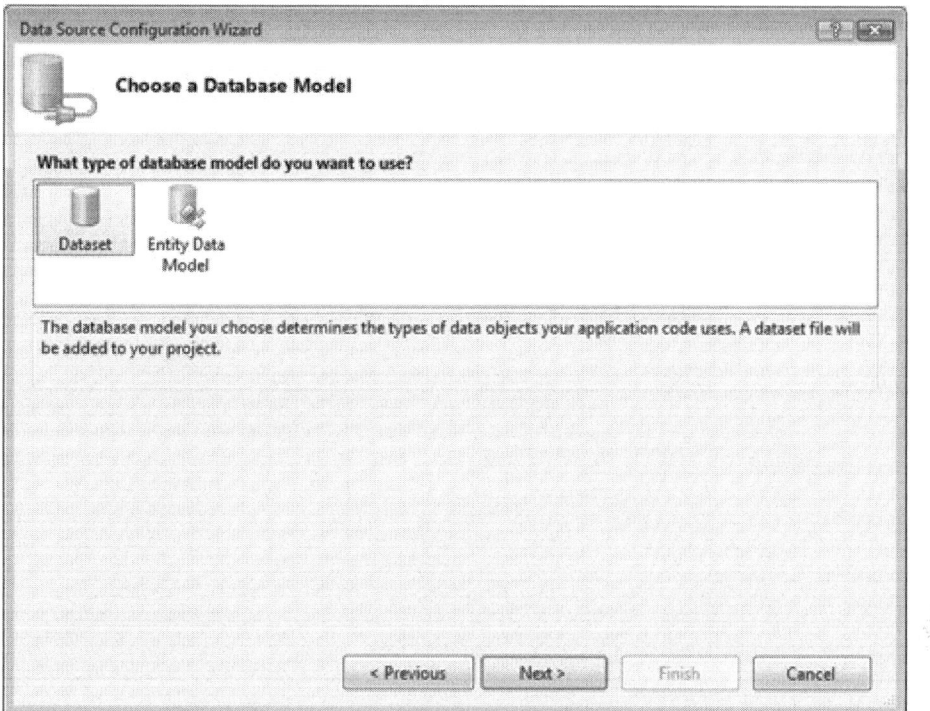

Select DataSet and click Next.

In both versions 2008 and 2010, you'll then see this screen:

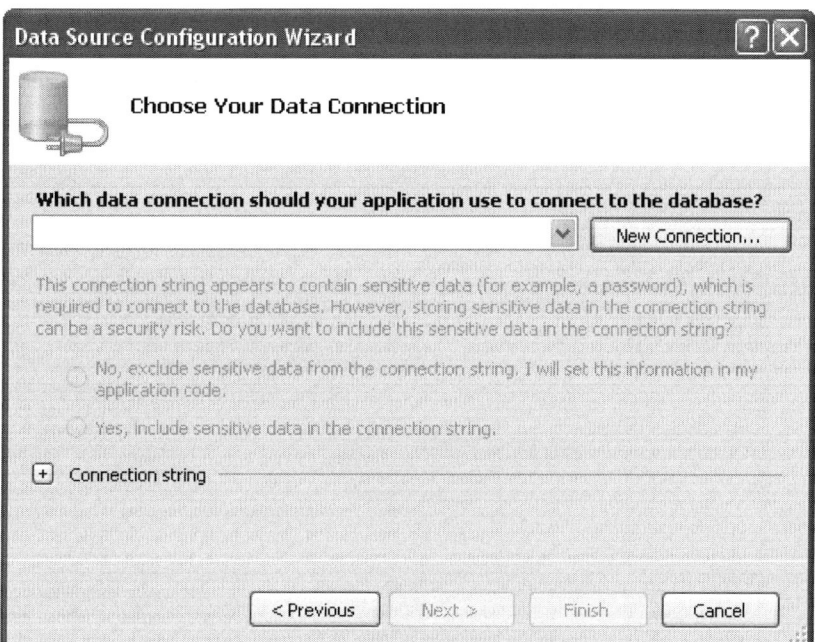

Click the **New Connection** button and another dialogue box pops up:

Click the **Change** button, because we want to connect to an Access database. (The default is for a SQL Server database.) When you click Change, you'll see this:

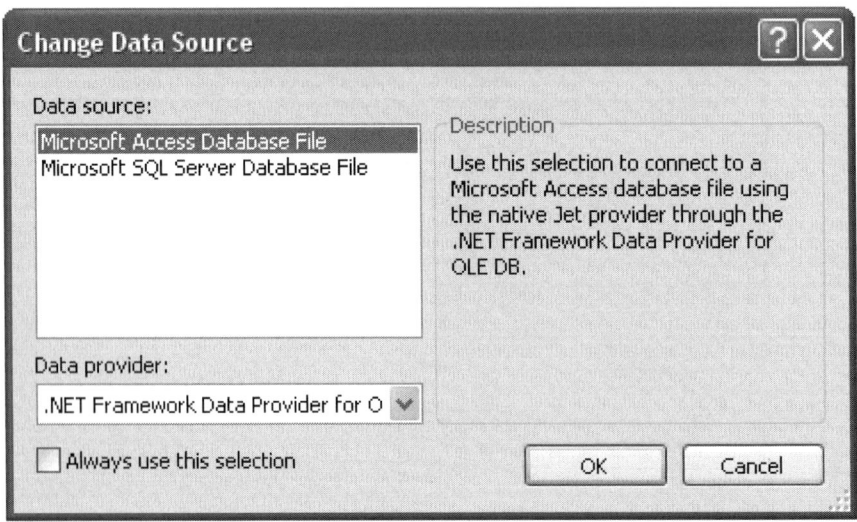

Select Microsoft Access Database File, then click OK. The previous dialogue box will then look like this:

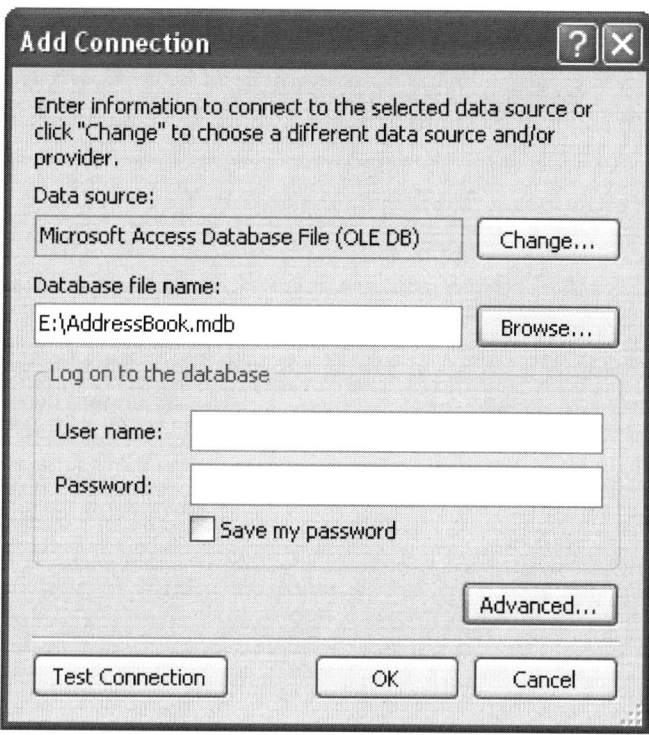

Click the **Browse** button and navigate to where on your computer you downloaded our Access Database called AddressBook.mdb. Click **Test Connection** to see if everything is OK, and you'll hopefully see this:

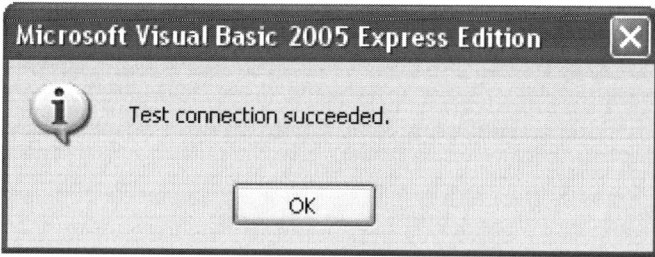

Click the OK button, then click the OK button on the Add Connection dialogue box as well. You will be returned to the Data Source Configuration Wizard, which should now look like this:

Click **Next** to move to the next step of the Wizard. You may see a message box appear, however. Click **No** on the message box to stop VB copying the database each time it runs. You should then see this:

Make sure there's a tick in the box for "Save the connection", and then click Next:

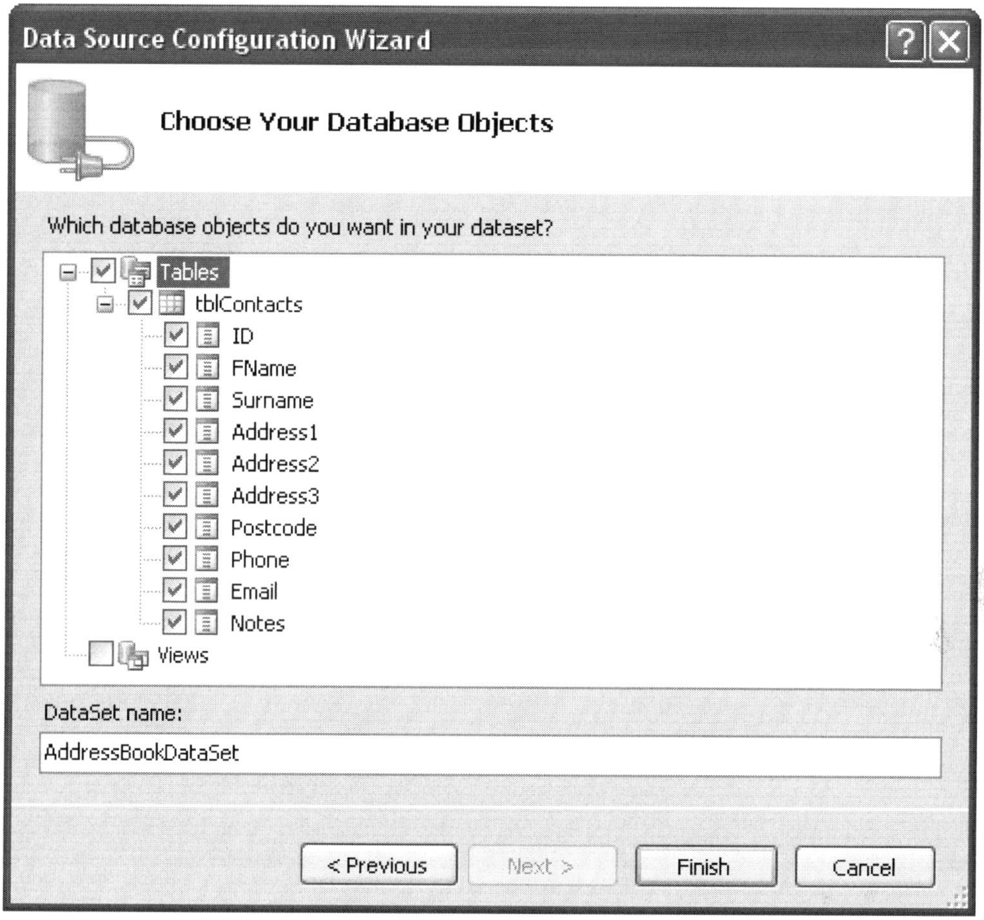

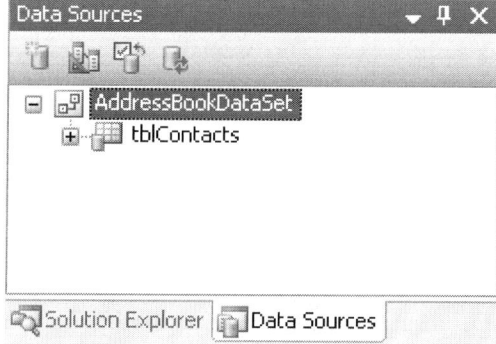

Here, you can select which tables and fields you want. Tick the Tables box to include them all. You can give your DataSet a name, if you prefer. Click Finish and you're done.

When you are returned to your form, you should notice the Solution Explorer has added your new Data Source:

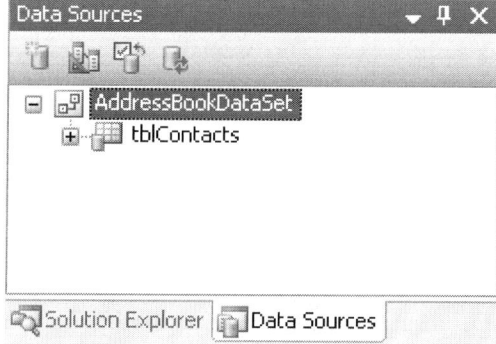

The Data Sources area of the Solution Explorer now displays information about your database. Click the plus symbol next to **tblContacts**:

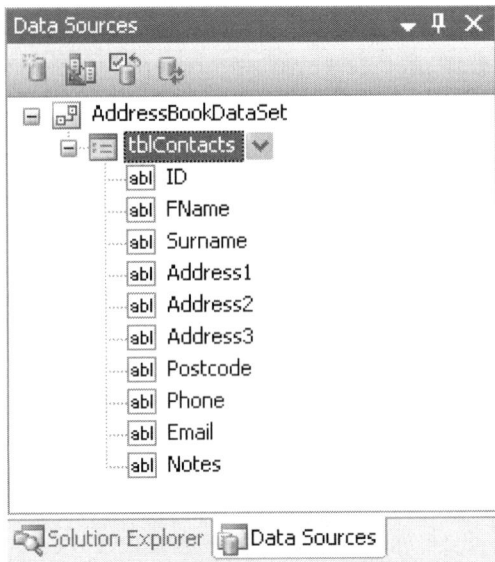

All the Fields in the Address Book database are now showing.

To add a Field to your Form, click on one in the list. Hold down your left mouse button, and drag it over to your form:

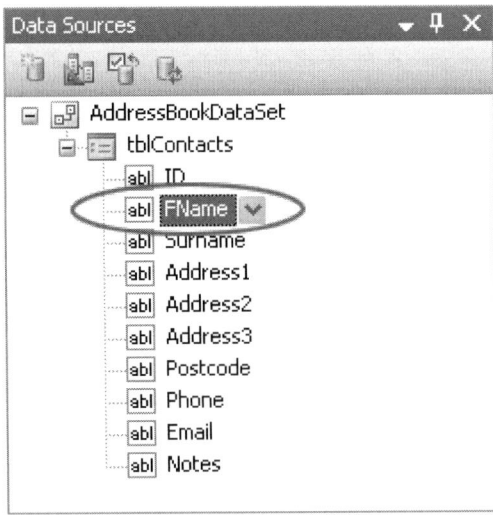

In the image above, the FirstName field is being dragged on the Form. Your mouse cursor will change shape.

When your Field is over the Form, let go of your left mouse button. A textbox and a label will be added. There are two other things to notice: a navigation bar appears at the top of the form, and a lot of strange objects have appeared in the object area at the bottom:

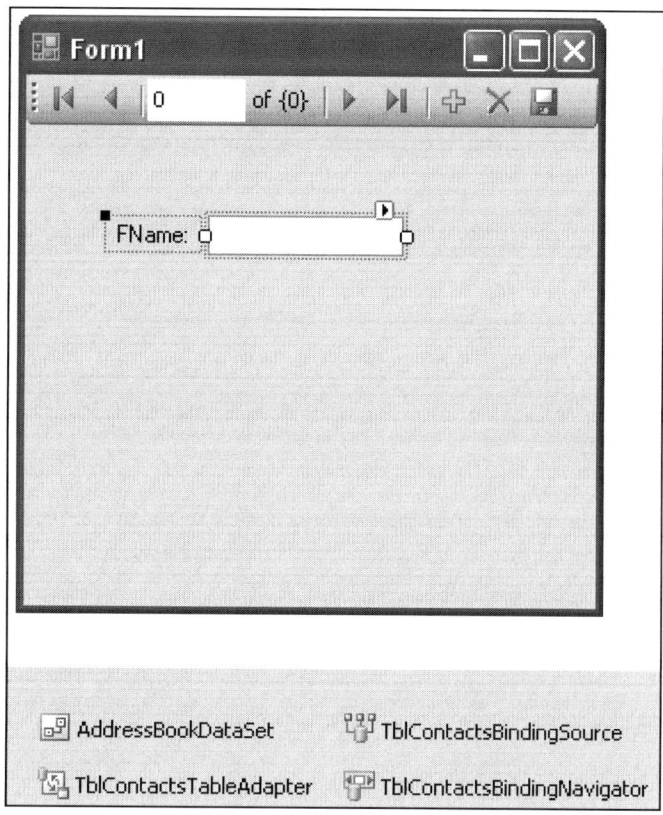

We'll explore the Objects in a later section. But notice the Navigation bar in blue. Run your programme by hitting the F5 key on your keyboard. You should see this:

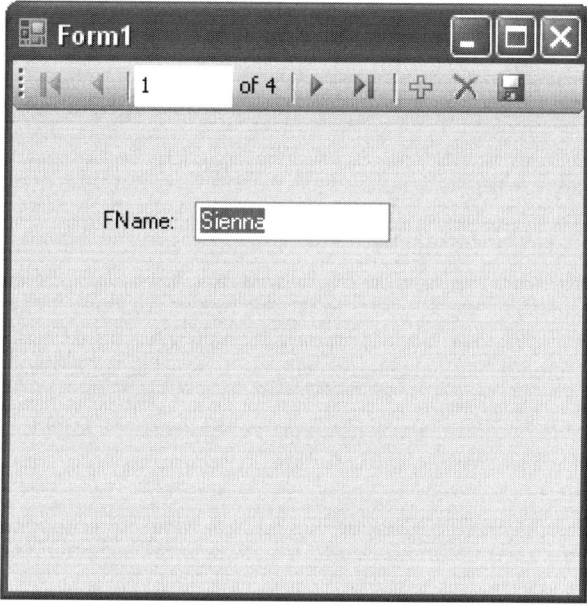

Click the Navigation arrows to scroll through the database. When you've played around with the controls, stop the form from running, and return to Design View.

Drag and Drop more Fields to your form. But don't align them yet. We'll see an easy way to do this. But once you've dragged the fields to your form, it might look like this:

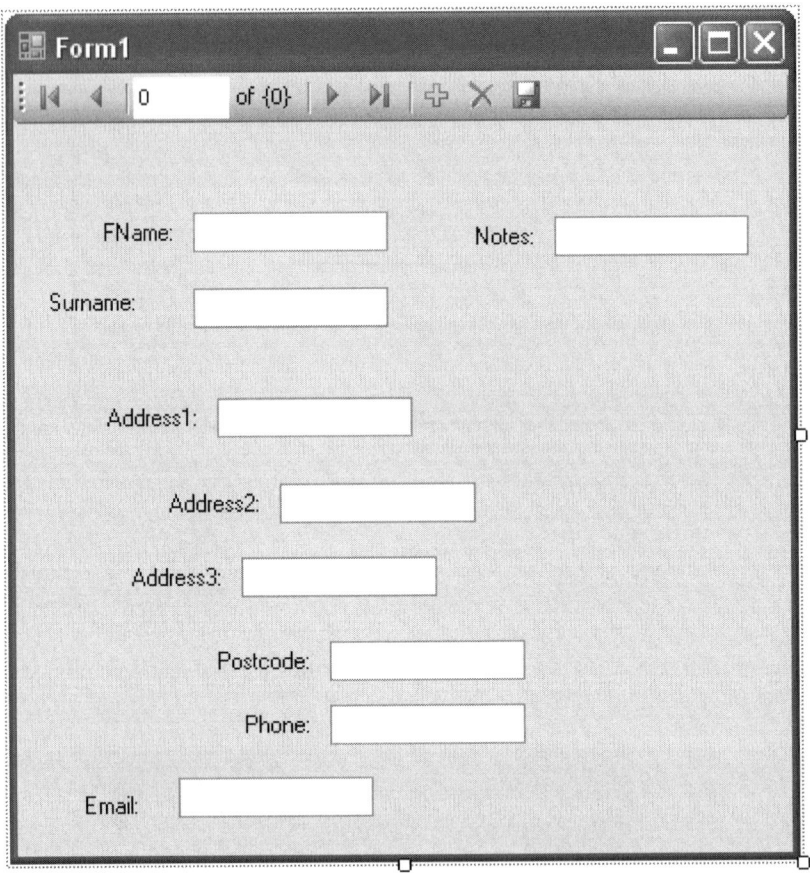

I'm sure you'll agree - that's a very untidy form. But there's a very easy way to align all your controls. Try this:

- Click on a Textbox and its label with your left mouse button
- Hold down the Ctrl key on your keyboard, and select a second Textbox and label
- With the Ctrl key still held down, click each Textbox and label in turn
- When all Textbox are selected, click on the **Format** menu at the top
- From the Format menu select **Align > Lefts**. The left edges of the Textboxes will align themselves
- From the Format menu select **Vertical Spacing > Make Equal**. The space between each textbox will then be the same

With your new controls added, and nicely aligned, press F5 to run your form. For the Notes Textbox, set the MultiLine property to True. Your form might then be something like this:

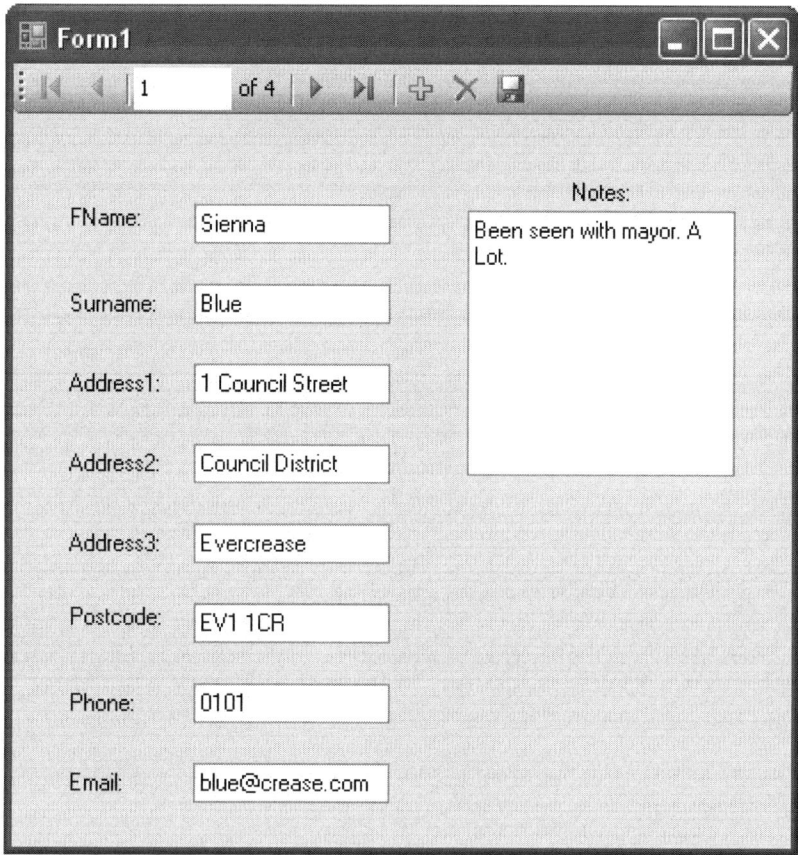

Click the Navigation icons to move backwards and forwards through your database.

In the next part, you'll move away from the Wizards and learn how to add your own programming code to open up and manipulate databases.

The Database Objects

In this next section, we'll take a look at the objects that you can use to open and read data from a Database. We'll stick with our Access database, the AddressBook.mdb one, and recreate what the Wizard has done. That way, you'll see for yourself just what is going on behind the scenes.

It is much better if we started on a new form. So close any current projects you have open, and create a new one. Give it whatever name you like, and let's begin.

The Connection Object

The Connection Object is what you need if you want to connect to a database. There are a number of different connection objects, and the one you use depends largely on the type of database you're connecting to. Because we're connecting to an Access database, we'll need something called the OLE DB connection object.

OLE stands for Object Linking and Embedding, and its basically a lot of objects (COM objects) bundled together that allow you to connect to data sources in general, and not just databases. You can use it, for example, to connect to text files, SQL Server, email, and a whole lot more.

There are a number of different OLE DB objects (called data providers), but the one we'll use is called "Jet". Others are SQL Server and Oracle.

So place a button on your form. Change the Name property to **btnLoad**. Double click your button to open up the code window. Add the following line:

Dim con As New OleDb.OleDbConnection

The variable **con** will now hold the Connection Object. Notice that there is a full stop after the **OleDB** part. You'll then get a pop up box from where you can select **OleDbConnection**. This is the object that you use to connect to an Access database. There are Properties and Methods associated with the Connection Object, of course. We want to start with the **ConnectionString** property. This can take MANY parameters. Fortunately, we only need a few of these.

We need to pass two things to our new Connection Object: the technology we want to use to do the connecting to our database, and where the database is. (If your database was password and user name protected, you would add these two parameters as well. Ours isn't, so we only need the two.)

The technology is called the Provider; and you use "Data Source" to specify where your database is. So add this to your code:

Dim dbProvider As String
Dim dbSource As String

dbProvider = "PROVIDER=Microsoft.Jet.OLEDB.4.0;"
dbSource = "Data Source = C:/AddressBook.mdb"

244

con.ConnectionString = dbProvider & dbSource

The first part specifies which provider technology we want to use to do the connecting (JET). The second part, typed after a semi-colon, points to where the database is. In the above code, the database is on the C drive, in the root folder. The name of the Access file we want to connect to is called AddressBook.mdb. (Note that "Data Source" is two words, and not one.)

If you prefer, you can have the provider and source on one line, as below (it's on two in this book because it won't all fit on one line):

con.ConnectionString = "PROVIDER=Microsoft.Jet.OLEDB.4.0;Data Source = C:\AddressBook.mdb"

But your coding window should now look like this:

```
Private Sub btnLoad_Click(ByVal sender As System.Object, _
                          ByVal e As System.EventArgs) _
                          Handles btnLoad.Click

    Dim con As New OleDb.OleDbConnection
    Dim dbProvider As String
    Dim dbSource As String


    dbProvider = "PROVIDER=Microsoft.Jet.OLEDB.4.0;"
    dbSource = "Data Source = C:/AddressBook.mdb"

    con.ConnectionString = dbProvider & dbSource

End Sub
```

This assumes that you have copied the AddressBook database over to the root folder of your C Drive. If you've copied it to another folder, change the "Data Source" part to match. For example, if you copied it to a folder called "databases" you'd put this:

Data Source = C:/databases/AddressBook.mdb

You can also specify a folder such as MyDocuments (or Documents in Vista and Windows 7). You do it like this:

dbSource = "Data Source = C:\Users\Owner\Documents\AddressBook.mdb"

Another way to specify a file path is this:

Dim fldr As String
fldr = Environment.GetFolderPath(Environment.SpecialFolder.MyDocuments) & "/AddressBook.mdb"

dbSource = "Data Source = " & fldr

On the second line, spread over two lines in the code above, we have this:

Environment.GetFolderPath( )

The folder path you're getting goes between the round brackets of **GetFolderPath**:

Environment.SpecialFolder.MyDocuments

The Special Folder in this case is the MyDocuments folder. Other special folders are:

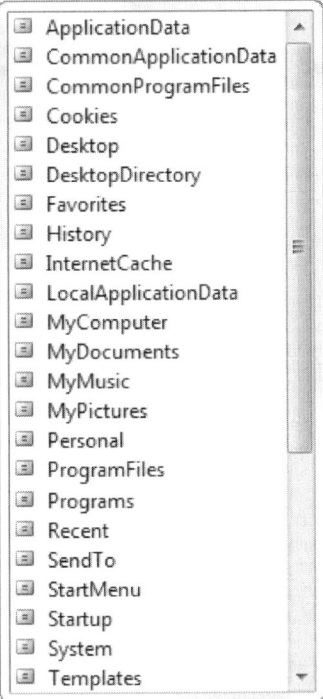

But back to our connection code.

ConnectionString is a property of the **con** variable. The **con** variable holds our Connection Object. We're passing the Connection String the name of a data provider, and a path to the database.

Now that we have a ConnectionString, we can go ahead and open the database. This is quite easy – just use the **Open** method of the Connection Object:

con.Open( )

Once open, the connection has to be closed again. This time, just use the **Close** method:

con.Close( )

Add the following four lines to your code:

```
       con.Open( )
       MsgBox("Database is now open")

       con.Close()
       MsgBox("Database is now Closed")
```

Your coding window will then look like this:

```
Private Sub btnLoad_Click(ByVal sender As System.Object, _
                          ByVal e As System.EventArgs) _
                          Handles btnLoad.Click

    Dim con As New OleDb.OleDbConnection
    Dim dbProvider As String
    Dim dbSource As String


    dbProvider = "PROVIDER=Microsoft.Jet.OLEDB.4.0;"
    dbSource = "Data Source = E:/AddressBook.mdb"

    con.ConnectionString = dbProvider & dbSource

    con.Open()

    MsgBox("Database is now open")

    con.Close()

    MsgBox("Database is now Closed")

End Sub
```

Test out your new code by running your programme. Click your button and the two message boxes should display. If they don't, make sure your Data Source path is correct. If it isn't, you might see this error message:

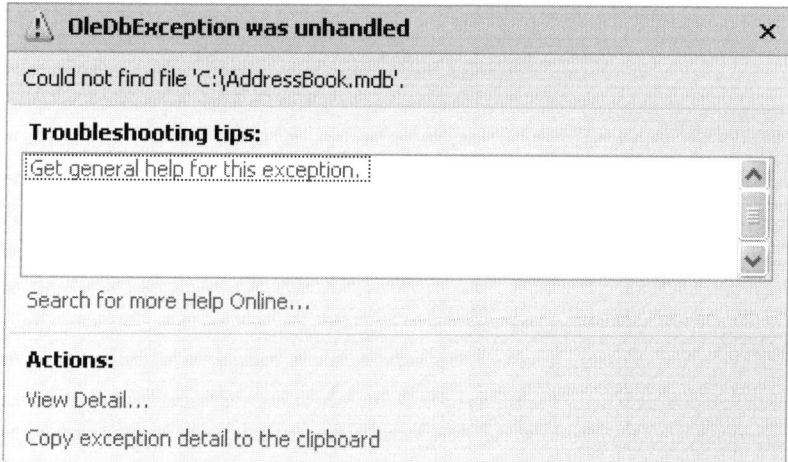

The error message is a bit on the vague and mysterious side. But what it's saying is that it can't find the path to the database, so it can't Open the connection. The line **con.Open** will then be highlighted in yellow. You need to specify the correct path to your database. When you do, you'll see the message boxes from our code, and not the big one above.

Now that we've opened a connection to the database, we need to read the information from it. This is where the DataSet and the DataAdapter come in.

Data Sets and Data Adapters

We've set up a Connection Object, and told NET how to connect to our database, and where it is. But that's not the end of it. The data from the database needs to be stored somewhere, so that we can manipulate it. ADO.NET uses something called a Data Set to hold all of your information from the database (you can also use a Data Table, if all you want to do is read information, and not have people write to your database.). But the Data Set (and Data Table) will hold a copy of the information from the database.

The Data Set is not something you can draw on your form, like a Button or a Textbox. The Data Set is something that is hidden from you, and just stored in memory. Imagine a grid with rows and columns. Each imaginary row of the Data Set represents a Row of information in your Access database. And each imaginary column represents a Column of information in your Access database (called a Field in Access).

This, then, is a Data Set. But what's a Data Adapter?

The Connection Object and the Data Set can't see each other. They need a go-between so that they can communicate. This go-between is called a Data Adapter. The Data Adapter contacts your Connection Object, and then executes a query that you set up. The results of that query are then stored in the Data Set.

The Data Adapter and Data Set are objects. You set them up like this:

Dim ds As New DataSet
Dim da As OleDb.OleDbDataAdapter

da = New OleDb.OleDbDataAdapter(sql, con)

The code needs a little explaining, though. First, the Data Adapter.

The Data Adapter is a property of the OLEDB object, hence the full stop between the two:

OleDb.OleDbDataAdapter

We're passing this object to the variable called **da**. This variable will then hold a reference to the Data Adapter.

Whereas the second line sets up a reference to the Data Adapter, the third line creates a new Data Adapter object. You need to pass two things in the Object declaration: Your SQL string (which we'll get to shortly), and your connection object. Our Connection Object is stored in the variable which we've called **con**. (Like all variable you can call it practically anything you like. We've gone for something short and memorable.) You then pass the New Data Adapter to your variable:

da = New OleDb.OleDbDataAdapter(sql, con)

We need something else, though. The **sql** in between round brackets is the name of a variable. We haven't yet set this up. So add this line to your code (near the top):

Dim sql As String

We need to put something in this string variable. But what? Let's have a brief look at SQL.

Structured Query Language

SQL (pronounced SeeKwel), is short for Structured Query Language, and is a way to query and write to databases (not just Access). The basics are quite easy to learn. If you want to grab all of the records from a table in a database, you use the SELECT word. Like this:

SELECT * FROM Table_Name

SQL is not case sensitive, so the above line could be written:

Select * From Table_Name

But your SQL statements are easier to read if you type the keywords in uppercase letters. The keywords in the lines above are SELECT and FROM. The asterisk means "All Records". **Table_Name** is the name of a table in your database. So the whole line reads:

"SELECT all the records FROM the table called Table_Name"

You don't need to select all (*) the records from your database. You can just select the columns that you need. For example, here's what the Address Book database looks like in Access:

FirstName	Surname	Address1	Address2	Address3	Postcode	Phone	Email	Notes
John	Smith	12 High Street	Town District	Evercrease	EV1 2CR	222	smith@crease.	Recently split up with wife. Not cop
Jane	Smith	11 High Street	Town District	Evercrease	EV1 2CR	2223	neesmith@cres	Recently split up with husband. Cor
Ira	Irate	2 Cold Pond La	Pond District	Evercrease	EV9 5CR	1122	none	Complains. A Lot.
Sienna	Blue	1 Council Stree	Council District	Evercrease	EV1 1CR	0101	blue@crease.ci	Been seen with mayor. A Lot.
John	Tucker	2 Copper Lane	Police District	Evercrease	EV12 9CR	9991	constabletucke	Local police officer. Been having pe

The name of the table in the database is **tblContacts**. If we wanted to select just the first name and surname columns from this table, we can specify that in our SQL String:

SELECT tblContacts.FirstName, tblContacts.Surname FROM tblContacts

When this SQL statement is executed, only the FirstName and Surname columns from the database will be returned.

There are a lot more SQL commands, but for our purposes this is enough. Add this new lines to your code.

sql = "SELECT * FROM tblContacts"

So we want to SELECT all (*) the records from the table called tblContacts. We pass this to the string variable we have called **sql**.

Your code window should now look like this (though the file path to your database might be different):

```
Private Sub btnLoad_Click(ByVal sender As System.Object, _
                          ByVal e As System.EventArgs) _
                          Handles btnLoad.Click

    Dim con As New OleDb.OleDbConnection
    Dim dbProvider As String
    Dim dbSource As String
    Dim ds As New DataSet
    Dim da As OleDb.OleDbDataAdapter
    Dim sql As String

    dbProvider = "PROVIDER=Microsoft.Jet.OLEDB.4.0;"
    dbSource = "Data Source = E:/AddressBook.mdb"

    con.ConnectionString = dbProvider & dbSource

    con.Open()

        sql = "SELECT * FROM tblContacts"
        da = New OleDb.OleDbDataAdapter(Sql, con)

    MsgBox("Database is now open")

    con.Close()

    MsgBox("Database is now Closed")

End Sub
```

Now that the Data Adapter has selected all of the records from the table in our database, we need somewhere to put those records – in the DataSet.

The Data Adapter can Fill a DataSet with records from a Table. You only need a single line of code to do this:

da.Fill(ds, "AddressBook")

As soon as you type the name of your Data Adapter, you'll get a pop up box of properties and methods. Select Fill from the list, then type a pair of round brackets. In between the round brackets, you need two things: the Name of your DataSet (ds, in our case), and an identifying name. This name can be anything you like. But it is just used to identify this particular Data Adapter Fill. We could have called it "Nice Sandwich", if we wanted:

da.Fill(ds, "Nice Sandwich")

The code above still works. But it's better to stick to something a little more descriptive than "Nice Sandwich"!

And that's it. The DataSet will now be filled with the records we selected from the table called tblContact. There's only one slight problem – nobody can see the data yet!

As we're trying to do the same thing that the Wizard did, we'll display the information in textboxes.

So add two textboxes to your form. Change the Name properties of your textboxes to txtFirstName and txtSurname. Go back to your code window, and add the following two lines:

txtFirstName.Text = ds.Tables("AddressBook").Rows(0).Item(1)
txtSurname.Text = ds.Tables("AddressBook").Rows(0).Item(2)

You can add them after the line that closes the connection to the database. Once the DataSet has been filled, the connection to the database can be closed.

Your code should now look like this:

```
Dim con As New OleDb.OleDbConnection
Dim dbProvider As String
Dim dbSource As String
Dim ds As New DataSet
Dim da As OleDb.OleDbDataAdapter
Dim sql As String

dbProvider = "PROVIDER=Microsoft.Jet.OLEDB.4.0;"
dbSource = "Data Source = E:/AddressBook.mdb"

con.ConnectionString = dbProvider & dbSource

con.Open()

sql = "SELECT * FROM tblContacts"
da = New OleDb.OleDbDataAdapter(sql, con)
da.Fill(ds, "AddressBook")

MsgBox("Database is now open")
con.Close()
MsgBox("Database is now Closed")

txtFirstName.Text = ds.Tables("AddressBook").Rows(0).Item(1)
txtSurname.Text = ds.Tables("AddressBook").Rows(0).Item(2)
```

Before the code is explained, run your programme and click the button. You should see "John Smith" displayed in your two textboxes.

So let's examine the code that assigns the data from the DataSet to the textboxes. The first line was this:

txtFirstName.Text = ds.Tables("AddressBook").Rows(0).Item(1)

It's rather a long line! But after the equals sign, you type the name of your DataSet (ds for us). After a full stop, select **Tables** from the popup list. The Tables property needs something in between round brackets. Quite bizarrely, this is NOT the name of your table! It's that identifier you used with the Data Adapter Fill. We used the identifier "AddressBook". If we had used "Nice Sandwich" then we'd put this:

ds.Tables("Nice Sandwich ")

But we didn't, so our code is:

ds.Tables("AddressBook")

Type a full stop and you'll see another list popping up at you. Select **Rows** from the list. In between round brackets, you need a number. This is a Row number from the DataSet. We want the first row, which is row zero in the DataSet:

ds.Tables("AddressBook").Rows(0)

Type full stop after **Rows(0)** and the popup list appears again. To identify a Column from the DataSet, you use **Item**. In between round brackets, you type which column you want:

ds.Tables("AddressBook").Rows(0).Item(1)

In the Access database, column zero is used for an ID. The FirstName column is the second column in the Access database. Because the Item collection is zero based, this is item 1 in the DataSet.

You can also refer to the column name itself for the Item property, rather than a number. So you can do this:

ds.Tables("AddressBook").Rows(0).Item("FirstName")
ds.Tables("AddressBook").Rows(0).Item("Surname")

If you get the name of the column wrong, then VB throws up an error. But an image might clear things up. The image below shows what the items and rows are in the database.

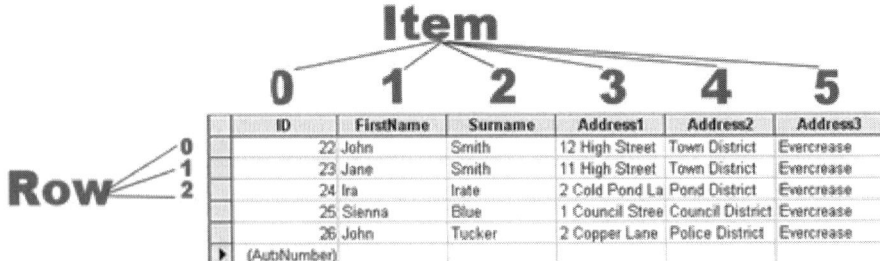

The image shows which are the Rows and which are the Items in the Access database Table. So the Items go down and the Rows go across.

However, we want to be able to scroll through the table. We want to be able to click a button and see the next record. Or click another button and see the previous record. You can do this by incrementing the Row number. To see the next record, we'd want this:

txtFirstName.Text = ds.Tables("AddressBook").**Rows(1).**Item(1)
txtSurname.Text = ds.Tables("AddressBook").**Rows(1).**Item(2)

The record after that would then be:

txtFirstName.Text = ds.Tables("AddressBook").**Rows(2).**Item(1)
txtSurname.Text = ds.Tables("AddressBook").**Rows(2).**Item(2)

So by incrementing and decrementing the Row number, you can navigate through the records. Let's see how that's done.

Navigating through the DataSet

To navigate through the dataset, let's change our form. By adding some navigation buttons, we can duplicate what the wizard did. We'll also need to move the code we already have. So let's start with that.

At the moment, all our code is in the Button we added to the form. We're going to delete this button, so we need to move it out of there. The variable declarations can be moved right to the top of the coding window. That way, any button can see the variables. So move your variables declarations to the top, as in the image below (don't forget to add the **Dim inc As Integer** line):

```
Public Class Form1

    Dim inc As Integer
    Dim con As New OleDb.OleDbConnection
    Dim dbProvider As String
    Dim dbSource As String
    Dim ds As New DataSet
    Dim da As OleDb.OleDbDataAdapter
    Dim sql As String
```

We can move a few lines to the Form Load event. So, create a Form Load event, as you did in a previous section. Now move all but the textbox lines to there. Your coding window should then look like this (you can delete the message box lines, or just comment them out):

```
(Form1 Events)                              Load
Public Class Form1

    Dim inc As Integer
    Dim con As New OleDb.OleDbConnection
    Dim dbProvider As String
    Dim dbSource As String
    Dim ds As New DataSet
    Dim da As OleDb.OleDbDataAdapter
    Dim sql As String

    Private Sub Form1_Load(ByVal sender As Object, _
                           ByVal e As System.EventArgs) _
                        Handles Me.Load

        dbProvider = "PROVIDER=Microsoft.Jet.OLEDB.4.0;"
        dbSource = "Data Source = E:/AddressBook.mdb"

        con.ConnectionString = dbProvider & dbSource

        con.Open()

        sql = "SELECT * FROM tblContacts"
        da = New OleDb.OleDbDataAdapter(sql, con)
        da.Fill(ds, "AddressBook")

        con.Close()

    End Sub
```

For your button, all you should have left are these two lines:

txtFirstName.Text = ds.Tables("AddressBook").Rows(inc).Item(1)
txtSurname.Text = ds.Tables("AddressBook").Rows(inc).Item(2)

Since we're going to be deleting this button, this code can be moved. Because all the buttons need to put something into the textboxes, the two lines we have left are an ideal candidate for a Subroutine. So add the following Sub to your code:

Private Sub NavigateRecords()

txtFirstName.Text = ds.Tables("AddressBook").Rows(inc).Item(1)
txtSurname.Text = ds.Tables("AddressBook").Rows(inc).Item(2)

End Sub

When we navigate through the DataSet, we'll call this subroutine.

Now that all of your code has gone from your button, you can delete the button code altogether. Return to you form, click on the button to select it, then press the delete key on your keyboard. This will remove the button itself from your form. (You can also right click on the button, and then select Delete from the menu.)

Here's what your coding window should like:

```
Public Class Form1

    Dim inc As Integer
    Dim con As New OleDb.OleDbConnection
    Dim dbProvider As String
    Dim dbSource As String
    Dim ds As New DataSet
    Dim da As OleDb.OleDbDataAdapter
    Dim sql As String

    Private Sub Form1_Load(ByVal sender As Object, _
                     ByVal e As System.EventArgs) _
                           Handles Me.Load

        dbProvider = "PROVIDER=Microsoft.Jet.OLEDB.4.0;"
        dbSource = "Data Source = E:/AddressBook.mdb"

        con.ConnectionString = dbProvider & dbSource

        con.Open()

        sql = "SELECT * FROM tblContacts"
        da = New OleDb.OleDbDataAdapter(sql, con)
        da.Fill(ds, "AddressBook")

        con.Close()

    End Sub
    Private Sub NavigateRecords()

        txtFirstName.Text = ds.Tables("AddressBook").Rows(inc).Item(1)
        txtSurname.Text = ds.Tables("AddressBook").Rows(inc).Item(2)

    End Sub

End Class
```

Now you can re-design the form. Add four new buttons, and change the Name properties to: btnNext, btnPrevious, btnFirst, and btnLast. Change the Text properties to >, <, <<, and >>. Your form will then look like this:

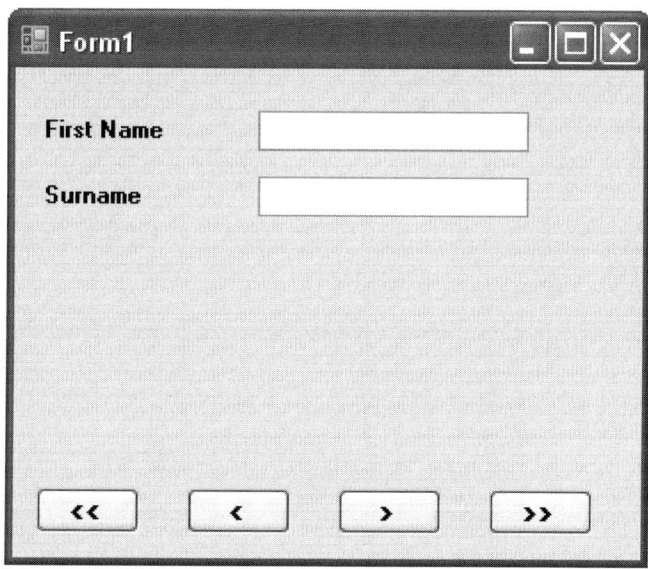

Just a couple of more things to set up before we get started. Add a new variable declaration to the top of your code, just under the **Dim inc As Integer** line. Add this:

Dim MaxRows As Integer

We can store how many rows are in the DataSet with this variable. You can get how many rows are in the DataSet with this:

MaxRows = ds.Tables("AddressBook").Rows.Count

So the Rows property has a Count Method. This simply counts how many rows are in the DataSet. We're passing that number to a variable called **MaxRows**. You can then test what is in the variable, and see if the **inc** counter doesn't go past it. You need to do this because VB throws up an error message if try to go past the last row in the DataSet. (Previous versions of VB had some called an EOF and BOF properties. These checked the End of File and Before End of File. These properties have now gone.)

Add the following two lines of code to the Form Load Event of Form1:

MaxRows = ds.Tables("AddressBook").Rows.Count
inc = - 1

Your code should then look like this:

```
Private Sub Form1_Load(ByVal sender As Object, _
                    ByVal e As System.EventArgs) _
                    Handles Me.Load

    dbProvider = "PROVIDER=Microsoft.Jet.OLEDB.4.0;"
    dbSource = "Data Source = E:/AddressBook.mdb"

    con.ConnectionString = dbProvider & dbSource

    con.Open()

    sql = "SELECT * FROM tblContacts"
    da = New OleDb.OleDbDataAdapter(sql, con)
    da.Fill(ds, "AddressBook")
    con.Close()

    MaxRows = ds.Tables("AddressBook").Rows.Count
    inc = -1

End Sub
```

Notice the other line of code for the Form Load event:

inc = - 1

This line sets the inc variable to minus one when the form loads. When the Buttons are clicked, this will ensure that we're moving the counter on by the correct amount.

We can now start to code for the Buttons.

Move Forward One Record at a Time

Double click your Next button (the one with the > on it) to access the code. Add the following If … Else Statement:

```
If inc <> MaxRows - 1 Then
        inc = inc + 1
        NavigateRecords( )
Else
        MsgBox("No More Rows")
End If
```

We're checking to see if the value in **inc** does not equal the value in **MaxRows – 1**. If they are both equal then we know we've reached the last record in the DataSet. In which case, we just display a message box. If they are not equal, these two lines get executed:

```
inc = inc + 1
NavigateRecords( )
```

First, we move the **inc** counter on by one. Then we call the Sub we set up:

```
NavigateRecords( )
```

Our Subroutine is where the action takes place, and the values from the DataSet are placed in the textboxes. Here it is again:

```
Private Sub NavigateRecords( )

        txtFirstName.Text = ds.Tables("AddressBook").Rows(inc).Item(1)
        txtSurname.Text = ds.Tables("AddressBook").Rows(inc).Item(2)

End Sub
```

The part that moves the record forward (and backwards soon) is this part:

```
Rows( inc )
```

Previously, we hard-coded this with:

```
Rows(0)
```

Now the value is coming from the variable called **inc**. Because we're incrementing this variable with code, the value will change each time the button is clicked. And so a different record will be displayed.

You can test out your Next button. Run your programme and click the button. You should now be able to move forward through the DataSet.

None of the other button will work yet, of course. So let's move backwards.

Move Back One Record at a Time

To move backwards through the DataSet, we need to decrement the **inc** counter. All this means is deducting 1 from whatever is currently in **inc**.

But we also need to check that **inc** doesn't go past zero, which is the first record in the DataSet. Here's the code to add to your btnPrevious:

```
If inc > 0 Then
        inc = inc - 1
        NavigateRecords( )
Else
        MsgBox("First Record")
End If
```

So the If statement first checks that **inc** is greater than zero. If it is, inc gets 1 deducted from it. Then the **NavigateRecords( )** subroutine gets called. If inc is zero or less, then we display a message.

When you've finished adding the code, test your programme out. Click the Previous button first. The message box should display, even though no records have been loaded into the textboxes. This is because the variable **inc** has a value of –1 when the form first loads. It only gets moved on to zero when the Next button is clicked. You could amend your IF Statement to this:

```
If inc > 0 Then
        inc = inc - 1
        NavigateRecords( )
ElseIf inc = -1 Then
        MsgBox("No Records Yet")
ElseIf inc = 0 Then
        MsgBox("First Record")
End If
```

This new If Statement now checks to see if **inc** is equal to minus 1, and displays a message if it does. It also checks if **inc** is equal to zero, and displays the "First Record" message box. All other values and **inc** gets decremented.

Moving to the Last Record in the DataSet

To jump to the last record in the DataSet, you only need to know how many records have been loaded into the DataSet: the MaxRows variable, in our code. You can then set the **inc** counter to that value, but minus 1. Here's the code to add to your btnLast:

> **If inc <> MaxRows - 1 Then**
> > **inc = MaxRows - 1**
> > **NavigateRecords( )**
>
> **End If**

The reason we're saying **MaxRows – 1** is that the row count might be 5, say, but the first record in the DataSet starts at zero. So the total number of records would be zero to 4. Inside of the If Statement, we're setting the inc counter to **MaxRows – 1**, then calling the **NavigateRecords( )** subroutine.

That's all we need to do. So run your programme. Click the **Last** button, and you should see the last record displayed in your textboxes.

Moving to the First Record in the DataSet

Moving to the first record is fairly straightforward. We only need to set the **inc** counter to zero, if it's not already at that value. Then call the Sub:

> **If inc <> 0 Then**
> > **inc = 0**
> > **NavigateRecords()**
>
> **End If**

Add the code to your btnFirst. Run your programme and test out all of your buttons. You should be able to move through the names in the database, and jump to the first and last records.

As yet, though, we don't have a way to add new records, to update records, or to delete them. Let's do that now.

Before we start the coding for these new buttons, it's important to understand that the DataSet is disconnected from the database. What this means is that if you're adding a new record, you're not adding it to the database: you're adding it to the DataSet. Similarly, if you're updating or Deleting, you doing it to the DataSet, and not to the database. After you have made all of your changes, you THEN commit these changes to the database. You do this by issuing a separate command. But we'll see how it works.

Add five more buttons to your form. Change the Name properties of the new Buttons to the following:

> **btnAddNew**
> **btnCommit**
> **btnUpdate**
> **btnDelete**
> **btnClear**

Change the Text properties of the buttons to "Add New", "Commit", "Update", "Delete", and "Cancel/Clear". Your form might look something like this:

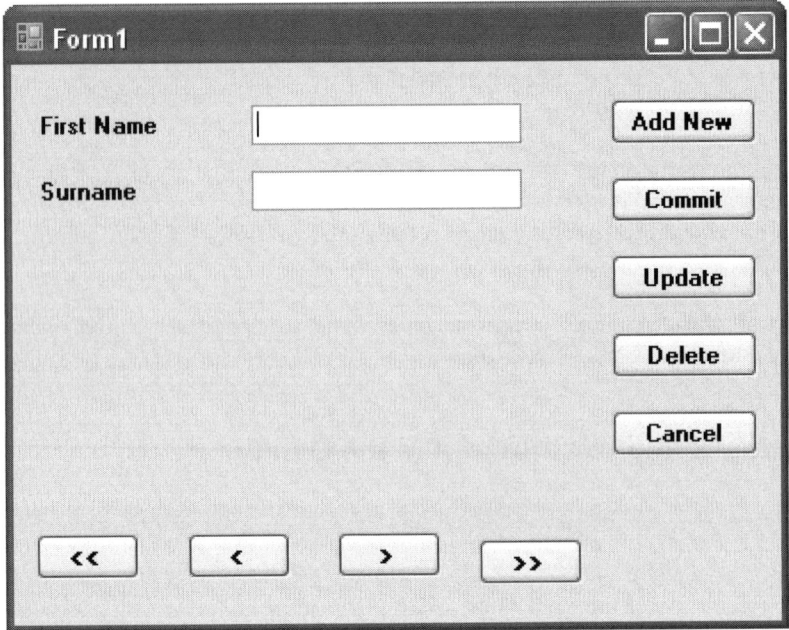

Updating a Record

To reference a particular column (item) in a row of the DataSet, the code is this:

ds.Tables("AddressBook").Rows(2).Item(1)

That will return whatever is at Item 1 on Row 2. As well as returning a value, you can also set a value. You do it like this:

ds.Tables("AddressBook").Rows(2).Item(1) = "Jane"

Now Item 1 Row 2 will contain the text "Jane". This won't, however, effect the database. The changes will just get made to the DataSet. To illustrate this, add the following code to your btnUpdate:

ds.Tables("AddressBook").Rows(inc).Item(1) = txtFirstName.Text
ds.Tables("AddressBook").Rows(inc).Item(2) = txtSurname.Text

MsgBox("Data updated")

Run your programme, and click the Next button to move to the first record. "John" should be displayed in your first textbox, and "Smith" in the second textbox. Click inside the textboxes and change "John" to "Joan" and "Smith" to "Smithy". (Without the quotes). Now click your Update button. Move to the next record by clicking your Next (>) button, and then move back (<) to the first record. You should see that the first record is now "Joan Smithy".

Close down your programme, then run it again. Click the Next (>) button to move to the first record. It will still be "John Smith". The data you updated has been lost. So here, again, is why:

"Changes are made to the DataSet, and <u>NOT</u> to the Database"

To update the database, you need some extra code. Amend your **btnUpdate** code to this (the new lines are in bold):

Dim cb As New OleDb.OleDbCommandBuilder(da)

ds.Tables("AddressBook").Rows(inc).Item(1) = txtFirstName.Text
ds.Tables("AddressBook").Rows(inc).Item(2) = txtSurname.Text

da.Update(ds, "AddressBook")

MsgBox("Data updated")

The first new line is this:

Dim cb As New OleDb.OleDbCommandBuilder(da)

To update the database itself, you need something called a Command Builder. The Command Builder will build a SQL string for you. In between round brackets, you type the name of your Data Adapter, **da** in our case. The command builder is then stored in a variable, which we have called **cb**.

The second new line is where the action is:

da.Update(ds, "AddressBook")

The **da** variable is holding our Data Adapter (which is the go-between for the database and the DataSet). One of the methods of the Data Adapter is Update. In between the round brackets, you need the name of your DataSet (**ds**, for us). The "AddressBook" part is optional. It's what we've called our DataSet, and is here to avoid any confusion.

But the Data Adapter will then contact the database. Because we have a Command Builder, the Data Adapter can then update your database with the values from the DataSet.

Without the Command Builder, though, the Data Adapter can't do its job. Try this. Comment out the Command Builder line (put a single quote before the "D" of Dim). Run your programme again, and then try and update a record. You'll get this error message:

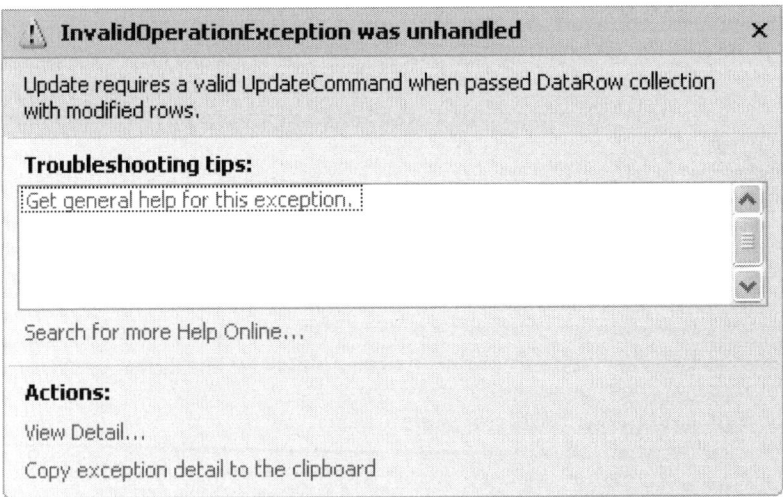

The error is because you haven't got a command builder – a Valid Update Command. Delete the comment from your Command Builder line and the error message goes away.

You should now be able to make changes to the database itself (as long as you haven't left the Access database as Read Only when you copied it to your hard drive).

Try it out. Run your programme, and change one of the records. Click the Update button. Then close the programme down, and load it up again. You should see your new changes displayed in the textboxes.

Exercise
There's one slight problem with the code above, though. Try clicking the Update button before clicking the Next (>) button. What happens? Do you know why you get the error message? Write code to stop this happening

Add a New Record

Adding a new record is slightly more complex. First, you have to add a new Row to the DataSet, then commit the new Row to the Database.

But the Add New button on our form is quite simple. The only thing it does is to switch off other buttons, and clear the textboxes, ready for a new entry. Here's the code for your Add New button:

```
btnCommit.Enabled = True
btnAddNew.Enabled = False
btnUpdate.Enabled = False
btnDelete.Enabled = False

txtFirstName.Clear( )
txtSurname.Clear( )
```

So three buttons are switched off when the Add New button is clicked, and one is switched on. The button that gets switched on is the Commit button. The Enable property of btnCommit gets set to True. But you need to set it to False for this to work. So return to your Form. Click btnCommit to select it. Then locate the Enabled Property in the Properties box. Set it to False. When the Form starts up, the button will be switched off.

The Cancel/Clear button can be used to switch it back on again. So add this code to your btnClear:

```
btnCommit.Enabled = False
btnAddNew.Enabled = True
btnUpdate.Enabled = True
btnDelete.Enabled = True

inc = 0
NavigateRecords( )
```

We're switching the Commit button off, and the other three back on. The other two lines just make sure that we display the first record again, after the Cancel button is clicked. Otherwise the textboxes will all be blank.

To add a new record to the database, we'll use the Commit button. So double click your btnCommit to access its code. Add the following:

```
If inc <> -1 Then
        Dim cb As New OleDb.OleDbCommandBuilder(da)
        Dim dsNewRow As DataRow

        dsNewRow = ds.Tables("AddressBook").NewRow()

        dsNewRow.Item("FirstName") = txtFirstName.Text
        dsNewRow.Item("Surname") = txtSurname.Text

        ds.Tables("AddressBook").Rows.Add(dsNewRow)

        da.Update(ds, "AddressBook")

        MsgBox("New Record added to the Database")

        btnCommit.Enabled = False
        btnAddNew.Enabled = True
        btnUpdate.Enabled = True
        btnDelete.Enabled = True
End If
```

The code is somewhat longer than usual, but we'll go through it.

The first line is an If Statement. We're just checking that there is a valid record to add. If there's not, the inc variable will be on minus 1. Inside of the If Statement, we first set up a Command Builder, as before. The next line is this:

Dim dsNewRow As DataRow

If you want to add a new row to your DataSet, you need a DataRow object. This line just sets up a variable called **dsNewRow**. The type of variable is a DataRow.

To create the new DataRow object, this line comes next:

dsNewRow = ds.Tables("AddressBook").NewRow( )

We're just saying, "Create a New Row object in the AddressBook DataSet, and store this in the variable called **dsNewRow**." As you can see, **NewRow()** is a method of **ds.Tables**. Use this Method to add rows to your DataSet.

The actual values we want to store in the rows are coming from the textboxes. So we have these two lines:

dsNewRow.Item("FirstName") = txtFirstName.Text
dsNewRow.Item("Surname") = txtSurname.Text

The dsNewRow object we created has a Property called Item. This is like the Item property you used earlier. It represents a column in your DataSet. We could have said this instead:

dsNewRow.Item(1) = txtFirstName.Text
dsNewRow.Item(2) = txtSurname.Text

The Item property is now using the index number of the DataSet columns, rather than the names. The result is the same, though: to store new values in these properties. We're storing the text from the textboxes to our new Row.

We now only need to call the Method that actually adds the Row to the DataSet:

ds.Tables("AddressBook").Rows.Add(dsNewRow)

To add the Row, you use the **Add** method of the Rows property of the DataSet. In between the round brackets, you need the name of your DataRow (the variable **dsNewRow**, in our case).

You should know what the rest of the code does. Here's the next line:

da.Update(ds, "AddressBook")

Again, we're just using the Update method of the Data Adapter, just like last time. The rest of the code just displays a message box, and resets the button.

But to add a new Row to a DataSet, here's a recap on what to do:

- Create a DataRow variable
- Cretae an Object from this variable by using the **NewRow** Method of the DataSet Tables property
- Assign values to the Items in the new Row
- Use the Add Method of the DataSet to add the new row

A little more complicated, but it does work! Try your programme out. Click your Add New button. The textboxes should go blank, and three of the buttons will be switched off. Enter a new record and then click the Commit button. You should see the message box telling you that a new record has been added to the database. To see the new record, close down your programme, and run it again. The new record will be there.

Deleting Records

The code to delete a record is a little easier. Double click your btnDelete and add the following:

```
Dim cb As New OleDb.OleDbCommandBuilder(da)

ds.Tables("AddressBook").Rows(inc).Delete()
MaxRows = MaxRows - 1

inc = 0
NavigateRecords( )
da.Update(ds, "AddressBook")
```

You've met most of it before. First we set up a Command Builder. Then we have this line:

ds.Tables("AddressBook").Rows(inc).Delete()

Just as there is an Add Method of the DataSet Rows property, so there is a Delete method. You don't need anything between the round brackets, this time. We've specified the Row to delete with:

Rows(inc)

The **inc** variable is setting which particular Row we're on. When the Delete method is called, it is this row that will be deleted.

However, it will only be deleted from the DataSet. To delete the row from the underlying database, we have this again:

da.Update(ds, "AddressBook")

The Command Builder, in conjunction with the Data Adapter, will take care of the deleting. All you need to is call the Update method of the Data Adapter.

The **MaxRows** line in the code just deducts 1 from the variable. This just ensures that the number of rows in the DataSet matches the number we have in the MaxRows variable.

We also reset the inc variable to zero, and call the NavigateRecords() subroutine. This will mean that the first record is displayed, after a record has been deleted.

Try out your programme. Click the Next (>) button a few times to move to a valid record. Then click the delete button. The record will be deleted from the DataSet AND the database. The record that is then displayed will be the first one.

There's another problem, though: if you click the Delete button before the Next (>) button, you'll get an error message. You can add an If Statement to check that the inc variable does not equal minus 1.

Another thing you can do is to display a message box asking users if they really want to delete this record. Here's one in action:

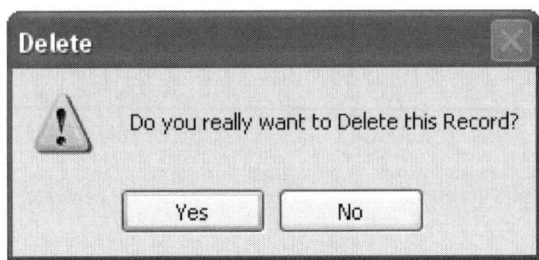

To get this in your own programme, add the following code to the very top of your Delete button code:

If MessageBox.Show("Do you really want to Delete this Record?", _
      "Delete", MessageBoxButtons.YesNo, _
      MessageBoxIcon.Warning) = Windows.Forms.DialogResult.No Then

      MsgBox("Operation Cancelled")
      Exit Sub

End If

The first three lines of the code are really one line. The underscore has been used to spread it out, so as to fit on this page.

But we're using the new message box function:

MessageBox.Show( )

In between the round brackets, we specifying the message to display, followed by a caption for the message box. We then have this:

MessageBoxButtons.YesNo

You won't have to type all that out; you'll be able to select it from a popup list. But what it does is give you Yes and No buttons on your message box.

After typing a comma, we selected the **MessageBoxIcon.Warning** icon from the popup list.

But you need to check which button the user clicked. This is done with this:

= Windows.Forms.DialogResult.No

Again, you select from a popup list. We want to check if the user clicked the No button. This will mean a change of mind from the user. A value of No will then be returned, which is what we're checking for in the If Statement.

The code for the If Statement itself is this:

MsgBox("Operation Cancelled")
Exit Sub

This will display another message for the user. But most importantly, the subroutine will be exited: we don't want the rest of the Delete code to be executed, if the user clicked the No button.

And that's it for our introduction to database programming. You not only saw how to construct a database programme using the Wizard, but how to write code to do this yourself. There is an awful lot more to database programming, and we've just scratched the surface. But in a beginner's book, that's all we have time for. To end, here's a Review that will test what you have learned in this section.

Review Nine

Finish off the database programme you have been working on. At the moment, you only have a first name and a surname displayed. Add textboxes so that the following fields from the database are displayed:

FirstName
Surname
Address1
Address2
Address3
Postcode
Phone
Email
Notes

When you are finished, your form might look like this (but feel free to come up with your own design):

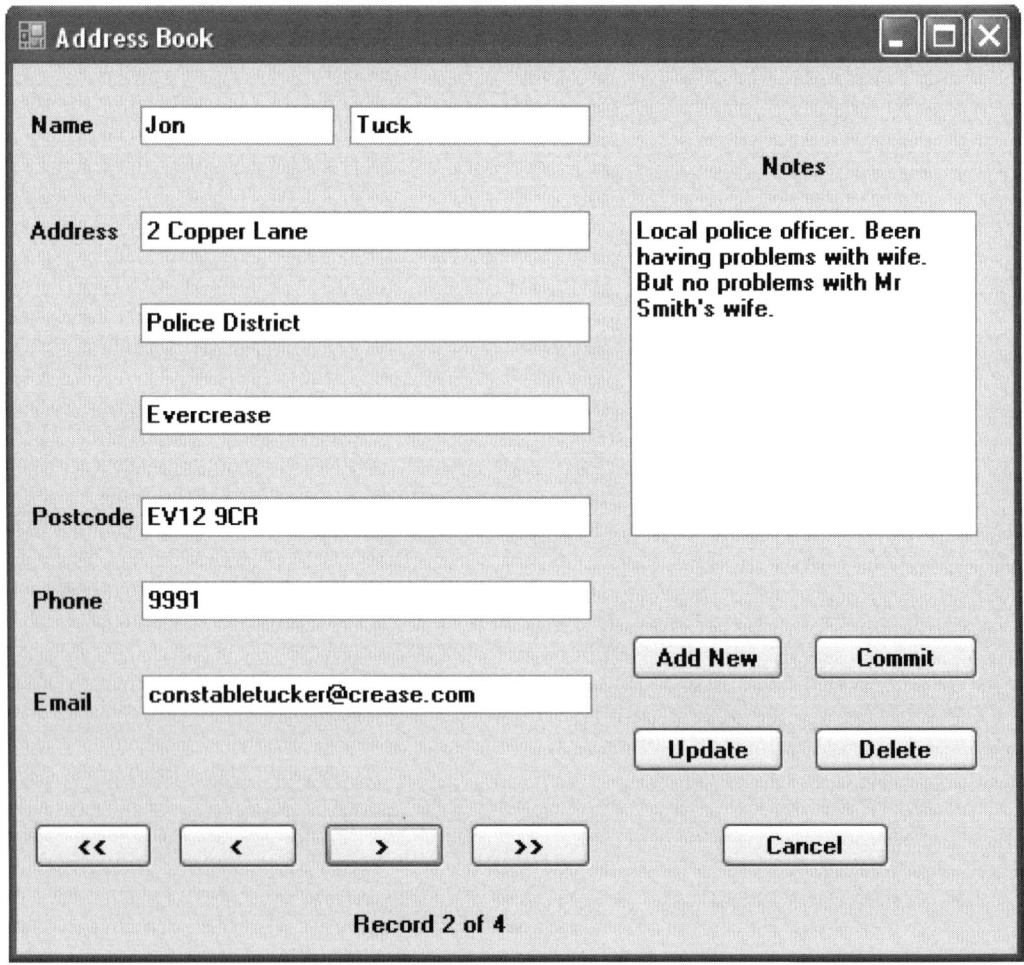

In your completed programme, a user should be able to do the following:

- Move through the records one at a time
- Move back through the records one at a time
- Jump to the last Record
- Jump to the first Record
- Update a record
- Add a new record
- Delete a record
- Cancel the adding a new record operation

Notice at the bottom of the form that it says "Record 2 of 4". Implement this in your own code. When you advance to the next record, it would then say "Record 3 of 4".

<u>NOTE</u>

For this project, it's better to copy the original AddressBook database, and paste it to the location "C:\" (Windows XP), or "C:\Users\Owner\Documents" (Vista/Windows 7). If you already have a file called AddressBook.mdb at this location, either move, rename or delete it. When you work from a fresh copy of the database, you won't get any "Type Casting" and Null value problems. You'll get these if you enter a fresh record in the database with only a First Name and a Surname, as you did when working on this section.

Working with Forms

In this final section of the course, we'll take a look at some of the extra things you can do with VB.NET forms. First, we'll take a look at the Anchor and Dock properties of a form.

Anchoring and Docking

The Anchor and Dock properties of a form are two separate properties. Anchor refers to the position a control has relative to the edges of the form. A textbox, for example, that is anchored to the left edge of a form will stay in the same position as the form is resized. Docking refers to how much space you want the control to take up on the form. If you dock a control to the left of the form, it will stretch itself to the height of the form, but its width will stay the same. Let's take a look at some examples, to clear things up.

Start a new windows project. Add two textboxes to your form, and set the MultiLine properties of both to True. Change the height of the boxes.

Click on Textbox1 and locate the Anchor property in the properties box:

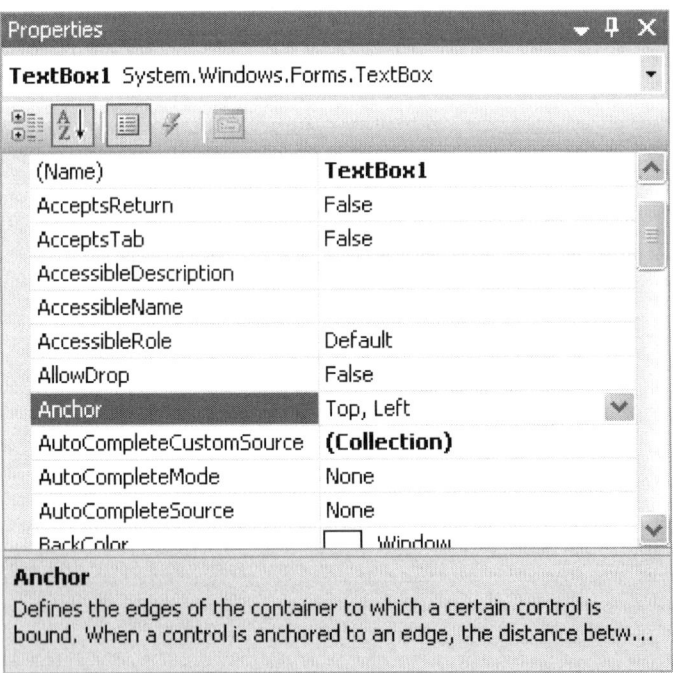

The default is to anchor the control to the Top, Left edge of the form. Click the arrow to reveal a curious drop down box:

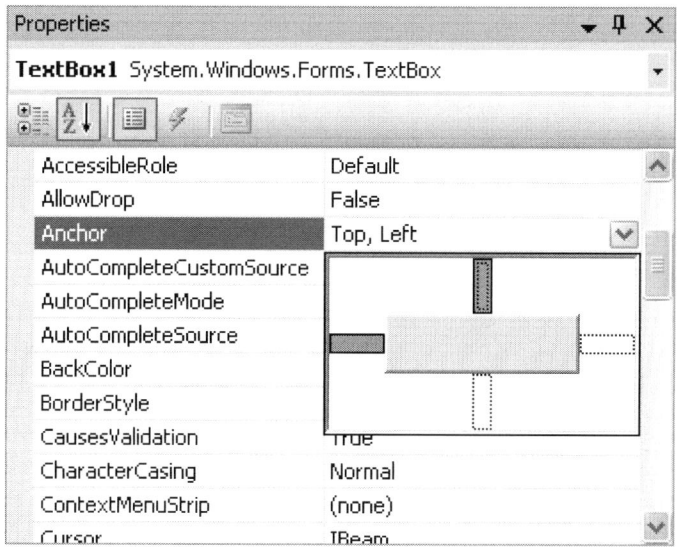

The button in the middle represents your control. The big white areas are rather confusing –
they don't actually do anything! To change the property, you click the smaller grey or white
rectangles between the big white rectangles. Click again to deselect it. In the image below, the
property has been changed so that the textbox is anchored to the Top, Left and Right sides of
the form:

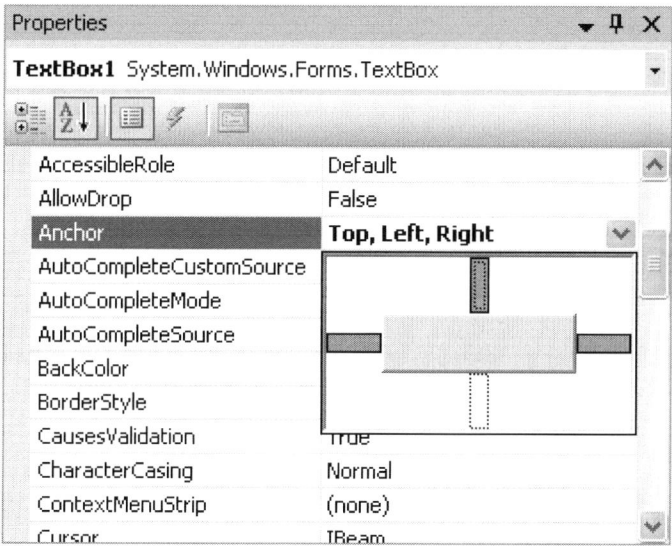

The next image has the textbox anchored to the Right and Bottom edges of the Form:

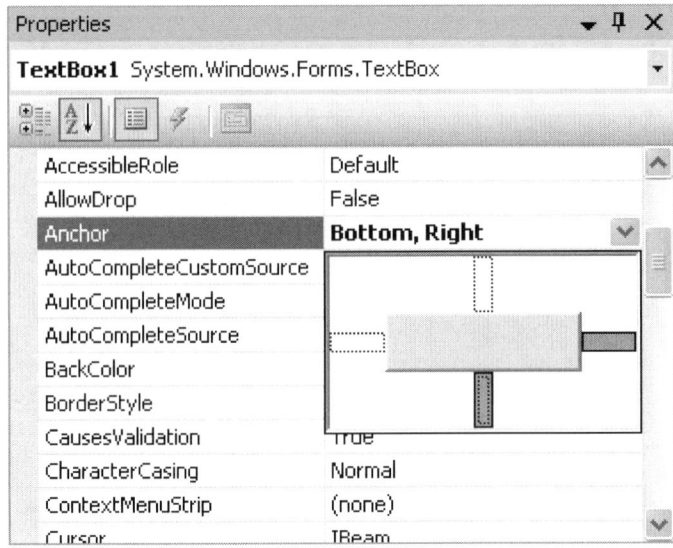

Click the arrow on the drop down box to confirm your choices.

To see what affect this all has, do the following:

- Set the Anchor property of Textbox1 on the default of Top, Left
- Change the Anchor property of Textbox2 to None (all the small rectangles should be white.)
- Run your programme and drag the edges of the Form outward. This will resize your form

What you should notice is that Textbox1 stays where it is, and that the left edge of Textbox2 moves.

Stop your programme from running. Change the Anchor properties of the two textboxes to anything you like. Run your form again and watch what happens. Try anchoring one textbox to the left and right of the form. Watch what happens.

But anchoring a control to an edge of the form is a useful property to get used to, if you have a form that can be resized and want your controls to stay where they are.

Docking

Docking is similar to Anchoring, but this time the control fills a certain area of the form. To see how it works, click on one of your textboxes and locate the Dock property. Click the arrow to reveal a drop down box:

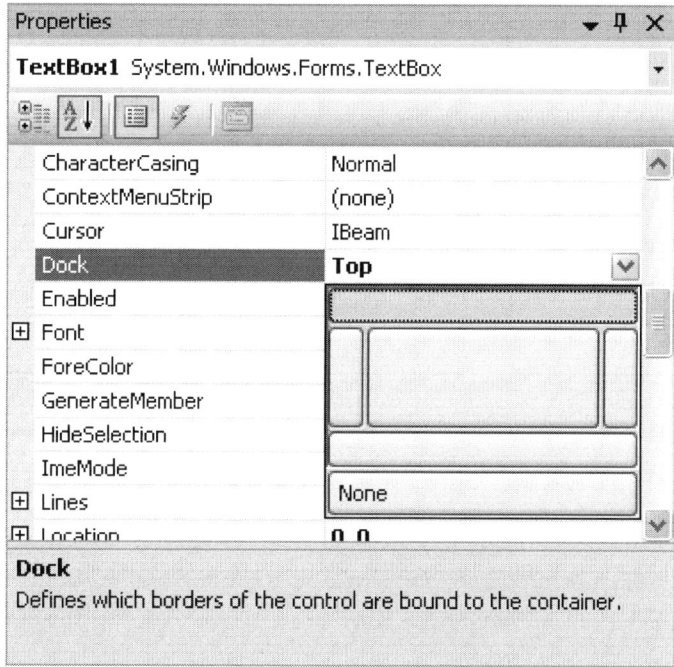

This time, all the rectangles are like buttons. You can only dock to one side at a time, and the default is None. Click a button to see what it does to your textbox. Click the middle one, and the textbox will Fill the whole form.

Docking is quite useful when used with the splitter control and panels, allowing you to create a Windows-style interface.

Toolbars

The toolbar is a very popular and much-used addition to a programme. It's difficult to think of a piece of software that doesn't make use of them. VB.NET lets you add toolbars to your forms, and the process is quite straightforward. Let's see how it's done:

Either start a new Windows project, or keep the one you currently have. To add a toolbar to the top of your form, expand the Toolbox and locate the **ToolStrip** control:

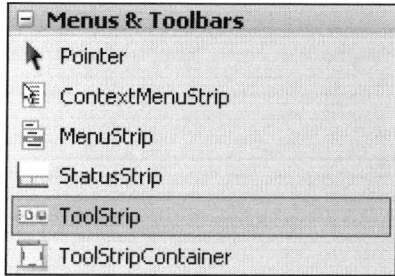

Double click the ToolStrip control, and it will be added to the top of your form:

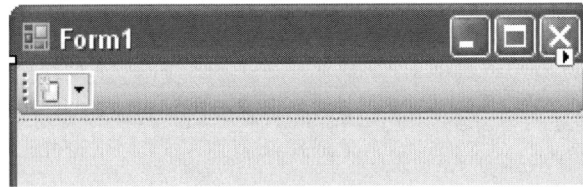

You should also notice the ToolStrip object that appears at the bottom of the window:

ToolStrips work by adding buttons and images to them. The button is then clicked, and an action performed.

Click on your ToolStrip to select it. In the property box for the ToolStrip, you'll notice that it has the default Name of ToolStrip1. We'll keep this Name. But locate the Items (Collection) property:

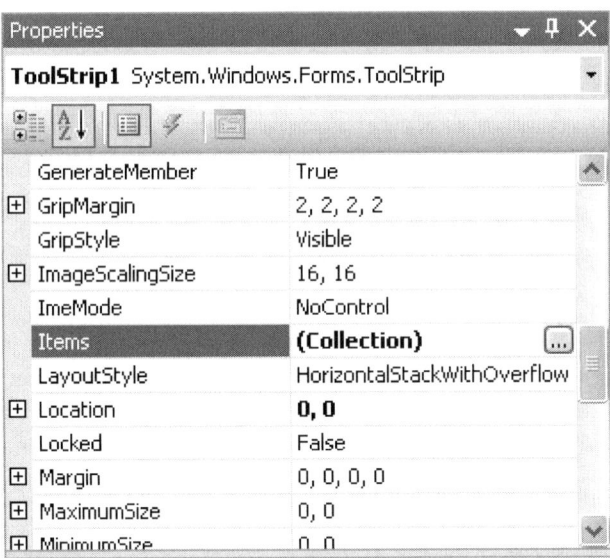

Click the button with the three dots in it. This brings up the Items Collection Editor:

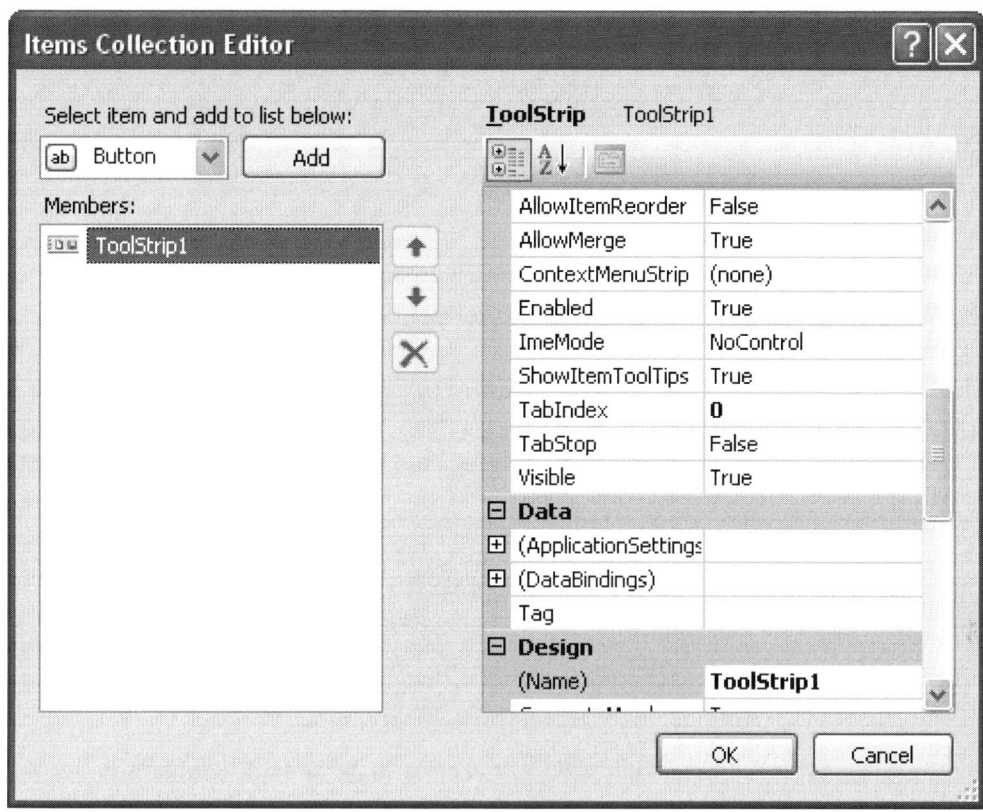

To add a new button to your ToolStrip, click the **Add** button at the top. The button appears in the **Members** box (ToolStripButton1):

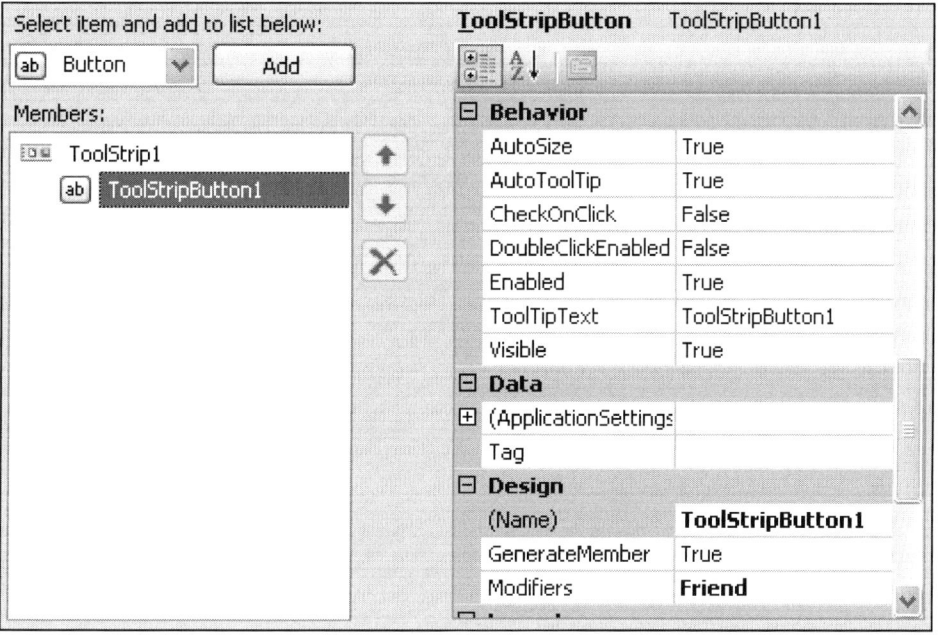

Notice that the new button has its own list of properties, just to the right. To add an image to this new button, locate the Image property:

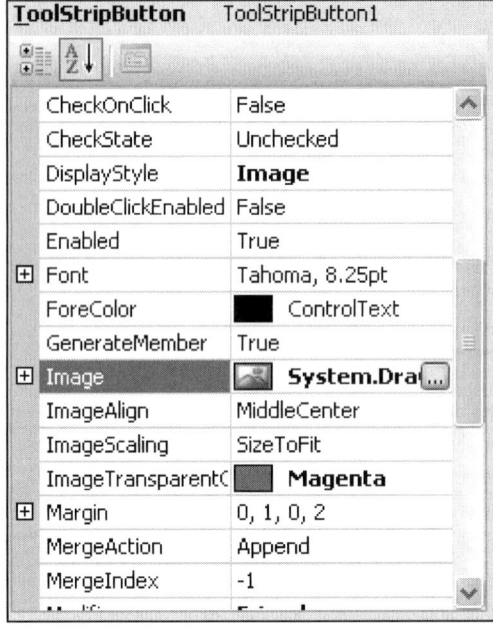

Click the small button with the 3 dots in it to bring up the **Select Resource** box:

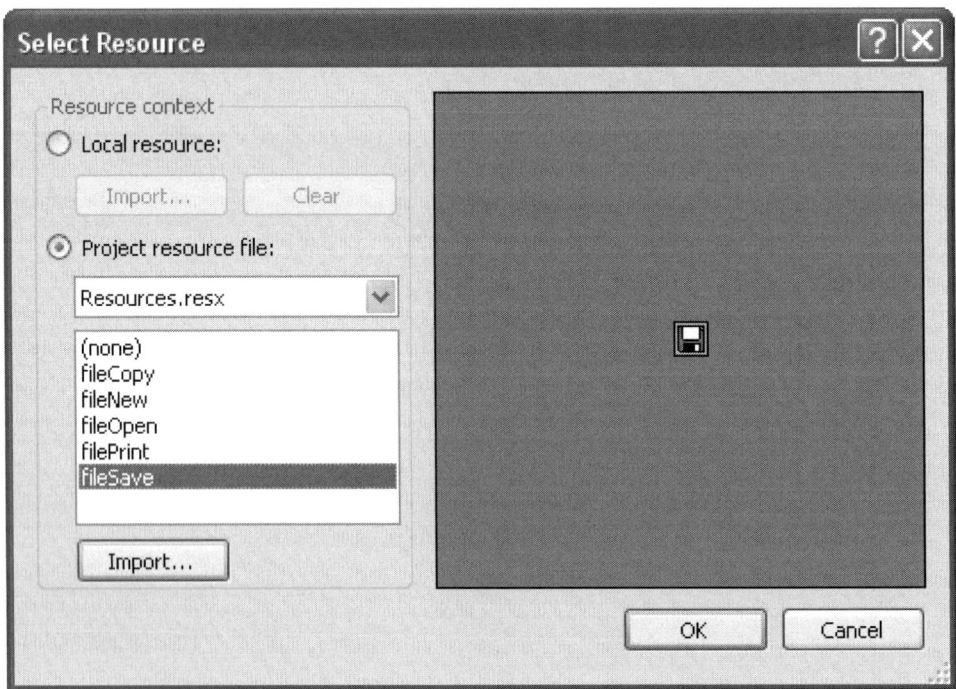

In the image above, we've selected "Project resource file", and then clicked the Import button. We then navigated to some Bitmap images and imported the five that you can see in the screenshot above. (The Bitmap folder is amongst the files you download at the start of this book.) Click OK when you have imported some images. You will be returned to the Item Collection Editor. Click OK on this, as well. The ToolStrip on your form will then look like this:

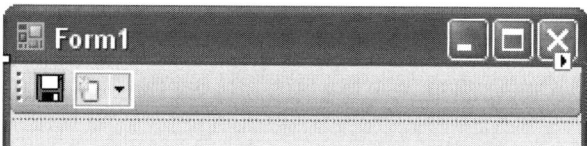

The second of those images is a dropdown list of available ToolStrip options:

So if you want, say, a separator instead of a button, select it from the list. This dropdown list will disappear when you run the form:

Repeat the steps outlined above, and add some more buttons to your ToolStrip. It should then look something like ours:

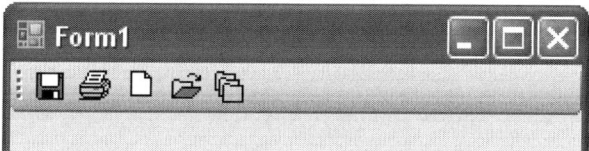

If your ToolStrip images have a grey background, you can get rid of this by bringing up the Image Collection Editor again. Select a button, and then locate the property called **ImageTransparentColor**. The default is Magenta. Change it to Silver, which is one of the Custom colours (second grey down, on the left).

Of course, if you click on the buttons nothing will happen. We need to write the code that gets them to work.

Coding For your Toolbar buttons

Return to the Design environment. Double click your first ToolStripbutton to bring up the coding window. It should look like this:

```
Private Sub ToolStripButton1_Click(ByVal sender As System.Object, _
                          ByVal e As System.EventArgs) _
                          Handles ToolStripButton1.Click


End Sub
```

You can place any code you like, here. Try a message box, as in the image below:

```
Private Sub ToolStripButton1_Click(ByVal sender As System.Object, _
                          ByVal e As System.EventArgs) _
                          Handles ToolStripButton1.Click


    MessageBox.Show("Save button clicked")

End Sub
```

Run your programme and click your ToolStrip button. You should see the message box display. In a real programme, however, the code would be the same code for a menu item – it's just shortcut, after all!

Creating other Forms

It's a rare programme that only has one form in it. Most programmes will have other forms. These other forms can be used for things like Find and Replace searches, extra formatting capabilities, to set Options for the programme, and a whole lot more besides. VB.NET lets you add as many forms as you want to your project. But the process is not quite so simple. We'll see how to do it, though.

You can use the form you already have for this, the one with the ToolStrip on it. But from the VB.NET design environment, click the **Project** menu. From the drop down menu, click **Add Windows Form**. The Add New Item dialogue box appears.

Select **Windows Form** under Templates. Then click inside the Name textbox at the bottom. Change the Name of the form to **frmSecond.vb**. Then click Add.

When you are returned to the design environment, your new form will be displayed:

To switch between forms, you can click the tabs. In the image, two tabs are displayed: Form1 (the original and first form), and our new form **frmSecond**.

We'll write code to get this new form to display. But it will only appear when a button is clicked on Form1.

So click the tab for Form1, and add a button to this form. Change the Name property of the button to **btnShowSecond**. Then double click the button to access the code for it.

In order to display the second form, you have to bear in mind that Forms are Classes. So **frmSecond** is a Class (as is Form1). You first have to create a new object from the class called frmSecond Class. Then call its Show method.

So add this code to your button:

Dim SecondForm As New frmSecond

SecondForm.Show( )

The first line Dims a variable called SecondForm. When you type "As New", you're asking VB.NET to create a New object. If you type a space, you'll see a pop up list. Type the **frm** of **frmSecond** and you should see it displayed on the list. You can double click the item in the list to add it to your code. But what the line does is create a new Object from the Class called **frmSecond**.

Once we have the Form Object stored in the variable, we can just use the Show method to display the form.

Run your programme and test it out. When you click your button, you should see the second form appear.

However, there's a problem with this code. Click the button again and another copy of **frmSecond** appears. Keep clicking the button and your screen will be filled with the second form!

To prevent this from happening, you can move the code that creates the form object. Move it right to the top of the coding window, just below **Public Class Form1**.

The only code left in the button is the line that Shows the form. A new form object will now not be created every time the button is clicked. If you try it out, you should see only one form appear when the button is clicked, and not multiple forms.

Modal and None Modal Forms

A modal from is one that has to be dealt with before a user can continue. An example is the Change Case dialogue box in Microsoft Word. If you try to click away from the dialogue box, you'll hear a beep to indicate an error. Until you click either the Cancel or OK buttons, the programme won't let you click anywhere else.

The second form you've just created is called a Modeless form. These are forms than can be hidden or sent to the taskbar. You can then return to the main form or programme and do things with it.

A Modal form is sometimes called a dialogue box. And we'll see how to create one of these now.

Add a second button to your Form1. Change the Name property of the new button to **btnDialogueBox**. Double click the new button and add the following code:

Dim frmDialogue As New frmSecond

frmDialogue.ShowDialog( )

To display a form as a Modal dialogue box, you use the ShowDialog method. If you use the Show method, the form is displayed as a Modeless form.

Run your programme. Click your new button, and the second form should display. Move it out the way and try to click a button on Form1. You won't be able to. The second form has to be dealt with before you can access Form1.

When the form is a Modal dialogue box, you can create OK and Cancel buttons for it. VB.NET then has a trick up its sleeve for these types of buttons. We'll see that trick now.

In the design environment, click the Tab for your **frmSecond**. When the form is displayed in the design window, add two buttons to it (make sure you're adding the buttons to the second form and NOT Form1). Change the Name property of the first button to btnOK, and the Name property of the second to btnCancel. Double click your OK button and add the following code to it:

Me.DialogResult = Windows.Forms.DialogResult.OK

The Me keyword refers to the current form. When you type a full stop, select DialogResult from the pop up list that appears. DialogResult is a property of the Form. It can accept a range of values. As soon as you type a space after the equals sign, you'll see a list with these values on it:

As you can see, one of these values is **Windows.Forms.DialogResult.OK**. This indicates that you want to use this button as an OK button. When the button is clicked, VB.NET will return a result of OK for this button.

Access the code for your Cancel button and add the following line:

Me.DialogResult = Windows.Forms.DialogResult.Cancel

For the Cancel button, we're just selecting **DialogResult.Cancel** from the list. When the button is clicked, VB.NET will return a result of Cancel for this button.

You can test to see what value is stored in **Me.DialogResult**. But you do that from the button that displays the form, Form1 for us.

So access your Form1 code, and locate the lines that display the second form. The two lines should be these:

Dim frmDialogue As New frmSecond
frmDialogue.ShowDialog( )

Change the second line to this:

If frmDialogue.ShowDialog() = Windows.Forms.DialogResult.OK Then
MsgBox("OK Button Clicked")
End If

To get at the value of the button clicked, you test to see what result the ShowDialog property is. If the ShowDialog property of frmDialogue is OK then you can execute the code that needs executing. If the Cancel button was clicked, however, you don't have to do anything: VB.NET will take care of closing your Modal dialogue box for you!

Run your programme and test it out. Click your button to bring up your Modal dialogue box. Click the OK button, and you should see the message box display. Bring the Modal dialogue box up a second time and then click the Cancel button. The form will just close down.

Getting at Values on other Forms

The form with OK and Cancel buttons on it is not doing much good. We need it do some work for us. Let's turn the form into a Change Case dialogue box.

Design a Form like the one in the following image (this is frmSecond):

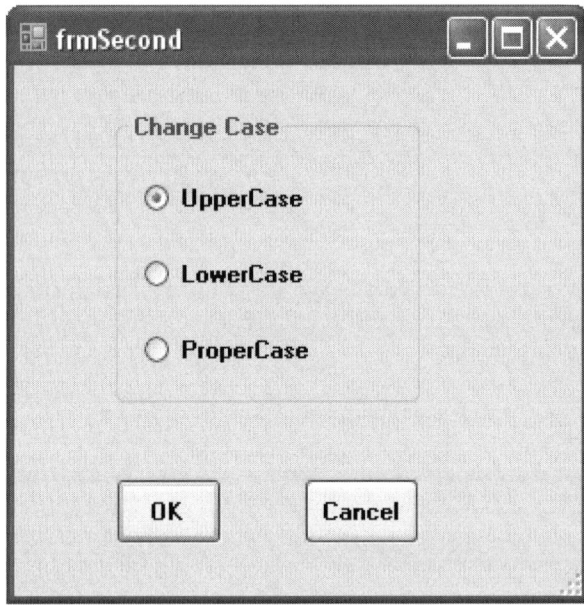

When you've designed your form, click back on Form1 and add a Textbox to it. When the button on Form1 is clicked, the dialogue box above will display. You can then select an option button to change the case to Upper, Lower or Proper. This will happen when the OK button is clicked. Whatever text is in Texbox1 on Form1 will be changed accordingly.

Double click the OK button on **frmSecond** to access the code. You should have the following:

Me.DialogResult = Windows.Forms.DialogResult.OK

If you want to refer to Texbox1 on Form1, you can't just do this:

Form1.Textbox1.Text

In previous version of VB, that code would be all right. You're saying "Access the Text property of Textbox1 on Form1." The problem in VB.NET is that forms are Classes. They don't become objects until one is created from a Class. So the **frmSecond** Class knows nothing about **Form1**. It has no idea what it is.

The solution is to create a textbox object variable on Form1, and assign Textbox1 to this variable. But this variable has to be something that all Classes in the project can see.

So add this near the top of your code window for Form1 (add it just below the **Public Class Form1** line):

Public Shared tb As TextBox

We're setting up a variable which we've called **tb**. A Textbox object is going to be stored in this variable. But notice that the variable is **Public Shared**. This way, **frmSecond** will be able to see the variable.

In the Form Load event for Form1, add the following line:

tb = Textbox1

When Form1 loads, the textbox called Textbox1 will be assigned to the **tb** variable. Now Textbox1 can be seen by **frmSecond**.

Go back to your code for the OK button on **frmSecond**. Add the following two lines at the top:

Dim ChangeCase As String
ChangeCase = Form1.tb.Text

We're setting up a String variable called **ChangeCase**. Whatever text is in Textbox1 of Form1 will then be assigned to the **ChangeCase** variable. But notice that as soon as you type a full stop after Form1, the **tb** variable will be available in the pop up list:

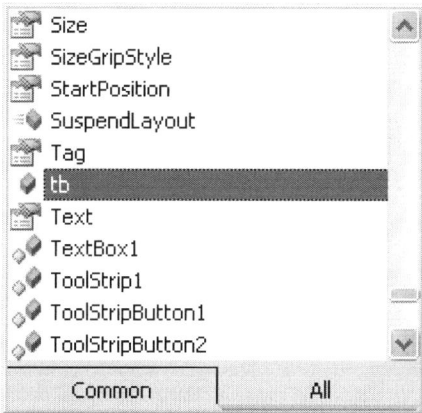

The Public variable called **tb** holds a reference to Textbox1 on Form1. When you type a full stop after the **tb**, you get a list popping up. The list is all the Properties and Methods that are available to Textbox1. One of these is the Text property.

We now only need to add the code that does the actual converting. So add this below the two lines you already have:

Dim ChangeCase As String
ChangeCase = Form1.tb.Text

If optUpper.Checked Then
        ChangeCase = ChangeCase.ToUpper
ElseIf optLower.Checked Then
        ChangeCase = ChangeCase.ToLower
ElseIf optProper.Checked Then
        ChangeCase = StrConv(ChangeCase, VbStrConv.ProperCase)
End If

Form1.tb.Text = ChangeCase

The three options buttons on our form were called optUpper, optLower and optProper. In the code, we're using an If Statement to see which of these was selected. The one that was chosen will have its Checked property set to True. We then store into the variable **ChangeCase** the converted text from the textbox. The final line puts the converted text back into Textbox1 on Form1. But you're coding window should look like this:

```
Private Sub btnOK_Click(ByVal sender As System.Object, _
                        ByVal e As System.EventArgs) _
                        Handles btnOK.Click

    Dim ChangeCase As String
    ChangeCase = Form1.tb.Text

    If optUpper.Checked Then

        ChangeCase = ChangeCase.ToUpper

    ElseIf optLower.Checked Then

        ChangeCase = ChangeCase.ToLower

    ElseIf optProper.Checked Then

        ChangeCase = StrConv(ChangeCase, VbStrConv.ProperCase)

    End If

    Form1.tb.Text = ChangeCase

    Me.DialogResult = Windows.Forms.DialogResult.OK

End Sub
```

Note that the DialogResult.OK line is the final line of the code. When you're writing your code, make sure that optUpper, optLower and optProper are changed to whatever you called your Radio Buttons.

When you're finished adding the code, run your programme. Enter some text into Textbox1. Then click the button that brings up the Change Case Dialogue box. Select an option from the three available, and then click OK. The text in Textbox1 should be converted.

Setting and Getting values from one form to another can be quite a tricky process at first. But once you get the hang of it you'll find it's not too difficult.

And that ends this section on forms. There's an awful lot more to learn about Windows Forms, and a bit of experimentation is needed before you become skilled in their use. But in a beginner's book, you've learned enough to be going on with.

Graphics and Visual Basic .NET

The NET framework comes with a lot of inbuilt classes to do with Graphics. You can use these classes to draw on forms, and on form objects such as Picture Boxes.

The first thing we'll do is to draw a line on a form when a button is clicked. This will teach you how to create objects from the various Graphics classes. It will also highlight a problem that needs to be solved.

Drawing lines on a form

To draw anything on a form or form object, you need to use a Graphics object. This will take care of all the tricky graphic card manipulation, and getting your drawing to the screen.

So start a new project. Put a button on your new form, somewhere on the right hand side. Make the form a little big bigger. Now double click your button to get at the coding window.

To set up a graphics object, add these two lines to your button code:

Dim graphicsObject As Graphics
graphicsObject = Me.CreateGraphics( )

The first line just sets up a variable of type **Graphics**. The second line sets the graphics object to the form (the **Me** part). If you wanted to draw a line on a Picture Box then the second line would be this, instead:

graphicsObject = PictureBox1.CreateGraphics( )

The graphics object would then attach itself to the Picture Box instead of the form.

Lines, and most other shapes, are drawn with Pen objects. Once you set up a Pen object, you then instruct the graphics object to draw a line with your chosen Pen. So add these two lines to your code:

Dim pen_one As Pen
pen_one = New Pen(Color.Black, 2)

The first line sets up a variable of type Pen. We've called ours **pen_one**. On the second line above, we're creating the Pen object with the **New** keyword. After the word **Pen**, you type a round bracket. The first thing you need to do is to specify a colour for your pen. As soon as you type the round bracket, you should see a list of colours to choose from:

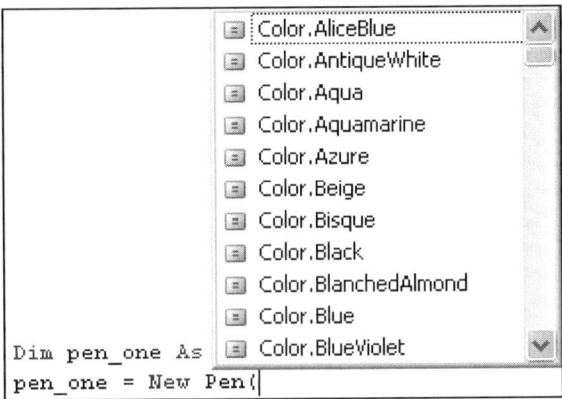

There's quite a lot! Select one from the list, then type a comma.

The second argument is for the width of your pen. The width value is a Single, so you can have 1.5, say, or 2.4. But type the number 2, then the final round bracket. If you prefer, you can keep the Pen code on one line:

Dim pen_one As New Pen(Color.Black, 2)

Your coding window should now look something like ours (The Private Sub line below has been edited to fit on this page):

```
Private Sub Button1_Click(ByVal sender As System.Object,
                          ByVal e As System.EventArgs)
                          Handles Button1.Click

    Dim graphicsObject As Graphics
    graphicsObject = Me.CreateGraphics()

    Dim pen_one As Pen
    pen_one = New Pen(Color.Black, 2)

End Sub
```

Now that we have a graphics object and a pen, we can tell the graphics object to draw the line. This is quite straightforward because the graphics object has a **Sub** called **DrawLine**.

Type the name of your graphics object, and then a dot. You should see a list of all the things that the graphics object can do:

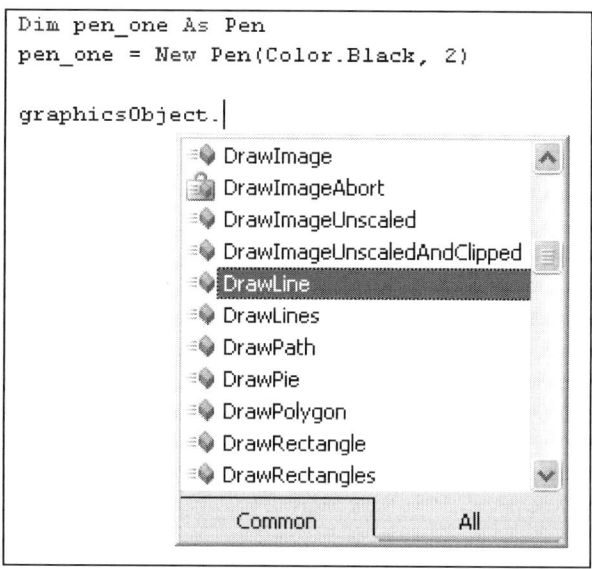

As you can see, the graphics object can draw lots of other things too. We'll meet a few more soon, but for now select DrawLine from the list. Then type a round bracket. You should see the colour list appear again. You'll also see 1 of 4 possible overloads. Keep it on the first one. Don't select a colour, though. Instead, type the name of your pen tool, which was pen_one for us. Now type a comma. You'll be invited to type in some number for the position of your line: X1, Y1, X2, Y2. The first two numbers, X1 and Y1, are for the start of your line. X1 is how far to the left you want to start drawing your line; Y1 is how far down you want to start drawing. Type 10, 10 for the first two numbers. The next set of numbers, X2 and Y2, are for the end of your line. Again, X2 is how far to the left, and Y2 is how far down. Type 100, 10 for the second two numbers. Then type the closing round bracket. You should have this:

graphicsObject.DrawLine(pen_one, 10, 10, 100, 10)

So what you're saying here is "Draw a line with the pen tool I've set up. Draw it at position 10, 10, 100, 10".

The entire code should now look like this:

```
Private Sub Button1_Click(ByVal sender As System.Object,
                          ByVal e As System.EventArgs)
                          Handles Button1.Click

     Dim graphicsObject As Graphics
     graphicsObject = Me.CreateGraphics()

     Dim pen_one As Pen
     pen_one = New Pen(Color.Black, 2)

     graphicsObject.DrawLine(pen_one, 10, 10, 100, 10)
End Sub
```

Run your programme and click your button. You should see the following straight line appear on your form:

So to recap. To draw a line on a form, you do the following:

- Set up a Graphics objects and point it to the current form by using the **Me** keyword.
- Set up a Pen object, and specify a colour and line width
- Use the **DrawLine** Subroutine using your Pen, and some position coordinates

To get some more practice, try the following exercises.

Exercise
How would you get the following diagonal line?

Exercise
And how would you get the following diagonal line?

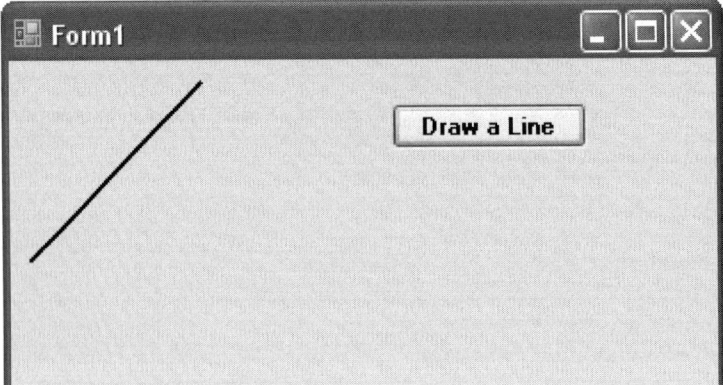

Exercise

Draw a vertical red line like the one in the image below:

The Paint Event

There is, however, a slight problem to be solved. Run your programme, and then either minimise it to the Taskbar at the bottom of the screen, or put another running programme over the top of it. Now bring your programme to the front of the screen again, making it the focus. Your line will have disappeared! You'll have to click the button again to get the line back.

The reason your lines have disappeared is because of the way graphics work in the Windows operating system. If you minimise a programme, Windows "forgets" about it. After all, there's no use wasting memory on a programme that is not displayed. But the Windows operating system will send a message to the programme that was minimised or hidden. It issues an Invalidate command, telling it that the programme has been invalidated and therefore needs to be redrawn.

To solve the problem, we'll use the Paint event of Forms. So, in design view, click on your form to select it. In the properties area on the right, click on the lightning bolt to see a list of all the events that a form has. You'll see the Paint event, as in the image below:

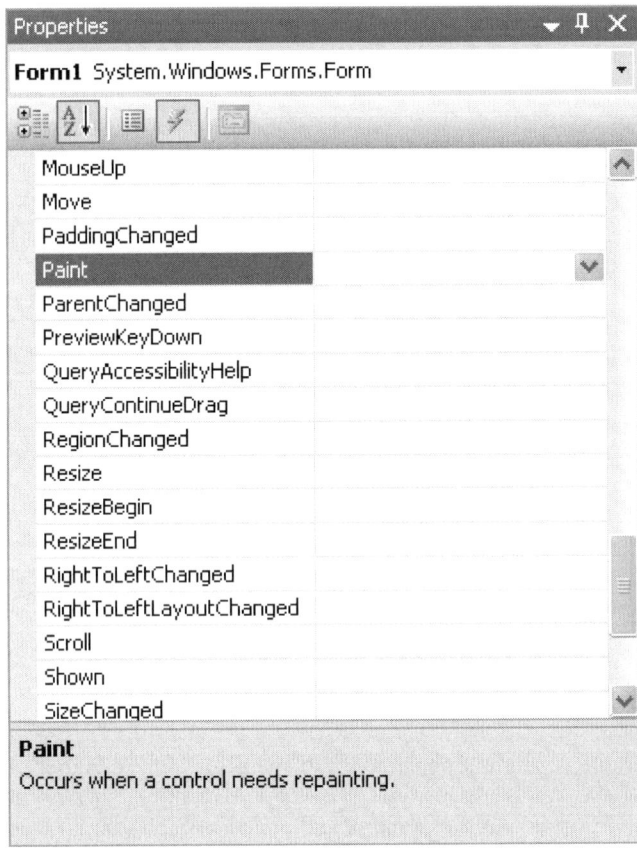

Double click on the word "Paint" and it will create a code stub for you:

```
Private Sub Form1_Paint(ByVal sender As System.Object, _
                        ByVal e As System.Windows.Forms.PaintEventArgs) _
                        Handles MyBase.Paint


End Sub
```

The Paint event gets called many times a second, ensuring that whatever objects you place on a form get drawn (Painted) without you noticing any problems. You can place your graphics code here, rather than in your button.

So move all your code from your button to the Paint event. Your coding window will now look like this:

```
Private Sub Button1_Click(ByVal sender As System.Object, _
                          ByVal e As System.EventArgs) _
                          Handles Button1.Click

End Sub

Private Sub Form1_Paint(ByVal sender As System.Object, _
                ByVal e As System.Windows.Forms.PaintEventArgs) _
                Handles MyBase.Paint

    Dim graphicsObject As Graphics
    graphicsObject = Me.CreateGraphics()

    Dim pen_one As Pen
    pen_one = New Pen(Color.Red, 4)

    graphicsObject.DrawLine(pen_one, 10, 10, 100, 10)

End Sub
```

Run your programme again. What you'll find is that the line is already drawn on the form, and that you don't need to click the button. That's because the Paint event fires as soon as the form is displayed on screen.

Minimise the form, though. Then bring it back up and make it the focus. The line will still be there. It is no longer getting erased!

However, we don't want the line to be drawn when the form loads. We want the line to be drawn when the button is clicked.

To get around this, we need to do two things: prevent the line being drawn when the form loads, and issue the Invalidate command when the button is clicked. We issue the Invalidate command to force the Paint event to be called. Once it's started, the Paint event will fire repeatedly, thus executing our code.

To prevent the line being drawn when the form loads, we can set up a variable that can be changed in various places. So add this line to the top of your coding window:

Dim draw_options As Integer = 0

Your coding window will then look like this:

```
Public Class Form1

    Dim draw_options As Integer = 0

    Private Sub Button1_Click(ByVal sender As System.Object, _
                              ByVal e As System.EventArgs) _
                              Handles Button1.Click




    End Sub
```

In the button code, we can change the value of the new variable. We can also issue the Invalidate command. Add these two lines to your code:

draw_options = 1
Me.Invalidate( )

Here's what your coding window will look like:

```
Public Class Form1

    Dim draw_options As Integer = 0

    Private Sub Button1_Click(ByVal sender As System.Object, _
                              ByVal e As System.EventArgs) _
                              Handles Button1.Click


        draw_options = 1
        Me.Invalidate()

    End Sub
```

The Me keyword refers the current form. Invalidate will automatically call the Paint event of Form1.

Except, we need to change the code in our Paint event. We can set up a Select Case statement to check the value of the draw_options variable. If it's zero, we won't draw anything. If it's 1, we can execute our code. So change your Paint event code to this:

```
Private Sub Form1_Paint(ByVal sender As System.Object, _
                        ByVal e As System.Windows.Forms.PaintEventArgs) _
                        Handles MyBase.Paint

    Dim graphicsObject As Graphics
    graphicsObject = Me.CreateGraphics()

    Dim pen_one As Pen
    pen_one = New Pen(Color.Red, 4)

    Select Case draw_options
        Case 1
            graphicsObject.DrawLine(pen_one, 10, 10, 100, 10)
        Case 0
    End Select

End Sub
```

So the DrawLine code has been moved to the **Case 1** option of the Select Case statement. When the form first loads, **draw_options** will have a value of 0. When you click the button, **draw_options** will be 1, thus executing the DrawLine code.

Run your programme and test it out. The line won't be visible when the form first loads. It will only appear when the button is clicked.

Minimise your form, and then bring it back on screen. Again, the line will still be there – it won't have vanished!

Exercise
Add a new button to your form. Set the Text property to "Clear the Form". Write code for the button so that when it's clicked, whatever is drawn on the form will be cleared.

There's a little bit of tidying up we can do to our code. Because the Paint event is fired repeatedly, you don't want to keep creating graphics objects and Pens, like our code does. So the first thing we can do is to move the Pen code out of there.

Move this line:

Dim pen_one As Pen

to the very top of the coding window, just below the line that sets **draw_options** to 0. The line that creates the Pen object can be moved to the button code. So move this line to your button:

pen_one = New Pen(Color.Red, 4)

Your coding window should then look like ours:

```
Dim draw_options As Integer = 0
Dim pen_one As Pen

Private Sub Button1_Click(ByVal sender As System.Object, _
                          ByVal e As System.EventArgs) _
                          Handles Button1.Click

    pen_one = New Pen(Color.Red, 4)
    draw_options = 1
    Me.Invalidate()

End Sub

Private Sub Form1_Paint(ByVal sender As System.Object, _
                        ByVal e As System.Windows.Forms.PaintEventArgs) _
                        Handles MyBase.Paint

    Dim graphicsObject As Graphics
    graphicsObject = Me.CreateGraphics()

    Select Case draw_options
        Case 1
            graphicsObject.DrawLine(pen_one, 10, 10, 100, 10)
        Case 0
    End Select

End Sub
```

We can also do something with the two lines that set up the Graphics objects.

If you have a look at the arguments for **Form1_Paint( )** you'll notice this one:

ByVal e As System.Windows.Forms.PaintEventArgs

The "**e**" is a variable, and has its own properties and Subs. One of these properties is a Graphics object. Which means you don't need to create a new one. You can just do this:

e.Graphics.DrawLine(pen_one, 10, 10, 100, 10)

So delete the two lines where we set up a new graphics objects. Change the line in **Case 1** from this:

graphicsObject.DrawLine(pen_one, 10, 10, 100, 10)

to this:

e.Graphics.DrawLine(pen_one, 10, 10, 100, 10)

Your Paint event will then look like this:

```
Private Sub Form1_Paint(ByVal sender As System.Object, _
                        ByVal e As System.Windows.Forms.PaintEventArgs) _
                        Handles MyBase.Paint

    Select Case draw_options
        Case 1
            e.Graphics.DrawLine(pen_one, 10, 10, 100, 10)
        Case 0
    End Select

End Sub
```

Run your programme and click your "Draw Line" button. You should find that it works OK.

Now that we've tidied the code up a bit, let's draws some rectangles and ellipses.

Rectangles and Ellipses

Rectangles, like lines, can be drawn with the Graphics object. First, though, you need to create a Rectangle object.

Add a new button to your form, and double click to get at the coding window. To set up a rectangle, add the following lines to the top of the coding window, just below the pen_one line:

Dim rectangle_one As Rectangle

This sets up a variable of type **Rectangle**. We now need to create a Rectangle object.

Click back inside of your new button code stub, and add the following:

rectangle_one = New Rectangle(10, 10, 100, 300)

The numbers between the round brackets of Rectangle are for the x position, the y position, the width of the rectangle, and the height. The x and y position are where you want to start drawing the upper right hand corner of the rectangle. In our code, we're saying "Have the upper right hand corner at position 10, 10. The width will be 100, and the height will be 300".

If you prefer, you can set up your rectangle like this:

rectangle_one = New Rectangle( )

rectangle_one.X = 10
rectangle_one.Y = 10
rectangle_one.Width = 100
rectangle_one.Height = 300

Here, we're just accessing the properties of a New Rectangle object and putting values into them.

But that just sets up a Rectangle object. To draw the rectangle, you still need a Pen. We'll use the Pen we have already set up. So add the following line to your button code:

pen_one = New Pen(Color.Blue, 1)

You can pick any colour you like for the Pen, but we've gone for Blue, with a line width of 1.

So that we can use our Select Case statement again, add this line:

draw_options = 2

We haven't got a Case 2 yet, but we'll add it next. The final line for the button code, though, is the Invalidate command:

Me.Invalidate( )

Your button code should now look something like ours:

```
Private Sub btnRectangle_Click(ByVal sender As System.Object, _
                               ByVal e As System.EventArgs) _
                               Handles btnRectangle.Click


    rectangle_one = New Rectangle(10, 10, 100, 300)
    pen_one = New Pen(Color.Blue, 1)

    draw_options = 2
    Me.Invalidate()

End Sub
```

You now need to amend the Select Case statement that is inside of your Paint event. Add a Case 2, and the following:

Case 2
        e.Graphics.DrawRectangle(pen_one, rectangle_one)

So you use DrawRectangle, which is a Subroutine of the Graphics object, just like DrawLine was. Inside of the round brackets of DrawRectangle you first specify the pen you want to use. The second argument is for the rectangle object you set up.

Your Paint event should now look something like ours:

```
Private Sub Form1_Paint(ByVal sender As System.Object, _
                        ByVal e As System.Windows.Forms.PaintEventArgs) _
                        Handles MyBase.Paint

    Select Case draw_options
        Case 0
        Case 1
            e.Graphics.DrawLine(pen_one, 10, 10, 100, 10)
        Case 2
            e.Graphics.DrawRectangle(pen_one, rectangle_one)
    End Select

End Sub
```

Run your programme and try it out. Click your new button, and a blue rectangle should appear on your form:

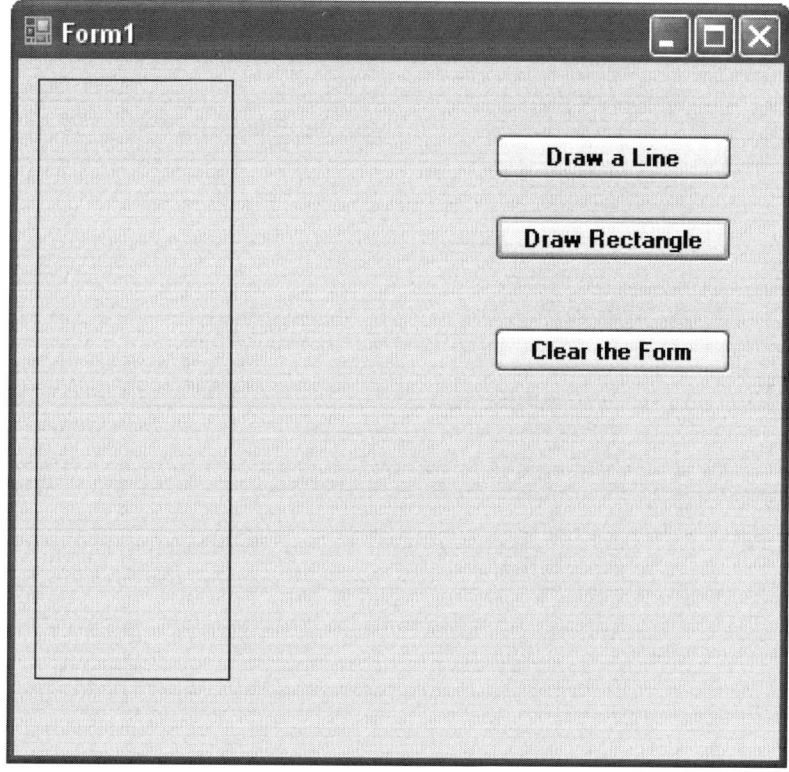

If you click your "Draw a Line" button, the rectangle will disappear to be replaced by your line.

Filled Rectangle

To draw a rectangle and fill it with a colour of your choice, you need another of the Subs available to the Graphics object – FillRectangle. The rectangle is then filled with a Brush.

Add the following to your Case 2 code, just below the DrawRectangle line:

e.Graphics.FillRectangle(Brushes.Blue**, rectangle_one)**

The first argument between the round brackets of **FillRectangle** is for the brush colour. The second argument is the rectangle you want to fill.

You can also set up a Brush object and use that, if you prefer. You do it like this:

Dim brush_one As Brush
brush_one = Brushes.Blue

e.Graphics.FillRectangle (brush_one, rectangle_one)

But whichever method you choose, when the programme is run, your rectangle should look like this, after the button click:

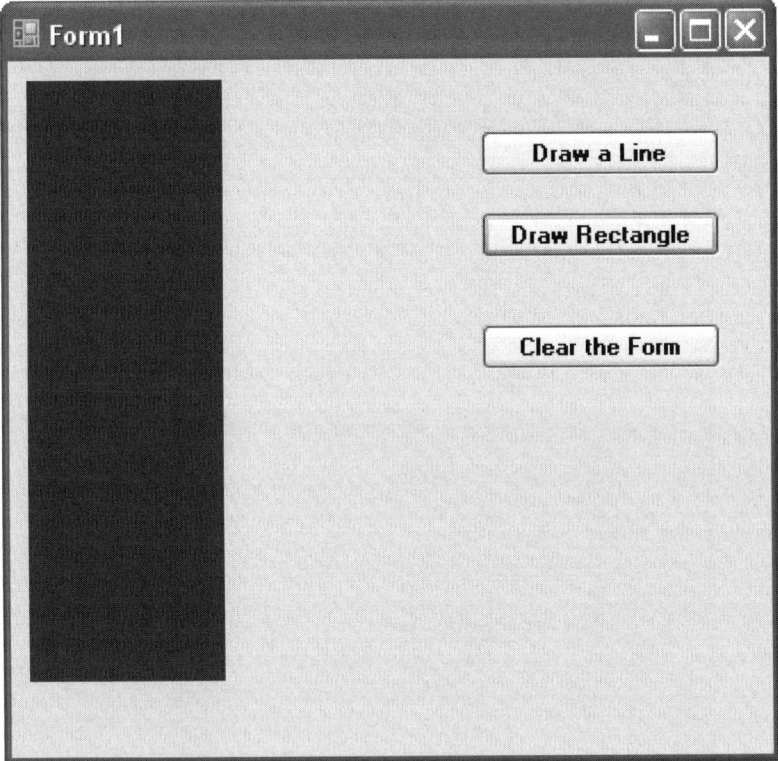

How to Draw an Ellipse

Ellipses are drawn in between the sides of rectangles. They are drawn like this:

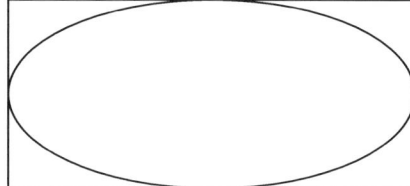

Erase the sides of the rectangle and you're left with an ellipse!

So add another button to your form. Double click to get at the coding window. Set up a second Rectangle variable at the top of the code, just below rectangle_one:

Dim rectangle_two As Rectangle

Add the following line to the button code:

rectangle_two = New Rectangle(10, 10, 150, 100)

So the width of the rectangle will be 150 and the height 100. Now set up the Pen, just below the rectangle line:

pen_one = New Pen(Color.DarkBlue, 2)

Add a new draw_option, and the Invalidate command with these two lines:

draw_options = 3
Me.Invalidate( )

Jump to your Paint event and add a new Case:

Case 3
        e.Graphics.DrawEllipse(pen_one, rectangle_two **)**

This time, we're selecting **DrawEllipse** from the list of available Graphics Subroutines. In between the round brackets of DrawEllipse, you need a Pen, followed by the rectangle that you want to turn into an ellipse.

Run your programme and click your Ellipse button. Your form will then look like this one:

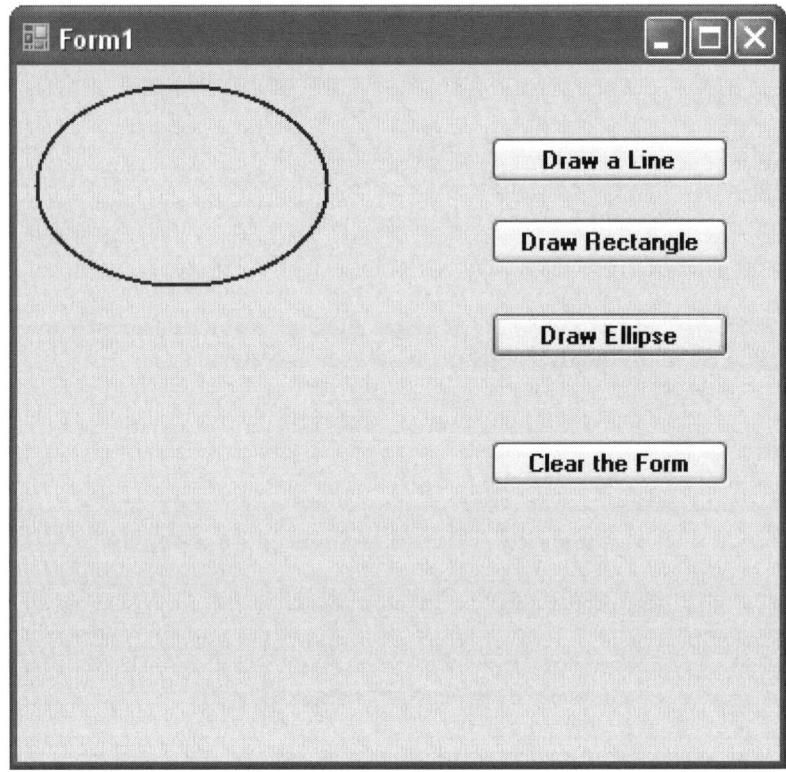

As you can see, though, the ellipse looks a little bit ragged. This is because of something called Aliasing. If you try to draw a curve onto a computer screen, it will get drawn in a grid. Like this:

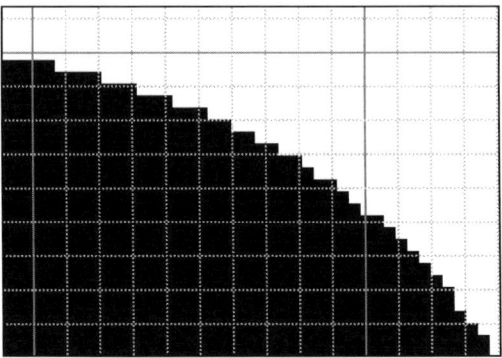

The Alias part is all those little steps – the jaggies, as they are known. Anti-Aliasing is filling in the steps to create a smooth curve. You can implement this in your code quite easily, with the SmoothingMode property. Add the following, just above your DrawEllipse line, but below **Case 3**:

e.Graphics.SmoothingMode = Drawing2D.SmoothingMode.AntiAlias

Your Paint event code should now look like this:

```
Private Sub Form1_Paint(ByVal sender As System.Object, _
                        ByVal e As System.Windows.Forms.PaintEventArgs) _
                        Handles MyBase.Paint

    Select Case draw_options
        Case 0
        Case 1
            e.Graphics.DrawLine(pen_one, 10, 10, 100, 10)
        Case 2
            e.Graphics.DrawRectangle(pen_one, rectangle_one)
            e.Graphics.FillRectangle(Brushes.Blue, rectangle_one)
        Case 3
            e.Graphics.SmoothingMode = Drawing2D.SmoothingMode.AntiAlias
            e.Graphics.DrawEllipse(pen_one, rectangle_two)
    End Select

End Sub
```

Run your programme and click your Ellipse button again. The ellipse should be a lot smoother:

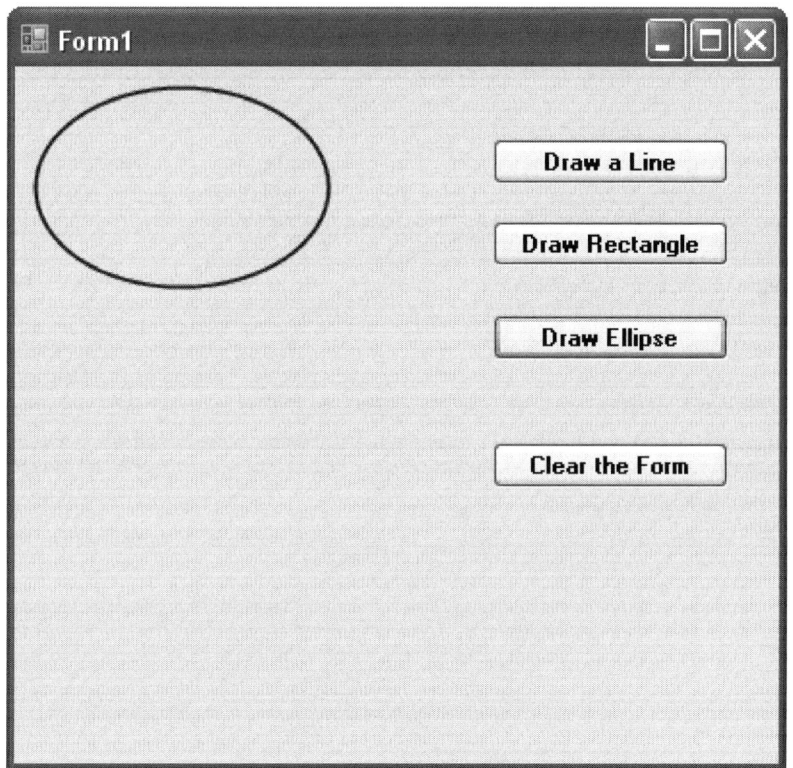

Now try these two exercises. You should find them quite easy!

Exercise
Fill your ellipse with a solid colour.

Exercise
Draw a circle to the form, instead of an ellipse.

Polygons

You can construct quite complex shapes by using Polygons. The idea is to set up an array of points for your polygon, and then pass the array to the DrawPolygon Subroutine of the Graphics objects. Let's see how it works by creating a polygon with five sides.

Add a new button to the form, with a Text property of "Draw Polygon". In the coding window, add this new line somewhere at the top, just under the Rectangle variables:

Dim polygon_points(5) As Point

We're setting up an array, here. But the type of variable we're setting up is a Structure of Points.

In your button code, add the following:

polygon_points(0) = New Point(

So every position in your array needs a new Point. But as soon as you have typed the left round bracket, you should see two arguments needed for the Point:

```
polygon_points(0) = New Point(|
```
▲ 1 of 3 ▼   New (**x As Integer**, y As Integer)
x: The horizontal position of the point.

The first argument, **x As Integer**, is how far from the left you want the point. The second argument, **y As Integer**, is how far down you want the point. The polygon we want to draw looks like this:

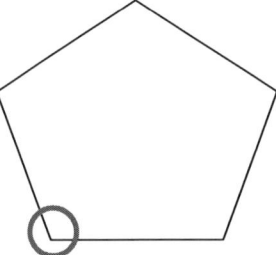

The highlighted point is the one we want to draw first (the ordering of the Points is not important). So the two points are at 50 for the x and 150 for the y. (We've just made these two figures up: there's not significance about them.) The first Point, then, is this:

polygon_points(0) = New Point(50, 150)

The other points are these. Add them to your button code:

polygon_points(1) = New Point(20, 65)
polygon_points(2) = New Point(100, 10)
polygon_points(3) = New Point(175, 65)
polygon_points(4) = New Point(150, 150)
polygon_points(5) = New Point(50, 150)

Notice how the last point above has the same coordinates as the first one. This is so that the polygon can be closed. Here's the polygon again, with the array positions:

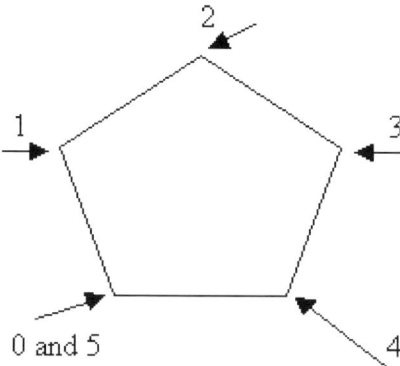

Now that we have a series of points, we can add a new draw option and an Invalidate command:

draw_options = 4
Me.Invalidate( )

Your button code should look like this:

```
Private Sub btnPolygon_Click(ByVal sender As System.Object, _
                        ByVal e As System.EventArgs) _
                        Handles btnPolygon.Click

    polygon_points(0) = New Point(50, 150)
    polygon_points(1) = New Point(20, 65)
    polygon_points(2) = New Point(100, 10)
    polygon_points(3) = New Point(175, 65)
    polygon_points(4) = New Point(150, 150)
    polygon_points(5) = New Point(50, 150)

    draw_options = 4
    Me.Invalidate()

End Sub
```

In your Paint event, add a **Case 4** option to your Select Case statement. Now add the following for it:

> **Case 4**
>   **e.Graphics.DrawPolygon(** Pens.Black, polygon_points **)**

So the Subroutine we're using is called **DrawPolygon**. The first argument between the round brackets is for the Pen you want to use. The second argument is the array of polygon points you want to use.

Run your programme and click your Polygon button. Your form should then look like ours below:

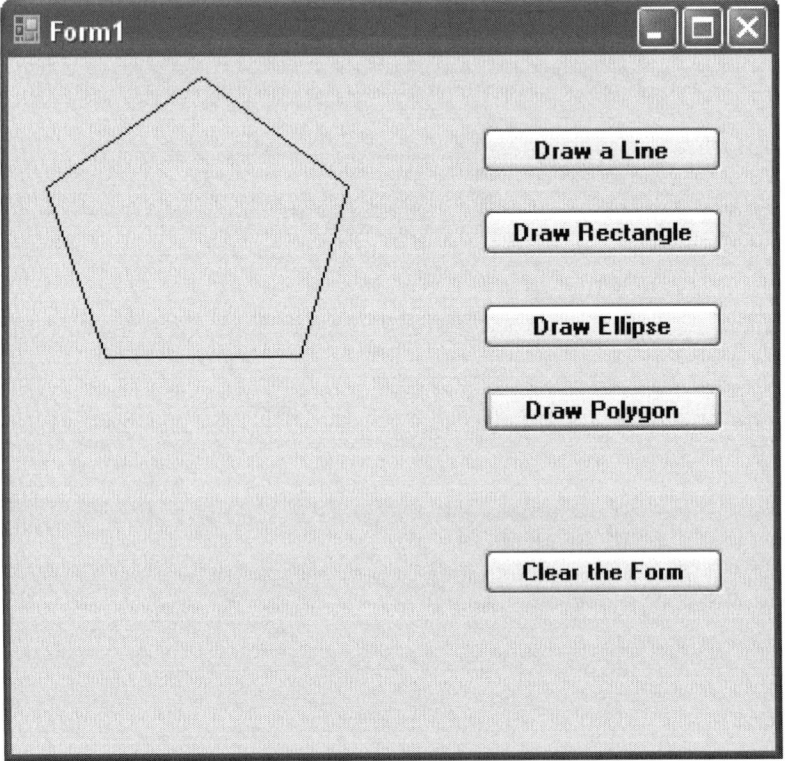

You can have as many polygon points as you want, creating some weird and wonderful shapes! Or if you can get hold of any map data, it usually comes as a series of polygon points, thereby enabling you to create your own area maps. At the time of writing, one such source of polygon data can be found at maplibrary.org (http://www.maplibrary.org/sources.php)

Other Fill Styles

You don't have to fill your shapes with solid colours. The NET framework allows you to set up something called a HatchBrush, which has lots more fill options for you. We'll see how it works by filling the Polygon we've just drawn with some cross-hatching.

The HatchBrush class is one of the Drawing2D classes. So add the following to the very top of your coding window, where you have the Rectangle variables and polygon points array set up:

Dim hatch_brush As System.Drawing.Drawing2D.HatchBrush

To create a new HatchBrush object, the syntax is this:

hatchBrush = New Drawing2D.HatchBrush(hatch_style, foreColour, backColour)

All of which makes a single line of code far too long for this page! But first type the following in your button code, just below the polygon lines:

hatch_brush = New Drawing2D.HatchBrush(

As soon as you type the round bracket, you'll see a list of the available styles:

As you can see, there's quite a lot to choose from! But go with the first one on the list, the Backward Diagonal. Then type a comma. You'll see a list of foreground colours you can choose from. Select any one you like, then type another comma. The background colours will appear. Again, select any one that takes your fancy. Then type the closing round bracket. When you're done, the code in round brackets will look something like this:

HatchBrush(Drawing2D.HatchStyle.BackwardDiagonal, Color.DarkCyan, Color.Aqua)

The whole of your Polygon button code should now be this (though we've had to manipulate the image a bit to fit it all on):

```
    Private Sub btnPolygon_Click(ByVal sender As System.Object, _
                                 ByVal e As System.EventArgs) _
                                 Handles btnPolygon.Click


        polygon_points(0) = New Point(50, 150)
        polygon_points(1) = New Point(20, 65)
        polygon_points(2) = New Point(100, 10)
        polygon_points(3) = New Point(175, 65)
        polygon_points(4) = New Point(150, 150)
        polygon_points(5) = New Point(50, 150)

        hatch_brush = New Drawing2D.HatchBrush(Drawing2D.HatchStyle. _
                    BackwardDiagonal, Color.DarkCyan, Color.Aqua)

        draw_options = 4
        Me.Invalidate()

    End Sub
```

Just like the FillRectangle option, there's a FillPolygon option for the Graphics Subroutine. Add the following to your Case 4 code, just below your DrawPolygon line:

e.Graphics.FillPolygon(hatch_brush, polygon_points)

The first argument for FillPolygon is the brush you want to use, which is a Hatch Brush for us. The second argument is the array of polygon points that you want to fill.

But your Paint event code should now be similar to ours:

```
Private Sub Form1_Paint(ByVal sender As System.Object, _
                  ByVal e As System.Windows.Forms.PaintEventArgs) _
                  Handles MyBase.Paint

    Select Case draw_options
        Case 0
        Case 1
            e.Graphics.DrawLine(pen_one, 10, 10, 100, 10)
        Case 2
            e.Graphics.DrawRectangle(pen_one, rectangle_one)
            e.Graphics.FillRectangle(Brushes.Blue, rectangle_one)
        Case 3
            e.Graphics.SmoothingMode = Drawing2D.SmoothingMode.AntiAlias
            e.Graphics.DrawEllipse(pen_one, rectangle_two)
        Case 4
            e.Graphics.DrawPolygon(Pens.Black, polygon_points)
            e.Graphics.FillPolygon(hatch_brush, polygon_points)

    End Select

End Sub
```

You can add another SmoothingMode line, if you want. But run your programme, and click your Polygon button. Your filled polygon should look something like ours:

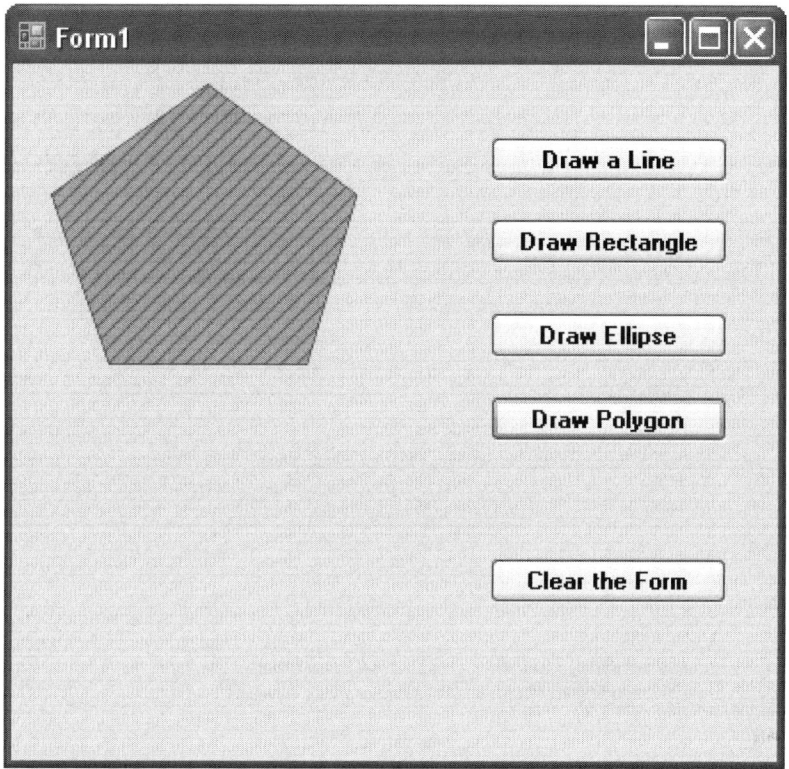

Drawing Text

You can also draw text directly to a form, or to a form object like a picture box. This will come in handy for the project at the end of this section, when we create a bar chart.

Drawing text is not as straightforward a process as you'd think. You need to set up a font object, a solid brush to draw the text, as well as setting up any optional string formats you may require.

Add another button to your form, and double click to get at the coding window. At the top of the coding window, along with all your other variables, add the following:

Dim Text_To_Draw As String
Dim chosen_font As Font
Dim solid_brush As SolidBrush
Dim string_format As StringFormat

So we're setting up four new variables. The type of variables we've set up are String, Font, SolidBrush, and StringFormat.

In your button code, set some text to draw:

Text_To_Draw = "Home and Learn"

Of course, you can change the text to anything you want. But the next thing to do is to specify the font you want to use. This is done by creating a new Font object:

chosen_font = New Font("Arial", 20, FontStyle.Bold)

Note the arguments, here. The first one is for the font. If you are using a font that you have on your system, then just enclose it in quotation marks, just like a string. The second argument, 20, is the size you want your font. The third argument sets the style of the font, Bold in our example. If you don't want a style, just have two arguments instead of three.

The brush for the font is easy enough to set up. Add this line to your button code:

solid_brush = New SolidBrush(Color.Black)

So you just create a New SolidBrush, and then specify a colour for it between the round brackets.

The string format class allows you to set up things like vertical text:

**string_format = New StringFormat(
StringFormatFlags.DirectionVertical)**

In between the round brackets of StringFormat, you set up a string format flag. Type a dot and you'll see the available options:

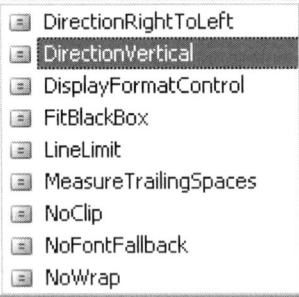

We've gone for Direction Vertical.

Finally for the button code, add a new draw option and an Invalidate command:

**draw_options = 5
Me.Invalidate( )**

Your button code should now look like this:

```
Private Sub btnDrawText_Click(ByVal sender As System.Object, _
                        ByVal e As System.EventArgs) _
                             Handles btnDrawText.Click


  Text_To_Draw = "Home and Learn"

  chosen_font = New Font("Arial", 20, FontStyle.Bold)
  solid_brush = New SolidBrush(Color.Black)
  string_format = New StringFormat(StringFormatFlags.DirectionVertical)

  draw_options = 5
  Me.Invalidate()

End Sub
```

Now, in your Paint event, add a **Case 5** option to your Select Case statement:

> **Case 5**
>> **e.Graphics.DrawString(** Text_To_Draw, chosen_font, solid_brush, 100, 10,
>> string_format **)**

We're now accessing the **DrawString** Subroutine of the Graphics object. In between the round brackets of DrawString, we first have the text we want to draw. After specifying a font and a brush, we have the numbers 100, 10. This is the X and Y coordinates for your string. In other words, where on your form you want to draw the string. The final argument we've specified is for the string format. This is optional, though, and you can miss it out. If you do, you get horizontal text.

Run your programme and test it out. Click your "Draw Text" button and your form should look something like ours:

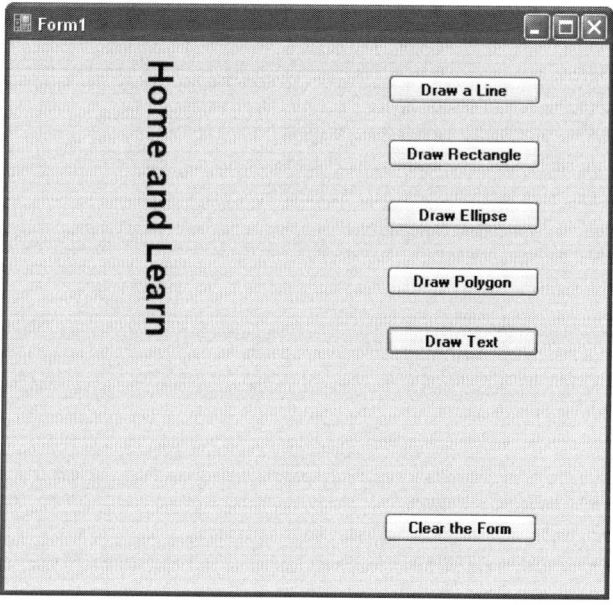

Putting it all together – A Bar Chart Project

Using all your new graphics knowledge, create the following bar chart.

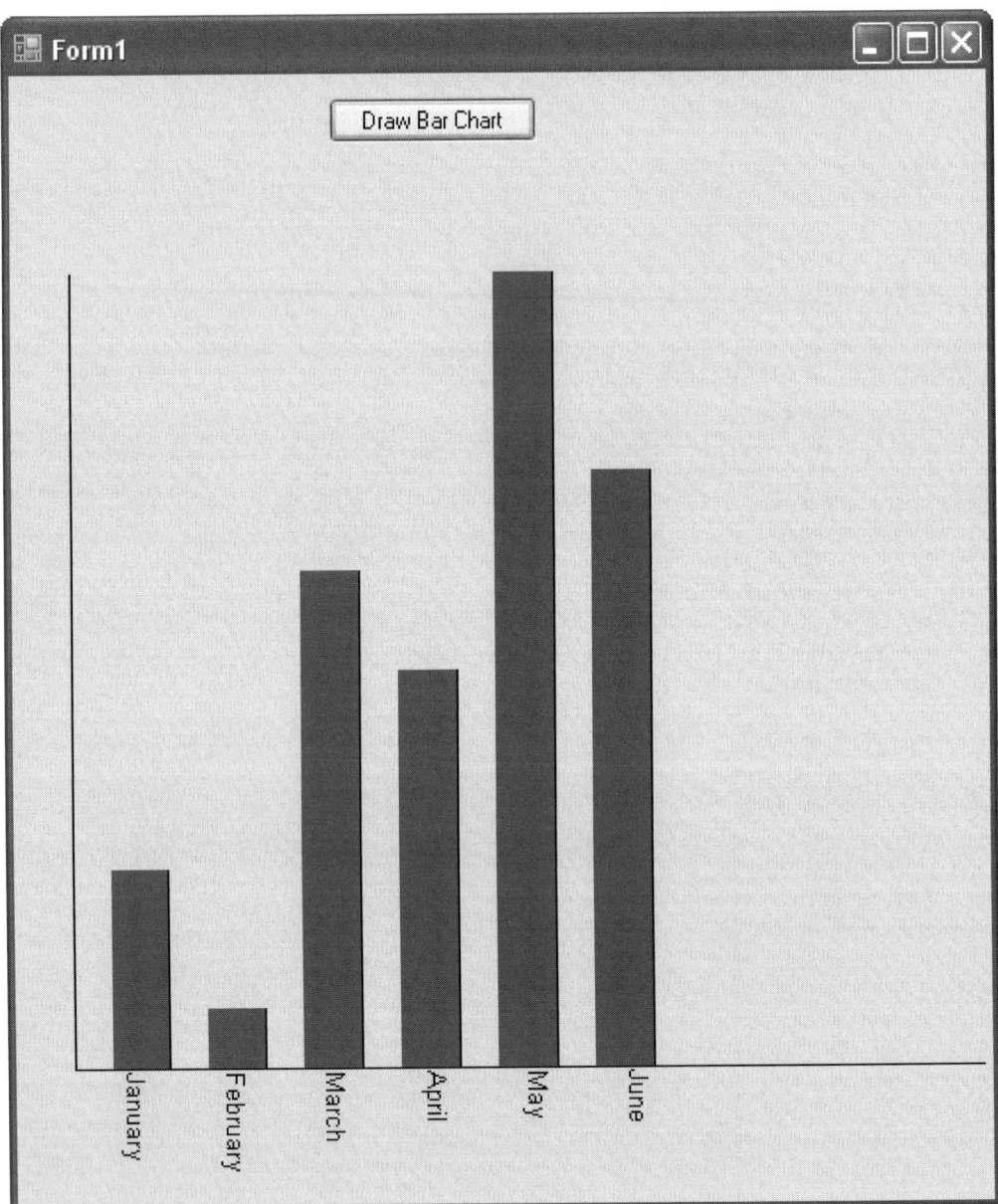

Help with this Project

We're not introducing anything new here, and all the knowledge you need has already been outlined.

When we drew the bars, we did so in a For loop. Create a new rectangle each time round the loop, fill it with a colour of your choice, then draw the text.

The tricky part is positioning your rectangles. When a rectangle is drawn, it is drawn starting at the top left corner. So if you specify a height of, say, 200 for the first rectangle and 100 for the second one, your bars would look like this:

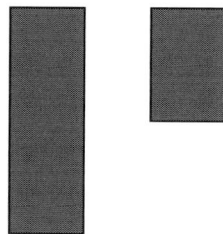

In other words, you'd have an upside down bar chart! You have to move them down to a baseline. Our solution was to get the maximum height of the bars, simply by noting the highest bar in the chart. We then had a drop value for the y position. The drop value is the maximum height minus the actually height for that particular bar. For example:

max_height = 200
bar_height = 100
bar_spacing = 50
bar_width = 30

drop_value = 100 + (max_height - bar_height)
new_rect = New Rectangle(bar_spacing, drop_value, bar_width, bar_height)

The figure of 100 for the drop_value is just so that the chart isn't right at the top of the form – we're shifting it down a little.

The values for the bars in your chart can be in an array:

Dim aryBarValues(5) As Integer

aryBarValues(0) = 100
aryBarValues(1) = 30
etc

The values we used were: 100, 30, 250, 200, 400, 300. The max_height is then 400. These array values can then be used in your For loop to get the height of the bars. (In a real-world scenario, you can get the values from a comma delimited text file, or straight from Excel.)

Draw two lines for the X and Y Axes, some vertical text for the months, and you're done!

If you need any help with this project, or would like to see our finished version, please send us an email.

How to Create a SQL Server Express Database

In an earlier section we used Access for the database lessons. But Access databases are rarely used in a professional environment. One database that is used is called SQL Server. The Express edition is free, and usually comes as part of the Visual Basic Express download.

In this section, you'll learn how to create a database in SQL Server Express. We'll then use this database in a project that uses a DataGrid.

Have you got SQL Server Express installed?

To see if you already have SQL Server Express, try this. Start a new project. When the form appears, click **Project** from the menu bars at the top of your Visual Basic .NET software. From the Project menu, select **Add New Item**:

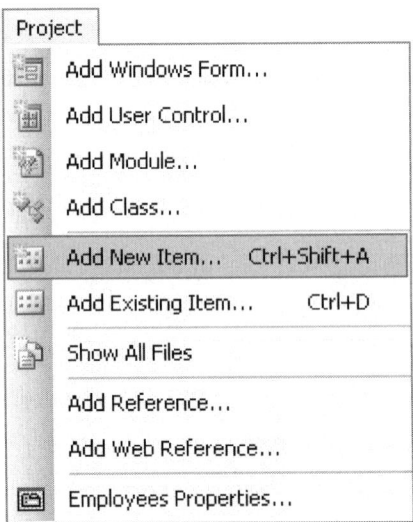

From the Add New Item dialogue box in version 2008, look for the Service-based Database item, as in the image below:

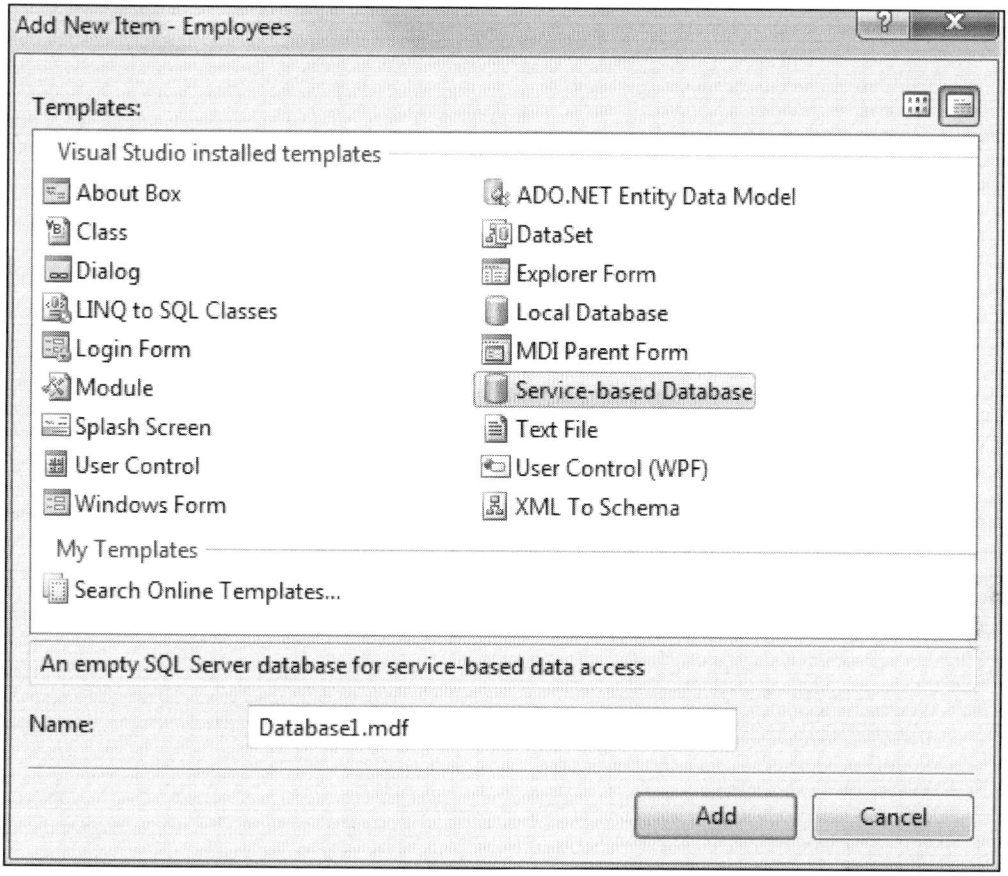

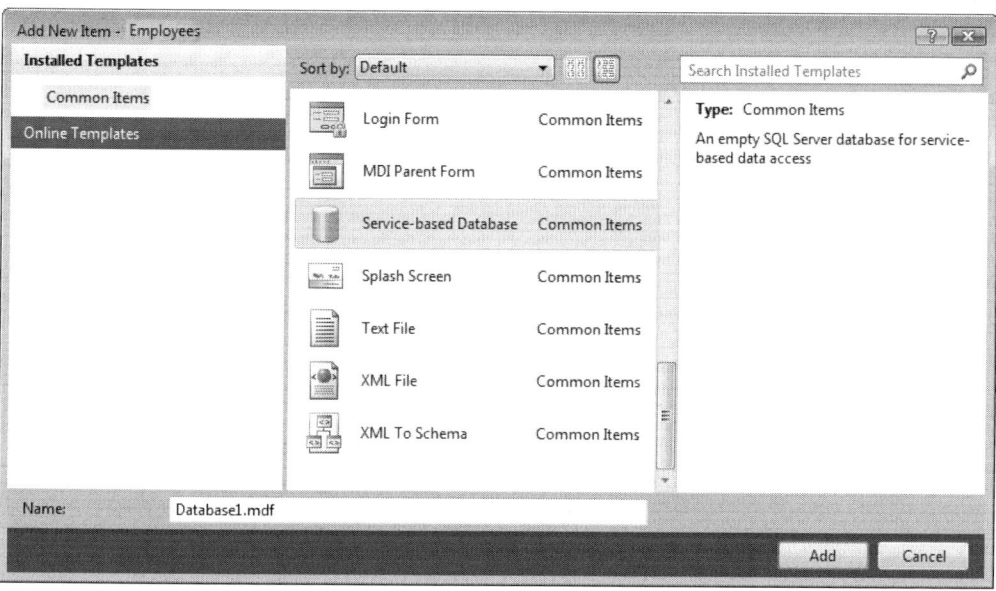

In VB NET 2010, you'll see this dialogue box:

Again, select "Service-based database".

If it's not there, then you may not have SQL Server Express installed. In which case, you need to download it. At the time of writing, the location is:

http://www.microsoft.com/sql/editions/express/default.mspx

How to Create a SQL Server database

If you see the Service-based Database item, click on it to select it. Note the file ending for a SQL Server database, though – it's an MDF file.

Change the name to this:

Employees.mdf

Now click the **Add** button. You should, eventually, see the Data Source Configuration Wizard appear. This one in version 2008:

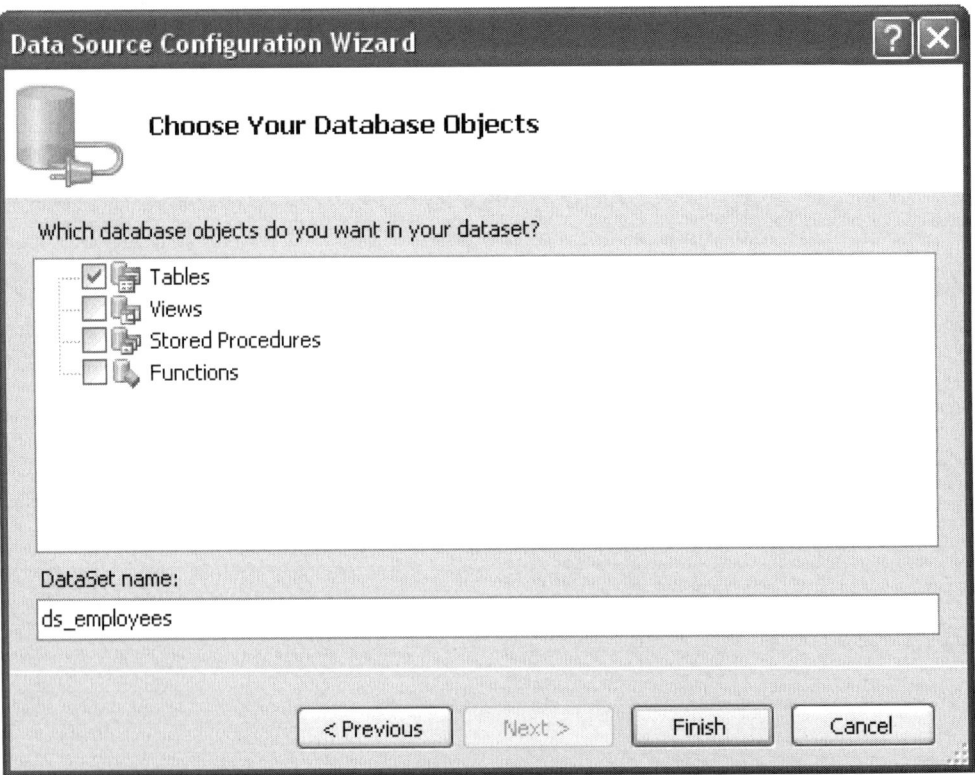

Put a tick in the box next to Tables, and then change the name of the dataset to this:

ds_employees

In version 2010 of the software, you'll see this instead:

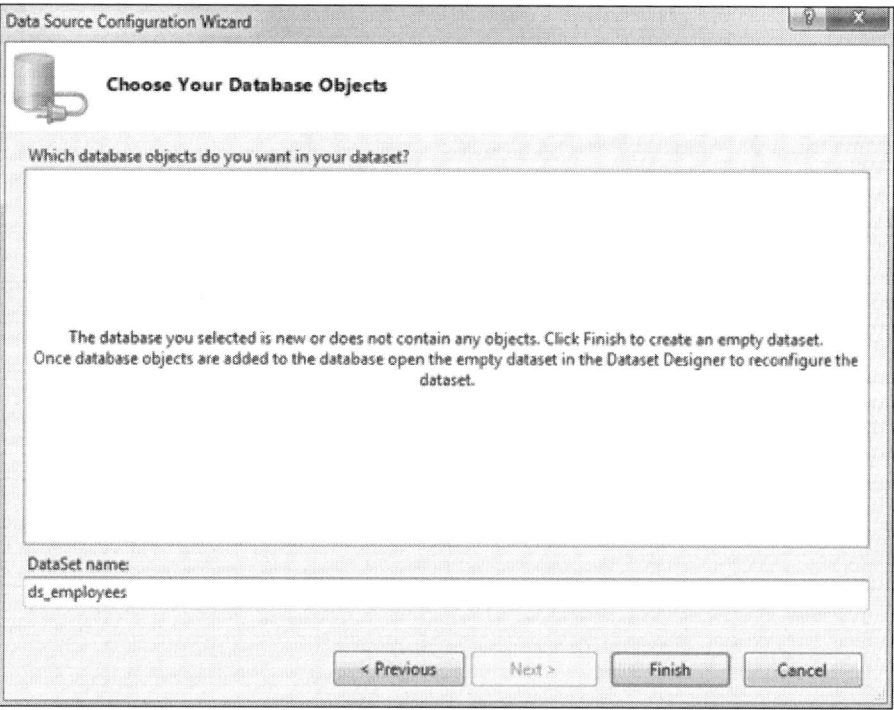

Again, change the name of the Data Set to **ds_employees**.

Click the Finish button.

It might look as though nothing has happened, after you click the Finish button. But have a look at the Solution Explorer at the top right of your screen. You should see your database there:

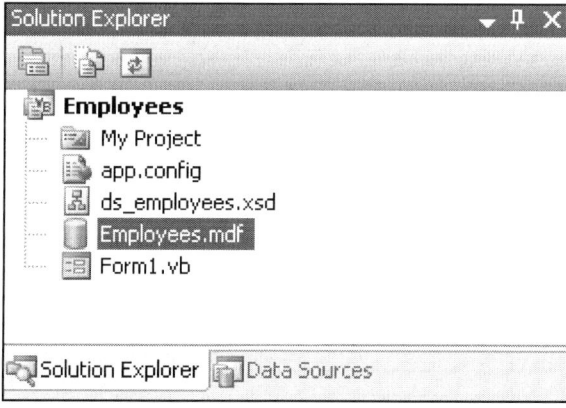

When you save your project, the database will get saved along with all the solution files.

How to Create Tables in your SQL Server Database

Now that you have created the database itself, you need to create at least one table to go in it.

To create a table, right click on the database in the Solution Explorer. From the menu that appears, select **Open**:

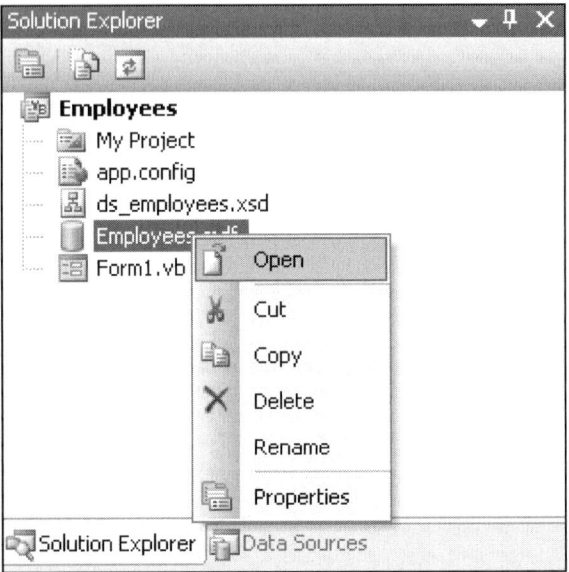

When you click **Open**, you'll see the Database Explorer appear on the left hand side of your screen:

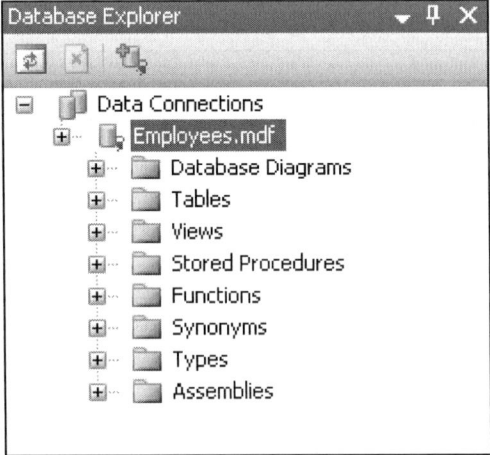

To create a new table, right click on **Tables**. From the menu that appears, select **Add New Table**, as in the image below:

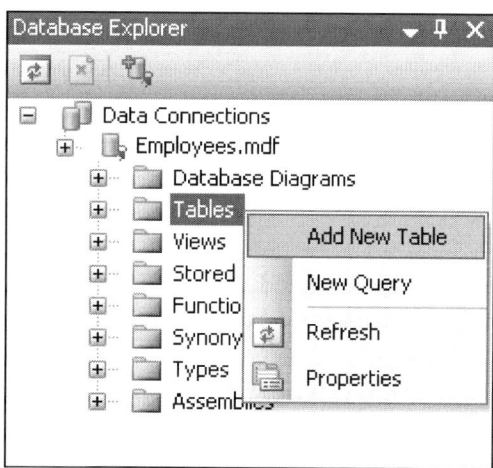

When you click Add New Table, you'll see a new Tab appear in your main window, where your Form is:

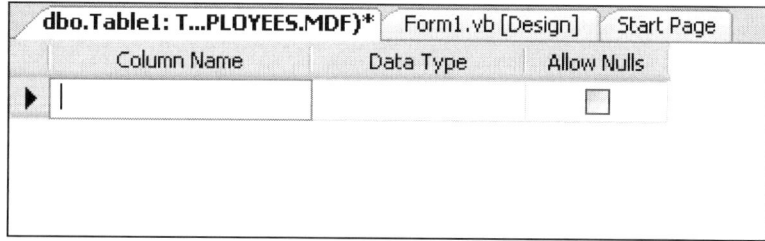

This screen is where you set up the Columns that go in the table. You'll get to enter the actual data later. But you need to tell SQL Server what kind of data (**Data Type**) is going into the each column.

So click into the Column Name box and type in **ID** as the name.

For Version 2008 VB NET Express users
Now that you have entered something, you'll be able to save the Table. Either right click the table Tab itself, or click the Save Table icon on the menu bar:

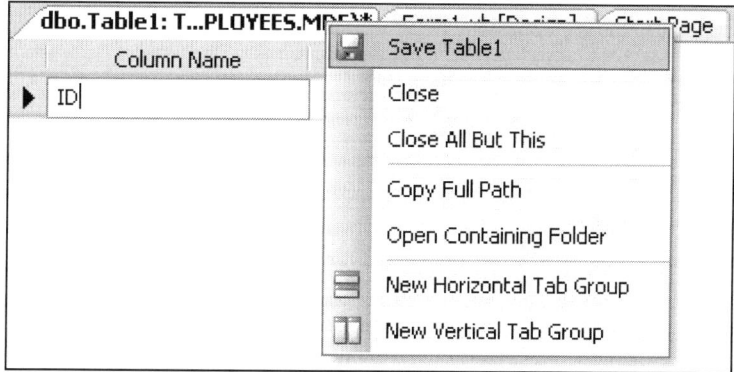

When you click Save Table, you'll see the following dialogue box appear:

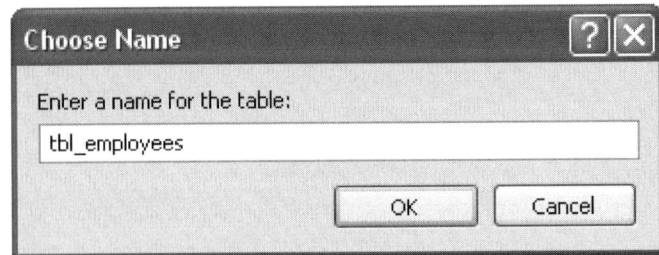

Type **tbl_employees** as the Name, and then click OK. Your table will then look like this:

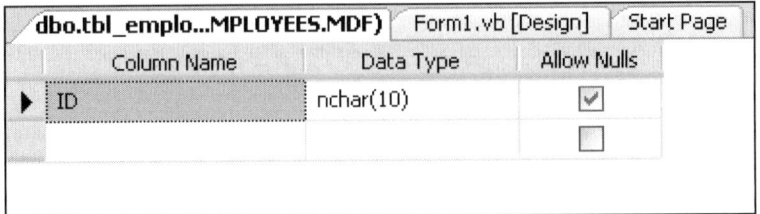

For Version 2010 VB NET Express users

If you have VB NET Express 2010, click Save All. You'll see a dialogue box appear asking you to save the table. Type a name for your table, then click Save.

If your table data disappears, expand the database tree in the Database explorer. Click the **Tables** item again. Then right-click the name of your table. From the menu, select **Open Table Definition**. The table should open up again.

All Users

Notice that the DataType for the ID Column has been filled in, and Allow Nulls has been checked. We want a different Data Type. First, though, uncheck **Allow Nulls**. This refers to the data going in to the column, and whether or not it needs to be filled in. Because this is an ID column, we always need it to be filled in.

Next, click on the Data Type area. You should see a dropdown list become available. Set it on **int**, which is short for integer:

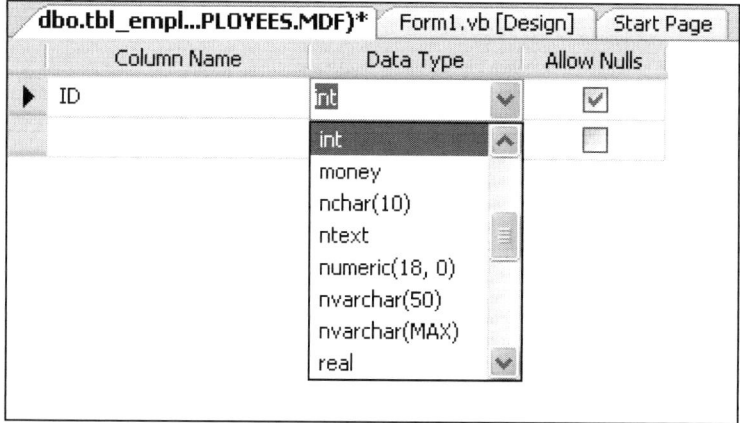

The ID column will need to have a new integer assigned every time a new entry is added to the table. In other databases, this is known as an auto increment number. So that this happens automatically without us having to worry about it, have a look at the bottom of your Table screen. You'll see a Column Properties area:

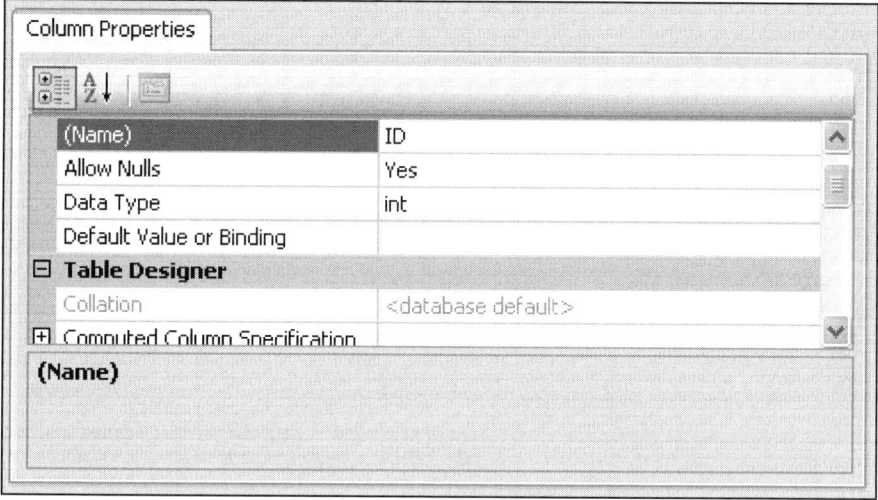

Click the AZ icon, and then scroll down until you come to **Identity Specification**. Set **Is Identity** to Yes:

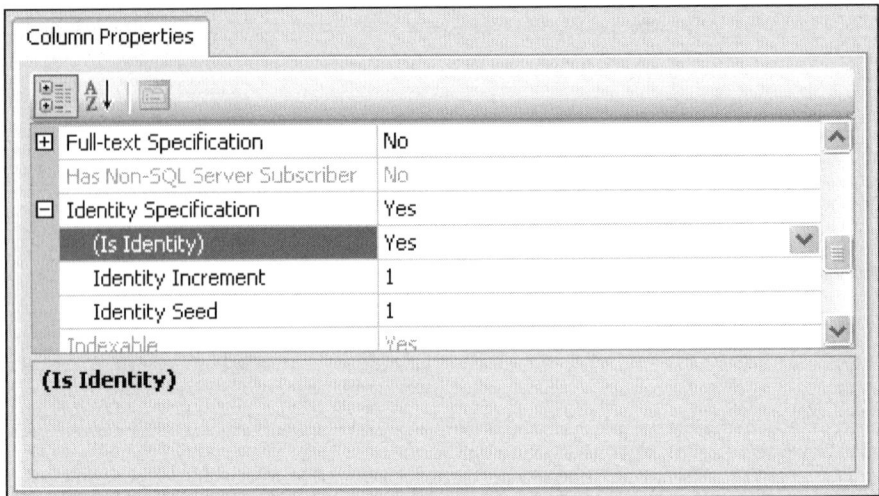

Because **Identity Increment** is on 1, then our ID column will get 1 added to it automatically when a new entry is made to the table. You'll see this in a moment. But your Table should now look like ours:

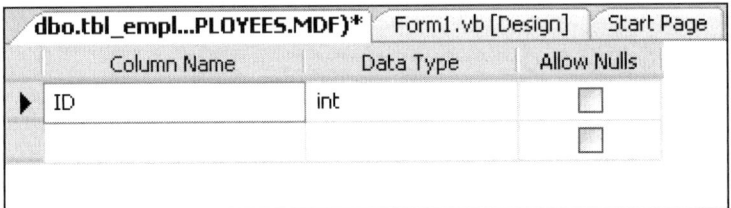

One final thing to do. In database tables, you can set what's called a Primary Key. This is used for things like linking tables together, indexing a long table, and for searching. To set a Primary Key, right click on the Column Name, where it says ID. From the menu that appears, select **Primary Key**. You should see a little Key icon appear next to the Column Name:

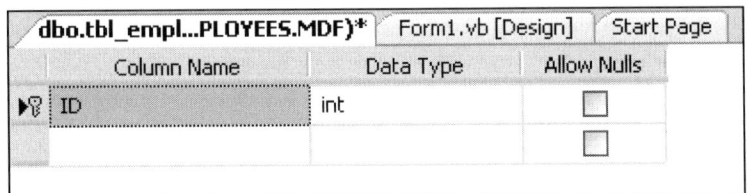

Save your work so far.

(In version 2010, if you get a dialogue box saying "You cannot save changes that would result in one or more tables being re-created", then follow the instructions below that. When the **Options** dialogue box appears, check the box at the bottom "show all settings")

Now have a look at the Database Explorer to the left. You should see your new table, and the one column we've just added:

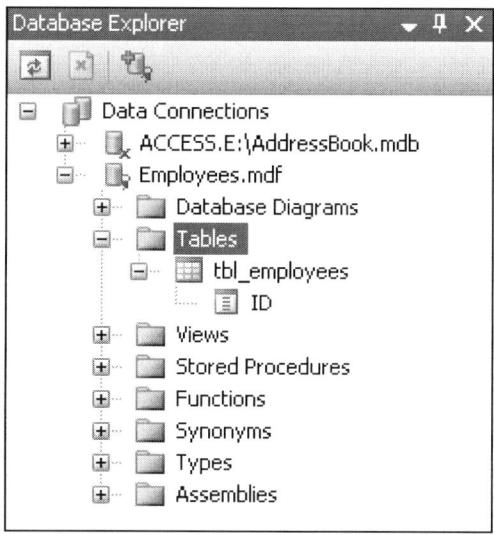

Using the same technique, create the following Column Names, Data Types, and Allow Null values:

Column Name	Data Type	Allow Nulls
first_name	nvarchar(50)	checked
last_name	nvarchar(50)	unchecked
job_title	ntext	unchecked
department	nvarchar(50)	unchecked

When you're done, your table should look like ours below:

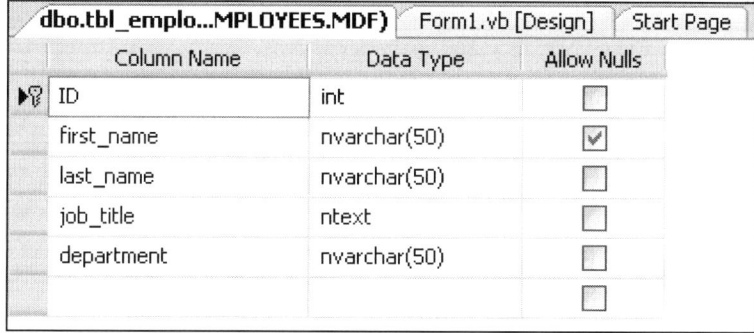

The **varchar**, by the way, is short for variable-length character string. With **nvarchar**, the n is short for Unicode, and the data will be stored in the UTF-16 format. Use nvarchar if you're going to be storing non-English characters. Otherwise, use varchar. The same is true of all the n's on the list.

Save your work again, and we can enter some data into the Table.

Adding Data to a SQL Server Database Table

To add entries to your SQL Server database, right click on your table name in the Database explorer. From the menu that appears, select **Show Table Data**:

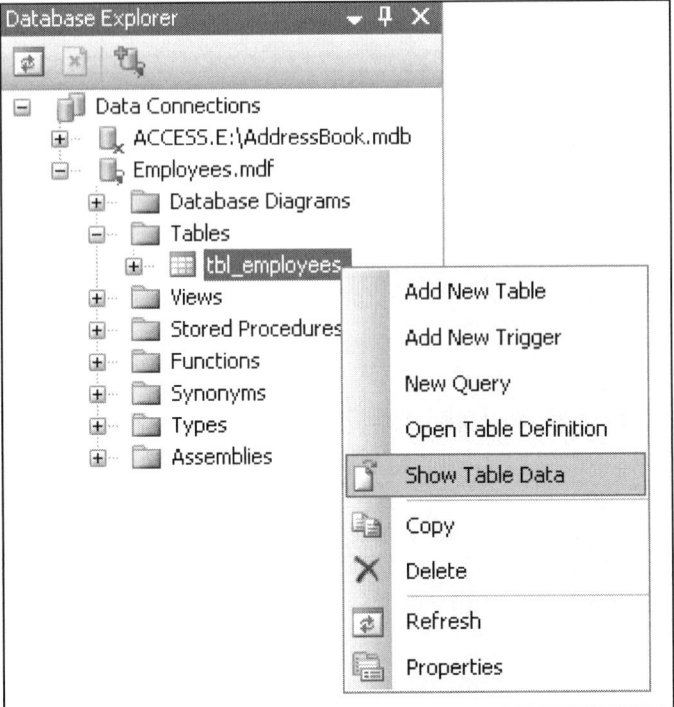

When you select **Show Table Data**, you'll see a new tab appear:

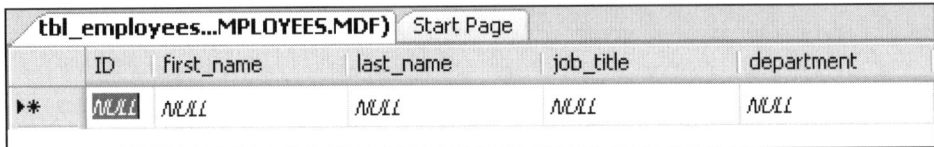

All our Column names are there, waiting to be filled in. To enter data, simply click inside a cell and start typing.

Click inside the first_name column. (The ID Column will take care of itself.) Type a first name. Click inside of last_name and type a last name. Click inside of job_title and enter a job title. Then enter a job description. You can enter the same details as ours, if you prefer (all made up):

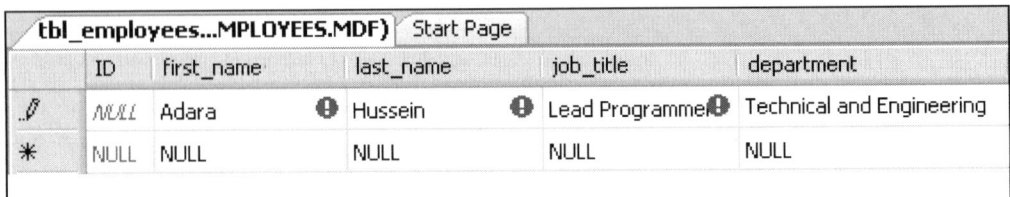

Notice the warning symbols in the cells. These appear when the cell data has changed. The ID is still NULL in the image above. When we click in the next row, however, notice that a number will appear in the first ID cell:

tbl_employees...MPLOYEES.MDF}	Start Page			
ID	first_name	last_name	job_title	department
1	Adara	Hussein	Lead Programmer	Technical and Engineering
NULL	NULL	NULL	NULL	NULL

The reason it does this is because we set **Is Identity** to Yes, and the **Identity Increment** to 1 – it's an Auto Increment field, in other words.

But we have now created one row in our database table. Fill out a few more rows. You can use the same details as ours, in the image below:

tbl_employees...MPLOYEES.MDF}	Start Page			
ID	first_na...	last_name	job_title	department
1	Adara	Hussein	Lead Programmer	Technical and Engineering
2	Bibi	Saleem	Head Writer	Creative Affairs
3	Hamal	Ata	Network Engineer	Technical and Engineering
4	Haris	Hameed	Systems Analyst	Technical and Engineering
5	Tansy	Lakshman	Writing Assistant	Creative Affairs
6	Orenda	Khan	Head of Tuition	Teaching and Education
7	Tadi	Patel	Network Engineer	Technical and Engineering
8	Zoe	Walker	Head of Design	Graphic Design
9	Alice	Thyne	Tutor	Teaching and Education
10	Jake	Jaloore	Graphic Artist	Graphic Design
NULL	NULL	NULL	NULL	NULL

Don't worry if your numbers for the ID column are not sequential (are not 1 to 10). If you make a mistake and delete a Row, you are given the next number after the deleted Row, and not the next number in your sequence.

Save your work, and you will have created your very first SQL Server Express database! But it's a huge subject, and whole books have been written about SQL Server. We can only touch on the very basics here. What we do have, though, is a database we can open with Visual Basic .NET programming code. We'll do that next, and use a DataGrid.

Databases and DataGrids

In a previous section, you saw how to connect to an Access database, and created a programme that allowed you to scroll through the records using buttons on a form. In this section, you'll see how to connect to a SQL Server Express database, and use a DataGrid instead of the buttons. Let's get started.

Close the entire Project down (File > Close Project), because we're going to be moving the database. We're doing this so that we don't run into any problems with this error:

"An attempt to attach an auto-named database ..."

Because SQL Server, as its name suggests, is supposed to be run on a Server, trying to get it work on a Local machine can be a real pain. For convenience's sake, then, we'll use a local hard drive location for the database connection.

To find your database, have a look in your Visual Studio Projects folder, usually located in the My Documents folder (XP). Find the folder with the name of the Project you just closed down. You should see the **Employees.mdf** file. If you can't find it that way, do a search through the Start menu of XP or Vista.

Once you've found the database, copy the file to your main hard drive. The file location would then be this, if your root folder is on the C drive:

C:\ Employees.mdf

The file path should then work for most users. Vista and Windows 7 users, however, may have a further problem, which we'll see later.

The DataGridView Control

But now that you have moved the database, create a New project in Visual Basic (**File > New Project**). Give it the name **employees_database**.

Add a **DataGridView** control to your new form. The DataGridView can be found under the Data category of the toolbox:

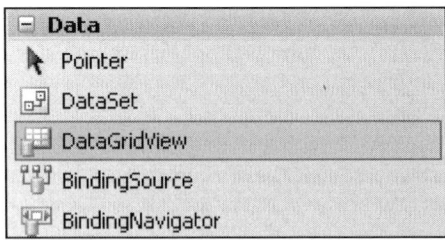

When you've added one to your form, it should look like this:

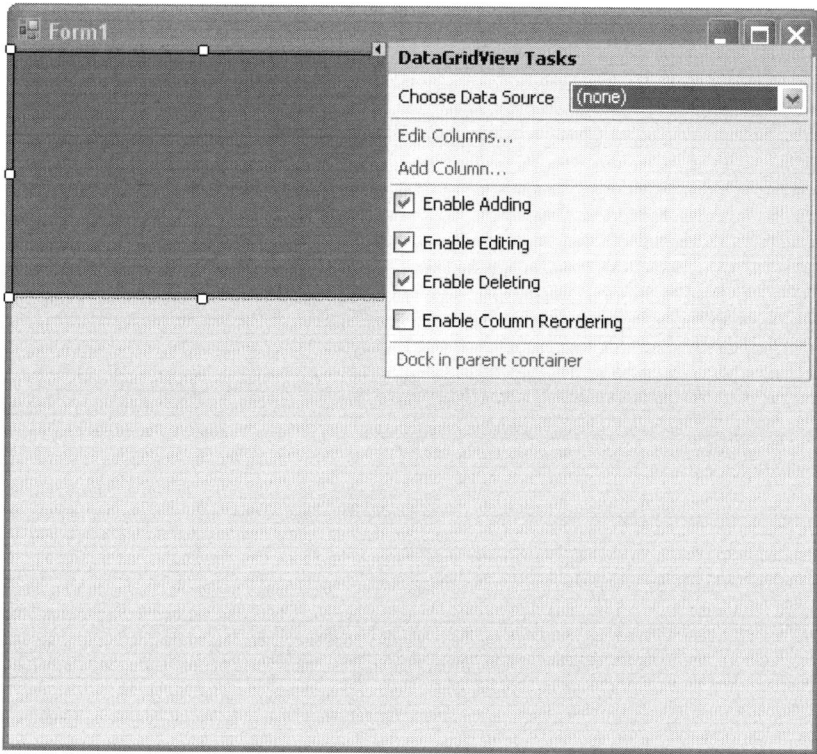

We're going to be doing the coding ourselves, so we don't need the DataGridView Tasks pane. To get rid of it, click the small, left-pointing arrow to the left of DataGridView Tasks. Resize your DataGridView control, and move it to the middle of your form.

The DataGrid itself is just a grid of white cells in Rows and Columns, rather like an Excel spreadsheet. When the form loads, we'll fill the grid with the data from a SQL Server database. To do that, we'll add something called a BindingSource object. The BindingSource object will contact the database on our behalf, and do all the tricky work for us. It means we don't have to write code to delete and add new rows – the BindingSource object will do that for us.

So double click anywhere on your form, and not on the DataGrid. This will create a Form Load event. At the top of your coding window, add the following two lines:

Private binding_source As New BindingSource( )
Private data_adapter As New SqlClient.SqlDataAdapter( )

The first line creates a New BindingSource object, while the second line creates a New Data Adapter object. The type of Data Adapter it is, though, is a SQL one, and not the OLEDB one we used for the Access database. (See a previous section for an explanation on Data Adapters.)

To bind the DataGridView, add the following line to your Form Load event:

Me.DataGridView1.DataSource = Me.binding_source

The Me keyword just refers to the current form. We're then setting the DataSource property of the DataGridView to our new BindingSource object. The BindingSource object has a DataSource property of its own. We'll point this to the real data soon.

To connect to the database, add the following line:

Get_DGV_Data("SELECT * FROM tbl_employees")

This is a Subroutine we need to create. We're going to be handing the Sub one thing: the SQL String that will be used to select records from the database. So create the following Sub just under your Form Load event:

Private Sub Get_DGV_Data(ByVal select_command As String)

End Sub

Your coding window should now look something like ours:

```
Public Class Form1

    Private binding_source As New BindingSource()
    Private data_adapter As New SqlClient.SqlDataAdapter()

    Private Sub Form1_Load(ByVal sender As System.Object, _
                       ByVal e As System.EventArgs) _
                     Handles MyBase.Load

        Me.DataGridView1.DataSource = Me.binding_source
        Get_DGV_Data("select * from tbl_employees")

    End Sub

    Private Sub Get_DGV_Data(ByVal select_command As String)

    End Sub

End Class
```

Connecting to a SQL Server Database

For the **Get_DGV_Data** Sub, we need a file path variable and a connection variable. So add the following to your Sub:

Dim filepath As String
Dim connect_string As String

For Windows XP users, the file path should be OK with this:

filepath = "C:\Employees.mdf;"

Don't forget the semicolon highlighted in red above.

For Vista and Windows 7 users, however, you may run into trouble with that file path. This is because Vista and Windows 7's new security measures may prevent you accessing files directly like this. In which case, you can move your database to the Documents folder. Then use this (put yours all on one line):

filepath = Environment.GetFolderPath(Environment.SpecialFolder.MyDocuments) & "\ Employees.mdf;"

Leave it on the shorter file path first, though. If you run into connection problems, try the longer path above.

For the connection string, add the following rather messy lines:

> **connect_string = "Data Source=.\SQLEXPRESS;"**
> **connect_string += "AttachDbFilename=" & filepath**
> **connect_string += "Integrated Security=True;"**
> **connect_string += "Connect Timeout=30;"**
> **connect_string += "User Instance=True;"**
> **connect_string += "Trusted_Connection=Yes;"**

We're just building up a string variable, here. SQL Server needs to know what kind of database you're connecting to (**Data Source=.\SQLEXPRESS;**). It also need to know where the database is (**AttachDbFilename=" & filepath**), as well as some other settings.

Finally, we can try to connect. To do that, we need to set up a SQL Adapter object, passing it our select command, and our connection string. So add the following **Try … Catch block** to your code:

Try

> **data_adapter = New SqlClient.SqlDataAdapter(select_command,** connect_string)

> **MsgBox("Connection OK")**

Catch ex As Exception
> **MsgBox(ex.Message)**
> **Exit Sub**
End Try

Your coding window should look like ours:

```
Private Sub Get_DGV_Data(ByVal select_command As String)

    Dim filepath As String
    Dim connect_string As String

    filepath = "C:\Employees.mdf;"

    connect_string = "Data Source=.\SQLEXPRESS;"
    connect_string += "AttachDbFilename=" & filepath
    connect_string += "Integrated Security=True;"
    connect_string += "Connect Timeout=30;"
    connect_string += "User Instance=True;"
    connect_string += "Trusted_Connection=Yes;"

    Try
        data_adapter = New SqlClient.SqlDataAdapter(select_command, _
                                                    connect_string)

        MsgBox("Connection OK")
    Catch ex As Exception
        MsgBox(ex.Message)
        Exit Sub
    End Try

End Sub
```

You can test it out, at this stage. Run your programme and see which message you get. Hopefully, it will be the "Connection OK" message.

If your connection is OK, then you can delete that particular message box. If you get any error messages, check that your file path is correct.

Now that we have a connection to the database, though, we can create a Data Table. The Data Table is where we place all the records from the database. This will then be bound to the DataGridView control, via the BindingSource we set up.

So add the following lines to your Sub:

```
Dim cb As New SqlClient.SqlCommandBuilder( data_adapter )
Dim data_table As New DataTable( )

Try
        data_adapter.Fill( data_table )
        binding_source.DataSource = data_table
Catch ex As Exception
        MsgBox(ex.Message)
End Try
```

The first line sets up a Command Builder object. (For an explanation of what this is, see the earlier database section.)

The second line sets up a Data Table object. The Data Table is like the Dataset that you have, if you've completed the first database section, already worked with. It's a Table with your Data in it!

(It's important to remember that Datasets and Data Tables are disconnected from the underlying database, once they are filled with data. This means that if you want to update the database, you have to reconnect to it.)

The **Try … Catch** block tries to fill the Data Table using the Data Adapter we set up.

The second line in the **Try … Catch** block is this:

binding_source.DataSource = data_table

As was mentioned, the BindingSource object has a DataSource property of its own. You just set this to the Data Table (or Dataset) that you have created. The BindingSource, remember, has already been configured earlier, when we added this line:

Me.DataGridView1.DataSource = Me.binding_source

So the DatagridView's DataSource is the BindingSource object. The BindingSource's DataSource is the data table.

Run your programme and test it out. You should find that your DataGridView is filled with all the data from your database. Your form should look like ours:

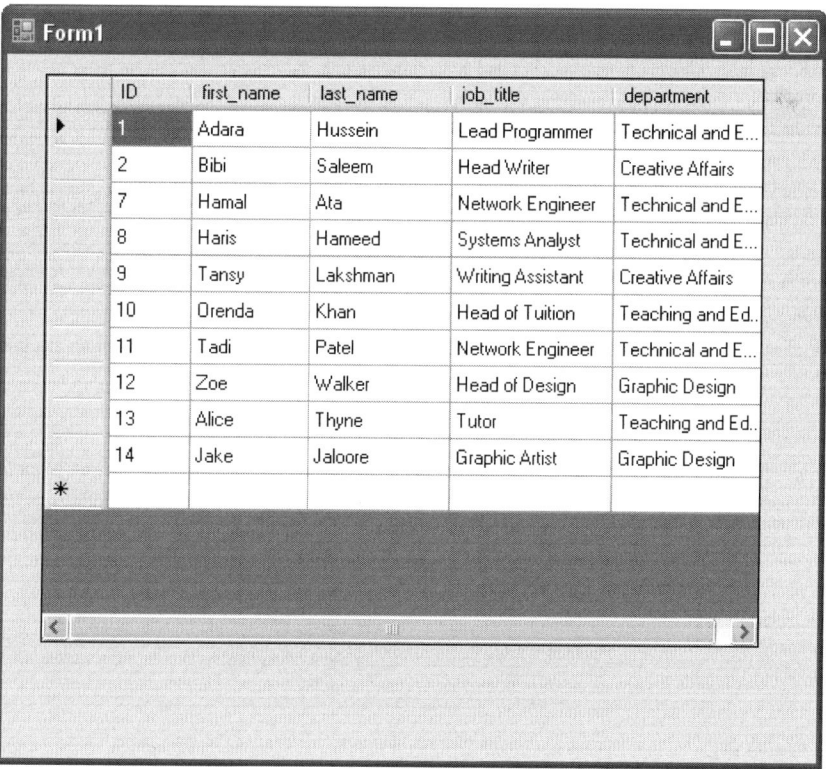

Your DataGrid will already have some functionality built into it. For example, you can resize the columns, and resize the rows.

You can also add new entries. Try it for yourself. Add a new record. (You'll have to start in the first name Column, and not the ID column)

		11	Tadi	Patel	Network Engineer	Techi
		12	Zoe	Walker	Head of Design	Graph
		13	Alice	Thyne	Tutor	Teac
		14	Jake	Jaloore	Graphic Artist	Graph
			Test	Person	Tutor	Teac
▶*						

Now close your programme down. Open it back up again and you'll find that the new record has vanished!

Likewise, run your programme and delete a record by clicking in the Row header to the left, indicated by the red circle in the image below:

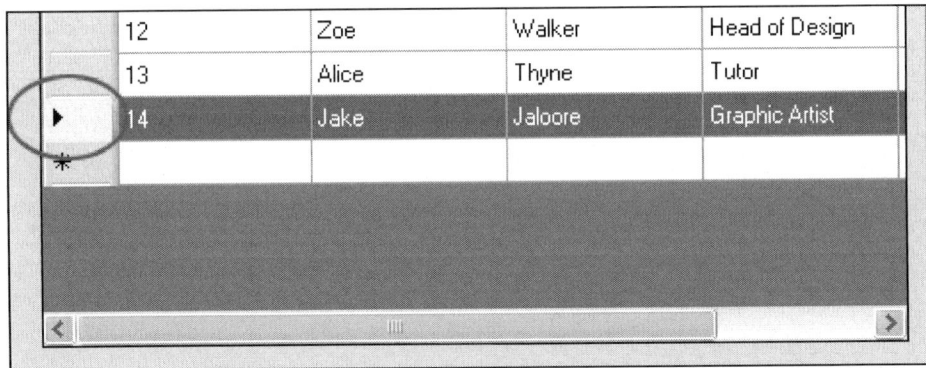

		12	Zoe	Walker	Head of Design
		13	Alice	Thyne	Tutor
▶		14	Jake	Jaloore	Graphic Artist
*					

Now press the delete key on your keyboard. The record gets deleted:

		11	Tadi	Patel	Network Engineer
		12	Zoe	Walker	Head of Design
▶		13	Alice	Thyne	Tutor
*					

When you close the programme down and then reopen it, however, the record will be back again!

This is because you're not doing anything to the underlying database – DataTables and Datasets are disconnected from the database. So we need to write some code to reconnect, and then update.

Add a button to your form. Change the Name property to **btnUpdate**. Change the Text property to **Update Changes**. Double click your button to open up its code stub.

The button, then, needs to do two things: issue the **Update** command against the underlying database, and refresh the connection.

Add the following two lines to your button code:

> **data_adapter.Update(CType(**binding_source.DataSource, DataTable**))**

> **Get_DGV_Data(data_adapter.SelectCommand.CommandText)**

The first line is the one that updates the database. Its done simply by typing the word **Update** after the name of your Data Adapter. In between the round brackets, though, you have to tell it what it is you're updating. Because we have a binding source object, we have to specify the DataSource property:

> **binding_source.DataSource**

However, the Data Adapter doesn't know what to do with this, so you have to convert it to a Type that it does understand – a DataTable:

> **CType(** binding_source.DataSource**, DataTable)**

The **CType** part means "Convert to Type". In between the round brackets, you add what it is you're trying to convert. After a comma, you add the Type you want to convert to, a DataTable for us. So we're saying, "Convert the DataSource of the BindingSource object to a DataTable".

The second line calls our **Get_DGV_Data( )** Sub again. Notice how we're getting the SQL command, though:

> **data_adapter.SelectCommand.CommandText**

So the Data Adapter has a SelectCommand property. This in turn has a CommandText property. The CommandText is a SQL Command, and it already knows what to do – get all the records from the database again.

Run your programme and try it out. You should now be able to add records, close the programme down, and still see them there. You should also be able to delete a row. When you click your Update Changes button, the row will be deleted from the database as well as the Data Table.

Get Cell Data from A DataGridView

Another thing you can do with programming code is to get the values of all the cells from a selected row. You could then pass these values on to a second form for further processing, or just display that person's details on a label or in a text box. Let's see how to do that.

Add another button to your form. Change the Name to **btnSelected**, and the Text to **Get Selected Row**. Double click the button to get at the code.

We need to set up some variables for this to work. So add the following to your button code:

Dim rowCount As Integer
Dim i As Integer

Now add the following line:

rowCount = DataGridView1.CurrentRow.Cells.Count

What we're going to do is to loop round all the cells in the row we have selected, and get each value. So we need to know how many cells there are. Quite handily, there's a property of DataGridViews that allows you to get the Current Row, and count how many cells it has. Which is what the above line does.

Now add the following For loop:

For i = 0 To rowCount – 1

        MsgBox(DataGridView1.CurrentRow.Cells(i).Value)

Next

So we're going from **0** to the **RowCount**, minus 1. The code for the loop then uses the loop counter to access the values at these positions in the Row:

DataGridView1.CurrentRow.Cells(i).Value

Run your programme and test it out. Select an entire row by clicking in the Row header (circled in red in a previous image). This selects the entire row. Now click your "Get Selected Row" button. You should see something like this:

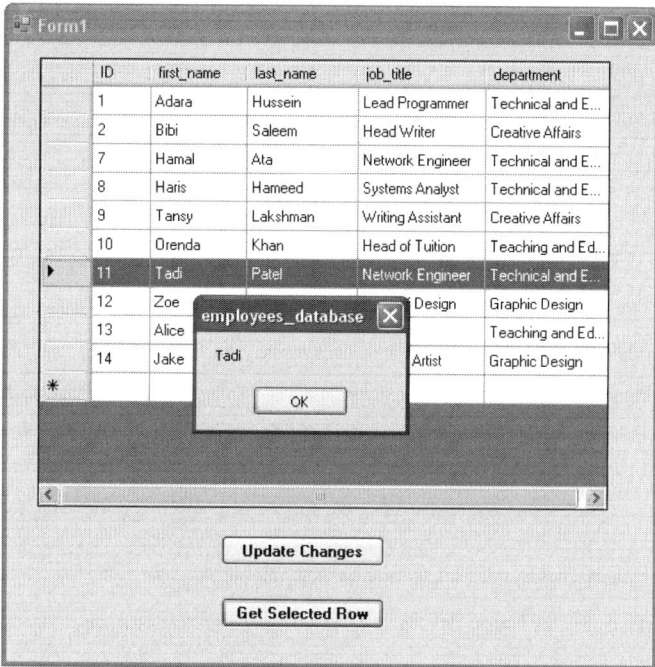

To finish off this section, try these exercises.

Exercise
Build up a string in your For loop, so that the message box displays the following:

Make sure you miss the ID cell out!

Exercise
Return to Design View. Click on your DataGridView control. Have a look at the properties area on the right, and explore the long list of properties available to the control. In particular, have a look at these properties:

AlternatingRowsDefaultCellStyle
AutoSizeColumnsMode
CellBorderStyle
Default Cell Size

Try to design a form like ours below:

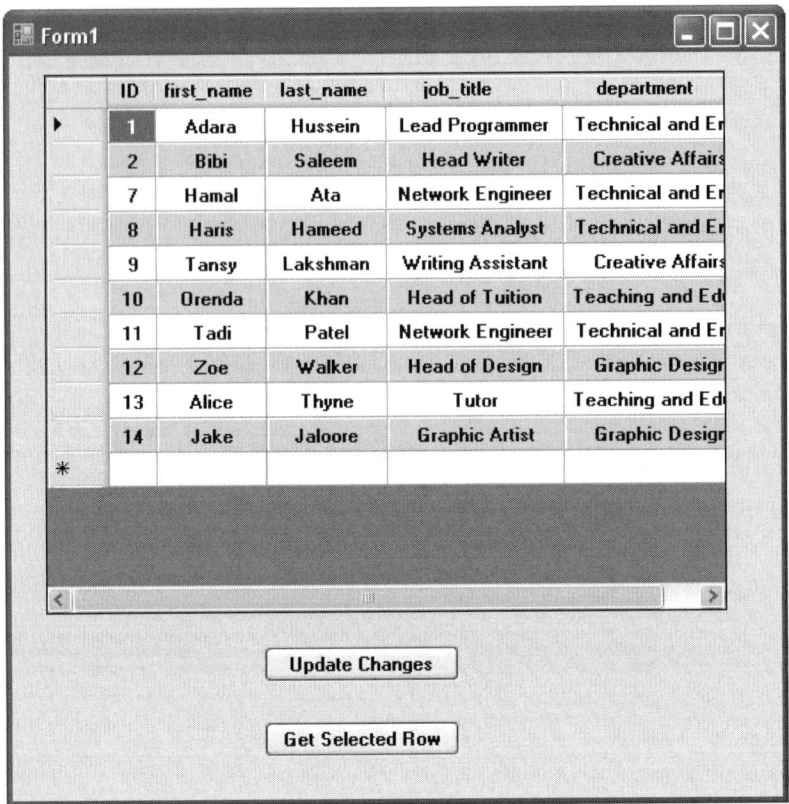

Notice that we've made the Column headers bold, centred everything, and had alternate colours for each row.

But we'll leave DataGrids there, and move on. Explore them further, though – they are quite handy for displaying data!

Picture Viewer – A Project

In this section, you'll create your very own Picture Viewer. It will look like this:

Down the left hand side, we have a ListView control. This allows us to display thumbnails of our chosen images. When you click an image in the ListView, the full size image appears on the right. If the image is too big for the form, scroll bars will appear. Our programme also has rudimentary zoom ability. When you right click the big image, the picture becomes smaller. When you left click the image, it will become bigger. You'll learn to use the following controls:

ListView
ImageList
Panels
Picture Box
Open File Dialogue Box

Let's make a start.

Adding the Controls to the Form

Start a new project. Make your Form nice and big. We made ours 950 wide by 800 high. Add a **Panel** control to the form. This can be found in the toolbox, in the **Containers** section:

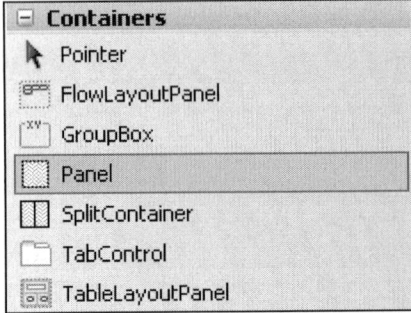

Draw the Panel any size you like. When you do, you'll see that it has a Move icon:

With the Panel selected, set the following properties for it:

Location:	160, 10
Size:	750, 720
Anchor:	Top, Bottom, Left, Right
AutoScroll:	True

The Panel will hold a PictureBox control. The reason we're adding a Panel is because the PictureBox doesn't have scrollbars of its own. We can dock a PictureBox to a Panel. When you make the PictureBox's image bigger than the Panel, the Panel will add the scrollbars automatically.

So add a PictureBox to your Panel. (The PictureBox is under the **Common** category in the Toolbox.) Just click the PictureBox once. Now draws out a PictureBox to fill your Panel.

Set the following Properties for your PictureBox:

Dock:	Top
SizeMode:	AutoSize

Your Picture Box should now be entirely inside of your Panel, right up to the edges.

Now add a button to your Form. Change the Name property to **btnLoadImages**, and set the Text to **Load Images**. Position the button somewhere in the top left of the form.

Just below the button, you can add a Label with the Text property of **Images**.

Add a ListView control to your form. The ListView is also under the **Common** category in the Toolbox. Resize your ListView control, and place it under your button and Label. (We made our Size 120, 300.) Leave the other properties on their defaults.

The next thing to add is a **OpenFileDialog** control. This can be found under the **Dialog** category of the Toolbox. Simply double click to add one to your project. You'll see it appear at the bottom of the project window:

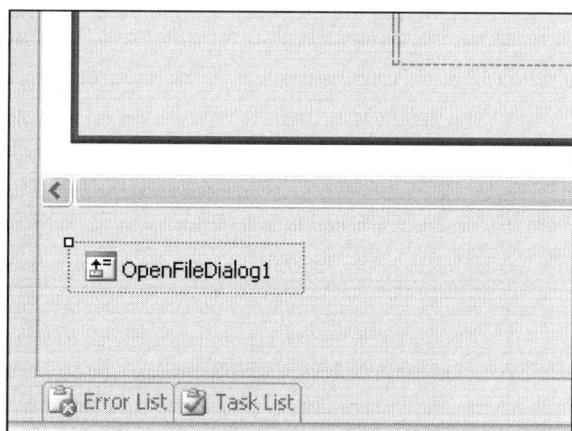

With the **OpenFileDialog** control selected, have a look at the Properties area on the right. Set the **Name** property to oFD1, and the **MultiSelect** property to True.

Finally, add an ImageList control. This can be found under the **Components** category of the Toolbox:

Double click ImageList to add one to your project. Again, it will get added to the bottom of the project Window:

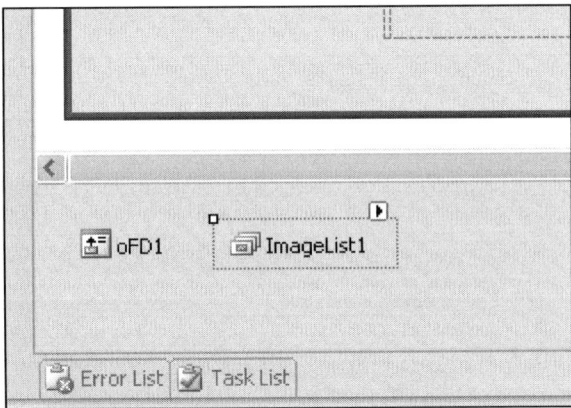

With your ImageList1 control selected, set its **ImageSize** property to 32, 32. The ImageList control, as its name suggests, holds a list of images. We'll use these images as the thumbnail images for the ListView.

Now that we have all our controls in place, we can start the coding.

Selecting Images

The first we'll do is to launch the Open File Dialogue box. You've done this before, in a previous section.

Double click your button to get at the code stub. The first two lines of code to add will clear the ImageList of its images, and clear the ListView. Add these two lines, then:

```
ImageList1.Images.Clear( )
ListView1.Clear( )
```

So we're just issuing the **Clear** command of the two objects.

To get the Open File Dialogue box to appear, add these lines:

```
oFD1.InitialDirectory = "C:\"
oFD1.Title = "Open an Image File"
oFD1.Filter = "JPEGS|*.jpg|GIFS|*.gif"

Dim ofdResults As Integer = oFD1.ShowDialog( )

        If ofdResults = Windows.Forms.DialogResult.Cancel Then
        Exit Sub
End If
```

You should know what these lines do by now, as you've met them before. But we're just setting the initial directory, adding a title to the dialogue box, and then specifying the type of files than can be opened. We have to handle the Cancel button being clicked, which is what the rest of the lines do.

You can try it out, if you like. The dialogue box should appear when you click your button, and you should be able to select more than one file.

As you learned earlier, though, the Open File Dialogue box doesn't actually open files. It just allows you to specify the names of the files you want to open.

Because you want the user to be able to load more than one file into the ListView area, you have to get at all the file names selected. This can be done with a **For ... Each** Loop. Add the following lines to the ones you already have:

```
Try
        Dim single_file As String

        For Each single_file In oFD1.FileNames

            MsgBox( single_file )

        Next


Catch ex As Exception
        MsgBox("Error opening files")
End Try
```

We've put it in a **Try ... Catch** block, to trap any errors. The first line sets up a string variable that we've called **single_file**. The **For ... Each** loop is this:

> **For Each single_file In oFD1.FileNames**
>
> **MsgBox(** single_file **)**
>
> **Next**

So the OpenFileDialog control has a property called FileNames. This gets you a list of all the files that the user selected. By using **For ... Each** you can loop round and get all the file names (which will include the file paths). The file names will be stored in the **single_file** variable.

Try your programme out again. Click your button, and select a few images on your computer. When you click the Open button, you should see the Message Box display, with all your file names and file paths displayed.

We need all those file names and file paths. We can then pass them to the ImageList control, for the thumbnails. But we'll also need them for the ListView control. To store the file names and file paths, we can use an array. Add the following to your **Try ... Catch** block, just under "Dim single_file As String":

> **Dim num_of_files As Integer = oFD1.FileNames.Length**
> **Dim aryFilePaths(num_of_files - 1) As String**

The **Length** property of **FileNames** gets you how many files were selected. In between the round brackets of **aryFilePaths**, we're using this number to set the size of the array. We're deducting 1 because arrays start at zero.

Add this third variable, just below the two above:

> **Dim counter As Integer = 0**

We can use the counter to access the array. In place of your Message Box, add this line to your **For ... Each** loop code:

> **aryFilePaths(** counter **) = single_file**

So the file names and paths will now be stored in the array we set up. Increment the counter on the line just below this one:

> **counter = counter + 1**

Your code should now look like this, though:

```
Private Sub btnLoadImages_Click(ByVal sender As System.Object, _
                                ByVal e As System.EventArgs) _
                                Handles btnLoadImages.Click

    ImageList1.Images.Clear()
    ListView1.Clear()

    oFD1.InitialDirectory = "C:\"
    oFD1.Title = "Open an Image File"
    oFD1.Filter = "JPEGS|*.jpg|GIFS|*.gif"

    Dim ofdResults As Integer = oFD1.ShowDialog()

    If ofdResults = Windows.Forms.DialogResult.Cancel Then
        Exit Sub
    End If

    Try
        Dim single_file As String
        Dim num_of_files As Integer = oFD1.FileNames.Length
        Dim aryFilePaths(num_of_files - 1) As String
        Dim counter As Integer = 0

        For Each single_file In oFD1.FileNames
            aryFilePaths(counter) = single_file
            counter = counter + 1
        Next

    Catch ex As Exception
        MsgBox("Error opening files")
    End Try

End Sub
```

Adding Images to an Images List

An ImageList control is something you need to add images to. You do this with the **Add** command. We can add all the images that the user selected. This can be done in your **For .. Each** loop:

```
For Each single_file In oFD1.FileNames
        aryFilePaths(counter) = single_file
        ImageList1.Images.Add( Image.FromFile( single_file ) )
        counter = counter + 1
Next
```

The new line to add is in bold text, above. The ImageList1 object has an **Images** collection. After a dot, use the word **Add**. In between the round brackets of **Add**, you specify the image that you want to add to your ImageList. For us, this was an image that the user selected, which is stored in the **single_file** variable.

You can't just use the file path, however. It has to be an Image. You can turn the file path into an image with the **Image** object. This has a **FromFile** function. In between the round brackets of FromFile, you specify a file path:

Image.FromFile(single_file **)**

So we're creating an image from the file path, and then adding it to the ImageList collection.

When the **For ... Each** loop is complete, you'll then have an ImageList filled with Images. The size of each image will be 32 by 32. Which is the size we set earlier.

After the **For ... Each** loop, you then need to attach the ImageList to the ListView control. There's only one line of code to add for this:

ListView1.LargeImageList = ImageList1

We're using the **LargeImageList** property of the ListView control. This, not surprisingly, will mean that the ListView can display large images. The large images are all in the ImageList.

Adding Images and File Paths to the ListView

So that the user can see the images, we still need to **Add** them as **Items** to the ListView. The previous line just attached the ImageList to the ListView object. But it won't do anything useful with them.

We need to add a **For** loop, now. We'll loop round adding new items to the ListView. The items we'll add are the images to display, as well as some text under the image. The text will be the file path of the image. (We'll be using this later.)

So add the following For loop to your code:

For i As Integer = 0 To counter - 1

ListView1.Items.Add(aryFilePaths(i), i)

Next i

The loop goes from 0 to the value of counter, minus 1. (The value of the counter variable is the same as the number of images in the array we set up.)

Inside the loop is where we add the Items to the ListView:

ListView1.Items.Add( )

You have a number of different options to choose from between the round brackets of **Add**. But remember what we're doing here: Adding **Items** to the ListView control.

The first thing we want to add is the Text that goes under the image:

aryFilePaths(i)

The second thing to add is the thumbnail image. This is stored in the ImageList, which the ListView now knows about. But the image we attached to the ListView are stored in a collection. You can access this collection either as a Key or as a number. The number is the position in the ImageList:

Add(aryFilePaths(i), i)

We're using the loop variable, here, which will start at 0. The first time round the loop, this will attach **image 0** in the ImageList collection to the ListView.

The full code for your button should now look like ours:

```vb
Private Sub btnLoadImages_Click(ByVal sender As System.Object, _
                                ByVal e As System.EventArgs) _
                                Handles btnLoadImages.Click
    ImageList1.Images.Clear()
    ListView1.Clear()

    oFD1.InitialDirectory = "C:\"
    oFD1.Title = "Open an Image File"
    oFD1.Filter = "JPEGS|*.jpg|GIFS|*.gif"

    Dim ofdResults As Integer = oFD1.ShowDialog()

    If ofdResults = Windows.Forms.DialogResult.Cancel Then
        Exit Sub
    End If

    Try
        Dim single_file As String
        Dim num_of_files As Integer = oFD1.FileNames.Length
        Dim aryFilePaths(num_of_files - 1) As String
        Dim counter As Integer = 0

        For Each single_file In oFD1.FileNames
            aryFilePaths(counter) = single_file
            ImageList1.Images.Add(Image.FromFile(single_file))
            counter = counter + 1
        Next

        ListView1.LargeImageList = ImageList1

        For i As Integer = 0 To counter - 1
            ListView1.Items.Add(aryFilePaths(i).ToString(), i)
        Next i

    Catch ex As Exception
        MsgBox("Error opening files")
    End Try

End Sub
```

Try it out. Run your programme and click your button. Select a few images to open. When you click the Open button on your Open File Dialogue box, your ListView control should look like ours below:

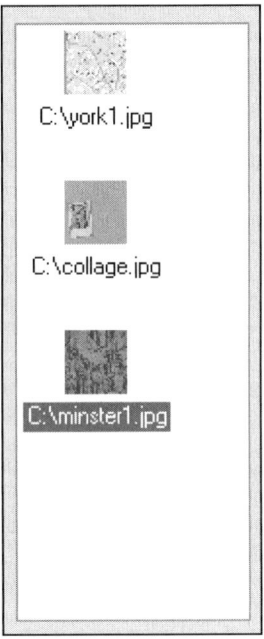

So we have a thumbnail image, and the file path of the image. We can use that file path for the bigger image.

The Bigger Picture

When you click on a thumbnail, you want the picture box on the right to display the full-size version of the image. To do this, you need to get just the file path to the image, which we displayed as text under the thumbnail. This is not quite as straightforward as it should be.

Clicking on a thumbnail fires the **SelectedIndexChanged** event of the ListView control. The Index refers to which complete item you clicked on: the thumbnail, the text, and anything else you have for that particular item. For example, clicking on the first thumbnail in the previous image above would get you a reference to not only the thumbnail image, but also the text "C:\york1.jpg". Because it's the first item in the ListView, the index would be 0.

The ListView, however, allows you to select more than one item. So in the image below, a user could select not only the A image but the B image as well.

Name ▲	Size	Type	Date Modified	Dimensions
01012008331.jpg	439 KB	JPEG Image	24/02/2008 23:31	2048 x 1536
01012008332.jpg	540 KB	JPEG Image	24/02/2008 23:30	2048 x 1536
01012008333.jpg	374 KB	JPEG Image	24/02/2008 23:30	2048 x 1536
01012008334.jpg	313 KB	JPEG Image	24/02/2008 23:30	2048 x 1536
A.jpg	414 KB	JPEG Image	24/02/2008 23:31	2048 x 1536
B.jpg	416 KB	JPEG Image	24/02/2008 23:31	2048 x 1536
collage.jpg	82 KB	JPEG Image	23/07/2007 19:10	1280 x 1024
minster1.jpg	756 KB	JPEG Image	23/07/2007 19:07	2048 x 1536
Thumbs.db	31 KB	Data Base File	05/09/2008 10:24	
York1.JPG	629 KB	JPEG Image	14/02/2003 00:03	1536 x 2048
York2.JPG	627 KB	JPEG Image	14/02/2003 00:06	2048 x 1536
York3.JPG	747 KB	JPEG Image	14/02/2003 00:11	2048 x 1536

You can loop round and get all the items that were selected by the user. For any one item, the options then available in the image above are:

Name
Size
Type
Date Modified
Dimensions

So, in Design View, click on your ListView control to select it. In the properties area on the right, click on the lightning symbol to display a list of available events, and locate **SelectedIndexChanged**:

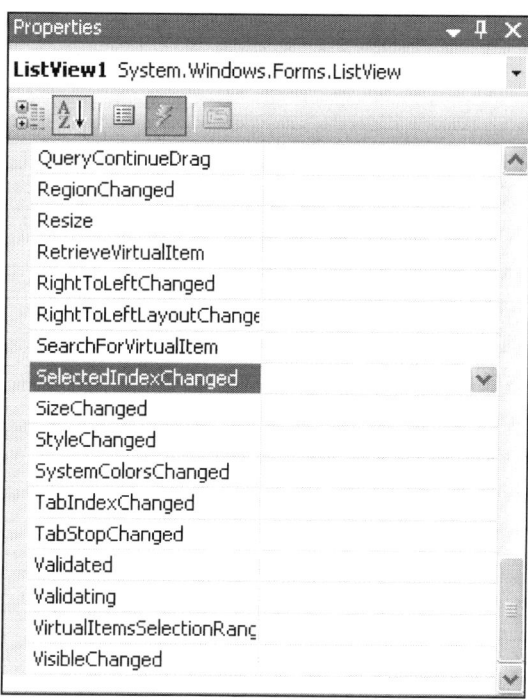

Double click to create the code stub. Now add the following line:

Dim big_filename As String

This just sets up a variable that we've called **big_filename**. The **For** loop is this:

For i As Integer = 0 To ListView1.SelectedItems.Count - 1
Next i

So we want to go round all the items that were selected. To get at the Text for an item, the code you need inside of your loop is this:

big_filename = ListView1.SelectedItems(i).Text

The **Text** for us was the file path to the thumbnail. The thumbnail is also the path to the bigger image. We can create a new image from the file path:

PictureBox1.Image = Image.FromFile(big_filename)

Again, we're using the **Image** object, and the **FromFile** function. In between the round brackets of **FromFile**, we're using our file path. Add the line to your **For** loop.

We only need one more line in the loop. Add this rather curious line:

Panel1.AutoScrollMinSize = New Size(PictureBox1.Image.Width, _
**   PictureBox1.Image.Height)**

The **AutoScrollMinSize** property of a Panel takes two arguments, a Width and a Height. It's used to get a minimum size for the AutoScroll of the Panel. If you don't include this line then you won't get the scroll bars, or you may just get a vertical scroll bar but no horizontal one.

But the code for your SelectedIndexChanged event should look like this:

```
Private Sub ListView1_SelectedIndexChanged(ByVal sender As System.Object, _
                        ByVal e As System.EventArgs) _
                        Handles ListView1.SelectedIndexChanged


    Dim big_filename As String

    For i As Integer = 0 To ListView1.SelectedItems.Count - 1

        big_filename = ListView1.SelectedItems(i).Text

        PictureBox1.Image = Image.FromFile(big_filename)
        Panel1.AutoScrollMinSize = New Size(PictureBox1.Image.Width, _
                                    PictureBox1.Image.Height)

    Next i


End Sub
```

Try it out. Run your programme and open some images. Click on a thumbnail in your ListView and you should find that the bigger image appears in the PictureBox on the right.

Zooming in and out

The first thing we'll do is to make the image smaller when the right mouse button is clicked on the image in the PictureBox (zooming out).

What we need to do, though, is to resize the image. We'll use the graphics object to do this, and create new bitmap objects. Tricky stuff!

Go back to Design View and select your PictureBox. Locate the MouseDown event in the properties area on the right (click the lightning symbol). Double click the event name to get the code stub. Now enter the following lines of code:

```
If e.Button = Windows.Forms.MouseButtons.Right Then

    Dim bmp As New Bitmap( PictureBox1.Image )

    Dim bmp_new As New Bitmap( CInt( PictureBox1.Image.Width / 2 ), _
        CInt( PictureBox1.Image.Height / 2 ) )

    Dim gr As Graphics = Graphics.FromImage( bmp_new )

    gr.DrawImage( bmp, 0, 0, bmp_new.Width, bmp_new.Height )

    PictureBox1.Image = bmp_new


    Panel1.AutoScrollMinSize = New Size( PictureBox1.Image.Width, _
        PictureBox1.Image.Height )

End If
```

The If Statement just detects if the Right mouse button was clicked. The first line in the If Statement is this:

Dim bmp As New Bitmap(PictureBox1.Image)

This creates a new Bitmap object, using the image from the PictureBox.

The second line also creates a new Bitmap object:

Dim bmp_new As New Bitmap(CInt(PictureBox1.Image.Width / 2 **), _**
CInt(PictureBox1.Image.Height / 2 **))**

This time, however, we're just specifying a new size for the bitmap. The new size is this:

CInt(PictureBox1.Image.Width / 2 **), CInt(** PictureBox1.Image.Height / 2 **)**

So we take the height of the image in the PictureBox and divide by 2. We then need to convert this to an Integer (**CInt**). We do the same for the Width. This will leave us with a blank image, but with the size we need.

The next line is this:

Dim gr As Graphics = Graphics.FromImage(bmp_new **)**

We're creating a graphics object here. The graphics object has a **FromImage** function. In other words, we're setting the new image to be the graphics object. It's still a blank image, though.

The next line is where we draw an image:

gr.DrawImage(bmp, 0, 0, bmp_new.Width, bmp_new.Height **)**

The **gr** variable is a graphics object containing an image. The image is blank, however, so we use the DrawImage function to draw an image onto it. In between the round brackets of DrawImage, we're drawing the original image, but at the new size. (The 0, 0 is the location to start drawing.)

After all this graphics manipulation, the variable we've called **bmp_new** will contain the original image at the new size. This is then used in the next line:

PictureBox1.Image = bmp_new

The final line is one you've met before – resize the panel's AutoScroll features.

Your coding window should look like ours, though:

```
Private Sub PictureBox1_MouseDown(ByVal sender As System.Object, _
                    ByVal e As System.Windows.Forms.MouseEventArgs) _
                    Handles PictureBox1.MouseDown


    If e.Button = Windows.Forms.MouseButtons.Right Then

        Dim bmp As New Bitmap(PictureBox1.Image)

        Dim bmp_new As New Bitmap( CInt(PictureBox1.Image.Width / 2), _
                                   CInt(PictureBox1.Image.Height / 2))

        Dim gr As Graphics = Graphics.FromImage(bmp_new)

        gr.DrawImage(bmp, 0, 0, bmp_new.Width, bmp_new.Height)

        PictureBox1.Image = bmp_new

        Panel1.AutoScrollMinSize = New Size(PictureBox1.Image.Width, _
                                    PictureBox1.Image.Height)


    End If

End Sub
```

Try it out. Run your programme and open a big image. Click the thumbnail to load it into your PictureBox. Now right click the PictureBox. Your image should resize.

Exercise

To finish your Picture Viewer, add a zoom in feature. The image in your PictureBox should get bigger when the user LEFT clicks on it. This exercise is a lot easier than you think!

And we'll leave our Picture View there. It's a bit rudimentary, but we hope you learned a lot from it! In the next part, you'll create your very own browser.

A Tabbed Browser

In this section, you'll create your very own tabbed browser. Let's get started!

Create a new project for this. Make your new Form nice and big. In the toolbox, locate the **TabControl**, which is under the Containers heading:

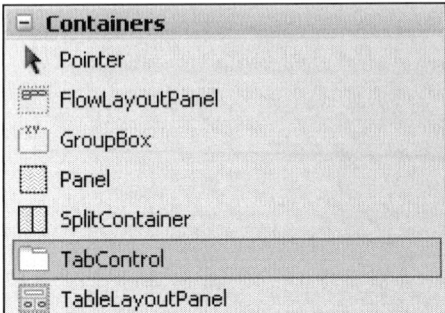

Add one to your form, and it should look like this:

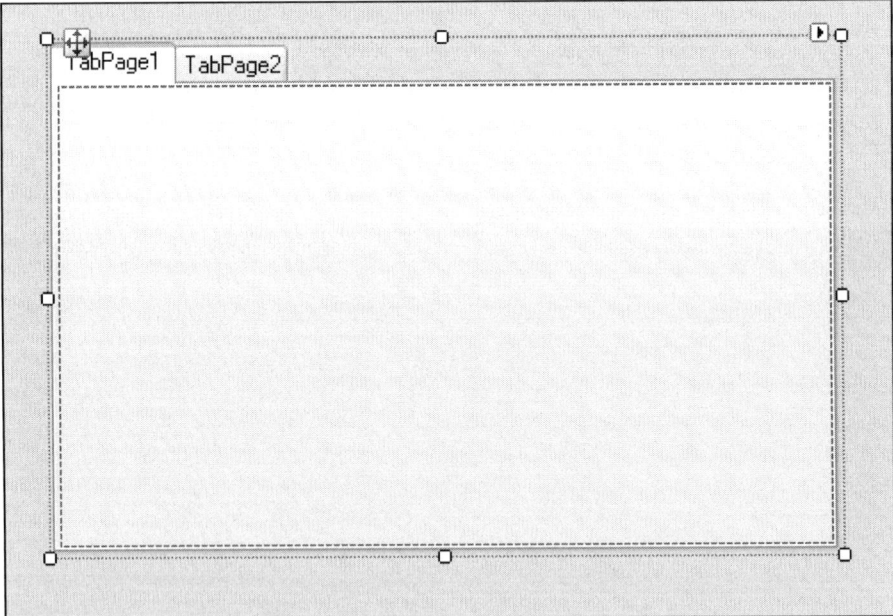

The default TabControl gives you two tabs. We're going to be creating a new tab when a button is clicked on the form, so we can delete one of the tabs.

To delete a tab, you can select it from the properties area on the right. Click the arrow on the drop down box:

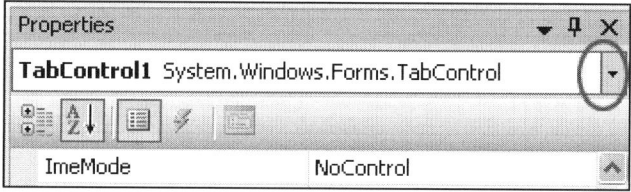

Locate TabPage2 and select it:

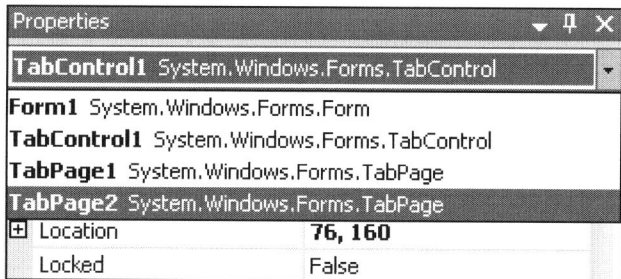

Now right click anywhere on TabPage2 except the tab header (where the TabPage2 text is). From the menu that appears, select the **Delete** option. If your whole TabControl disappears, click **Edit > Undo** from the menu bars at the top of the Visual Basic .NET software.

You should now have a TabControl with just one tab. Select this tab from the drop down box in the properties window. We'll add a browser to it.

The WebBrowser Control

Adding a Browser to a Tab is quite easy. Locate the **WebBrowser** control in the toolbox, in the Common Controls category (we've chopped a few controls out, in the image below):

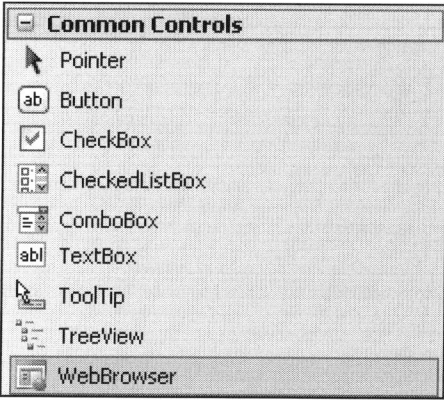

Click the control once to select it. Now draw out a browser in your TabPage1. It should fill the whole tab, and look like this:

The web browser you have just added is an instance of Internet Explorer. It will take the same settings as those from the Internet Options dialogue box in your control panel. So, for example, if you have scripting turned on in Internet Options, it will still be turned on in the WebBrowser control you have just added to the tab.

To see if it works as a browser, though, add a text box and button to your form. Change the Name of the text box to **txtAddress**, and type a web address for the Text property. Change the Name property of the button to **btnGo**, and the Text to **GO**. Aim for something like this:

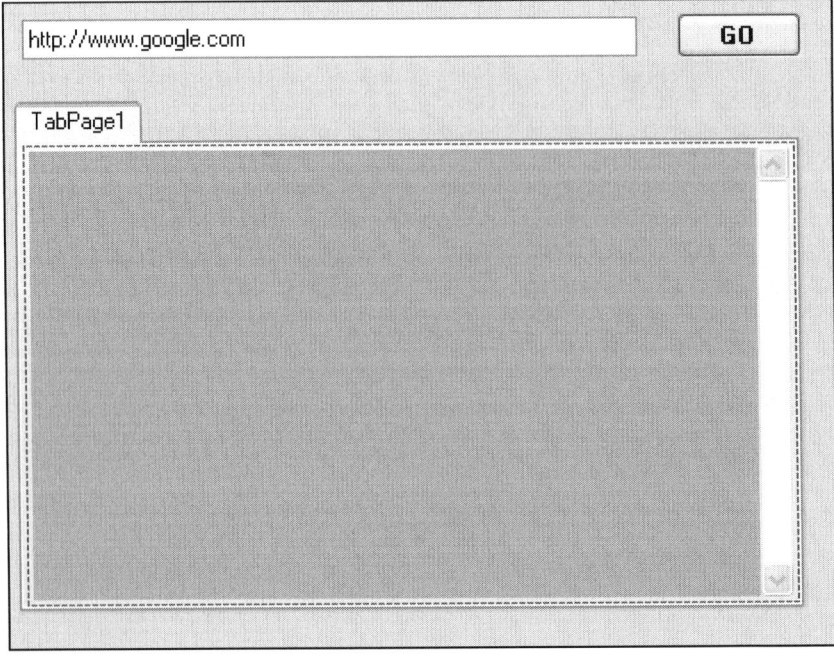

Now double click your new button to get at the code stub.

The WebBrowser control has a Subroutine called **Navigate**. You use it to navigate to a web page that you specify. So add these two lines to your button code:

Dim WebPage As String = Trim(txtAddress.Text)

Me.WebBrowser1.Navigate(WebPage)

We're just getting the web page address from the text box. You would need to do some error checking here, though, testing for things like blank strings and valid web addresses.

The page you want to navigate to goes between the round brackets of the **Navigate** Subroutine. And that's it!

Test it out. Run your programme and click your button. You should find that the web page that you typed in the text box appears in the web browser that you placed on TabPage1. If it doesn't, make sure that your firewall is not blocking your Visual Basic .NET software. Here's what ours looks like:

Navigation Buttons

We'll add some navigation buttons, now. The buttons we'll add will allow us to go back one page, move forward one page, go to the home page, cancel the page loading, and refresh the page. Instead of having text on our buttons, we'll have images.

For the button images, we'll have an ImageList that will allow us to select a picture for all the buttons on the form.

You'll need some images for your buttons. We're using the free icon set from this web page:

http://stemplate.com/icons.html

However, the file is a Photoshop PSD file. You then create smaller image in Photoshop. If you haven't got Photoshop, you should be able to get hold of some free icons by Googling the term "free icons" (with the quote marks). Or search your hard drive for suitable images. You can search for files that end in, say, GIF by entering ***.gif** in the Windows search box. Go for an image size no bigger than 64 pixels high by 64 pixels wide. Image types supported by the ImageList control are JPEG, GIF, BMP, PNG and ICO.

So, add an ImageList object to your project (under the **Components** category in the toolbox).

The ImageList has a **ColorDepth** property that we need to change. Our images are in the PNG-24 format, where the 24 stands for the number of bits. You'd think, then, that we'd need to set the ColorDepth to 24Bit. However, they look awful at this Depth. When we switch to 32Bit, they look fine! But if your images look awful, change the ColorDepth property.

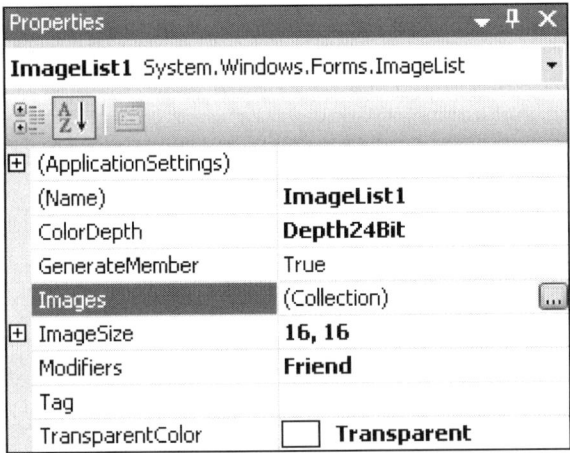

To add images to your image list, click the **Images** button in the Properties area, just to the right of Collection, in the image above.

When you click the small button, you'll see the following dialogue box appear:

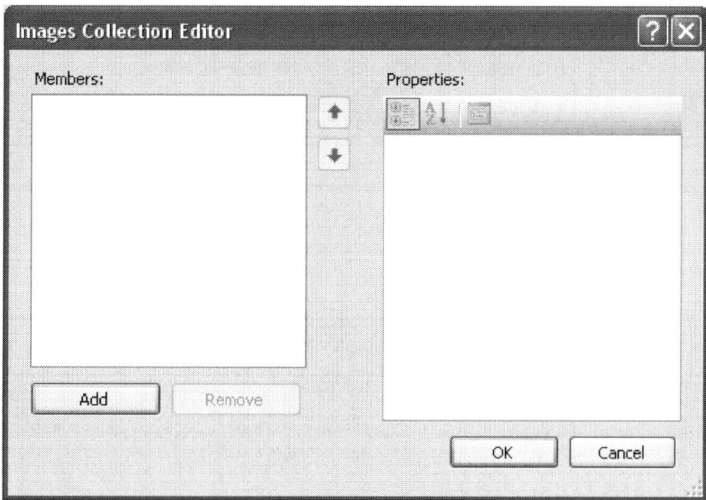

Click the Add button to add some image to your ImageList. We've added five to ours, in the image below:

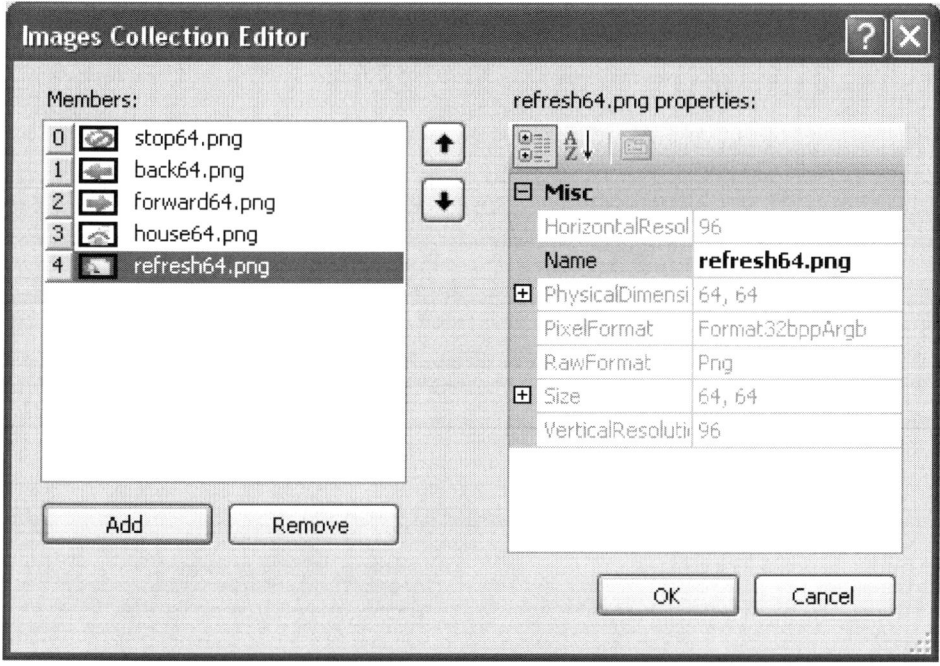

Click OK when you're done.

Our images are 64 pixels high by 64 pixels wide. We can change to that size in the ImageList properties area. The default is to have the images 16 by 16. Type the new size into the ImageSize property, if you need to:

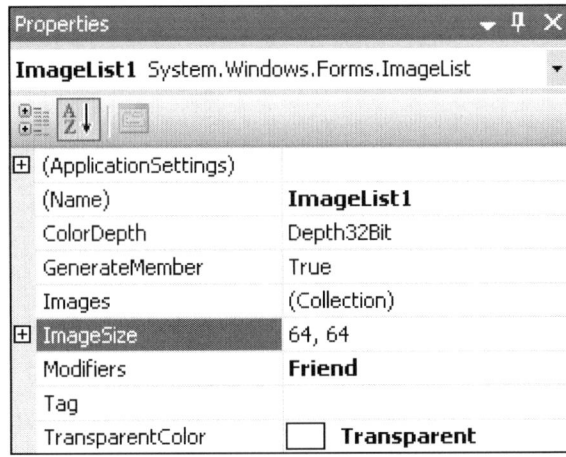

Graphic Buttons

Adding graphics to your buttons is quite easy. Add a button to your form, using the toolbox area on the left. Change the Name property to **btnBack**. Delete the default text from the Text property of the button, leaving it blank. Resize your button to a suitable size.

To add an image from your ImageList, locate the ImageList property. From the dropdown box, select the name of your ImageList:

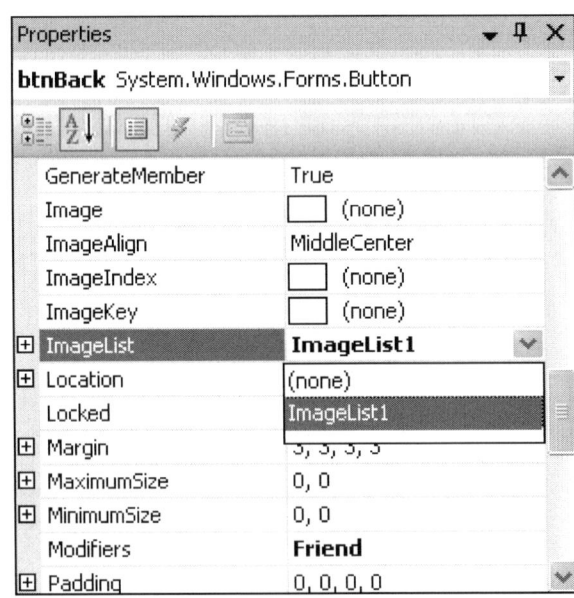

Now locate the **ImageIndex** property. Click the dropdown box and you'll see a list of all your available images. Select the image you're going to use for your Back button. We're using a left-pointing green arrow for ours, which has the ImageIndex of 1:

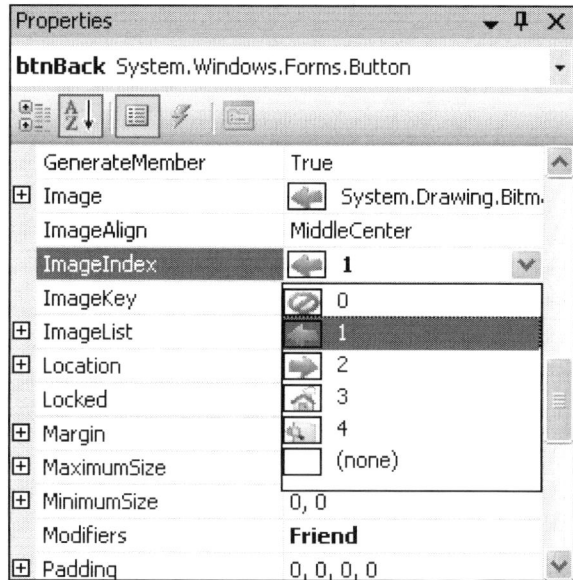

Once you've selected an image, take a look at your button. It should have your picture on it:

The code for the back button is quite simple. So double click your button to get at the coding window. Add the following:

If WebBrowser1.CanGoBack Then

WebBrowser1.GoBack( )

End If

We're using an If statement first to check whether there is a page to go back to. This is done with the **CanGoBack** property of the WebBrowser object.

If there is a page to go back to, we then use the built-in **GoBack** function. This will force the browser to go back to the page you were previously looking at.

Exercise

Add four more buttons to your Form. Set up the following properties for your buttons:

Name:	btnForward
Image:	An image of your choice

Name:	btnHome
Image:	An image of your choice

Name:	btnStop
Image:	An image of your choice

Name:	btnRefresh
Image:	An image of your choice

When you're done, your form may look something like ours:

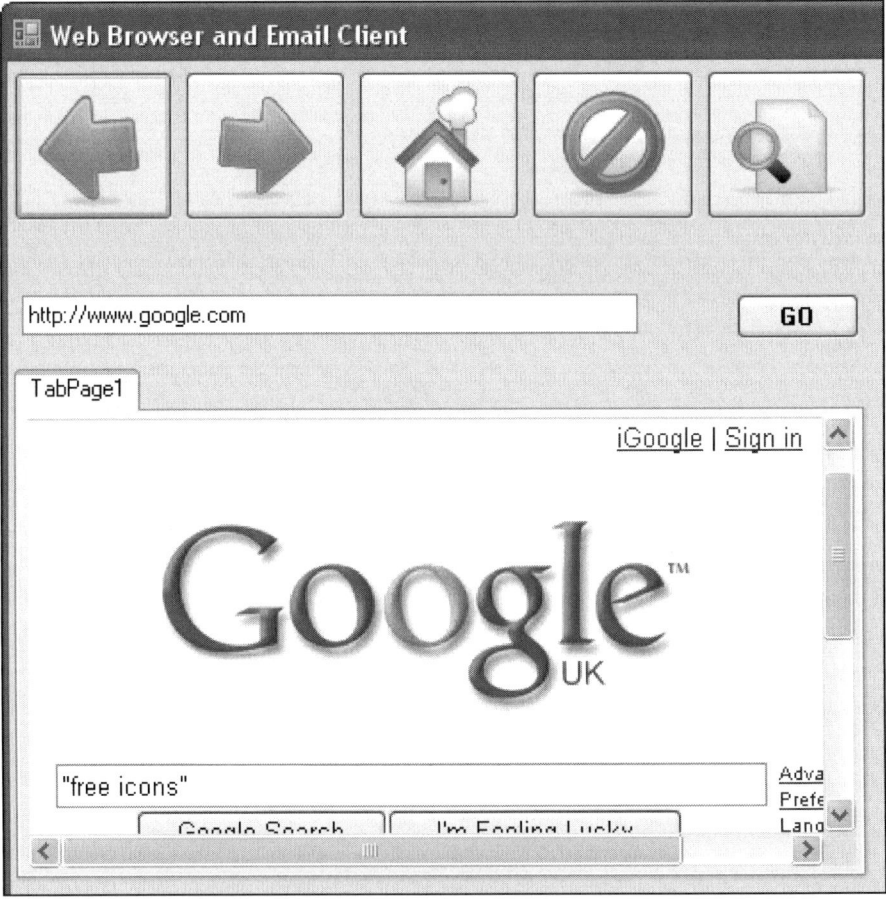

Test out your programme, though. Navigate to a web page like Google. Enter something in the search page, just so as to bring up a second page. Now click your Back button. You should be taken back to the previous page.

Exercise

Below, you'll find four pieces of code. Add the right code to the appropriate button:

> **If Me.WebBrowser1.CanGoForward Then**
>   **Me.WebBrowser1.GoForward( )**
> **End If**
>
> **WebBrowser1.Stop( )**
>
> **WebBrowser1.GoHome( )**
>
> **WebBrowser1.Refresh( )**

So you're adding code to each of your remaining four buttons. When you're done, all four buttons should work, when you run your programme.

Adding ToolTips

When you hold your mouse over a button, it would be nice to have a ToolTip display. The ToolTip will tell the user what the button does. Sadly, adding a ToolTip is not quite as straightforward as it should be. But what we want to add looks like this (the yellow box in the image below):

To get ToolTips, you need to create a ToolTip object. You then pass it the name of the form object you want the ToolTip for, and the text you want to display.

The ToolTip object can be added using the toolbox. It's under the **Common Controls** category:

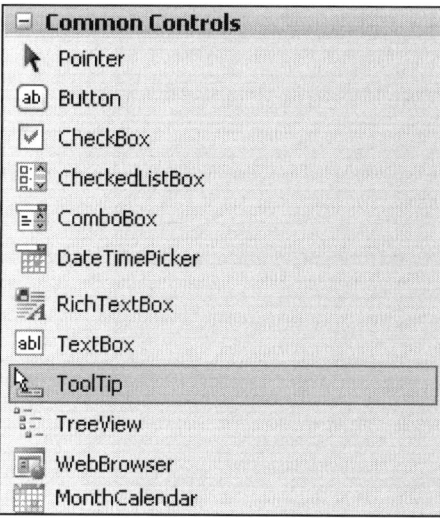

Double click to add one to your project, and you'll see it appear at the bottom of the screen, rather than on the form.

You want the text of the ToolTip to appear when the mouse is over a button. Buttons have a Hover event, so we can use that for the code.

To get to the Hover event, click on a button to select it. In the properties area on the right, click the lightning bolt icon to see a list of event. Locate the MouseHover event:

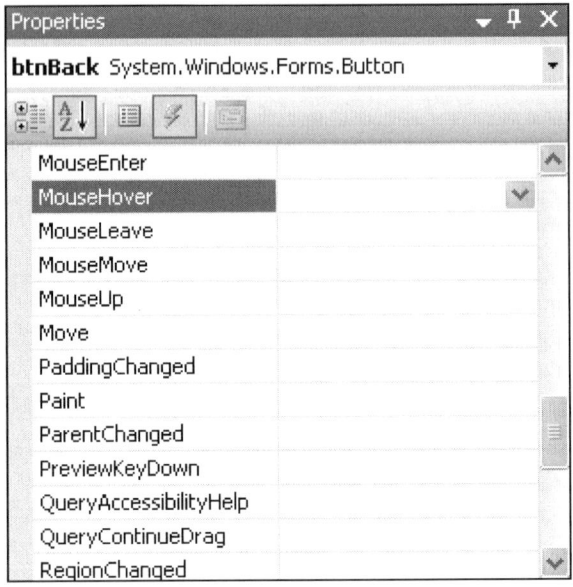

Double click where it says MouseHover, and it will open up the code stub. Now enter the following code:

```
Private Sub btnBack_MouseHover(ByVal sender As System.Object, _
                              ByVal e As System.EventArgs) _
                              Handles btnBack.MouseHover

        ToolTip1.SetToolTip(btnBack, "Back One Page")

End Sub
```

So the ToolTip has an in-built Subroutine called **SetToolTip**. In between the round brackets of SetToolTip you need two things: the name of the object you want the ToolTip for, and the Text to go in the yellow box. We called our button btnBack, so that's we put as the first argument. The text comes after a comma, and in quote marks.

Run your programme and test it out. Hold your mouse over your button and you should (eventually) see your ToolTip:

Exercise

Add ToolTips for your other four buttons. You can have any text you want for your ToolTips.

Exercise

If you wanted to, you could have a Rollover effect for your buttons. This is when the image on the button changes when the mouse hovers over it. When you take your mouse away, it will go back to the original image. The only thing you need for your MouseHover event is this:

btnBack.Image = ImageList1.Images.Item(2)

What you're doing here is setting the **Image** property of the button to one of the images from your Image list, Item 2 in the code above. You can get the item number from the dropdown list you saw earlier, for the ImageIndex property of the button. Use the MouseLeave event to reset the image to the original.

Creating New Tabs

We want to create a new tab in our browser when a button is clicked on the form. To do this, you create a new TabPage object. You then set some properties for your Tab, before adding the page to the TabControl. But we also need to add a WebBrowser control to the TabPage. This is done in the same way.

So add a new button to your Form. You can add an image to it, if you want. But set the Name property for your new button to **btnAddTab**. Double click your button to get at the code stub.

To create a new TabPage object, the code is this:

Dim new_tab As System.Windows.Forms.TabPage

new_tab = New System.Windows.Forms.TabPage( )

So we're setting up a variable called **new_tab**. The type of variable we're creating is a TabPage. The second line creates a new object from the variable.

Add some text to your Tab with the Text property:

new_tab.Text = "New Tab"

You also need to specify a size for your new tab. You can do this by creating a new Size object:

new_tab.Size = **New Size(** TabControl1.Width, TabControl1.Height **)**

The Size property needs a Height and a Width. Visual Basic .NET has a Size object you can use to set both of these values at once. After **New Size**, we're setting the Width and Height to be the same as TabControl1.

Finally, you need to add the new tab to the TabControl1 object:

TabControl1.Controls.Add(new_tab **)**

In between the round brackets of Add, you type the name of the control you want to add.

You do more or less the same for the WebBrowser, except the WebBrowser needs to be added to the new tab, rather than the main TabControl itself. Add these four lines of code:

WebBrowser1 = **New System.Windows.Forms.WebBrowser**
WebBrowser1.Height = **new_tab.Height**
WebBrowser1.Width = **new_tab.Width**

new_tab.Controls.Add(WebBrowser1 **)**

You should be able to work out what's going on: create a new WebBrowser object, set a height and width (a different way, this time), then add the control to the new tab object. Your coding window should look like this one, though:

```
Private Sub btnAddTab_Click(ByVal sender As System.Object, _
                            ByVal e As System.EventArgs) _
                        Handles btnAddTab.Click

    Dim new_tab As System.Windows.Forms.TabPage

    new_tab = New System.Windows.Forms.TabPage()

    new_tab.Text = "New Tab"
    new_tab.Size = New Size(TabControl1.Width, TabControl1.Height)

    TabControl1.Controls.Add(new_tab)

    WebBrowser1 = New System.Windows.Forms.WebBrowser
    WebBrowser1.Height = new_tab.Height
    WebBrowser1.Width = new_tab.Width

    new_tab.Controls.Add(WebBrowser1)

End Sub
```

Test your programme out. When you click your "New Tab" button, you should see a new tab appear in your browser, ready for a web page. Here's ours:

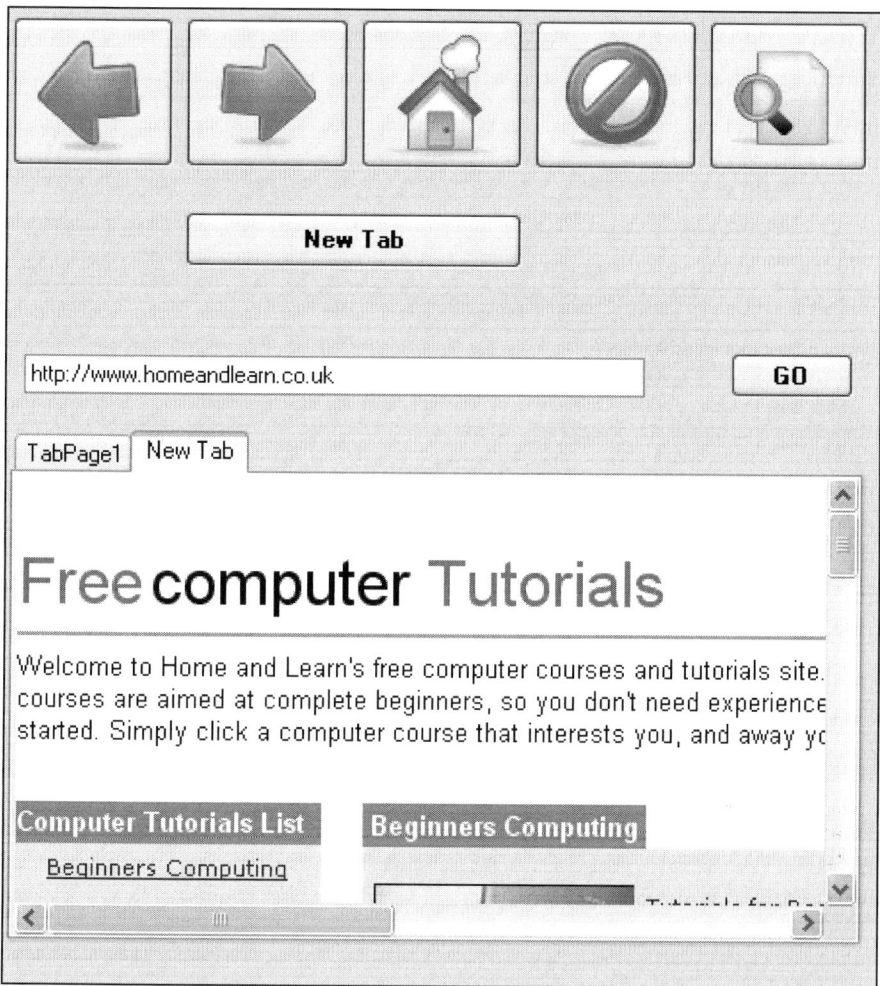

Notice that we haven't added an image button, though, and the form looks a little bit messy. Hopefully, yours is better!

In the next section, you'll see how to send and receive emails with Visual Basic .NET. If you want to, you can add tabs to your browser for this.

Sending Email with Visual Basic .NET

Visual Basic .NET has inbuilt classes that allow you to send emails. For this project, you can either create a new tab in your browser, or use a new form. The email form or tab to design should look something like this one:

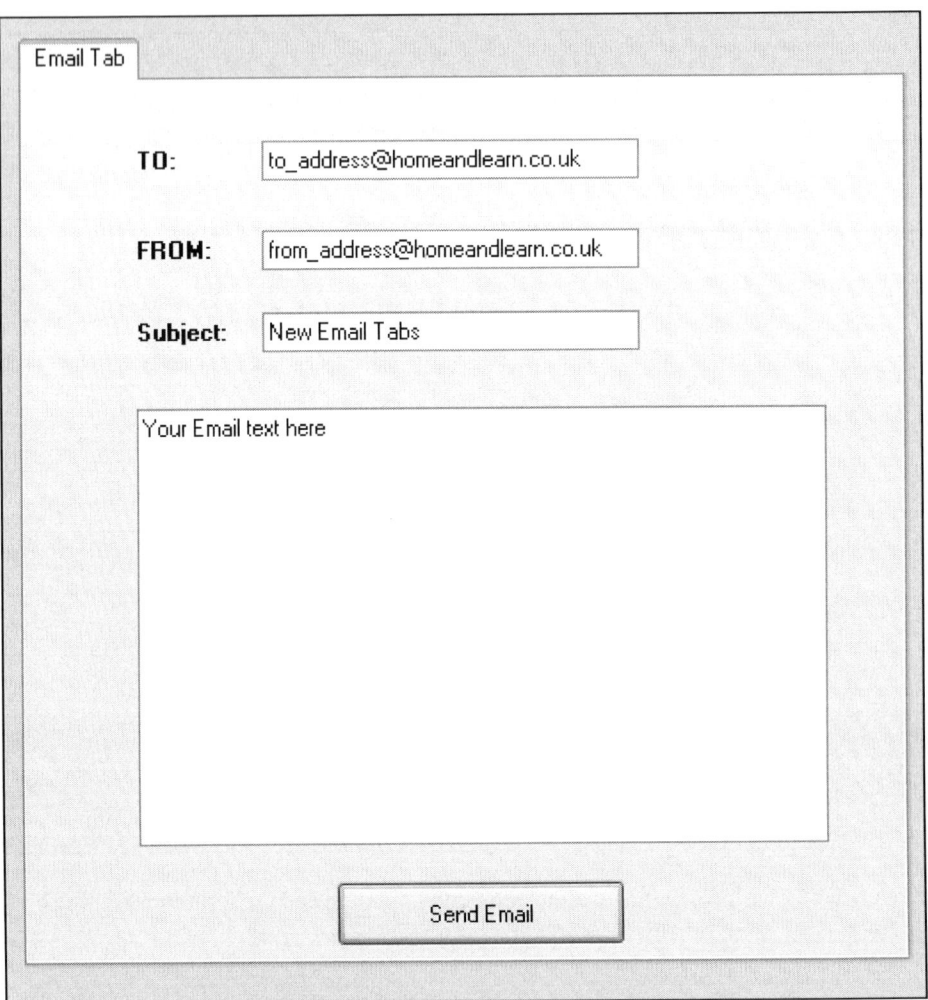

The controls to draw on your form or tab are:

4 TextBoxes
3 Labels
1 Button

Set the following properties for the controls:

TextBox1

Name:	txtEmailTo
Height:	20
Width:	200
Text:	An Email Address of your Choice

TextBox2

Name:	txtEmailFrom
Height: 20	
Width: 200	
Text:	An Email Address of your Choice

TextBox3

Name:	txtEmailSubject
Height:	20
Width:	200
Text:	Any Text of your choice

TextBox4

Name:	txtEmailBody
Height:	200
Width:	350
Text:	Blank
MultiLine:	True

Label 1

Text:	To

Label 2

Text:	From

Label 3

Text:	Subject

Button

Name:	btnSend
Text:	Send Email

When you've finished adding all the controls, double click your button to get at the code stub.

The first thing to do is to get all the text from the textboxes. So set up the following variables in your code:

```
Dim email_to As String
Dim email_from As String
Dim email_subject As String
Dim email_body As String
```

And then get the text from the text boxes:

```
email_to = Trim(txtEmailTo.Text)
email_from = Trim(txtEmailFrom.Text)
email_subject = Trim(txtEmailSubject.Text)
email_body = Trim(txtEmailBody.Text)
```

You can add error checking, if you like (and you should). We'll leave it out, though, for convenience's sake.

To send emails, VB NET has a class called SmtpClient. This is in the Mail namespace. So add the following to your code:

Dim smtpServer As New System.Net.Mail.SmtpClient

This sets up an object of type **SmtpClient** that we've called **smtpServer**.

The SmtpClient needs a few things from you: a host address, a logon username, and a logon password. There are also a few optional extras you can specify.

If you're with an ISP, the Host address is the one they gave you to set up your email account. It can be found in Outlook Express or Windows Mail by clicking on **Tools > Accounts**. Select an email account and then click **Properties**. You'll see a dialogue box appear. Select the **Servers** tab. The Host you need is the address for Outgoing Mail (SMTP). In the Image below, it's **smtp.my_isp.net**.

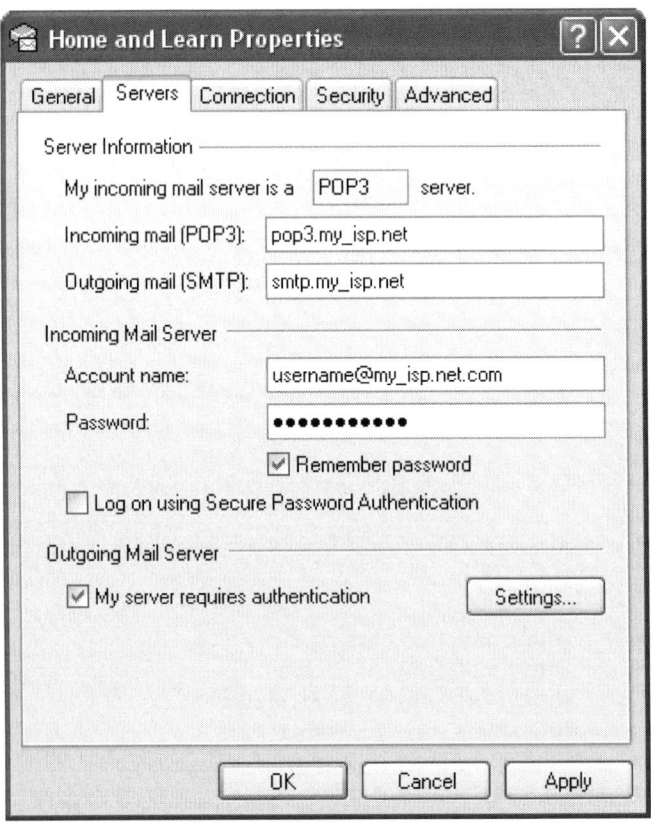

If your server requires authentication, and it probably does these days, then click the Settings button. Note down the username and password, because we'll need them shortly. But these are usually the same as for the Incoming Mail Server, in the image above.

Click on the **Advanced** tab, as well. Note the server port number for outgoing mail. The default is Port 25, but yours may be different.

OK, now that we have all the details, we can set up our SmtpClient. Add the Host with this line of code:

smtpServer.Host = "**smtp.my_isp.net**"

Obviously, you should substitute **smtp.my_isp.net** for whatever your Host is.

You can also set a TimeOut:

smtpServer.Timeout = 60

The TimeOut property is in second, and is the length of time that VB will wait before giving up sending the email.

If your Port number is not 25, then you can set it with this:

smtpServer.Port = 25

Port 25 is the default, so you don't need this line, unless it's not 25.

You can also set a delivery method for your email:

smtpServer.DeliveryMethod = Net.Mail.SmtpDeliveryMethod.**Network**

There are only two other options: Pickup directory from IIS, and Specified Pickup directory. We're assuming that you want to send your email through the Network directly to a SMTP server.

The final thing we need to do is to specify our SMTP logon credentials. Set up two string variables for this:

Dim username As String = "my_username"
Dim password As String = "my_password"

Again, specify your own Authentication details here.

The SmtpClient object we created has a **Credentials** property. This needs a NetworkCredential object. You set it up like this:

smtpServer.Credentials = New Net.NetworkCredential(username**,** password **)**

In between the round brackets of NetworkCredential, you need your username and password to log on to your SMTP server.

Your code should now look something like ours:

```
Private Sub btnSend_Click(ByVal sender As System.Object, _
                          ByVal e As System.EventArgs) _
                          Handles btnSend.Click

    Dim email_to As String
    Dim email_from As String
    Dim email_subject As String
    Dim email_body As String

    email_to = Trim(txtEmailTo.Text)
    email_from = Trim(txtEmailFrom.Text)
    email_subject = Trim(txtEmailSubject.Text)
    email_body = Trim(txtEmailBody.Text)


    Dim smtpServer As New System.Net.Mail.SmtpClient

    smtpServer.Host = "smtp.my_isp.net"
    smtpServer.Timeout = 60
    smtpServer.DeliveryMethod = _
                    Net.Mail.SmtpDeliveryMethod.Network

    Dim username As String = "my_username"
    Dim password As String = "my_password"

    smtpServer.Credentials = _
                New Net.NetworkCredential(username, password)



End Sub
```

Create a New Mail Message

Now that you've set up your SmtpClient, it's time to create a Mail Message. This is done through the **MailMessage** Class. Add this to your code:

Dim message As New Net.Mail.MailMessage(email_from, email_to)

So we're setting up an object called **message**, which is a MailMessage object. In between the round brackets of MailMessage we first specify who is sending the email. After a comma, we specify who the email is going to. We got these details from the textboxes.

Once we have a message object, we can specify the Subject of the email and the Body. Add these two lines:

> message.Subject = email_subject
> message.Body = email_body

The message object, then, has a Subject property and a Body property. After an equals sign, we're setting these to the details we got from the text boxes.

You can also specify an encoding type for your email:

message.BodyEncoding = System.Text.Encoding.UTF8

Here, we're setting the Encoding to UTF8. Others are ASCII, UTF7 and UTF32.

These days, if your email has no Headers, it may get flagged as spam. You can add a **Reply-To** header and an **Organisation** header:

message.Headers.Add("Reply-To", email_from **)**
message.Headers.Add("X-Organization", "Home and Learn" **)**

We're almost ready to send the email. However, there's a slight problem: We have no way of knowing if the email has been sent. If there's a problem with, say, the credentials, we need VB to report back to us. Otherwise, it will appear as though nothing has happened, even though no email will get through to the recipient.

The way you get VB to report back is a bit complicated. But you need to add something called an Event Handler. This allows you to use the **SendCompleted** event of the **SmtpClient** object you set up. You tell the Event Handler which Subroutine you want to call when the Sending of the email has been Completed.

Add this line to your code:

AddHandler smtpServer.SendCompleted, AddressOf doSendCompleted

The **AddHandler** part means "Add an Event Handler". The **AddressOf** part tells VB which Subroutine to call when the email has been sent. You need to add this Subroutine yourself. So, after the **End Sub** of you button code, add the following Sub:

```
Private Sub doSendCompleted(ByVal sender As Object, _
        ByVal e As System.ComponentModel.AsyncCompletedEventArgs)

    Dim token As String = e.UserState.ToString

    If e.Error IsNot Nothing OrElse e.Cancelled Then
        MsgBox("Error " & token)
    Else
        MsgBox("Message Sent " & token)
    End If

End Sub
```

This event we've created means that a message box will be displayed when the email has been sent. The **UserState** in the code above is used to identify which email was sent.

You will probably have noticed the curious **token** string variable we've set up in the code. To see why, add these two final lines of code to your Send button:

Dim user_state As String = " – Mail Message"

smtpServer.SendAsync(message, user_state)

First, we've set up a string variable (string object) called **user_state**. The Send method we're using is **SendAsync**. The Async stands for Asynchronous, and means the programme is not kept waiting for the email to be sent – it can get on with other things while sending. However, it needs two things, the message to send, and a UserState token. The token can be just about any object. But we're using a string.

The result of all this is that VB sends the email message using the SMTP details you set up. If there's a problem, you'll see an error message like this:

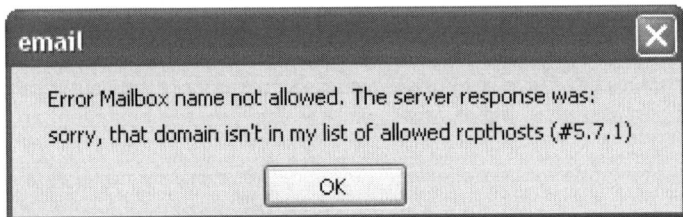

If all is OK, then the message will be this:

With the problem email, we didn't fill in our credentials correctly. Although the error message we got back is a bit mysterious, at least we got something back!

But the whole of your email code should look something like the one on the next page (we've amended it slightly at the top):

```
Private Sub btnSend_Click(ByVal sender As System.Object, _
                          ByVal e As System.EventArgs) _
                          Handles btnSend.Click

    Dim email_to As String = Trim(txtEmailTo.Text)
    Dim email_from As String = Trim(txtEmailFrom.Text)
    Dim email_subject As String = Trim(txtEmailSubject.Text)
    Dim email_body As String = Trim(txtEmailBody.Text)
    Dim smtpServer As New System.Net.Mail.SmtpClient

    smtpServer.Host = "smtp.my_isp.net"
    smtpServer.Timeout = 60
    smtpServer.DeliveryMethod = _
                    Net.Mail.SmtpDeliveryMethod.Network

    Dim username As String = "my_username"
    Dim password As String = "my_password"

    smtpServer.Credentials = _
                New Net.NetworkCredential(username, password)

    Dim message As New Net.Mail.MailMessage(email_from, email_to)

    message.Subject = email_subject
    message.Body = email_body
    message.BodyEncoding = System.Text.Encoding.UTF8
    message.Headers.Add("Reply-To", email_from)
    message.Headers.Add("X-Organization", "Home and Learn")

    AddHandler smtpServer.SendCompleted, AddressOf doSendCompleted

    Dim user_state As String = " - Mail Message"

    smtpServer.SendAsync(message, user_state)

End Sub

Private Sub doSendCompleted(ByVal sender As Object, _
            ByVal e As System.ComponentModel.AsyncCompletedEventArgs)

    Dim token As String = e.UserState.ToString

    If e.Error IsNot Nothing OrElse e.Cancelled Then
        MsgBox("Error " & e.Error.Message)
    Else
        MsgBox("Message Sent " & token)
    End If

End Sub
```

You can test out your programme, now. Hopefully, you'll be able to send emails!

Adding Attachments

You can add attachments to your emails, as well. What we need is an Open File Dialogue box that allows a user to select the files to attach. We'll then put the file names in an array. The **Net.Mail** namespace has an Attachments class that we can use along with our MailMessage object.

To make this work, add a new button to your form or tab. Add a textbox, as well. (This will just display the file names that the user selected.) Add an OpenFileDialog to your project by double-clicking its entry in the toolbox (under Dialog). Change the Name property of your OpenFileDialog to oFD1, and set the MultiSelect property to True.

Your form or tab may look something like this:

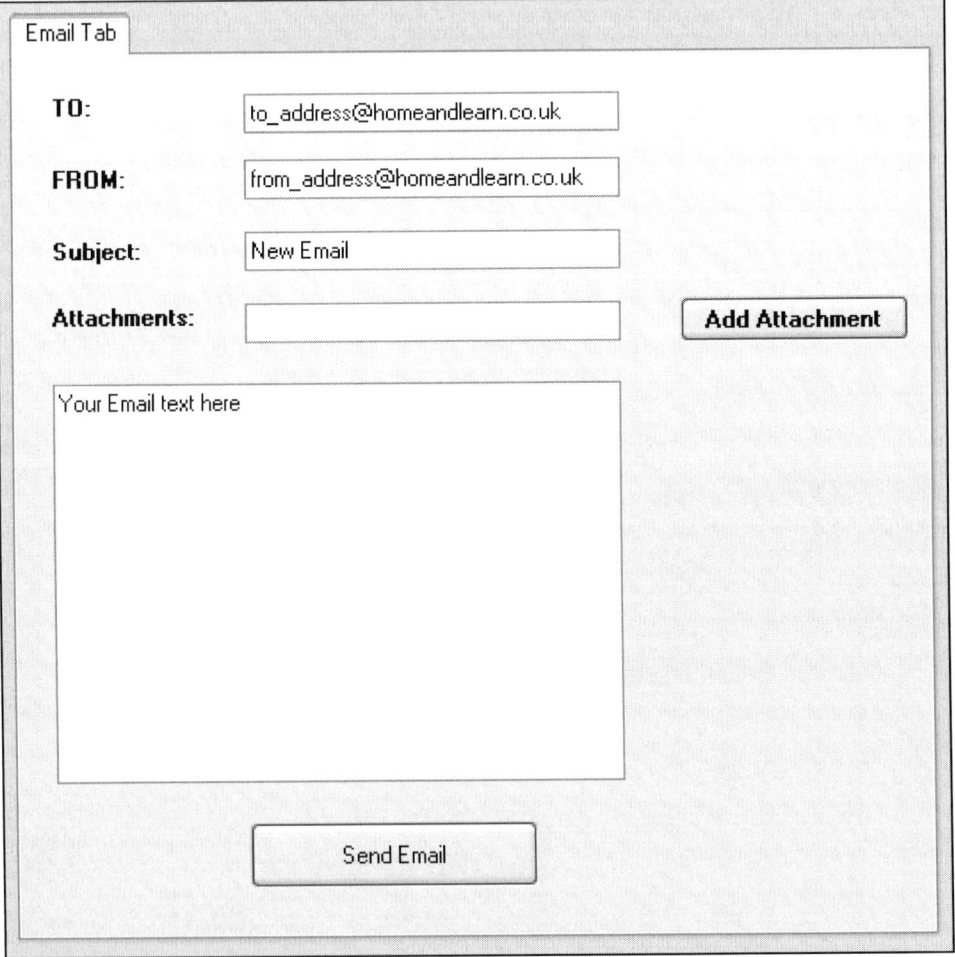

Double click your new button to open its code stub. At the very top of the coding window, in the Declarations area, set up the following two variables:

Dim HasAttachment As Boolean = False

```
Dim aryAttachments( ) As String
```

The first one is a Boolean flag that we can use to check if the user has added an attachment or not. The second one is the array that will contain all the file names chosen.

In the code for your new button, add the following lines:

```
txtAttachments.Text = ""

oFD1.InitialDirectory = "C:\"
oFD1.Title = "Open a Text File"
oFD1.Filter = "PDF Files |*.pdf|Text Files|*.txt|All Files|*.*"
Dim ofdResults As Integer = oFD1.ShowDialog( )

If ofdResults = Windows.Forms.DialogResult.Cancel Then
        HasAttachment = False
        Exit Sub
End If
```

The first line just clears our new text box. The other lines are ones you've already met: set some properties for the Open File Dialogue box, display it, and then check if the cancel button was clicked. We're also making sure to set **HasAttachment** to False.

We now need to get at the files that the user selected, putting each file name into the array. Add the following code:

```
Try
        Dim fNum As Integer = oFD1.FileNames.Length
        Dim single_file As String
        Dim file_counter As Integer = 0

        ReDim aryAttachments( fNum – 1 )

        For Each single_file In oFD1.FileNames
          aryAttachments( file_counter ) = single_file
          txtAttachments.Text += single_file & " "
          file_counter = file_counter + 1
        Next

        HasAttachment = True

Catch ex As Exception
        MsgBox("Error opening files")
End Try
```

The first line in the **Try ... Catch** block gets how many files the user selected, while the next two lines set up some variables, a string and an integer.

The fourth line is this:

```
ReDim aryAttachments( fNum -1 )
```

What we're doing here is resizing the array. We need to set it to the number of files that the user selected, one position in the array for each file. We're deducting 1 because arrays in VB NET start at zero.

The **For ... Each** loop get each file name than the user selected, and places it in the variable we've called **single_file**. The **file_counter** variable is used to access each position in the array. We then place a file name at this position:

aryAttachments(file_counter) = single_file

Next, we build up the text in the text box, displaying each file name:

txtAttachments.Text += single_file & " "

The final thing to do in the **Try** part of the **Try ... Catch** block is to set **HasAttachment** to **True**. The code for your attachment button should now look like this:

```
Private Sub btnAttachments_Click(ByVal sender As System.Object, _
                             ByVal e As System.EventArgs) _
                                 Handles btnAttachments.Click

    txtAttachments.Text = ""

    oFD1.InitialDirectory = "C:\"
    oFD1.Title = "Open a Text File"
    oFD1.Filter = "PDF Files |*.pdf|Text Files|*.txt|All Files|*.*"

    Dim ofdResults As Integer = oFD1.ShowDialog()

    If ofdResults = Windows.Forms.DialogResult.Cancel Then
        HasAttachment = False
        Exit Sub
    End If

    Try
        Dim fNum As Integer = oFD1.FileNames.Length
        Dim single_file As String
        Dim file_counter As Integer = 0

        ReDim aryAttachments(fNum - 1)

        For Each single_file In oFD1.FileNames
            aryAttachments(file_counter) = single_file
            txtAttachments.Text += single_file & " "
            file_counter = file_counter + 1
        Next

        HasAttachment = True

    Catch ex As Exception
        MsgBox("Error opening files")
    End Try

End Sub
```

If someone clicks your Attachment button, **HasAttachment** will either be True or False. In your **Send Email** button code, you can test for a True value. If it's True, add the attachments the user selected.

The way we'll add the attachments is to loop round and get each file name from our array. To add an attachment to your message, though, the code is this:

Dim file_attach As New Net.Mail.Attachment(attachments **)**
message.Attachments.Add(file_attach **)**

The first line sets up a **New Attachment** object. The **Attachment** class is part of the **Net.Mail** namespace in VB NET. In between the round brackets of Attachment, you type the name of the file you want to attach.

The second line uses the **message** object we set up earlier. It has an Attachments property. This in turn has an **Add** subroutine. In between the round brackets of **Add**, you again specify the name of the attachment.

Here's some code to add to your **Send Email** button. Add it just before your AddHandler line:

If HasAttachment Then
    Dim i As Integer

    For i = 0 To aryAttachments.Length - 1
        Dim file_attach As New Net.Mail.Attachment(aryAttachments(i) **)**
        message.Attachments.Add(file_attach **)**
    Next
End If

The code at the bottom of your **Send Email** button should look like this:

```
Dim message As New Net.Mail.MailMessage(email_from, email_to)

message.Subject = email_subject
message.Body = email_body
message.BodyEncoding = System.Text.Encoding.UTF8
message.Headers.Add("Reply-To", email_from)
message.Headers.Add("X-Organization", "Home and Learn")

If HasAttachment Then
    Dim i As Integer
    For i = 0 To aryAttachments.Length - 1
        Dim file_attach As New Net.Mail.Attachment(aryAttachments(i))
        message.Attachments.Add(file_attach)
    Next
End If


AddHandler smtpServer.SendCompleted, AddressOf doSendCompleted

Dim user_state As String = " - Mail Message"

smtpServer.SendAsync(message, user_state)
```

The **message** object will take care of adding the attachments for you. When you run your programme, you should now be able to send emails with an attachment.

You can also receive emails with Visual Basic .NET, but the process is quite complicated. Even more so than sending emails! You'll see how to do it in the next section.

Receive emails with VB NET

You have just seen how to send emails through a SMTP server. What we're going to do now is to connect to a POP3 server like the ones you have with your ISP or your web host, and check if there's any emails waiting. If there are, then we'll download them. You need to know something about how POP3 servers work first, though.

POP3 servers

When you receive emails with a client like Outlook, Outlook Express or Windows Live Mail what you are doing is talking to a POP3 server. The POP3 server is listening all the time on port 110 for any incoming connections. When you try to connect for the first time, you enter what's known as the Handshake process. This is when you send a command to the server asking if it's available. If it is, the server will say so, and ask for your login credentials. If they are accepted, the connection to the server stays open, waiting for your commands. There are generally 4 steps in the whole process:

Connection
Authorisation
Transaction
Update

The **Connection** step is when you wake the POP3 server up with your handshake. The **Authorisation** step is when you send the POP3 server your credentials. If these are accepted, the POP3 server waits for your commands. This is the **Transaction** step. When you are finished, you issue a Quit command. The server then takes care of any **Updates** you made, such as deleting emails. (If the POP3 Server doesn't receive the Quit command then no updates get made. It might not receive an Update command, for example, if your programme crashes.)

The response you get for a POP3 server is either +**OK** or –**ERR**.

POP3 Commands

Most POP3 servers will recognise the following commands (not case sensitive):

USER
PASS
LIST
STAT
NOOP
RETR
RSET
DELE
QUIT

Here's a rundown of what they do. You can probably guess most of them!

USER
Your username to logon to the POP3 server.

PASS
Your Password to logon to the POP3 server.

LIST
Gets a list of all the emails you have waiting for you.

STAT
Gets statistics about the emails. These are how many emails are waiting, and the total size. The total size is in Octets. This is important for your programming. An Octet is a group of eight bits (1 Byte), so we're going to have to work with bit manipulation when dealing with the POP3 server. It's not too painful, though!

NOOP
Stands for No Operation. You can issue the NOOP command just to check if the server's still there.

RETR
Used to retrieve email messages from the server.

DELE
Used to delete emails from the server.

QUIT
Starts the update process on the POP3 server, and then ends a session. If you've issued any delete commands, they won't get executed until the server receives the QUIT command. Otherwise, the server doesn't get updated.

Now that you have a general idea of how POP3 servers work, let's get started on some programming.

Opening a Connection to a POP3 server

Start a new programme, or add a new tab to your TabControl, if you're using one. Add the following controls:

Button
  Name: btnConnect
  Text: Connect

Button
  Name: btnDelete
  Text: Delete

Button

Name:	btnQuit
Text:	Quit

ListBox

Name:	ListBox1 (the default name)

TextBox

Name:	txtServerResponse
Multiline:	True
Scrollbars:	Vertical
Text:	Blank

TextBox

Name:	txtEmail
Multiline:	True
Scrollbars:	Vertical
Text:	Blank

Label

Name:	lblEmailList
Text:	Email List

Label

Name:	lblServerResponse
Text:	Server Response

Label

Name:	lblEmail
Text:	Email

When you're finished, your form may look something like this:

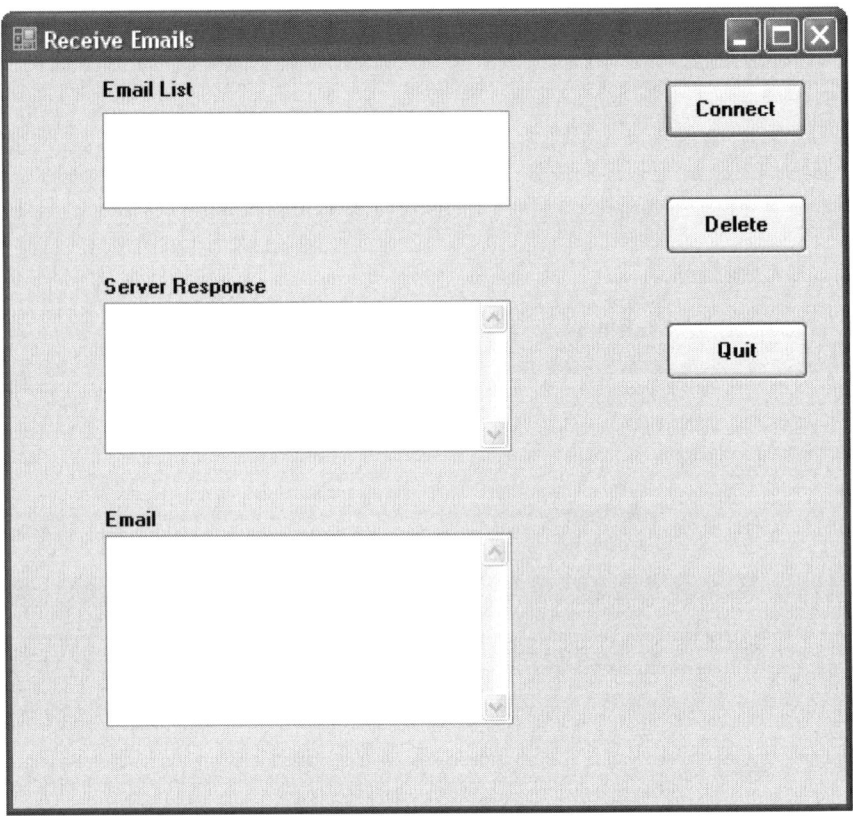

Double click your Connect button to get at a coding window. At the very top of your coding window, before Public Class Form1, enter the following two lines:

Imports System.Net.Sockets
Imports System.IO

The first Import statement is used to connect to the POP3 server; the second one is for dealing with the all the text we get back.

Just below Public Class Form1, in the Declaration area, enter these lines of code:

Dim network_stream As NetworkStream
Dim read_stream As StreamReader

The first line sets up a variable we've called **network_stream**. The type is **NetworkStream**. This is used to deal with the data to and from the POP3 server. The second variable sets up a StreamReader. You've used these before in a previous section.

Your coding window should look like this:

```
Imports System.Net.Sockets
Imports System.IO

Public Class Form1

    Dim network_stream As NetworkStream
    Dim read_stream As StreamReader

    Private Sub btnConnect_Click(ByVal sender As System.Object, _
                                 ByVal e As System.EventArgs) _
                                 Handles btnConnect.Click



    End Sub
End Class
```

Just below the End Sub of your button code, set up the following Function:

```
Private Sub btnConnect_Click(ByVal sender As System.Object, _
                             ByVal e As System.EventArgs) _
                             Handles btnConnect.Click


End Sub

Private Function PopCommand(ByRef network_stream As NetworkStream, _
                            ByVal server_command As String) As String



End Function
```

For the first argument of the **PopCommand** function, we want to change the underlying network stream. That's why it's ByRef and not ByVal. But we're setting up this function to deal with the POP3 server, and then getting its response back as a String. (Don't worry if your "End Function" has a green wavy line under it – it's because we haven't added any code for it yet.)

Click inside the code stub for your button. Add the following variable declarations:

> **Dim pop_server As New TcpClient( )**
> **Dim pop_host As String = "your_host"**
> **Dim username As String = "your_username"**
> **Dim password As String = "your_password"**

The first variable sets up a New **TcpClient** object. TcpClient is a class belonging to **Net.Sockets**. It can be used to communicate with a POP3 server.

The next three variables are all Strings, and you should replace the values above with your own. The Host would be something like **pop.your_isp.com**. But you can get the details from the

Outgoing Server section of Outlook or Outlook Express. The **username** and **password** are the ones you normally use to collect your emails.

The next thing we need to do is to try to connect to the POP3 server. Enter the following three lines in a **Try … Catch** block:

```
pop_server.Connect( pop_host, 110 )
network_stream = pop_server.GetStream( )
read_stream = New StreamReader( network_stream )
```

The first line is the one that tries to Connect to the POP3 Server. In between the round brackets of **Connect**, you type the Host you want to connect to, followed by the port number.

The second line gets the data from the pop server and then places it in our **network_stream** object:

```
network_stream = pop_server.GetStream( )
```

The variable **pop_server** is a TcpClient object, remember, and is dealing with the fetching and carrying of the data to and from the server. We're assigning all the data to the **NetworkStream** object we set up.

The third line uses our StreamReader to read the stream of text we get back. In between the round brackets of **StreamReader**, you need the name of your NetworkStream object.

To check if all this is working or not, add the following three lines:

```
Dim return_string As String

return_string = read_stream.ReadLine( ) + vbCrLf
txtServerResponse.Text = return_string
```

The important line above is this one:

```
return_string = read_stream.ReadLine() + vbCrLf
```

The line of text we got back from the server is now in our StreamReader object. We're using ReadLine to read the line of text that the POP3 server gave us back. (We're at the Handshake stage, here.) The **vbCrLf** at the end adds a Linefeed.

Your code so far should look like ours:

```
Private Sub btnConnect_Click(ByVal sender As System.Object, _
                            ByVal e As System.EventArgs) _
                            Handles btnConnect.Click

    Dim pop_server As New TcpClient()
    Dim pop_host As String = "your_host"
    Dim username As String = "your_username"
    Dim password As String = "your_password"

    Try
        pop_server.Connect(pop_host, 110)
        network_stream = pop_server.GetStream()
        read_stream = New StreamReader(network_stream)

        Dim return_string As String

        return_string = read_stream.ReadLine() & vbCrLf
        txtServerResponse.Text = return_string

    Catch ex As Exception
        MessageBox.Show(ex.Message)
    End Try

End Sub
```

To see what all this code does, start your programme. Click your Connect button. If you've correctly entered your Host details, you should see this in your Server Response text box (though you may have different text after the +OK part):

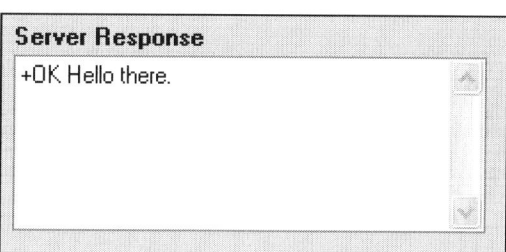

We haven't yet sent the username and password, so the response is always +OK. But only if you have correctly entered the Host details. If you didn't, the **Catch** part of your **Try ... Catch** block will activate, and you'll see an error message: "No such host exists".

We'll now try to logon with a username and password. For that, we'll need to add some code for our **PopCommand** function.

POP3 Server Authentication

Our **PopCommand** function will deal with all the commands we send to the POP3 server, and the responses we get back. As was mentioned, the data you send and the data you get back is in Octets (bytes). So we first need to convert the command string we're sending to the server into an array of bytes. In the **Try** part of a **Try … Catch** block, add these two lines to your **PopCommand** function:

> **server_command = server_command & vbCrLf**

> **Dim server_bytes( ) As Byte = _**
> **System.Text.Encoding.ASCII.GetBytes(server_command)**

The first line just adds a linefeed character to the end of the command we're going to send. The second line (spread out over two in this book) sets up a Byte array:

> **Dim server_bytes( ) As Byte**

We've called this array server_bytes. After an equals sign, we have this:

> **System.Text.Encoding.ASCII.GetBytes(server_command)**

This part encodes ASCII characters. It converts the text that's in the variable server_command and turns each character into bytes for the array. The first of the server commands we're going to send is USER your_username. Instead of it being in text, however, the above lines will turn them into bytes. The server won't be able to read the text, if you don't.

We can set up a new StreamReader and a string variable next, so as to deal with the response we get back from the server. Add these two lines:

> **Dim read_stream2 As StreamReader**
> **Dim server_response As String**

Now add the following rather tricky four lines:

> **network_stream.Write(server_bytes, 0, server_bytes.Length)**
> **read_stream2 = New StreamReader(network_stream)**
> **server_response = read_stream2.ReadLine( )**

> **Return server_response**

The NetworkStream object we set up will be dealing with the commands we send to the server:

> **network_stream.Write(server_bytes, 0, server_bytes.Length)**

In between the round brackets of Write, we have 3 values. The first one is the array of Bytes. But we're actually writing to a Buffer (an area of memory). The location in the Buffer that we want to write to is at the start, so we type a 0 as the second value of Write. The final value is the size of the buffer we want to create.

In case that's a little confusing, here's what's happening:

- The NetworkStream object contacts the POP3 server for us
- To write to the network stream, you need to set up a buffer and fill it with Bytes. The bytes you're sending are the commands you want the POP3 server to execute
- The NetworkStream object sends your command to the server as a series of bytes

- The POP3 Server sees the NetworkStream object, and tries to execute the command
- It returns a response that the NetworkStream object can deal with

So that we can do something with the response that the POP3 server sends back to us, we have these two lines:

read_stream2 = New StreamReader(network_stream)
server_response = read_stream2.ReadLine( )

The first of these two lines sets up a StreamReader. In between the round brackets of StreamReader, we type the name of our network stream. The StreamReader converts the bytes from the network stream into text. We then Read the Line or lines that were sent back, putting them into the string variable we've called server_response.

The final line to add to your PopCommand function is for the Catch part of your Try … Catch block:

Return ex.Message

This returns any errors thrown up. Your function should look like this, though:

```
Private Function PopCommand(ByRef network_stream As NetworkStream, _
                    ByVal server_command As String) As String

    Try
        server_command = server_command & vbCrLf
        Dim server_bytes() As Byte = _
                        System.Text.Encoding.ASCII.GetBytes(server_command)

        Dim read_stream2 As StreamReader
        Dim server_response As String

        network_stream.Write(server_bytes, 0, server_bytes.Length)
        read_stream2 = New StreamReader(network_stream)
        server_response = read_stream2.ReadLine()

        Return server_response

    Catch ex As Exception
        Return ex.Message
    End Try

End Function
```

Now that we have a function to deal with the POP3 server, we can call it into action.

To try our username on the server, the code is this:

PopCommand(network_stream**, "USER "** & username **)**

So we pass the function our network stream object. After a comma, we issue the POP3 command **USER**. The server is expecting the keyword **USER**. After a space it needs your username:

USER your_username

Add the following line to the code for your **Connect** button (We've split the line into two, by using an underscore (_) character):

txtServerResponse.Text += _
    PopCommand(network_stream**, "USER "** & username**) & vbCrLf**

Underneath this, you can try your password. The line is almost identical:

txtServerResponse.Text += _
    PopCommand(network_stream**, "PASS "** & password **) &**
vbCrLf

This time, the POP3 server needs the keyword **PASS**, followed by a space, then your password:

PASS your_password

The **Try ... Catch** block for your button code should now look like this:

```
Try
    pop_server.Connect(pop_host, 110)
    network_stream = pop_server.GetStream()
    read_stream = New StreamReader(network_stream)

    Dim return_string As String

    return_string = read_stream.ReadLine() & vbCrLf
    txtServerResponse.Text = return_string

    txtServerResponse.Text += _
            PopCommand(network_stream, "USER " & username) & vbCrLf

    txtServerResponse.Text += _
        PopCommand(network_stream, "PASS " & password) & vbCrLf

Catch ex As Exception
    MessageBox.Show(ex.Message)
End Try
```

We could do some error checking, here. Instead of returning the value from the function directly to the text box, we could test the return value for the –ERR string. For example:

```
Dim RetVal as String

RetVal  = PopCommand( network_stream,  "PASS" & password )

If RetVal.Substring( 0, 4 ) = "-ERR" Then
        txtServerResponse.Text = "Invalid Password"
        Exit Sub
End If
```

The code above grabs 4 characters from the start of the string that the server returned, and checks if it has a value of "-ERR".

Note that we're checking the password and not the username. That's because some servers give an +OK response, even though the username is not valid. They don't check until both username and password have been given. But in the code above, we're bailing out if the password is not accepted by the server.

Quitting the POP3 Server

We're almost ready to try it out. Before you do, create a Sub called **QuitServer**. Add the following for its code:

```
Private Sub QuitServer( )

        Try
                Dim server_response As String = ""
                server_response = PopCommand( network_stream, "QUIT" )
                MessageBox.Show( server_response )
                Catch ex As Exception
                MessageBox.Show( ex.Message )
        End Try

    End Sub
```

All we need to do here is to call the **PopCommand** function and pass it first the network stream object, then the command. In this case the server command is just **QUIT**.

In the code for your Quit button, call your new Sub:

Call QuitServer( )

It's a good idea to call the Sub when the form is closing, as its all too easy to forget to click a button. And if you forget to issue the Quit button the POP3 Server won't update.

Here's what your new code should look like (you could get rid of the Quit button altogether, if you have a Form Closing Event):

```
Private Sub btnQuit_Click(ByVal sender As System.Object, _
                          ByVal e As System.EventArgs) _
                      Handles btnQuit.Click

    Call QuitServer()

End Sub

Private Sub QuitServer()

    Try
        Dim server_response As String = ""
        server_response = PopCommand(network_stream, "QUIT")
        MessageBox.Show(server_response)
    Catch ex As Exception
        MessageBox.Show(ex.Message)
    End Try

End Sub

Private Sub Form1_FormClosing(ByVal sender As System.Object, _
              ByVal e As System.Windows.Forms.FormClosingEventArgs) _
                Handles MyBase.FormClosing

    Call QuitServer()

End Sub
```

Try it all out. Run your programme and click your Connect button. If your Authentication details are all right, you should see this in your text box:

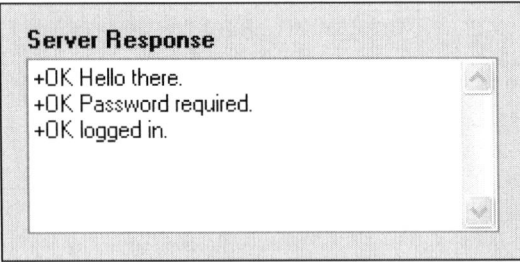

Click your Quit button and you should see this (though the message after +OK may differ):

If you get your Authentication details wrong, you may see something like this:

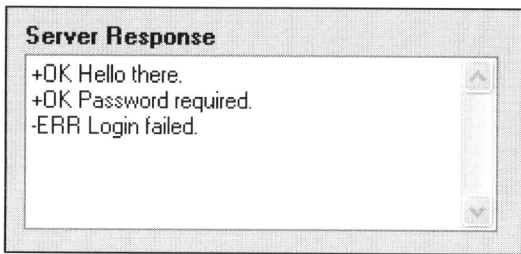

When you quit after failing to logon, you may see this rather polite message:

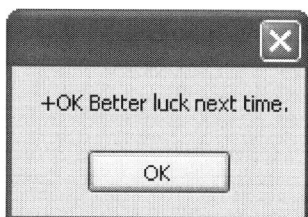

Do You Have Mail?

To check if you have any emails waiting, you use the STAT command. This will get you how many emails are on the server, and the total size (in octets). Let's see how it works.

Add the following function stub to your code:

Private Function GetMailStats( ) As String
End Function

We need a string variable for the stats, so add this variable to your function:

Dim stats_response As String

To issue the STAT command to the POP3 server, we only need to use our **PopCommand** function. Again, though, we need our NetworkStream object as the first parameter.

stats_response = PopCommand(network_stream, "STAT" **)**

The final line for this function is the return value:

Return stats_response

You coding window should look like this:

```
Private Function GetMailStats() As String

    Dim stats_response As String

    stats_response = PopCommand(network_stream, "STAT")

    Return stats_response

End Function
```

Add a call to this function from your Connect button, just under your USER and PASS lines:

Dim server_stats As String
server_stats = GetMailStats( )

Place the string in the textbox, just so that you can see what the response is:

txtServerResponse.Text += server_stats & vbCrLf

The bottom of your **Try ... Catch** block should then look like ours:

```
    txtServerResponse.Text += _
        PopCommand(network_stream, "PASS " & password) & vbCrLf

    Dim server_stats As String
    server_stats = GetMailStats()

    txtServerResponse.Text += server_stats & vbCrLf

Catch ex As Exception
    MessageBox.Show(ex.Message)
End Try
```

Before running your programme and trying out the new code, send yourself an email or two, just so that you have something waiting. When you click your Connect button, your Server Response text box should show you the STATs about your emails:

```
Server Response
+OK Hello there.
+OK Password required.
+OK logged in.
+OK 2 3639
```

After the +OK response we have the number of emails (2) followed by the number of octets (3639). Note the spaces in the line of text, one after +OK and one after the 2. We need to parse this line to get how many emails there are. We need the number of emails for the LIST command.

To get at the number of emails, add the following three lines to your button code:

```
Dim aryStats(2) As String
aryStats = server_stats.Split(" ")
txtServerResponse.Text += "number of emails: " & aryStats(1) & vbCrLf
```

The first line sets up a String array with three positions in it. The second line splits the server stats based on where the space is. This will get you three values. The first value is the +OK response, while the next two are the number of emails and the octet size. The third line in the code above displays the number of emails on a line of its own in the text box.

Getting a List of Messages

The next thing to do is to get a list of messages on the server. Not surprisingly, you use the LIST command for this. What we'll do is to loop round all the messages we have waiting and put each one in the ListBox at the top of our form.

Add the following Sub to your code:

```
Private Sub GetMailList( ByVal num_of_emails As Integer )


End Sub
```

In between the round brackets of the Sub, we have the number of emails as an argument. We'll pass the figure we got from the server. Add this call to your Connect button code:

```
Call GetMailList( Integer.Parse( aryStats(1) ) )
```

Because we need the number of emails as an integer, we need to convert it to a number:

```
Integer.Parse( )
```

In between the round brackets of Parse( ), you type what it is you're trying to convert. For us, this was the string in aryStats(1).

The code for your new Sub is this:

```
Dim list_response As String
Dim i As Integer

For i = 1 To num_of_emails
        list_response = PopCommand( network_stream, "LIST " & i.ToString )
        ListBox1.Items.Add( list_response )
    Next i
```

What we're trying to do here is to loop round issuing the LIST command to the POP3 server. The LIST command works like this:

```
LIST 1
```

This will get the server to LIST email number 1. We're then adding the server response to the ListBox at the top of our form. Our loop goes from 1 to the number of emails we have received.

There is, however, a problem with our code. Suppose we get no emails? The loop would then be going from 1 To 0, which would cause an error. The solution is to not call the Sub if the number emails equals 0. Change your calling line to this:

If Integer.Parse(aryStats(1)) > 0 Then
        Call GetMailList(Integer.Parse(aryStats(1)) **)**
End If

So we just add an IF statement and check if the value in aryStats(1) is greater than zero.

Your Connect button code should look like this, at the bottom:

```
    txtServerResponse.Text += _
        PopCommand(network_stream, "PASS " & password) & vbCrLf

    Dim server_stats As String
    server_stats = GetMailStats()

    txtServerResponse.Text += server_stats & vbCrLf

    Dim aryStats(2) As String
    aryStats = server_stats.Split(" ")
    txtServerResponse.Text += "number of emails: " & aryStats(1) & vbCrLf

    If Integer.Parse(aryStats(1)) > 0 Then
        Call GetMailList(Integer.Parse(aryStats(1)))
    End If

Catch ex As Exception
    MessageBox.Show(ex.Message)
End Try
```

And your new Sub should look like this:

```
Private Sub GetMailList(ByVal num_of_emails As Integer)

    Dim list_response As String
    Dim i As Integer

    For i = 1 To num_of_emails
        list_response = PopCommand(network_stream, "LIST " & i.ToString)
        ListBox1.Items.Add(list_response)
    Next i

End Sub
```

When you run your programme, you should see something like this appear in the ListBox at the top of your code:

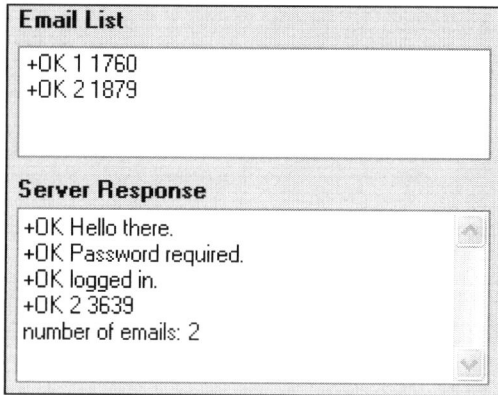

After the +OK, the ListBox shows the email number, followed by the size in octets of each email.

Getting the Message

To get the actual message itself, we need to use the ListBox. When an item is clicked in the ListBox, we'll call a Subroutine to get the email chosen. We'll put all of it in the text box at the bottom of the form.

ListBoxes have a **SelectedIndexChanged** event that is quite handy for us. The Index number of a ListBox is the item's position in the list. The count starts at zero, though. So item 1 on the Email List above is Index 0 and item 2 is Index 1.

Create a code stub for the SelectedIndexChanged event of your ListBox (you should know how to do this by now). Add the following code:

```
Dim index_number As String
Dim strRetrieve As String

txtEmail.Text = ""

Try
        index_number = ( ListBox1.SelectedIndex + 1 ).ToString
        strRetrieve = "RETR " + index_number + vbCrLf
        GetEmail(strRetrieve)
Catch ex As Exception
        MessageBox.Show(ex.Message)
End Try
```

First we set up two string variables, and then clear the Email text box. Inside of a **Try … Catch** block, we get the index number of the item on the list that was selected:

index_number = (ListBox1.SelectedIndex + 1).ToString

We have to add 1 to the SelectedIndex because, as was mentioned, items in a listbox start at zero. We're going to be retrieving emails from the server. If you tried to retrieve email 0 you'd get an error.

The second line is this:

strRetrieve = "RETR " + index_number + vbCrLf

This builds up a string for the POP3 command. The command we need is RETR. It works like this:

RETR 1

The 1 after RETR is the email number you want to retrieve. The server will then give you back the whole of the email. The first line of the server response will be something this, however:

+OK 120 octets

So you get the +OK response followed by the size in octets of the email you are retrieving. The rest of the response is the email's header and the body.

After building up a string for the POP3 command, we have this line:

GetEmail(strRetrieve)

This is a Subroutine you haven't created yet. We've called the Sub **GetEmail**. In between the round brackets of the Sub, we're passing in the POP3 Command.

But the code for your SelectedIndexChanged event should look like this:

```
Private Sub ListBox1_SelectedIndexChanged(ByVal sender As Object, _
                          ByVal e As System.EventArgs) _
                          Handles ListBox1.SelectedIndexChanged

     Dim index_number As String
     Dim strRetrieve As String

     txtEmail.Text = ""

     Try
          index_number = (ListBox1.SelectedIndex + 1).ToString
          strRetrieve = "RETR " + index_number + vbCrLf
          GetEmail(strRetrieve)
     Catch ex As Exception
          MessageBox.Show(ex.Message)
     End Try

End Sub
```

You now need to create the **GetEmail** Sub. Add the following code stub:

Private Sub GetEmail(ByVal server_command As String)

End Sub

In the code for the GetEmail Sub, we're going to be repeating most of what our PopCommand function does. However, this function returns a single line. The server response this time will be multiple lines. Creating a new Sub to deal with just the email also means we can loop through it, without cluttering up the PopCommand function. So add this code to your new Sub:

```
Dim server_bytes( ) As Byte = _
          System.Text.Encoding.ASCII.GetBytes(server_command)


Dim stream_reader As StreamReader
Dim TextLine As String = ""

Try

          network_stream.Write( server_bytes, 0, server_bytes.Length )
          stream_reader = New StreamReader( network_stream )

          Do While stream_reader.Peek() <> -1

                    TextLine += stream_reader.ReadLine( ) & vbNewLine

          Loop

          txtEmail.Text = TextLine

Catch ex As Exception
          MessageBox.Show( ex.Message )
End Try
```

You've already met most of this code when we set up the PopCommand function. The thing that's different is the **Do … While** loop:

```
Do While stream_reader.Peek() <> -1

          TextLine += stream_reader.ReadLine( ) & vbNewLine

Loop
```

The **Peek( ) <> –1** part looks one character ahead. If there are no more characters to be read then a value of –1 is returned. We're looping while the value is not –1.

Inside of the **Do … While** loop, we're reading each line from the stream reader and building up the TextLine string variable.

After the loop has finished, we place the email contents into the text box:

txtEmail.Text = TextLine

Run your programme and test it out. Click your Connect button to check your emails. Now select an email from the ListBox at the top. You should see the entire contents of your email appear in the text box at the bottom of the form (we've made the bottom text box a little bit bigger in the image below):

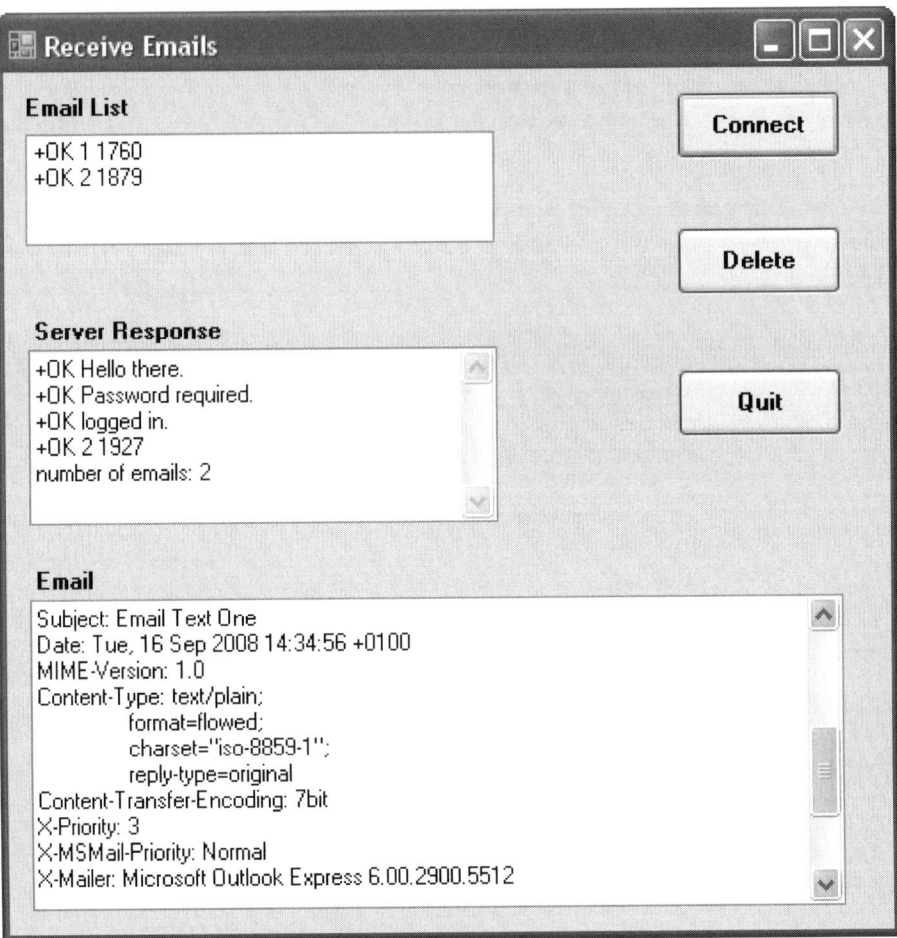

Parsing the Email

In the email above, we placed both the email Header and the email Body all in the same text box. You can, however, parse the email and separate the two. You do so by searching for two line feed characters (vbCrLf & vbCrLf). Here's some code:

```
Dim line_feeds As Integer
line_feeds = InStr( 1, TextLine, vbCrLf & vbCrLf )
```

If you remember your string manipulation techniques, InStr is short for "In String", and is used to find the position of one string inside of another. In the code above we're searching for the two linefeed characters in the TextLine string. We're starting at position 1. If the string is found, line_feeds will contain the position number of the string. If the string is not found then 0 will be returned. We can use this to separate the Headers from the Body:

Dim email_header As String
Dim email_body As String

If line_feeds <> 0 Then
      email_header = TextLine.Substring(0, line_feeds - 1)
      email_body = TextLine.Substring(line_feeds + 1, TextLine.Length -
      email_header.Length - 3)

    End If

You could then place the Header in one text box and the Body inside of another

If you just want to get the Header then there is another POP3 command available on some, if not most, servers: **TOP**.

The TOP command returns the Header of the email and an optional number of lines. It is used like this:

TOP 1 2

The first number after TOP is the message number. The second number is how many lines from the Body of the email you want. In the code above, we want the Header from email 1, plus 2 lines from the Body. Both numbers are required. If you don't want any lines from the body, you'd have this:

TOP 1 0

That's not TOP ten, it's TOP followed by a 1 and then a 0. A space separates the two. You can use your PopCommand function to try it out.

One thing you may want to do is to get at the Subject line of the Header. You can then decide if it's likely to be spam, and delete it. By using TOP, you're not sifting through the entire email, but just the Header. (To get at the Subject, search each line for "Subject:" and place the returned value into a text box.)

Deleting Emails

You can also delete emails that are on the POP3 server. For this, the DELE command is used:

DELE 2

The number after DELE is the email number you want to delete.

The problem we face is that emails are not actually deleted when you issue the DELE command – they are only marked for deletion. They only get deleted when you issue the QUIT command. But we can indicate that an email is marked for deletion by adding text to the item that was selected in the ListBox. Let's see how it works.

So open up the code stub for your Delete button. The first thing to do is to get which item was selected in the ListBox. You can this with the selected index property:

```
Dim i As Integer
i = ListBox1.SelectedIndex + 1
```

Again, we're adding 1 to the selected index. This is because we need to get a message number to delete, and ListBoxes start counting at zero.

Now add the following code:

```
Try
        Dim server_response As String
        server_response = PopCommand( network_stream, "DELE " & i.ToString )
        txtServerResponse.Text += server_response & vbCrLf

        ListBox1.Items.Item( i – 1 ) += " Marked for Deletion"

        txtEmail.Text = ""

Catch ex As Exception
        MessageBox.Show(ex.Message)
End Try
```

Inside the Try … Catch block, we send the **DELE** command to the POP3 server:

```
server_response = PopCommand( network_stream, "DELE " & i.ToString )
```

The **i** variable holds which email number needs deleting. This has to be converted to a string.

The next line just adds the response to the textbox, so that we can see what came back from the server.

To mark the email as "for deletion", we have this:

```
ListBox1.Items.Item(i - 1) += " Marked for Deletion"
```

All we're doing here is adding some text to what is already there for that Item. The final line just clears the text box at the bottom of the form.

Your Delete button code should look like this:

```
Private Sub btnDelete_Click(ByVal sender As System.Object, _
                            ByVal e As System.EventArgs) _
                            Handles btnDelete.Click


    Dim i As Integer
    i = ListBox1.SelectedIndex + 1

    Try
        Dim server_response As String
        server_response = PopCommand(network_stream, "DELE " + i.ToString)
        txtServerResponse.Text += server_response & vbCrLf

        ListBox1.Items.Item(i - 1) += " Marked for Deletion"

        txtEmail.Text = ""

    Catch ex As Exception
        MessageBox.Show(ex.Message)
    End Try

End Sub
```

Before you run your programme, send yourself at least two emails. Now run your programme and click Connect. Then select an email. Click your Delete button and you should see something like this. Note the Server Response:

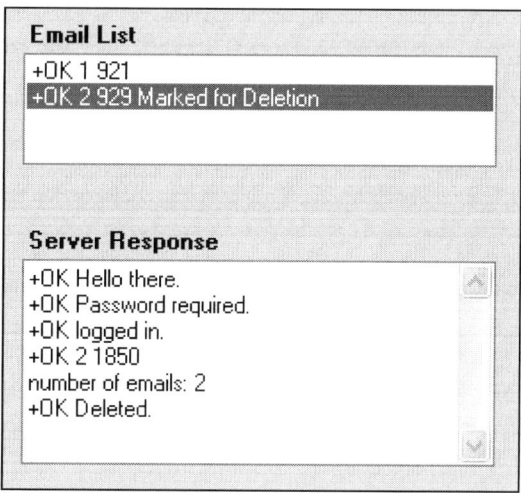

Even thought the response is "+OK Deleted", the email has not actually been deleted. To finalise things at the server level, you would click your Quit button.

However, click on a second email, and then back on the email that is marked for deletion. You should see an error message appear in your Email text box at the bottom:

The reason for the error is that emails marked for deletion can no longer be read. But what if you made a mistake and actually want to read it again?

Reset the Pop3 Server

If you want to go back and unmark an email you had previously marked for deletion, you can issue the RSET command. This, you won't be surprised to hear, stands for Reset.

Add another button to your form, and change the Name property to **btnReset**. Add some text to your button and then double click it to get at the code stub. Now enter the following code:

```
Dim server_response As String
server_response = PopCommand( network_stream, "RSET" )
txtServerResponse.Text += server_response & vbCrLf
```

All the code does, then, is to send the RSET command to the server.

Try it out. Mark an email for deletion. Then click your Reset button. Your Server Response text box will say something like this (final line):

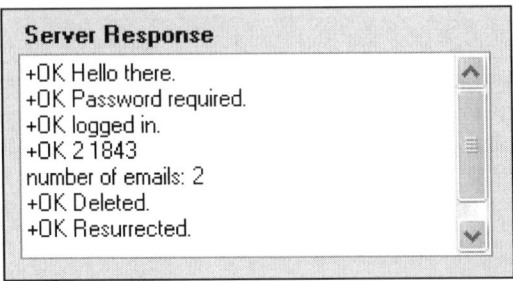

Exercise

In the ListBox, your email will still say "Marked for Deletion", even though you have reset the server. How would you solve this problem?

And that completes this rather long section on receiving emails – a bit tricky, wasn't it! In the next section we'll take a look at how Visual Basic .NET handles printing. Before we leave, though, here's the complete code for this section. (Next Page). It might be an idea to print it all out and study it. There are four pages.

Email Code Page 1

```vb
Imports System.Net.Sockets
Imports System.IO

Public Class Form1
    Dim network_stream As NetworkStream
    Dim read_stream As StreamReader
    Dim delete_button_clicked As Boolean = False

  Private Sub btnConnect_Click(ByVal sender As System.Object, _
                               ByVal e As System.EventArgs) _
                               Handles btnConnect.Click

    Dim pop_server As New TcpClient()
    Dim pop_host As String = "your_host"
    Dim username As String = "your_username"
    Dim password As String = "your_password"

    Try
      pop_server.Connect(pop_host, 110)
      network_stream = pop_server.GetStream()
      read_stream = New StreamReader(network_stream)

      Dim return_string As String

      return_string = read_stream.ReadLine() & vbCrLf
      txtServerResponse.Text = return_string

      txtServerResponse.Text += _
              PopCommand(network_stream, "USER " & username) & vbCrLf

      txtServerResponse.Text += _
          PopCommand(network_stream, "PASS " & password) & vbCrLf

      Dim server_stats As String
      server_stats = GetMailStats()

      txtServerResponse.Text += server_stats & vbCrLf

      Dim aryStats(2) As String
      aryStats = server_stats.Split(" ")
      txtServerResponse.Text += "number of emails: " & aryStats(1) & vbCrLf

      If Integer.Parse(aryStats(1)) > 0 Then
          Call GetMailList(Integer.Parse(aryStats(1)))
      End If

    Catch ex As Exception
        MessageBox.Show(ex.Message)
    End Try

End Sub
```

Email Code Page 2

```vbnet
Private Sub GetMailList(ByVal num_of_emails As Integer)

    Dim list_response As String
    Dim i As Integer

    For i = 1 To num_of_emails
        list_response = PopCommand(network_stream, "LIST " & i.ToString)
        ListBox1.Items.Add(list_response)
    Next i

End Sub
```

```vbnet
Private Function GetMailStats() As String

    Dim stats_response As String

    stats_response = PopCommand(network_stream, "STAT")

    Return stats_response

End Function
```

```vbnet
Private Sub GetEmail(ByVal server_command As String)

    Dim server_bytes() As Byte = _
                    System.Text.Encoding.ASCII.GetBytes(server_command)

    Dim stream_reader As StreamReader
    Dim TextLine As String = ""

    Try
        network_stream.Write(server_bytes, 0, server_bytes.Length)
        stream_reader = New StreamReader(network_stream)

        Do While stream_reader.Peek() <> -1
            TextLine += stream_reader.ReadLine() & vbNewLine
        Loop

        txtEmail.Text = TextLine

    Catch ex As Exception
        MessageBox.Show(ex.Message)
    End Try

End Sub
```

Email Code Page 3

```vb
Private Sub ListBox1_SelectedIndexChanged(ByVal sender As Object, _
                            ByVal e As System.EventArgs) _
                            Handles ListBox1.SelectedIndexChanged

    Dim index_number As String
    Dim strRetrieve As String

    txtEmail.Text = ""

    Try
        index_number = (ListBox1.SelectedIndex + 1).ToString
        strRetrieve = "RETR " + index_number + vbCrLf
        GetEmail(strRetrieve)
    Catch ex As Exception
        MessageBox.Show(ex.Message)
    End Try


End Sub
```

```vb
Private Function PopCommand(ByRef network_stream As NetworkStream, _
                            ByVal server_command As String) As String

    Try
        server_command = server_command & vbCrLf
        Dim server bytes() As Byte =
                System.Text.Encoding.ASCII.GetBytes(server_command)

        Dim read_stream2 As StreamReader
        Dim server_response As String

        network_stream.Write(server_bytes, 0, server_bytes.Length)
        read_stream2 = New StreamReader(network_stream)
        server_response = read_stream2.ReadLine()

        Return server_response

    Catch ex As Exception
        Return ex.Message
    End Try
End Function
```

```vb
Private Sub btnQuit_Click(ByVal sender As System.Object, _
                            ByVal e As System.EventArgs) _
                            Handles btnQuit.Click

    Call QuitServer()

End Sub
```

Email Code Page 4

```
Private Sub QuitServer()

    Try
        Dim server_response As String = ""
        server_response = PopCommand(network_stream, "QUIT")
        MessageBox.Show(server_response)
    Catch ex As Exception
        MessageBox.Show(ex.Message)
    End Try

End Sub
```

```
Private Sub Form1_FormClosing(ByVal sender As System.Object, _
            ByVal e As System.Windows.Forms.FormClosingEventArgs) _
                Handles MyBase.FormClosing

    Call QuitServer()

End Sub
```

```
Private Sub btnDelete_Click(ByVal sender As System.Object, _
                            ByVal e As System.EventArgs) _
                                Handles btnDelete.Click
    Dim i As Integer
    i = ListBox1.SelectedIndex + 1

    Try
      Dim server_response As String
      server_response = PopCommand(network_stream, "DELE " + i.ToString)
      txtServerResponse.Text += server_response & vbCrLf
      ListBox1.Items.Item(i - 1) += " Marked for Deletion"
      txtEmail.Text = ""
    Catch ex As Exception
        MessageBox.Show(ex.Message)
    End Try

End Sub
```

```
Private Sub btnReset_Click(ByVal sender As System.Object, _
                           ByVal e As System.EventArgs) _
                               Handles btnReset.Click
    Dim server_response As String
    server_response = PopCommand(network_stream, "RSET")
    txtServerResponse.Text += server_response & vbCrLf

End Sub
End Class
```

Printing in VB NET

Printing in the Visual Basic programming language has never been easy, and Visual Basic .NET seems to carry on this tradition. If all you want to do is to print one page of text from a text box, then that's relatively simple, with not much code to write. It's when you want to print multiple pages that the difficulties arise.

First off, we'll try some simple printing, just so that you can undertand how it all works. Then we'll have a go at printing multiple pages, and you'll quickly see how complex it can get!

If you don't have a printer, or would rather not waste lots of ink and paper during these lessons, then we highly recommend installing some PDF creation software like the free CutePDF, or Bullzip PDF Printer. When it's time to print, you'll be able to choose to print as PDF file rather than sending the document to a physical printer.

Simple Printing

Start a new project for this. Add a button to your form. Set the Name property to **btnPrint**, and add some text. Now add a Text box or a RichTextBox control. Leave it on the default Name, but add some text to your text box.

To print documents, you need a few objects from the toolbox on the left. The first one to add is rather curious – the PrintDocument object:

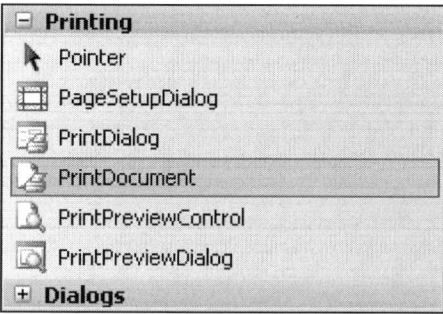

Double click to add one to your project, and it will appear at the bottom of the Visual Basic software.

The PrintDocment object handles all the events related to printing, and represents the entire document you want to print. The most important event it has is called **PrintPage**. This gets fired for every page in your document.

Before you see how it works, add a PrintDialog control to your project. Again, this will get added to the bottom of your project, alongside your PrintDocment object:

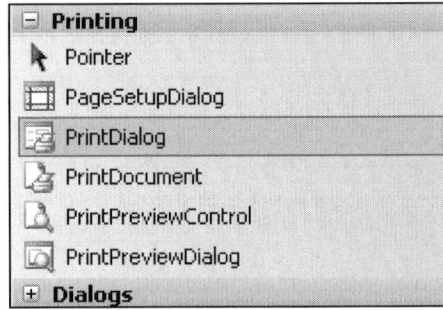

Leave both objects on their default names. Double click your button to create a code stub.

To display the Print Dialogue Box, add the following code:

```
If PrintDialog1.ShowDialog = Windows.Forms.DialogResult.OK Then
        PrintDocument1.Print( )
End If
```

The If statement is standard code to display a dialogue box, and you've met it before in a previous section. Inside of the If statement, though, we have this line:

PrintDocument1.Print( )

The PrintDocument object you added has a **Print** Subroutine. Calling this Sub will cause the **PrintPage** event to be fired.

You can try your code out. Run your programme and click your button. You should see this dialogue box appear:

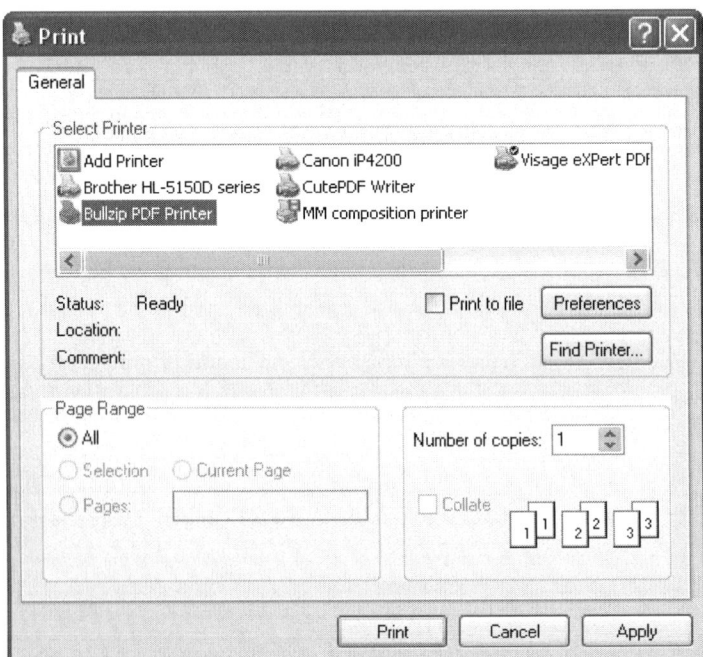

If you click the Print button on the dialogue box then no errors will occur, even though we have yet to tell the programme what it is we want printing. All that will happen is that you get a blank page for your printed document. We'll solve that in a moment. But there is, however, another problem.

If you have more than one printer installed, or preferably a PDF printer, try selecting that. When you click Print, your choice will be completely ignored. That's because VB prints to the default printer, unless you specify otherwise. To set a different printer, amend your code to this:

PrintDialog1.PrinterSettings.PrinterName = "Bullzip PDF Printer"

If PrintDialog1.ShowDialog = Windows.Forms.DialogResult.OK Then
    PrintDocument1.PrinterSettings = PrintDialog1.PrinterSettings
    PrintDocument1.Print( )
End If

Obviously, change the **PrinterName** to something you have in your dialogue box. The line that sets the printer, though, is this one:

PrintDocument1.PrinterSettings = PrintDialog1.PrinterSettings

What you're doing here is transferring the settings from the dialogue box to the **PrinterSettings** of PrintDocument. It's PrintDocument, remember, that will handle all the printing, not the dialogue box.

You can set other values that a user selected from the dialogue box. To get the number of copies, for example, the code would be this:

PrintDialog1.PrinterSettings.PrinterName = "Bullzip PDF Printer"
Dim num_copies As Short = PrintDialog1.PrinterSettings.Copies

If PrintDialog1.ShowDialog = Windows.Forms.DialogResult.OK Then
    PrintDocument1.PrinterSettings.Copies = num_copies
    PrintDocument1.PrinterSettings = PrintDialog1.PrinterSettings
    PrintDocument1.Print( )
End If

Whichever settings you receive from the printer dialogue box, though, you need to transfer them to the PrinterSettings property of your PrintDocument object.

The PrintPage Event

When you click the Print button on the dialogue box, the PrintPage event will fire for your PrintDocument object. It's here that you specify what it is you want to print. You do so with the **DrawString** Subroutine of the Graphics object.

Return to Design view, and select your PrintDocument object at the bottom of the VB software. Now, in the properties window on the right, click the lightning bolt icon to see a list of events for the PrintDocument object. There's only four:

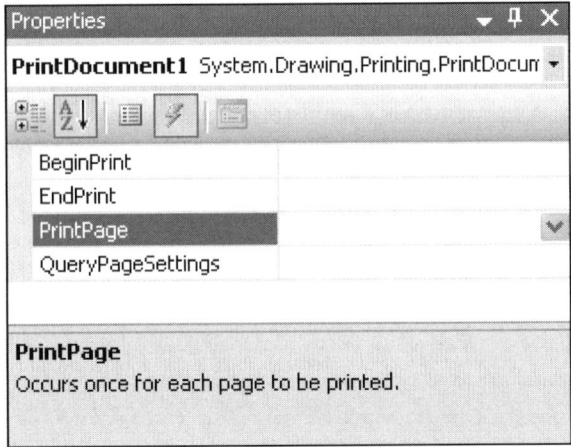

Double click the **PrintPage** event to create a code stub. Notice that one of the parameters for the event is this:

ByVal e As System.Drawing.Printing.PrintPageEventArgs

This sets up a variable of type **PrintPageEventArgs**. One of these arguments is the Graphics object. If you remember the section on Graphics at the start of these extra contents, you'll know that the Graphics object has a DrawString Subroutine:

e.Graphics.DrawString( )

In between the round brackets of DrawString, you have quite a few options available. Add the following between the round brackets:

RichTextBox1.Text, RichTextBox1.Font, Brushes.Black, 50, 50

The first thing to add is the text you want to print. In the code above, this was the Text from RichTextBox1 (change this if you added a Text Box instead). Next, we need a Font. We're using the same Font that was chosen for RichTextBox1. The third parameter is what colour you want to use to draw the text. The two numbers at the end (50, 50) are where you want to start drawing your text. The first 50 is how far to the left of the page (left margin), and the next 50 is how far down the page (top margin).

Your code should look like this (we've split ours over multiple lines so that it will fit on this page):

```
Private Sub PrintDocument1_PrintPage(ByVal sender As System.Object, _
              ByVal e As System.Drawing.Printing.PrintPageEventArgs) _
              Handles PrintDocument1.PrintPage

    e.Graphics.DrawString(RichTextBox1.Text, RichTextBox1.Font, _
                                            Brushes.Black, 50, 50)

End Sub
```

Try it out. Run your programme and click your button. When the print dialogue box appears, click Print. This time, the text you had in your Text Box or RichTextBox should be printed.

Now that you have some experience with simple printing (yes, that was the simple version!) let's move on to printing multiple pages.

Printing Multiple Pages

The problem with printing multiple pages is that the PrintPage event doesn't know how many pages worth of text you have in your document. It doesn't do the calculations for you. Instead, you have to work this out for yourself, and then tell the PrintPage event when to stop printing. If you don't, the event will only fire once, and you'll just get the first page of text, but not the rest.

To make this work, add another control to your project – the **PageSetupDialog** control. You'll find this in the toolbox, under the **Printing** category:

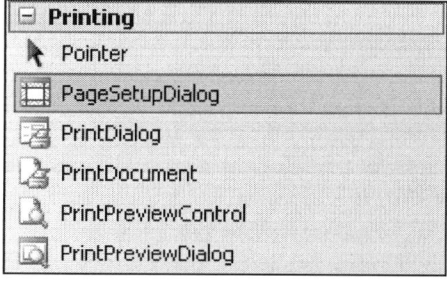

This object will allow us to get the settings for the pages to be printed. The settings we want are all the margins, and the paper size. This will allow us to create a Rectangle of the correct size. We can then pass the rectangle to DrawString, instead of typing 50, 50 for the start of the printing position.

Add another button to your form. Give it the Name **btnPageSetup**, and set the Text property to **Page Setup**. Double click your new button to get at the code.

We need to set up some variables at the top of the coding window, in the Declarations area. So add the following variables:

> **Dim num_of_pages As Integer**
> **Dim rectangle1 As Rectangle**

Dim aryTextFile() As String
Dim lineCounter As Integer = 0
Dim lines_per_page As Integer

We'll also be doing some file manipulation. So add an **Imports** statement at the very top of the code window, above everything else:

Imports System.IO

Your coding window should look like this:

```
Imports System.IO

Public Class Form1

    Dim num_of_pages As Integer
    Dim rectangle1 As Rectangle
    Dim aryTextFile() As String
    Dim lineCounter As Integer = 0
    Dim lines_per_page As Integer


    Private Sub btnPageSetup_Click(ByVal sender As System.Object, _
                              ByVal e As System.EventArgs) _
                                   Handles btnPageSetup.Click



    End Sub
```

What we're going to be doing is getting the contents of a file, and then printing that, rather than printing the contents of a TextBox or RichTextBox. We'll also place the contents of the file into the RichTextBox, though, just so that we can see what's being printed.

The array in the variable declarations above will be used to hold the contents of the file, one array position for every line in the file. The methodology we'll be using is this:

- Get the total number of lines in the file
- Get the maximum number of lines per page
- Get how many pages need to be printed by dividing the total number of lines by the number of lines per page
- For each page that needs to be printed, pull the correct lines from the array

Most of these details can be pulled from the Page Setup dialogue box. In the code for your Page Setup button, add the following:

PageSetupDialog1.PageSettings = PrintDocument1.DefaultPageSettings

Dim dbResult As Integer = PageSetupDialog1.ShowDialog( )

If dbResult = Windows.Forms.DialogResult.Cancel Then
         Exit Sub
End If

The first line transfers the **DefaultPageSettings** of the PrintDocument to the **PageSettings** property of the Page Setup dialogue box. The rest of this code just displays the dialogue box, exiting the Subroutine if the Cancel button is clicked.

Try it out by running your programme and clicking your Page Setup button. You should see a dialogue box like this one:

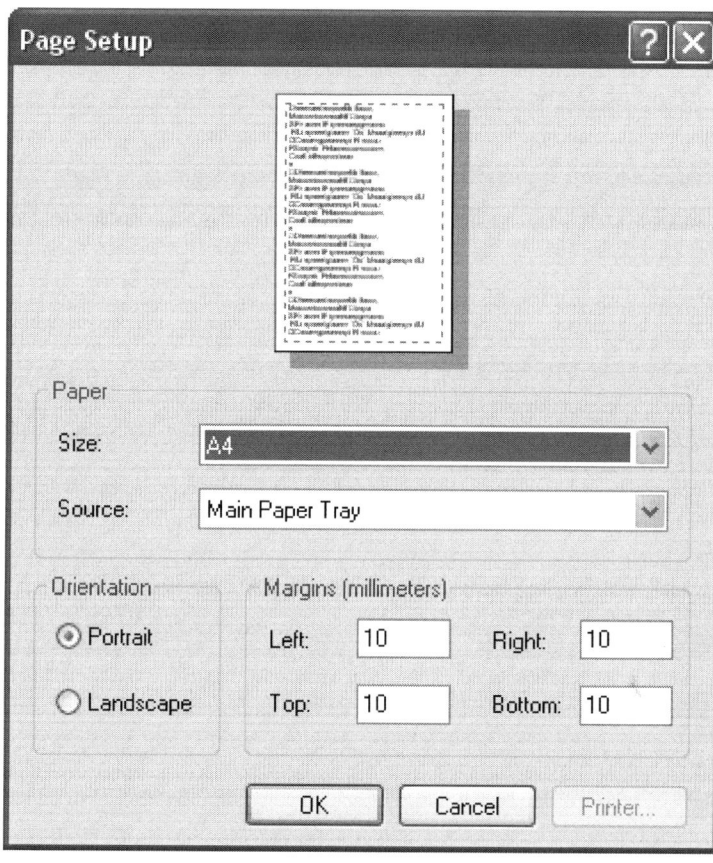

We need the Margins, here, and the Size of the paper that the user selects. We won't worry about Landscape printing, but just have Portrait.

When the OK button is clicked, we can get at the values from the dialogue box. To get the chosen margins, add this to your Page Setup button code:

```
Dim leftMargin As Integer
Dim topMargin As Integer
Dim rightMargin As Integer
Dim bottomMargin As Integer

leftMargin = PageSetupDialog1.PageSettings.Margins.Left
topMargin = PageSetupDialog1.PageSettings.Margins.Top
rightMargin = PageSetupDialog1.PageSettings.Margins.Right
bottomMargin = PageSetupDialog1.PageSettings.Margins.Bottom
```

To get a margin, then, you access the **Margins** property of **PageSettings**. After a dot, you then add which margin you're trying to access: left, right, top, or bottom.

(If you were to examine the values in the margins, however, you'd find that they don't match the millimetre values from the dialogue box. That's because VB converts the values for you, and uses hundreds of an inch. So 10 millimetres would equal 39 hundredths of an inch.)

The next thing to do is to get the height and width of the paper that the user selected:

Dim paperHeight As Integer
Dim paperWidth As Integer

paperHeight = PageSetupDialog1.PageSettings.PaperSize.Height
paperWidth = PageSetupDialog1.PageSettings.PaperSize.Width

When you add the code above, your Page Setup button will look like this:

```
Private Sub btnPageSetup_Click(ByVal sender As System.Object, _
                    ByVal e As System.EventArgs) _
                        Handles btnPageSetup.Click

    PageSetupDialog1.PageSettings = PrintDocument1.DefaultPageSettings
    Dim dbResult As Integer = PageSetupDialog1.ShowDialog()

    If dbResult = Windows.Forms.DialogResult.Cancel Then
        Exit Sub
    End If

    Dim leftMargin As Integer
    Dim topMargin As Integer
    Dim rightMargin As Integer
    Dim bottomMargin As Integer

    leftMargin = PageSetupDialog1.PageSettings.Margins.Left
    topMargin = PageSetupDialog1.PageSettings.Margins.Top
    rightMargin = PageSetupDialog1.PageSettings.Margins.Right
    bottomMargin = PageSetupDialog1.PageSettings.Margins.Bottom

    Dim paperHeight As Integer
    Dim paperWidth As Integer

    paperHeight = PageSetupDialog1.PageSettings.PaperSize.Height
    paperWidth = PageSetupDialog1.PageSettings.PaperSize.Width


End Sub
```

The reason we need all these values is so that we can set up a Rectangle object. The Rectangle can then be used in **DrawString** for the size of the printing area.

So add the following code to set up the Rectangle object:

```
Dim rectWidth As Integer
Dim rectheight As Integer

rectheight = paperHeight - (topMargin + bottomMargin)
rectWidth = paperWidth - (leftMargin + rightMargin)
rectangle1 = New Rectangle( leftMargin, topMargin, rectWidth, rectheight )
```

To get the height of the rectangle, you deduct the size of the top and bottom margins from the paper height. To get the width of the rectangle, you deduct the left and right margin sizes from the paper width.

We created a rectangle in a previous section. But the values you need between the round brackets are these:

X Value
Y Value
Width
Height

To place anything inside of a rectangle, you need to specify an X value (how far to the left you want to position the contents) and a Y value (how far down you want to position the contents). For our rectangle, we're taking the size of the left margin for X, and the size of the top margin for Y.

The next thing to do is to get how many lines this size rectangle can support. To do that, you need to set up a font object, and give it a size. You then divide the height of the rectangle by the height of the font. Add the following two lines to your code:

```
Dim chosen_font As New Font("Arial", 12)

lines_per_page = rectheight / chosen_font.Height
```

Here, we're using an Arial font at 12 points in size. This will be the font used for the entire document. (We're not going to be handling different font sizes, weight and styles, as this would make the code insanely complex!)

The final thing to do is to get the number of pages that need to be printed:

```
num_of_pages = System.Math.Ceiling(lineCounter / lines_per_page)
```

We're using **Math.Ceiling** to round up, as VB NET doesn't have an inbuilt Round function. But to get the number of pages, you just divide the total number of lines by the number of lines per page. (The total number of lines is something we still need to do.)

OK, that's it for the Page Setup button. Here's what your code should look like:

```
Private Sub btnPageSetup_Click(ByVal sender As System.Object, _
                               ByVal e As System.EventArgs) _
                               Handles btnPageSetup.Click

    PageSetupDialog1.PageSettings = PrintDocument1.DefaultPageSettings
    Dim dbResult As Integer = PageSetupDialog1.ShowDialog()

    If dbResult = Windows.Forms.DialogResult.Cancel Then
        Exit Sub
    End If

    Dim leftMargin As Integer
    Dim topMargin As Integer
    Dim rightMargin As Integer
    Dim bottomMargin As Integer

    leftMargin = PageSetupDialog1.PageSettings.Margins.Left
    topMargin = PageSetupDialog1.PageSettings.Margins.Top
    rightMargin = PageSetupDialog1.PageSettings.Margins.Right
    bottomMargin = PageSetupDialog1.PageSettings.Margins.Bottom

    Dim paperHeight As Integer
    Dim paperWidth As Integer

    paperHeight = PageSetupDialog1.PageSettings.PaperSize.Height
    paperWidth = PageSetupDialog1.PageSettings.PaperSize.Width

    Dim rectWidth As Integer
    Dim rectheight As Integer

    rectheight = paperHeight - (topMargin + bottomMargin)
    rectWidth = paperWidth - (leftMargin + rightMargin)
    rectangle1 = New Rectangle(leftMargin, topMargin, rectWidth, rectheight)

    Dim chosen_font As New Font("Arial", 12)
    lines_per_page = rectheight / chosen_font.Height

    num_of_pages = System.Math.Ceiling(lineCounter / lines_per_page)

End Sub
```

Loading a File to be Printed

We can now load a text file into our array, and get how many lines we need to print. The text file we're using is one of the files that you download with the book, in the NetFiles folder. The file is **dictionary.txt**. But you can use any long file on your computer.

The code for this is something you've already met previously, so we won't go through it all. But create a Form Load event. Then add this code:

```
Private Sub Form1_Load(ByVal sender As System.Object, _
                       ByVal e As System.EventArgs) _
                       Handles MyBase.Load

    Try
        RichTextBox1.LoadFile("C:\dictionary.txt", _
                              RichTextBoxStreamType.PlainText)

        Dim stream As New StreamReader("C:\dictionary.txt")
        Dim TextLine As String = ""
        Dim lines As String

        '=======================================================
        '   CALCULATE THE NUMBER OF LINES TO BE PRINTED
        '=======================================================
        Do While stream.Peek() <> -1
            TextLine = stream.ReadLine()
            lineCounter += 1
        Loop

        stream.Close()

        '=======================================================
        '   READ ALL THE LINES INTO THE ARRAY
        '=======================================================
        Dim stream2 As New StreamReader("C:\dictionary.txt")
        ReDim aryTextFile(lineCounter - 1)
        Dim i As Integer = 0

        Do While stream2.Peek() <> -1
            lines = stream2.ReadLine()
            aryTextFile(i) = lines
            i += 1
        Loop

        stream2.Close()

    Catch ex As Exception
        MsgBox(ex.Message)
    End Try
End Sub
```

The first thing we're doing is just loading the text file into the RichTextBox. You need to specify what type of file it is, PlainText in our case.

We then set up a StreamReader, and specify the file path between the round brackets. To count the number of lines, we're using a **Do … While** loop. The number of lines in the file is going into the variable we've called **lineCounter**.

Because of the difficulties of working with StreamReaders, we've created a second one. We use this second one to loop round the text file and place each line into our array.

After the form loads, then, we'll have an array filled with the lines from the text file, and a count of how many lines need to be printed.

Instead of hard-coding everything like this, you could have an Open File dialogue box and select a file to be read into the StreamReaders. We've left this out for simplicity's sake. But it would be a nice addition to your programme!

Printing the File

To print our selected file, we need the PrintPage event again. This is where your DrawString code is. Because this event gets fired for every page, we can set up some Static variables to keep track of what has been printed. Add these lines to the top of your PrintPage event code:

```
Static pages_printed As Integer
Static startVal As Integer
Static endVal As Integer
Dim chosen_font As New Font("Arial", 12)
Dim i As Integer
Dim textToPrint As String = ""
```

A Static variable will retain its contents when the code is executed again. If you have a Dim variable then the contents get erased. We need to keep a count of how many pages have been printed.

We also need to keep track of where we are in our array. The **dictionary.txt** file has more than 230 lines. With our page margins, we'll only get 57 lines per page. When the PrintPage event fires, we first need lines 1 to 57. The second time it fires, we need to get lines 58 to 114, and so on. We're going to keep track with the two variables startVal and endVal.

To pull the correct lines from the array, add the following code:

```
endVal = endVal + lines_per_page

For i = (startVal) To endVal
        If i <= (lineCounter - 1) Then
                textToPrint += aryTextFile(i) & vbNewLine
        End If

Next

startVal = ( startVal + lines_per_page ) + 1
```

The code looks a bit complex, but we're just trying to get some lines to print from our array. The first time that the PrintPage event fires, the loop will go from 0 to how many lines per page we can print. We're increasing this value for each page printed:

```
endVal = endVal + lines_per_page
```

The starting value for the loop will be zero at first. We then increase this value after the loop:

startVal = (startVal + lines_per_page) + 1

Can you see why it needs to go after the loop and not before it?

Inside the loop, though, we're just building up a variable called **textToPrint**. This will have a new line each time round the loop.

The next thing to do is to adapt your DrawString code. We also need a new value for it:

Dim fmt As New StringFormat(StringFormatFlags.LineLimit)

e.Graphics.DrawString(textToPrint, chosen_font, Brushes.Black, rectangle1, fmt)

The line we've added creates a new **StringFormat** object. This allows you to specify that only entire lines are laid out in the rectangle.

Amend your DrawString code to the same as ours above. The text that we want to print is pulled from the array, in that for loop code. This is now in the variable **textToPrint**. After specifying a font and a Brush, we use the rectangle object we set up, **rectangle1**. The string format goes at the end.

The final thing we need to do is to tell the PrintPage event whether there are more lines to be printed or not. This is done with the **HasMorePages** property. If this is set to True then the event will fire again. If it's set to False, it won't. Add these lines to your code:

If pages_printed = (num_of_pages - 1) Then

e.HasMorePages = False

Else

e.HasMorePages = True

End If

pages_printed += 1

So we keep track of the number of pages that have already been printed and compare that to the total number of pages in our text file. If **pages_printed** is equal to **num_of_pages** (minus 1 because of all that rounding) then the print run has finished. If it's not, we keep printing.

The final line advances the **pages_printed** counter.

The whole of the code for your PrintPage event should look like this:

```
Private Sub PrintDocument1_PrintPage(ByVal sender As System.Object, _
              ByVal e As System.Drawing.Printing.PrintPageEventArgs) _
              Handles PrintDocument1.PrintPage

    Static pages_printed As Integer
    Static startVal As Integer
    Static endVal As Integer
    Dim chosen_font As New Font("Arial", 12)
    Dim i As Integer
    Dim textToPrint As String = ""

    endVal = endVal + lines_per_page

    For i = (startVal) To endVal
        If i <= (lineCounter - 1) Then
            textToPrint += aryTextFile(i) & vbNewLine
        End If
    Next

    startVal = (startVal + lines_per_page) + 1

    Dim fmt As New StringFormat(StringFormatFlags.LineLimit)
    e.Graphics.DrawString(textToPrint, chosen_font, Brushes.Black, _
                                        rectangle1, fmt)

    If pages_printed = (num_of_pages - 1) Then
        e.HasMorePages = False
    Else
        e.HasMorePages = True
    End If
    pages_printed += 1

End Sub
```

But you can try it out now. Run your programme and click your Page Setup button. Set the margins and paper size. Click OK, then print. You should find that you can now print multiple page documents.

There are, of course, one or two things you can change about the programme. The first thing you may want to do is to solve the problem of clicking the Print button without clicking Page Setup. (Can you see why it would cause problems? And how to solve it?)

Also, you may find that too many lines are being printed. This seems to be a problem with the size of fonts and line spacing. For example, take the following:

> **Dim chosen_font As New Font("Arial", 12)**
> **Dim fontHeight As Integer** = chosen_font.**Height**
> **MsgBox(** fontHeight **)**

The Height value also includes the space between two lines of text. Because we chose an Arial font size of 12, the value of the font height plus the line spacing is 19. Change your font to

Verdana and the message box will display a value of 20. If you have the Arial Black font on your computer, the message box will display a value of 23 for a 12 point font!

If you find that too many lines are being printed, try replacing this line:

lines_per_page = rectheight / chosen_font.Height

with this:

lines_per_page = rectheight / (chosen_font.Height * 1.1)

Or deduct 3 or 4 lines per page:

lines_per_page = lines_per_page - 4

Another thing you'll have to solve in our code is to reset the variables if you want to print again. At the moment, you have to close the programme down and open it back up again.

But we'll leave printing there. We're sure you'll agree that this section has thrown up some of the problems you'll have when it comes to printing. Perhaps in the next version of the software, Microsoft will make the process easier!

Code Libraries

In this final section of the extra contents, we're going to take a look at some of the things you can do before saying goodbye to your programmes, and handing them off to other people. First up is code libraries.

Creating your own code libraries

If you have created some useful code that you want to save and use in other programmes, you can create your own code libraries. Your useful code can be saved as a Dynamic Link Library (DLL) file, and easily imported into other projects. Let's see how it's done.

Start a new project. From the Open Project dialogue box, don't select Windows Application, but **Class Library**.

In the **Name** box at the bottom, type a name for your library. This will be used as its Namespace, so make sure it's something descriptive. We've called ours StringFunctions:

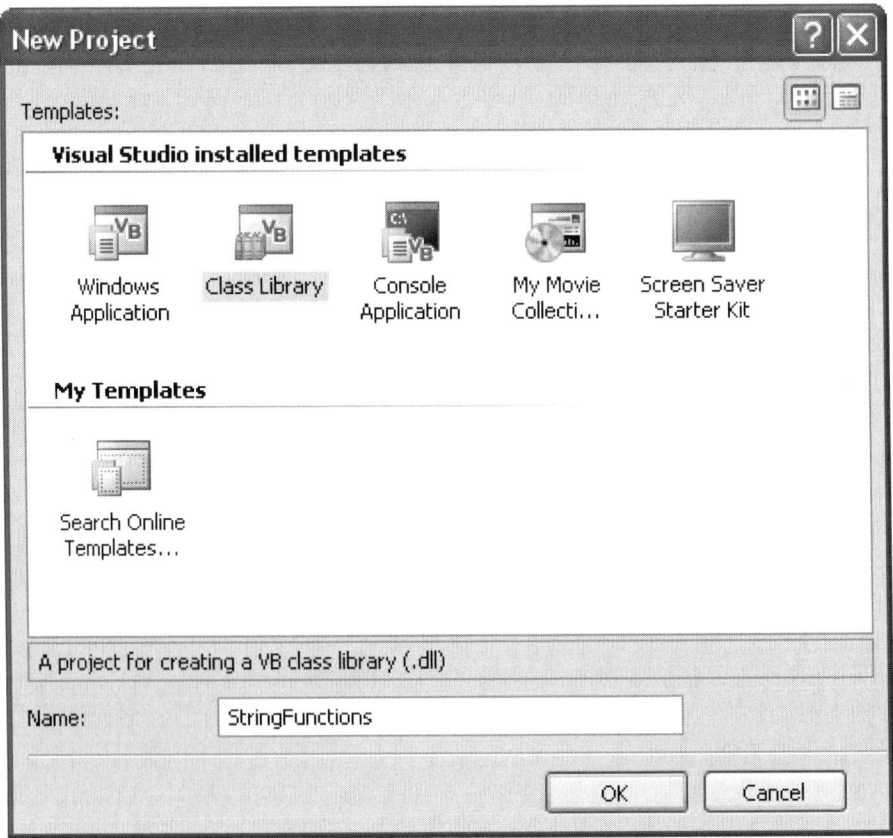

When you click OK, you should see a code window appear:

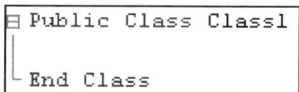

```
Public Class Class1

End Class
```

Class1 is the default name for the new Class. To change it, have a look at the properties area on the right:

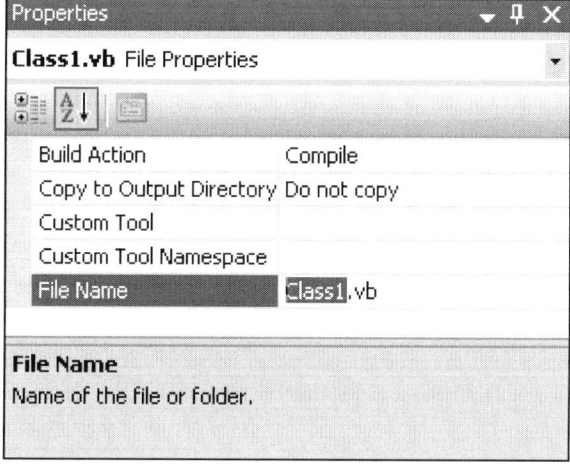

Change the **FileName** property from the default to something of your own, not forgetting the **.vb** at the end of the name.

Our Class is to do with Authentication, so we've called it **Authentication.vb**:

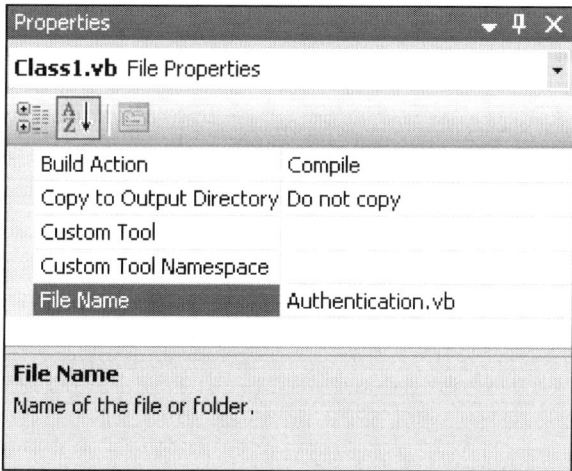

Notice that the name will change in the Solution Explorer in the top right, as well as in the main coding window:

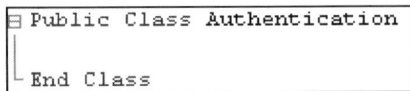

```
Public Class Authentication

End Class
```

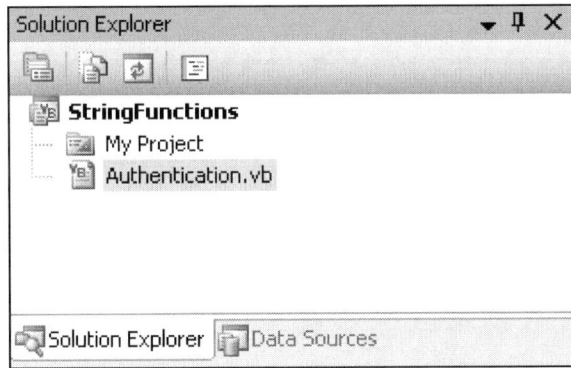

You are now ready to type the code for your class. In our code below, we've just added some Public Functions. (This is a quick and easy way to create code libraries, but it's not the recommended way to create classes. We're doing it this way just for simplicity's sake):

```vbnet
Public Class Authentication

    '''<Summary>Checks if a string is blank or not</Summary>
    '''<Returns>True or False</Returns>
    '''<Remarks>None</Remarks>
    Public Function isBlankString(ByVal check_string As String) As Boolean
        If check_string = "" Then
            Return True
        Else
            Return False
        End If
    End Function

    '''<Summary>Checks a string for invalid characters</Summary>
    '''<Returns>True or False</Returns>
    '''<Remarks>char_list should contain the characters you
    ''' want to allow</Remarks>
    Public Function InvalidChars(ByVal check_string As String, _
                                 ByVal char_list As String) As Boolean

        Dim i As Integer
        Dim counter As Integer = 0
        Dim endVal As Integer = Trim(check_string.Length)
        Dim temp As String

        InvalidChars = False

        For i = 1 To endVal
            temp = Mid(check_string, i, 1)
            counter = InStr(char_list, temp)
            If counter = 0 Then
                Return True
            End If
        Next

    End Function
End Class
```

Notice the comments at the top of each function. These are XML comments that VB recognises, and can be used for XML documentation. But the Intellisense list will use the Summary and Remarks to provide extra information about your function. They'll also help you to remember what your code does when you come to view the file months down the line. Notice, too, that each line starts with three single quotes.

You can add more Classes in this file. In the code below, we've added a second class. This second class will check for valid email addresses. There are only a few lines of code for it, in our example, because email address checking can get quite complex:

```
Public Class Authentication

    '''<Summary>Checks if a string is blank or not</Summary>
    '''<Returns>True or False</Returns>
    '''<Remarks>None</Remarks>
    Public Function isBlankString(ByVal check_string As String) As Boolean
        If check_string = "" Then
            Return True
        Else
            Return False
        End If
    End Function

    '''<Summary>Checks a string for invalid characters</Summary>
    '''<Returns>True or False</Returns>
    '''<Remarks>char_list should contain the characters you
    ''' want to allow</Remarks>
    Public Function InvalidChars(ByVal check_string As String, _
                                 ByVal char_list As String) As Boolean
        Dim i As Integer
        Dim counter As Integer = 0
        Dim endVal As Integer = Trim(check_string.Length)
        Dim temp As String

        InvalidChars = False

        For i = 1 To endVal
            temp = Mid(check_string, i, 1)
            counter = InStr(char_list, temp)
            If counter = 0 Then
                Return True
            End If
        Next
    End Function
End Class

Public Class EmailAddress

    Public Function IsValidEmailSddress(ByVal email As String) As Boolean
        If email = "" Then
            Return True
        Else
            Return False
        End If
    End Function

End Class
```

Once you have your useful code, it's time to turn it into a DLL file. This is quite simple. From the menu bars at the top of VB, click **Build**. From the Build menu, select the **Build** item:

It may appear as though nothing has happened, after you click Build. But take a look at your Solution Explorer. Click the **All Files** icon, circled in red below. Expand the **Release** item, and your DLL file will be there:

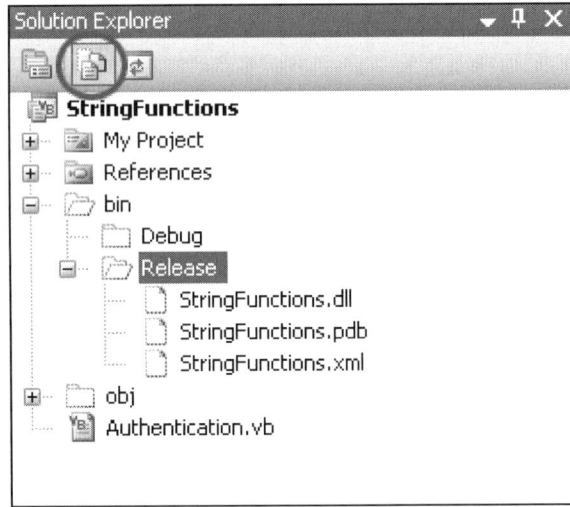

Save your work, and remember where you saved it all too. Now close this project down. You'll now learn how to use the DLL file you've just created.

How to use your DLL file

Now that you have created your own Class library, it's time to put it to some use. Create a new Windows Application.

To use your new DLL file, you need to add a reference to it. So from the VB menu at the top of the screen, click the **Project** item. From the Project menu, select **Add Reference**:

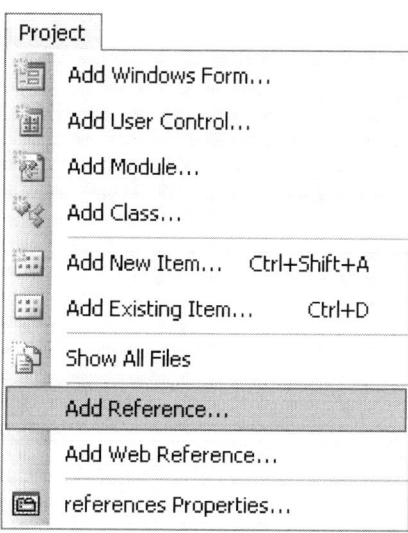

When you click **Add Reference**, you'll see a dialogue box appear. Click the **Browse** tab:

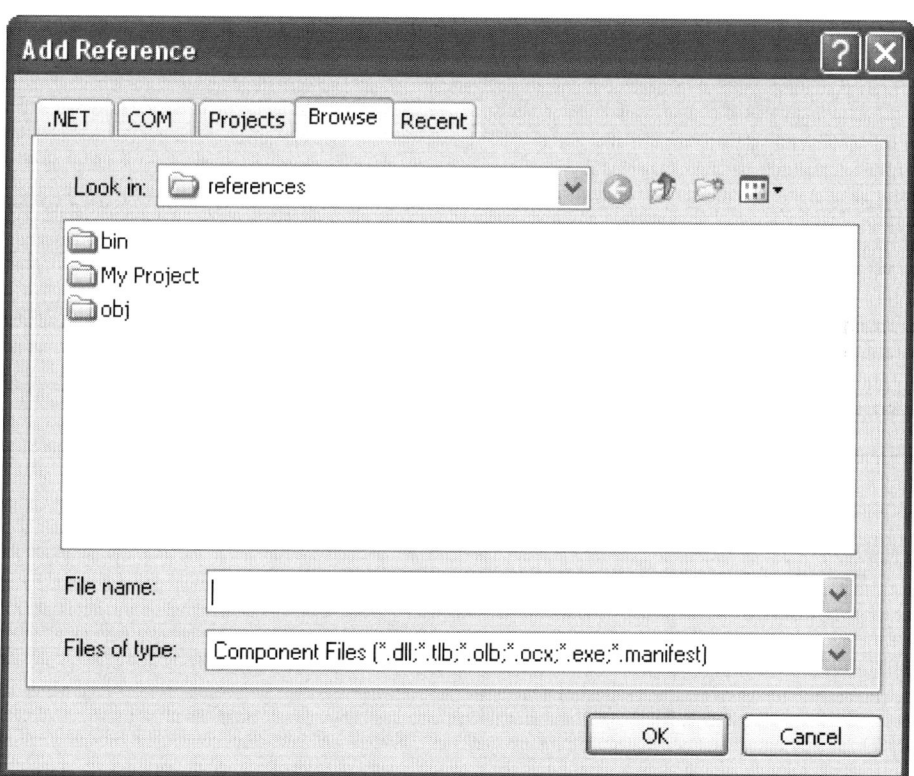

Search for you DLL file. It will be in the **Bin\Release** folder where you saved your Class Library project file:

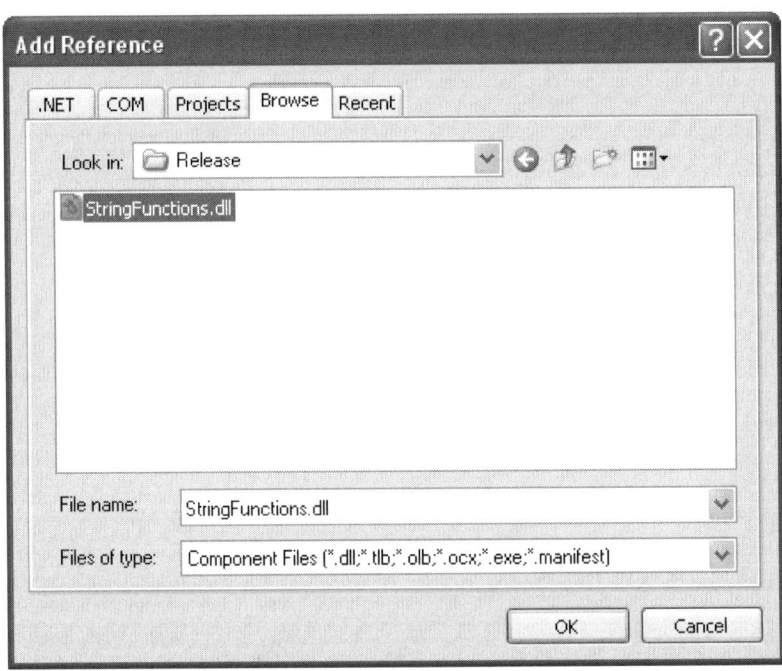

Look for a file that ends in DLL. Click OK when you've found it. To see if it has been added, click the **All Files** icon in the Solution Explorer in the top right. Your DLL file should be under **References**:

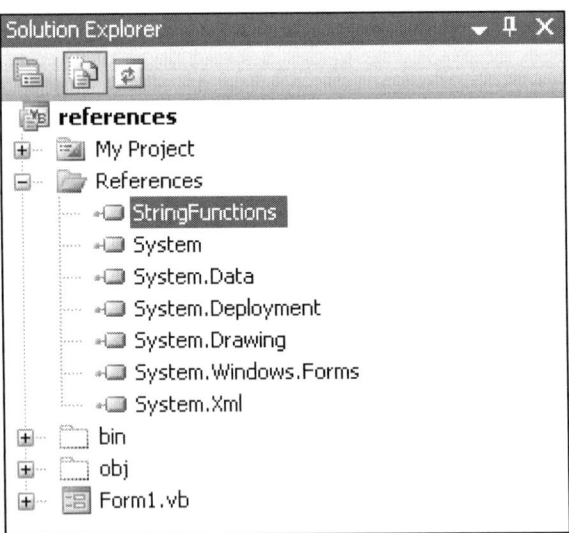

Once you've added a reference to you DLL file, you can put it to work.

Add a button to your new form. Double click to get at the coding window. Now create a New object:

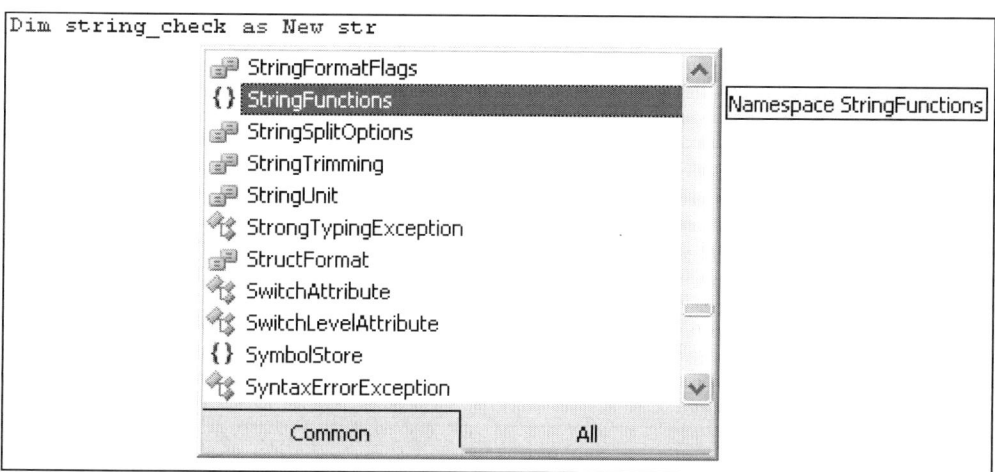

What you should see after you type the **New** keyword is that your Namespace is on the IntelliSense list. Double click your Namespace, then type a dot. You should then see any Classes you created in your Namespace:

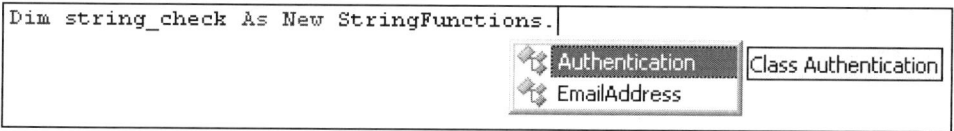

In the image above, you can see the two classes we created earlier. Double click to add a class to your code.

When you use your new class, you should see the functions that you created:

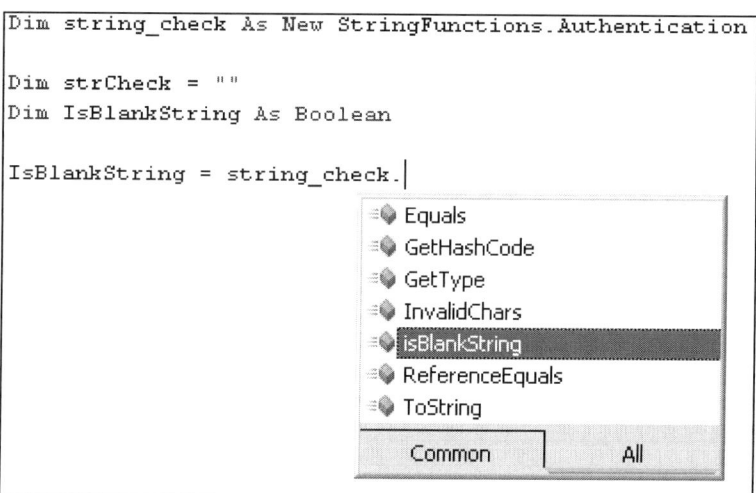

And there you have it – an easy way to reuse your code. You can copy the DLL file and paste to a library folder. That way, you can reference it for other projects, or even send it to others!

Deploying your apps

If you want others to install your programmes, then you need to prepare them inside of the VB environment. Before doing so, however, there's one or two things you may want to take care of

Vista's/Win 7 Authentication Issues

If your users will be installing on Windows Vista or Windows 7, then there are security issues to consider. Visa and Windows 7 have something called User Account Control (UAC) that makes the operating system more secure. If your programme does something like writing a text file to the hard drive, then you may run in to problems if you don't create a manifest file. You add one of these to your project to tell Vista or Windows 7 to display the Authenticate dialogue box. The user can then either accept or decline.

To create a manifest file for your project, right click your project name in the Solution Explorer. From the menu that appears, select **Add New Item**:

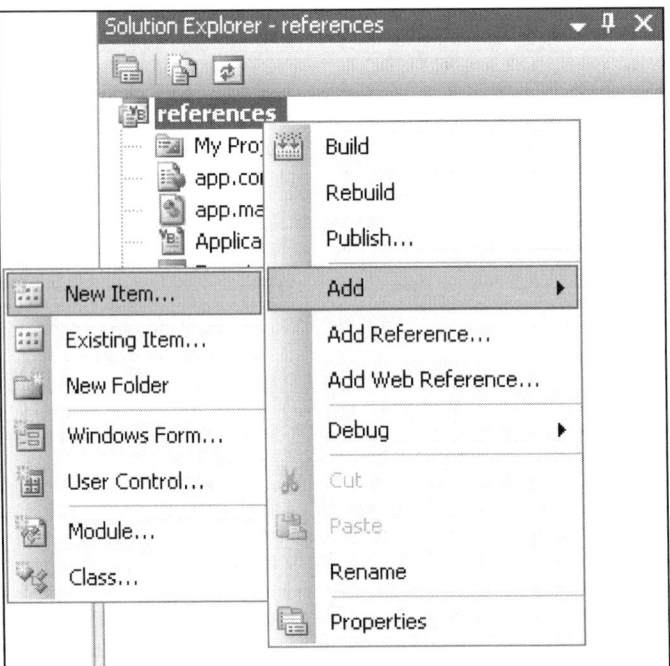

When you see the Add New Item dialogue box, select **Text File**.

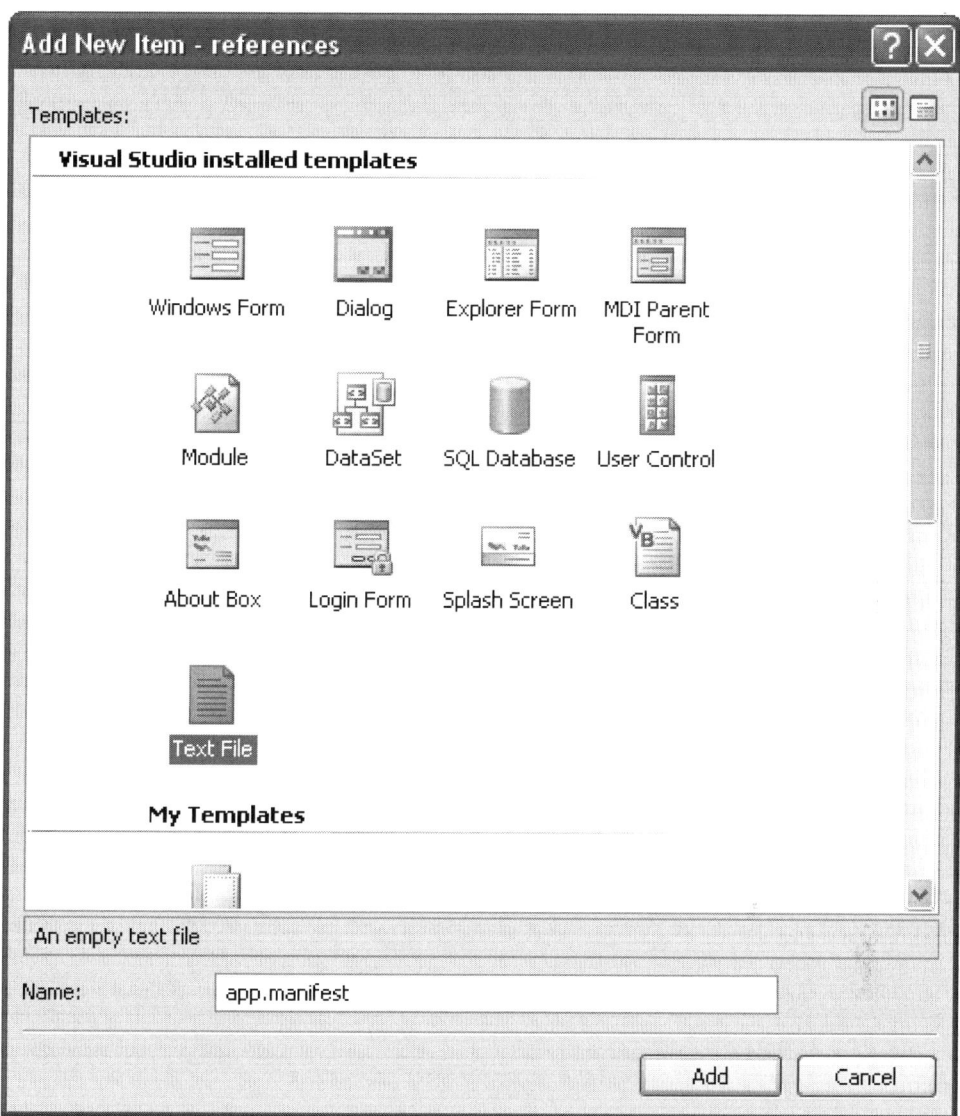

In the Name box, type **app.manifest**.

When you click **Add**, you'll see a blank file appear in the main window. In the Solution Explorer, an **app.manifest** file will be created.

A manifest is an XML file that can be used to tell Windows about any special considerations your programme may need. For us, this is an addition about Vista's UAC policy. The following is a bare minimum of what your manifest needs to contain.

Add the following to your manifest file. It's a bit long!

<?xml version="1.0" encoding="utf-8"?>
<assembly xmlns="urn:schemas-microsoft-com:asm.v1" manifestVersion="1.0">
<trustInfo xmlns="urn:schemas-microsoft-com:asm.v3">

```
        <security>
                <requestedPrivileges>
                        <requestedExecutionLevel level="asInvoker" />
                </requestedPrivileges>
        </security>
</trustInfo>
</assembly>
```

So you're trying to access the **requestedPrivileges** area. **requestedExecutionLevel** can be set to **as invoker**. This means whoever happens to be logged in at the time (User Account).

Save your file, and we can test if VB Net has any problems with this manifest.

To check the security levels, click the **Project** menu at the top of the VB NET software. From the Project menu, select the **Properties** item at the bottom of the menu item. You should see a new tab appear. The tab will have lots of options on the left hand side:

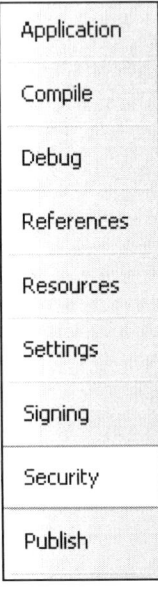

Click on the **Security** option. If there are problems with your manifest file, a large message box will pop up warning you of them. In which case, amend your manifest. You should be OK with ours above, though.

Setting an Icon for your programme

Instead of using the default icon for your programmes, you can specify your own. Click on **Application**, of the options in the image above. You should see something like this:

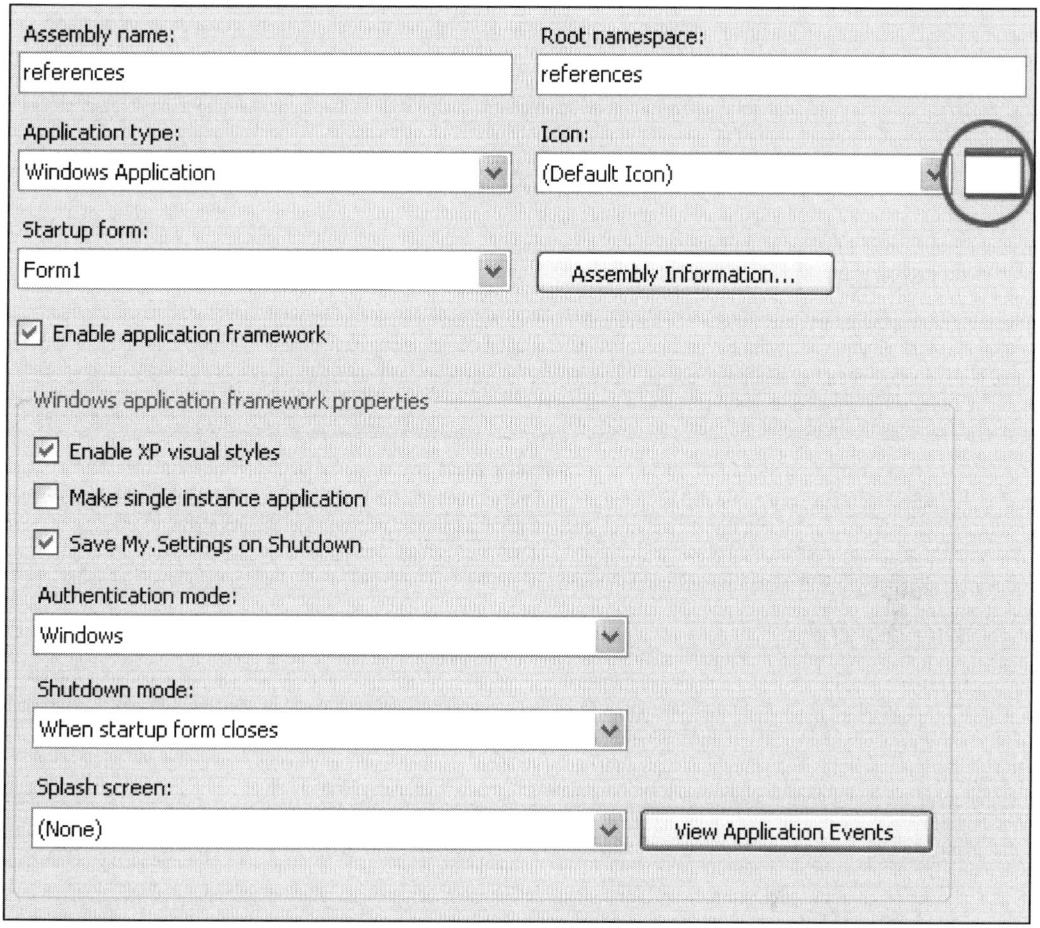

Assembly name: Root namespace:
references   references

Application type: Icon:
Windows Application   (Default Icon)

Startup form:
Form1   Assembly Information...

☑ Enable application framework

Windows application framework properties

  ☑ Enable XP visual styles
  ☐ Make single instance application
  ☑ Save My.Settings on Shutdown

  Authentication mode:
  Windows

  Shutdown mode:
  When startup form closes

  Splash screen:
  (None)   View Application Events

The default icon is highlighted by a red circle, in the image above. Icons need to be created in an image editor that supports the saving as ICO files. A good freeware icon editor is "Greenfish Icon Editor Pro". It can be found here:

http://greenfish.extra.hu/downloads.php

Greenfish is donation supported. You can make a donation via PayPal, if you want to support the programmers (not us!).

We created a simple icon in Greenfish, with a size of 32 by 32. To let VB know that you want to use your icon, click the dropdown box under **Icon**. Then select **Browse**:

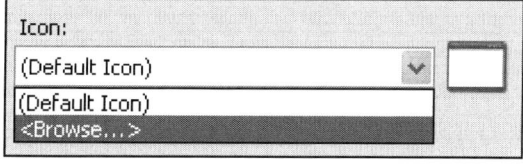

Browse for your new icon, and then click the **Open** button. The icon image should change:

This icon will now be used when your programme is installed.

Publish your Programme

VB already creates an executable file for your project, in the **Bin\Debug** folder, so there's no need to create a separate one. But you can package all your files together and create a setup file that can double-clicked on to install.

To create your installation file, click **Build** from the main VB menu bars at the top. By default, VB NET Express 2010 doesn't have a Build menu. To get it, click **Tools > Settings > Expert Settings**. The Build menu will appear at the top. Now click **Build > Build project_name**. This will create an executable in the Release folder in the Solution Explorer. Now click **Build > Publish**.

When you click **Publish**, you'll see the first step of a wizard appear:

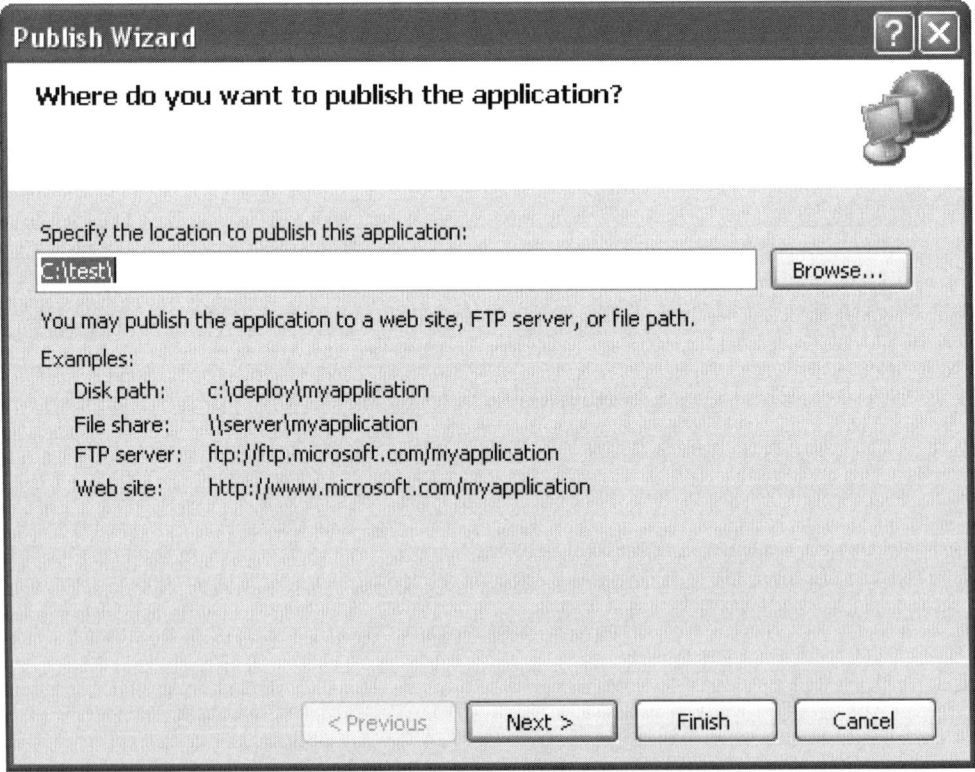

The location to publish is just any folder that you want to use to save all the setup files. It's not the location that the user will install to. We've just created a folder called **test** and are going to save all the setup file to there.

Click **Next** when you've specified your location, and you'll see this:

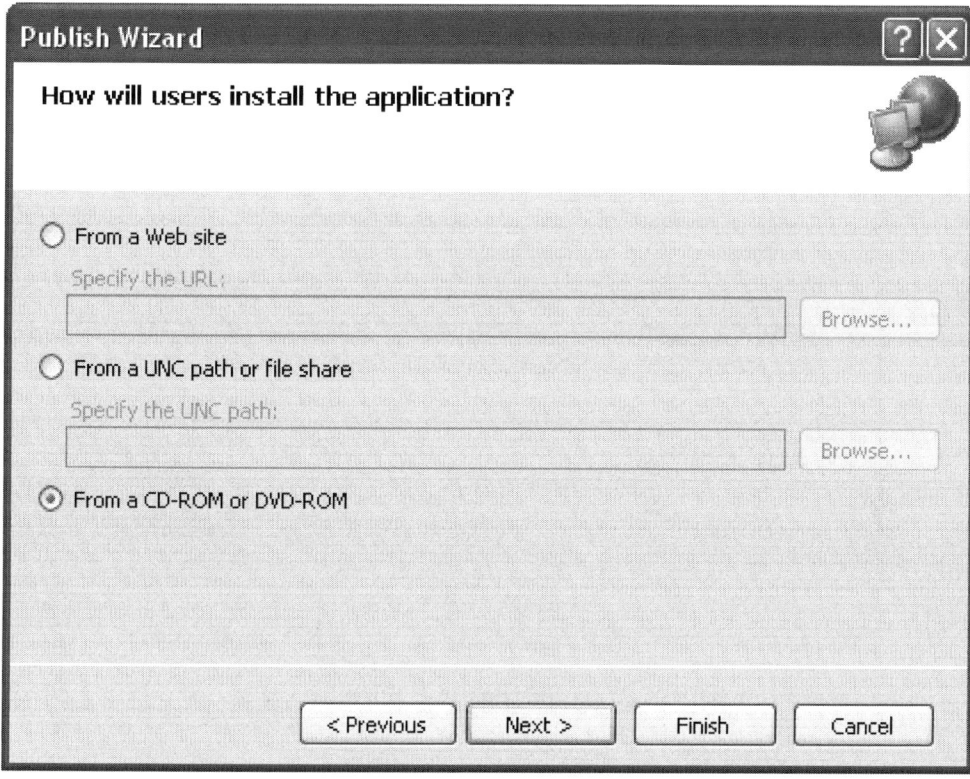

You can select the third option if users will be installing from a hard drive or a portable drive. It doesn't have to be a CD or DVD ROM.

When you click **Next**, you'll see this step:

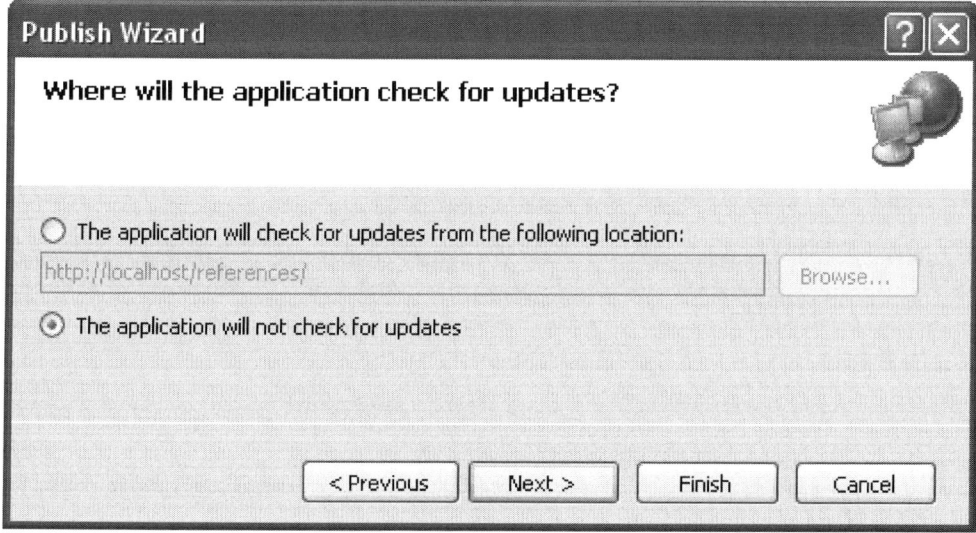

The default is not to check for updates. Leave it on this, and then click **Next**:

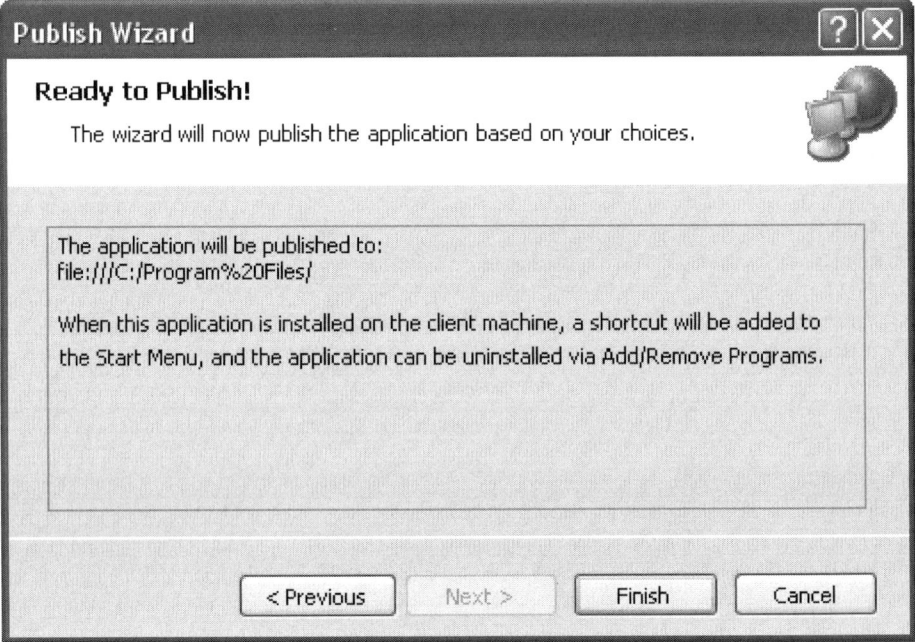

This is the final step. Click Finish and your setup file will be created.

To see all your new files, use an explorer window to navigate to where you saved your files to in step one:

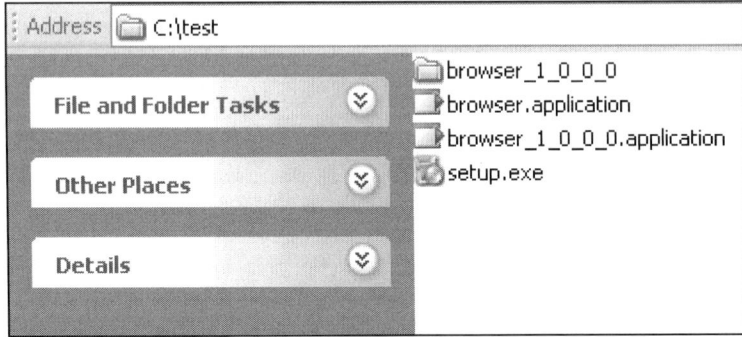

You can send your users all these files. When they double click on **setup.exe**, the windows installer should launch.

Final Word

And that's it for this Home and Learn book on Visual Basic .NET. You have come a long way since you first started this course, and should feel very proud of yourself for getting this far. You now have a good working knowledge of Microsoft's newest programming strategy – NET. This is very much the future of programming on a windows machine. By completing this course, you've given yourself a terrific advantage. Of course, there is an awful lot more to learn about NET. But the skills you have acquired should stand you in good stead, should you wish to take it further. We wish you every success in your programming endeavours.